Communications
in Computer and Inf

MW01600295

Rationale

The CCIS series is devoted to the publication of proceedings of computer science conferences. Its aim is to efficiently disseminate original research results in informatics in printed and electronic form. While the focus is on publication of peer-reviewed full papers presenting mature work, inclusion of reviewed short papers reporting on work in progress is welcome, too. Besides globally relevant meetings with internationally representative program committees guaranteeing a strict peer-reviewing and paper selection process, conferences run by societies or of high regional or national relevance are also considered for publication.

Topics

The topical scope of CCIS spans the entire spectrum of informatics ranging from foundational topics in the theory of computing to information and communications science and technology and a broad variety of interdisciplinary application fields.

Information for Volume Editors and Authors

Publication in CCIS is free of charge. No royalties are paid, however, we offer registered conference participants temporary free access to the online version of the conference proceedings on SpringerLink (http://link.springer.com) by means of an http referrer from the conference website and/or a number of complimentary printed copies, as specified in the official acceptance email of the event.

CCIS proceedings can be published in time for distribution at conferences or as post-proceedings, and delivered in the form of printed books and/or electronically as USBs and/or e-content licenses for accessing proceedings at SpringerLink. Furthermore, CCIS proceedings are included in the CCIS electronic book series hosted in the SpringerLink digital library at http://link.springer.com/bookseries/7899. Conferences publishing in CCIS are allowed to use Online Conference Service (OCS) for managing the whole proceedings lifecycle (from submission and reviewing to preparing for publication) free of charge.

Publication process

The language of publication is exclusively English. Authors publishing in CCIS have to sign the Springer CCIS copyright transfer form, however, they are free to use their material published in CCIS for substantially changed, more elaborate subsequent publications elsewhere. For the preparation of the camera-ready papers/files, authors have to strictly adhere to the Springer CCIS Authors' Instructions and are strongly encouraged to use the CCIS LaTeX style files or templates.

Abstracting/Indexing

CCIS is abstracted/indexed in DBLP, Google Scholar, EI-Compendex, Mathematical Reviews, SCImago, Scopus. CCIS volumes are also submitted for the inclusion in ISI Proceedings.

How to start

To start the evaluation of your proposal for inclusion in the CCIS series, please send an e-mail to ccis@springer.com.

Juan Carlos Figueroa-García ·
German Hernández ·
Diego Fernando Suero Pérez ·
Elvis Eduardo Gaona García
Editors

Applied Computer Sciences in Engineering

11th Workshop on Engineering Applications, WEA 2024
Barranquilla, Colombia, October 23–25, 2024
Proceedings, Part II

 Springer

Editors
Juan Carlos Figueroa-García 🆔
Universidad Distrital Francisco José de
Caldas
Bogotá, Colombia

German Hernández 🆔
National University of Colombia
Bogotá, Colombia

Elvis Eduardo Gaona García 🆔
Universidad Distrital Francisco José de
Caldas
Bogotá, Colombia

Diego Fernando Suero Pérez 🆔
Universidad Libre
Bogotá, Colombia

ISSN 1865-0929   ISSN 1865-0937 (electronic)
Communications in Computer and Information Science
ISBN 978-3-031-74597-3   ISBN 978-3-031-74598-0 (eBook)
https://doi.org/10.1007/978-3-031-74598-0

This Springer imprint is published by the registered company Springer Nature Switzerland AG
The registered company address is: Gewerbestrasse 11, 6330 Cham, Switzerland

If disposing of this product, please recycle the paper.

Preface

The 11th edition of the Workshop on Engineering Applications (WEA 2024) was focused on computer science, artificial intelligence, operations research, optimization and simulation. WEA 2024 was one of the flagship events of the Faculty of Engineering of the Universidad Distrital Francisco José de Caldas, the Universidad Libre de Colombia, the Faculty of Engineering of the National University of Colombia and the Universidad Externado de Colombia.

WEA 2024 was held from October 23–25 in hybrid mode due to some authors' request. In total, 97 submissions were received from authors in 11 countries on topics such as computer science, artificial intelligence, operations research/optimization, simulation systems and their applications. The peer review process for all submissions was rigorous: every paper was reviewed by one Program Committee member who assigned at least 3 external reviewers in a single-blind manner, and as a result a total of 42 papers were accepted for oral presentation at WEA 2024. The Program Committee organized all the accepted papers into two volumes and four sections to increase the readability and the impact of these volumes published in Springer's Communications in Computer and Information Sciences (CCIS) series, where this second volume is dedicated to optimization, simulation and their applications with a total of 21 papers.

The Faculty of Engineering of the Universidad Distrital Francisco José de Caldas, the Universidad Libre de Colombia, the Faculty of Engineering of the National University of Colombia and the Universidad Externado de Colombia made significant efforts to guarantee the success and continuity of the conference.

We would like to thank all members of the Program Committee for their commitment to help in the review process and for spreading the WEA 2024 call for papers and the team at Springer for their helpful advice, guidance and continuous support in publishing the proceedings. Also, we would also like to thank all the authors for supporting WEA 2024 as without all their high-quality submissions the conference would not be possible. Finally, we are especially grateful to the IEEE Universidad Distrital Francisco José de Caldas Student Branch, the Laboratory for Automation and Computational Intelligence (LAMIC), the GITUD and the Emerging Technologies for Electrical Microgrids with High Penetration of Renewable Energies research groups of the Universidad Distrital Francisco José de Caldas, the Algorithms and Combinatorics (ALGOS) research group of the Universidad Nacional de Colombia and the Observatory for Economics and Numerical Operations (ODEON) of the Universidad Externado de Colombia.

October 2024

Juan Carlos Figueroa-García
German Hernández
Diego Fernando Suero Pérez
Elvis Eduardo Gaona García

Organization

General Chair

Juan Carlos Figueroa-García   Universidad Distrital Francisco José de Caldas, Colombia

Technical Chairs

Diego Fernando Suero Pérez   Universidad Libre, Colombia
Elvis Eduardo Gaona García   Universidad Distrital Francisco José de Caldas, Colombia
Germán Hernández-Pérez   Universidad Nacional de Colombia, Colombia

Program and Track Chairs

Carlos Franco   Universidad del Rosario, Colombia
Diego Fernando Suero Pérez   Universidad Libre, Colombia

Publication Chair

Alvaro David Orjuela-Cañnon   Universidad del Rosario, Colombia

Organizing Committee Chairs

Alexander Parody   Universidad Libre, Colombia
Ricardo de la Hoz   Universidad Libre, Colombia
Diana Suárez   Universidad Libre, Colombia
Erick Jassir   Universidad Libre, Colombia

Plenary Speakers

Roman Neruda	Czech Academy of Sciences, Czech Republic
Rafael Bello Pérez	Universidad Central "Marta Abreu" de las Villas, Cuba
Juan D. Velasquez	University of Chile, Chile
Nabil Absi	Mines Saint-Étienne, France

Program Committee

Adil Usman	Indian Institute of Technology at Mandi, India
Adolfo Jaramillo-Matta	Universidad Distrital Francisco José de Caldas, Colombia
Alvaro David Orjuela-Cañon	Universidad del Rosario, Colombia
Andres Gaona	Universidad Distrital Francisco José de Caldas, Colombia
Aparna Mehra	Indian Institute of Technology at Delhi, India
Carlos Osorio-Ramírez	Universidad Nacional de Colombia, Colombia
Christian Schwede	University of Applied Sciences and Arts (HSBI), Germany
David Becerra	McGill University, Canada
David Pelta	Universidad de Granada, Spain
De-Shuang Huang	Tongji University, China
Diana Ovalle	Universidad Distrital Francisco José de Caldas, Colombia
Diego Ismael León Nieto	Universidad Externado, Colombia
Fabián Garay	ESINF, Colombia
Feizar Javier Rueda-Velazco	Universidad Distrital Francisco José de Caldas, Colombia
Francisco Ramis	Universidad del Bío-Bío, Chile
Guadalupe González	Universidad Tecnológica de Panamá, Panama
I-Hsien Ting	National University of Kaohsiung, Taiwan
Jair Cervantes-Canales	Universidad Autónoma de México, Mexico
Jairo Soriano-Mendez	Universidad Distrital Francisco José de Caldas, Colombia
Javier Arturo Orjuela-Castro	Universidad Distrital Francisco José de Caldas, Colombia
Javier Sandoval	Universidad Externado, Colombia
J. J. Merelo	Universidad de Granada, Spain
John Leonardo Vargas Mesa	Universidad del Rosario, Colombia
Jose Luís Gonzalez-Velarde	Instituto Tecnológico de Monterrey, Mexico

Jose Ignacio Rodríguez Molano	Universidad Distrital Francisco José de Caldas, Colombia
Jose Luis Villa Ramírez	Universidad Tecnológica de Bolívar, Colombia
Jose Luis Gonzalez-Velarde	Instituto Tecnológico de Monterrey, Mexico
Jose Ignacio Rodríguez	Molano Universidad Distrital Francisco José de Caldas, Colombia
Jose Luis Villa Ramírez	Universidad Tecnológica de Bolívar, Colombia
Jose Luis Gonzalez Velarde	Instituto Tecnológico de Monterrey, Mexico
Leonardo Bobadilla	Florida International University, USA
Lindsay Alvarez	Universidad Distrital Francisco José de Caldas, Colombia
Mabel Frías	Universidad de las Villas "Marta Abreu", Cuba
Mario Enrique Duarte-Gonzalez	Universidad Antonio Nariño, Colombia
Martha Centeno	University of Turabo, Puerto Rico
Martin Pilat	Charles University, Czech Republic
Martine Ceberio	University of Texas at El Paso, USA
Miguel Melgarejo	Universidad Distrital Francisco José de Caldas, Colombia
Nelson L. Diaz Aldana	Universidad Distrital Francisco José de Caldas, Colombia
Paulo Alonso Gaona	Universidad Distrital Francisco José de Caldas, Colombia
Pavel Novoa	Universidad de Granada, Spain
Rafael Bello-Pérez	Universidad de las Villas "Marta Abreu", Cuba
Rodrigo Linfati	Universidad del Bío-Bío, Chile
Roman Neruda	Charles University and Czech Academy of Sciences, Czech Republic
S. Dharmaraja	Indian Institute of Technology at Delhi, India
Sebastián Jaramillo-Isaza	Universidad Antonio Nariño, Colombia
Sergio Rojas-Galeano	Universidad Distrital Francisco José de Caldas, Colombia
Vladik Kreinovich	University of Texas at El Paso, USA
Wilson Rodríguez Calderón	ESAP, Colombia
Yesid Díaz-Gutierrez	Universidad Santo Tomás de Aquino, Colombia
Yurilev Chalco-Cano	Universidad de Tarapacá, Chile

Contents – Part II

Simulation

Applications

Contents – Part I

Optimization

Location-Allocation of Relief Service Facilities: A Case Study for Bogotá - Colombia

Natalia Chacón-Tibaduiza[1], Diana C. Guzmán-Cortés[1],
Juan Carlos Figueroa-García[2], and Carlos Franco[3]

[1] School of Engineering, Science and Technology, Universidad del Rosario,
Bogotá, Colombia
{giseth.chacon,dianacar.guzman}@urosario.edu.co
[2] Faculty of Engineering, Universidad Distrital Francisco José de Caldas,
Bogotá, Colombia
jcfigueroag@udistrital.edu.co
[3] School of Management and Business, Universidad del Rosario, Bogotá, Colombia
carlosa.franco@urosario.edu.co

Abstract. Effective resource allocation during natural disasters and response strategies are crucial to mitigate impacts and save lives. This paper presents a comprehensive mathematical model, which is designed to optimize disaster response operations. The proposed model integrates various components, including the demand for different types of relief services, facilities distributed by zones, as well as the assessment of resource requirements, and optimization of the location capacities per zone. We propose the use of mixed-integer linear programming (MILP), where we propose three different objective functions. The model was tested over a real case in Bogotá-Colombia and we evaluate different scenarios to analyze the performance of the model and obtained results. The proposed framework offers a strategic tool for policymakers and emergency managers to enable data-driven decision-making in disaster preparedness and response planning.

Keywords: location-allocation · optimization · relief service facilities · humanitarian logistics

1 Introduction

A disaster is defined as a significant disruption to the functioning of a community due to hazardous events that result in human, material, economic, and environmental losses and impacts, and that may exceed the response capacity of the community, requiring external assistance at the regional, national or international level [16].

According to [6], 2023 had 399 disaster events and a higher mortality rate than the average of the last 20 years (64148 deaths) and the median value (19290

J. C. Figueroa-García et al. (Eds.): WEA 2024, CCIS 2223, pp. 3–14, 2025.
https://doi.org/10.1007/978-3-031-74598-0_1

deaths), specifically due to the earthquake in Türkiye and Syria, this natural disaster event represented two-thirds of the total deaths for the year.

Colombia has experienced an increase in the frequency of natural disasters, as well as an increase in the number of deaths, injuries, and missing people because of these events [2]. The period 1998–2007 presented an average of 632 natural disasters per year and the number of people seriously affected was 3866, whereas for the period 2008–2017, the annual average increased to 1804 events (excluding the La Niña phenomenon in 2010–2011, the annual average is 1603 events) and the number of people seriously affected increased to 5410 [2].

Although 94% of the natural disaster events correspond to landslides, floods, and windstorms [2], Colombia faces a seismic threat related to the convergence of the Nazca, the South American, and the Caribbean lithospheric plates. The dynamic of these plates has caused earthquakes of different magnitudes and has a high destructive potential in the country, a record of earthquakes in Colombia can be found in [15]

According to [1], Bogotá, the capital of Colombia, is classified as a zone of medium seismic threat and the sources of contribution to the hazard are the frontal faults of the Cordillera Oriental, Benioff and Salinas. Furthermore, the rural and urban areas of Bogotá are close to the zone of high seismic threat.

This seismic threat to Bogotá implies a great challenge for the decision-makers, governmental institutions, and humanitarian organizations involved in different activities of the disaster management cycle such as prevention, mitigation, preparedness, disaster impact, response, recovery, and development [5].

In this paper, we determine the location of different relief service facilities to provide humanitarian assistance to the affected population in the event of a disaster situation, specifically an earthquake, by focusing on the preparedness and response phases. We consider relief service facilities such as shelters, mobile and fixed field hospitals, and points of distribution (PODs), facilities that usually need to be located to support humanitarian relief operations [8].

Thus, we propose a mixed-integer programming (MIP) formulation for the location/allocation of these facilities, considering a damage scenario due to a 7.0 magnitude frontal fault earthquake in Bogotá [7], with different objective functions focused on the early opening of the relief services locations and the minimum movement of people between localities of the city.

2   Literature Review

Several studies have addressed the problem of location-allocation of services in case of disasters. For example, [11] developed a mathematical model to select communities to be served and to design the routes to distribute health services, authors use mobile clinics as a product to be distributed over the population. This work is related with our approach, nevertheless our focus is to locate-allocate different relief service facilities and we don't take into account the routing immerse in the problem. In [3] authors address the problem of multi-period mobile facility location with mobile demand (MM-FLP-MD) within the framework of refugee migration. Their objective is to minimize the travel and setup costs associated with mobile clinics over the planning horizon. To solve this problem, they propose the use of an algorithm that is tested over a real case in Honduras.

In [12] authors examine the provision of mobile healthcare services in rural regions, targeting remote villages that lack nearby healthcare facilities. The objective of this paper is to enhance healthcare accessibility for these isolated communities. Authors aim to determine the village assignments for doctors, their monthly visit schedules, and the base hospitals from which they commence and conclude their tours. On the other hand [4] present a capacitated set-covering formulation in their study on multi-period location routing, specifically applied to the planning of mobile clinic operations in Iraq. They address the uncertainty related to patients who move to access healthcare services. The authors employ robust optimization techniques, utilizing Benders decomposition and constraint generation to solve the problem. Their algorithm is tested on instances based on a case study from rural Germany.

To analyze more studies related to location problems in humanitarian supply chains, readers can see the work developed in [8]. Finally, there are also studies with other types of approaches rather than mathematical modeling, for example [9] study the community-based mobile hearing clinic through a retrospective, cross-sectional pilot study.

The contribution of this work can be summarized as follows:

– We propose a multi-period, multi-service optimization planning problem.
– We analyze different types of services based on human needs in case of a disaster.
– We contrast two different objective functions in order to evaluate the satisfaction of needs in terms of time and movements of people to cover their needs.
– We analyze the impact of different capacities given the different types of services.
– We analyze our proposal in Bogotá city to analyze the performance of the results in case of a disaster.

3   Problem Description and Mathematical Model

3.1   Problem Description

To model our problem, we have considered different types of relief services in order to satisfy the demand of the affected population. Therefore, we consider a set of relief service facilities S which consist of shelters of different capacities, as well as mobile hospitals and points of distribution of relief aids. Also, we consider a set O aggregate relief services. In our case we model the problem to make decisions in a period of time T of one week. We consider also a set of zones defined by L, given the cadastral division of Bogotá. We use two types of binary variables, $X_{s,l,t}$ and $Z_{s,l,t}$ to determine if a relief service is opened and the earliest opening time respectively. Also, we consider the integer variables $Y_{l,i,s,t}$ and $W_{s,l,t}$ to define the amount of relief service facilities opened and the amount of affected population located in zones.

3.2 Mathematical Model

– **Sets**

– T : Set of time periods : $\{t = 1, ..., 7\}$
– S : Set of type of relief services: $\{s = 1, ..., 6\}$
– L : Set of zones : $\{l, i = 1, ..., 19\}$
– O : Set of aggregate relief services: $\{o = 1, ..., 4\}$
– N_o : Sub-set of aggregate relief services of $o \in O$

– **Decision variables**

– $X_{s,l,t} = \begin{cases} 1 \text{ if the type of relief services } \in \text{ S is opened in zone l } \in \text{ L} \\ \qquad\qquad \text{in the time period t } \in \text{ T} \\ \qquad\qquad\qquad 0 \text{ otherwise} \end{cases}$

– $Y_{l,i,s,t}$ = Amount of affected population of zone $l \in$ L located in zone $i \in$ L for the type of relief service $s \in$ S in time period $t \in$ T.

– $W_{s,l,t}$ = Amount of relief services $s \in$ S, opened in zone $l \in$ L in time period $t \in$ T.

– $Z_{s,l,t} = \begin{cases} 1 \text{ if in the time period t } \in \text{ T an early opened of the relief service} \\ \qquad\qquad s \in \text{ S in the zone l } \in \text{ L is made} \\ \qquad\qquad\qquad 0 \text{ otherwise} \end{cases}$

– **Parameters:**

– C_s: maximum capacity of the relief service $s \in$ S.
– $D_{l,o}$: demand in zone $l \in$ L of the aggregate relief service $o \in$ O.
– $M_{s,l}$: Maximum number of relief service facilities $s \in$ S that can be opened in the zone $l \in$ L.

– **Mathematical model:**

– **Objective Functions:**

OF1:

$$\text{Min} \sum_{s \in S} \sum_{t \in T} \sum_{l \in L} t \cdot Z_{s,l,t} \tag{1}$$

OF2:

$$\text{Min} \sum_{i \in L} \sum_{l \in L:i \neq l} \sum_{s \in S} \sum_{t \in T} Y_{i,l,s,t} \tag{2}$$

OF3:

$$\text{Min} \sum_{s \in S} \sum_{t \in T} \sum_{l \in L} \frac{t \cdot Z_{s,l,t}}{OF1} + \sum_{i \in L} \sum_{l \in L:i \neq l} \sum_{s \in S} \sum_{t \in T} \frac{Y_{i,l,s,t}}{OF2} \tag{3}$$

Constraints:

$$W_{s,l,t} = W_{s,l,t+1} \quad \forall t \in T \mid t < 7, \quad \forall l \in L, \quad \forall s \in S \mid s = 4 \tag{4}$$

$$\sum_{l \in L} \sum_{a \in N_o} \sum_{t \in T} Y_{i,l,a,t} = D_{i,o} \quad \forall i \in L, \quad \forall o \in O \tag{5}$$

$$\sum_{i \in L} Y_{i,l,s,t} \leq C_s \cdot W_{s,l,t} \quad \forall t \in T, \quad \forall l \in L, \quad \forall s \in S \tag{6}$$

$$W_{s,l,t} \leq W_{s,l,t+1} \quad \forall t \in T \mid t < 7, \quad \forall l \in L, \quad \forall s \in S \mid s < 4 \tag{7}$$

$$W_{s,l,t} \leq M_{s,l} \cdot X_{s,l,t} \quad \forall t \in T, \quad \forall l \in L, \quad \forall s \in S \tag{8}$$

$$\sum_{t \in T} Z_{s,l,t} \leq 1 \quad \forall l \in L, \quad \forall s \in S \tag{9}$$

$$X_{s,l,t} \geq Z_{s,l,t} \quad \forall t \in T, \quad \forall l \in L, \quad \forall s \in S \tag{10}$$

$$\sum_{t \in T} X_{s,l,t} \leq |T| \cdot Z_{s,l,t} \quad \forall l \in L, \quad \forall s \in S \tag{11}$$

$$X_{s,l,t} \in \{0,1\} \quad \forall s \in S, \quad \forall l \in L, \quad \forall t \in T \tag{12}$$

$$Y_{l,i,s,t} \in \mathbb{Z}^+ \quad \forall l \in L \quad \forall i \in L \quad \forall s \in S, \quad \forall t \in T \tag{13}$$

$$W_{s,l,t} \in \mathbb{Z}^+ \quad \forall s \in S, \quad \forall l \in L, \quad \forall t \in T \tag{14}$$

$$Z_{s,l,t} \in \{0,1\} \quad \forall s \in S, \quad \forall l \in L, \quad \forall t \in T \tag{15}$$

We propose the use of three objective functions separately. The first objective function aims to minimize the early opening of relief services and is presented in Eq. 1. The second objective function (Eq. 2) aims to minimize the number of affected population allocated out of their region to satisfy their needs. Finally, in the third objective function proposed (Eq. 3) we combine these two objective functions by normalizing the values.

In Eq. 4 we establish that fixed locations must remain over the planning horizon. On the other hand Eq. 5 determines that the demand for aggregate relief services must be satisfied. Eq. 6 restricts the number of relief facilities that can be opened. Constraint 7 determines that opened locations can't be closed where the relationship between the integer variables $W_{s,l,t}$ and binary variables $X_{s,l,t}$ are presented in Eq. 8.

Constraints 9 determine that there is only possible to choose one value for the early opening of relief facilities services, where Eq. 10 determines the lower bound and Eqs. 11 the upper bound of variables $Z_{s,l,t}$. Finally, Eq. 12, 13, 14 and 15 determine the types of variables used in the problem.

3.3   Data Description

In this section, we explain how the different parameters of the model were set for this work. We take the study developed by [7], which presents a damage scenario for a 7.0 magnitude frontal fault earthquake in Bogotá. Because the damage estimations were based on the 2010 population, we updated these values with the forecasted population for 2024 [13], which considered the 2018 census. In Table 1 we present the percentage change in the population for each locality in Bogotá.

Table 1. Percentage Change for each zone of Bogotá

Code	Zone	Population 2010	Population 2024	Percentage of change
1	Usaquén	488850	594611	21,6%
2	Chapinero	142753	182103	27,6%
3	Santa Fe	100177	107906	7,7%
4	San Cristóbal	387010	409106	5,7%
5	Usme	335777	414995	23,6%
6	Tunjuelito	173235	184492	6,5%
7	Bosa	619699	733740	18,4%
8	Kennedy	980198	1037929	5,9%
9	Fontibón	338086	408155	20,7%
10	Engativá	784404	819441	4,5%
11	Suba	1055912	1313453	24,4%
12	Barrios Unidos	161921	156268	–3,5%
13	Teusaquillo	140098	165438	18,1%
14	Los Mártires	79597	83001	4,3%
15	Antonio Nariño	90640	84979	–6,2%
16	Puente Aranda	242970	258034	6,2%
17	La Candelaria	18750	18675	–0,4%
18	Rafael Uribe Uribe	363581	391588	7,7%
19	Ciudad Bolivar	589290	666809	13,2%
20	Sumapaz	3938	3926	–0,3%

The demand for shelters was estimated taking into account the affected population with a damage index higher than 60%, since [7] identified them as the population without a home after the earthquake.

The demand for field hospitals was estimated by considering the average number of injured people when the earthquake occurred during the day and the number of injured people when the earthquake occurred during the night. It is assumed that 60% of the injured will need fixed field hospitals and the rest will need mobile field hospitals.

The demand for points of distribution (PODs) was estimated considering the population affected with a damage index between 30% and 60%, without the average of the injured people and the average of deaths, both of them taking into account the numbers when the earthquake occurred during the day and at night.

In Table 2 we present the summary of the demand for each type of relief service facility.

Table 2. Demand (population) for each type of relief service facility

Code	Zone	Shelters	Mobile field hospitals	Fixed field hospitals	Points of Distribution (POD)
1	Usaquén	19397	1412	2119	20762
2	Chapinero	10346	2028	3042	16012
3	Santa Fe	9871	1603	2403	41177
4	San Cristóbal	31418	4137	6205	164356
5	Usme	2359	1953	2929	57157
6	Tunjuelito	545	661	993	44522
7	Bosa	359	2620	3929	113277
8	Kennedy	0	856	1282	46990
9	Fontibón	0	0	0	0
10	Engativá	0	31	47	1355
11	Suba	6910	1377	2065	34190
12	Barrios Unidos	0	0	0	0
13	Teusaquillo	0	41	61	1840
14	Los Mártires	20	154	231	5844
15	Antonio Nariño	0	50	74	2431
16	Puente Aranda	0	0	0	0
17	La Candelaria	1575	388	583	11203
18	Rafael Uribe Uribe	88578	3402	5103	127309
19	Ciudad Bolivar	9803	3558	5338	143267

The capacity for shelters was set according to [14], we have three types of shelters A, B, and C with capacities of 100, 500, and 1000 people respectively. The capacities of fixed and mobile field hospitals are set at 80 and 50 people according to information from [10]. In the case of the points of distribution (PODs) we vary their capacity in terms of people in the values of 5000, 10000, 15000, and 20000.

To determine the maximum number of relief service facilities that can be opened for each zone we take the ceil of the demand for each zone and each type of relief service facility divided by the capacity of each relief service facility. In the case of shelters, given that there are three types with different sizes, we consolidate the total capacity with 1600 people, estimate the ceiling using this value, and then distribute the maximum number in equal proportions. Then, we reduce the base values for the maximum number of facilities considering three factors, 75%, 50%, and 25%.

4   Numerical Results and Analysis

We coded and solved the instances using IBM ILOG CPLEX Optimization Studio 22.1.1.0. Results are summarized and presented in Tables 3, 4 and 5. We organize the results showing different variations in the parameters compared to the total results for each period of time. Therefore we organize the tables as follows: in column 1 we present the combination of the capacity of Point of Distributions, in Column 2 we give details about the period of time (in days). Then, for each of the three objective functions presented we show the number of services (summarized) opened, the total amount of demand that is satisfied by the same zone and the total amount of demand that is covered with other regions. Finally, we present the number of locations that are opened early. Then we present the same results obtained by varying the maximum number of facilities.

In Table 3 it can be analyzed if the maximum number of facilities is fixed to 25% in the Objective Function 1, where the total number of services opened remains almost constant in overall analyzed instances, these results are somewhat expected given that the model attempts to reach the population in an early stage population but this is restricted to the maximum possible number of facilities, therefore, it uses the maximum value as possible, thus most of the services are opened early in the first period. On the other hand, regarding the movements of the affected population in OF 1, most of the population was assigned to a different area. On the other hand for Objective Function 2, which is related to the minimization of movements of affected population outside of the region, it is clear that the number of services opened increases when assigning the maximum population to the region of residence in contrast to the values of the OF1, in contrast, the number of early openings is split over the time periods. Finally, in the Objective Function 3, it can be observed that the results of the metrics are in between of those obtained from the two objective functions.

In Table 4 it can be analyzed results if the maximum number of facilities is fixed to 50%. We conclude that the results exhibit behavior similar to those summarized in Table 3. In terms of the objective functions used, it can be concluded that the results show an increase in the opening of services (for the OF1) and a reduction in the initial opening quantity. For the OF2, the overall demand is satisfied in the same area (given that it is increased the capacity), and the same behavior is obtained for OF3, where the initial opening quantity

Table 3. Summary of results 1

Max number of facilities 25%

Capacity of POD	Period of Time	FO1				FO2				FO3			
		Total Services	Internal Demand	External Demand	Initial Opening Quantity	Total Services	Internal Demand	External Demand	Initial Opening Quantity	Total Services	Internal Demand	External Demand	InitialOpening Quantity
5000	1	194	1197	153433	33	359	289789	4800	43	321	211557	7881	58
	2	194	67878	86753	0	354	279264	5780	14	285	121023	5984	0
	3	194	3758	150872	0	353	259530	5308	12	296	169899	6269	0
	4	194	8880	145750	0	343	149897	6500	12	248	148414	7320	0
	5	194	13316	138273	0	185	19191	5954	7	298	202545	5138	0
	6	194	8550	140258	0	189	19300	6000	17	282	116515	6388	0
	7	194	37978	116652	0	199	14981	7254	9	196	57829	6786	0
10000	1	187	2830	155620	33	338	330633	3700	52	296	325451	6024	58
	2	187	9517	120065	0	333	306080	4680	10	286	284248	5930	0
	3	187	8000	156382	0	331	237974	5000	15	289	197976	7127	0
	4	187	1800	162522	0	321	104484	6754	11	228	107891	5683	0
	5	187	60072	104558	0	185	18000	6800	14	290	58074	6623	0
	6	187	9550	118001	0	187	19800	6500	9	292	31293	7994	0
	7	187	7718	156913	0	187	14981	8162	3	292	22849	6385	0
15000	1	183	2830	162860	33	330	331836	4800	45	292	161815	7584	58
	2	183	75879	70113	0	323	284828	6621	14	272	154685	5541	0
	3	183	8000	161274	0	321	253889	4167	11	234	99000	6121	0
	4	183	1800	126901	0	314	107727	6500	10	223	100594	5814	0
	5	183	44630	125000	0	185	18772	6373	7	280	182604	6798	0
	6	180	9550	115081	0	187	19800	5500	16	268	206118	5992	0
	7	183	52717	116913	0	200	15100	7635	11	255	122966	7916	0
20000	1	182	59125	115705	33	328	377260	5529	45	261	293856	6430	58
	2	182	49600	55462	0	319	312372	4880	14	150	25534	5449	0
	3	182	8900	157761	0	318	223804	7325	11	150	44985	5331	0
	4	182	40900	116765	0	308	63666	3956	9	150	243946	6258	0
	5	182	71627	103203	0	189	19305	7354	9	248	230180	7198	0
	6	182	14934	125349	0	187	20245	5455	17	229	111868	5698	0
	7	182	7100	147117	0	199	15300	7097	9	227	68413	9402	0

increases compared with the values obtained when the number of facilities is fixed to 25%.

Finally, in Table 5 it can be analyzed results if the maximum number of facilities is fixed to 75%. It can be concluded that the results are higher in terms of the opening of locations, given that it can be used more capacity, in this sense the time of the initial openings is lower than those obtained in the previous results. In terms of the demand satisfaction, and as expected, the overall

Table 4. Summary of results 2

Max number of facilities 50%

Capacity of POD	Period of Time	FO1				FO2				FO3			
		Total Services	Internal Demand	External Demand	Initial Opening Quantity	Total Services	Internal Demand	External Demand	Initial Opening Quantity	Total Services	Internal Demand	External Demand	InitialOpening Quantity
5000	1	206	104000	40910	12	664	529579	0	46	618	503874	0	62
	2	191	19011	101179	0	658	444026	0	19	618	307327	0	0
	3	206	0	190146	0	335	38400	0	6	601	29347	0	0
	4	191	40460	77242	0	334	30020	0	6	614	29348	0	0
	5	206	9653	138078	0	360	20945	0	9	618	91657	0	0
	6	206	6687	187346	0	352	10578	0	18	624	82623	0	0
	7	206	34298	115538	0	335	0	0	6	625	29372	0	0
10000	1	188	61756	103014	12	623	565423	0	50	577	539718	0	50
	2	188	18120	147270	0	616	408182	0	19	577	250493	0	19
	3	188	0	165160	0	334	38400	0	5	560	29347	0	5
	4	188	3000	161398	0	343	30020	0	7	575	46338	0	7
	5	188	58553	106216	0	335	20945	0	7	577	86657	0	7
	6	154	35683	118514	0	335	10578	0	14	583	82623	0	14
	7	181	70000	24864	0	337	0	0	8	584	29372	0	8
15000	1	193	72321	106740	12	608	576626	0	48	562	550921	0	62
	2	193	17112	130745	0	600	396979	0	20	502	253290	0	0
	3	193	11145	125798	0	337	38400	0	7	545	29347	0	0
	4	193	0	114747	0	343	30020	0	7	560	46338	0	0
	5	193	53010	146654	0	335	20945	0	7	502	81657	0	0
	6	193	6344	135716	0	335	10578	0	14	568	82623	0	0
	7	193	10723	142493	0	336	0	0	7	569	29372	0	0
20000	1	183	19000	147722	12	603	632638	0	46	557	606933	0	62
	2	183	39528	175502	0	594	340967	0	19	557	212278	0	0
	3	183	56006	159024	0	335	38400	0	6	540	29347	0	0
	4	178	83422	31609	0	334	30020	0	6	556	36338	0	0
	5	183	50996	163523	0	357	20945	0	9	557	76657	0	0
	6	142	2591	29880	0	348	10578	0	18	563	82623	0	0
	7	178	11983	102762	0	335	0	0	6	564	29372	0	0

population can be assigned to the same zone of residence (OF 2), and this behavior remains for the third objective function.

Table 5. Summary of results 3

Max number of facilities 75%

Capacity of POD	Period of Time	FO1				FO2				FO3			
		Total Services	Internal Demand	External Demand	Initial Opening Quantity	Total Services	Internal Demand	External Demand	Initial Opening Quantity	Total Services	Internal Demand	External Demand	Initial Opening Quantity
5000	1	239	155603	5757	8	984	776307	0	52	899	725272	0	60
	2	188	7500	151570	0	970	236078	0	13	899	143939	0	0
	3	188	10863	122829	0	521	41730	0	8	874	29347	0	0
	4	188	2299	156771	0	552	19393	0	8	893	36338	0	0
	5	188	54356	86785	0	494	20	0	6	901	56657	0	0
	6	188	15740	143330	0	494	20	0	8	905	52623	0	0
	7	241	17652	142493	0	497	0	0	15	907	29372	0	0
10000	1	215	97505	30053	8	922	808081	0	53	837	757046	0	60
	2	215	106003	58450	0	905	204304	0	11	837	112165	0	0
	3	167	0	125024	0	526	41730	0	9	812	29347	0	0
	4	215	18150	147454	0	552	19393	0	8	834	36338	0	0
	5	167	3455	158529	0	494	20	0	6	839	56657	0	0
	6	167	19080	144350	0	497	20	0	9	843	52623	0	0
	7	216	22239	143256	0	494	0	0	14	845	29372	0	0
15000	1	219	25081	128747	8	901	827970	0	51	816	776935	0	60
	2	171	6883	106069	0	880	184415	0	11	816	104266	0	0
	3	171	6883	161987	0	525	41730	0	8	791	29347	0	0
	4	171	87606	44928	0	552	19393	0	8	813	29348	0	0
	5	171	101655	67416	0	496	20	0	7	818	51657	0	0
	6	171	15741	151482	0	498	20	0	10	822	52623	0	0
	7	172	21110	147960	0	495	0	0	15	824	29372	0	0
20000	1	217	29528	128622	8	893	872117	0	53	808	821082	0	60
	2	166	4883	148471	0	866	140268	0	10	808	105705	0	0
	3	166	10883	134880	0	568	41730	0	7	783	29347	0	0
	4	166	98886	55184	0	558	19393	0	9	806	29348	0	0
	5	166	70058	84012	0	494	20	0	6	804	29348	0	0
	6	166	15352	138718	0	495	20	0	9	814	29346	0	0
	7	171	15431	138640	0	498	0	0	16	816	29372	0	0

5   Conclusions and Future Research

In this work, we have proposed the use of a mathematical model for the multi-period multi-relief service location-allocation problem. We considered three different objective functions aiming to evaluate the early opening of facilities, allocation of affected population, and a balance between these two objectives. To analyze the performance of our model, we tested over real data in the case of Bogotá-city in Colombia. Through the estimation of the demand during a disaster, we found how relief service locations must be opened and how to allocate the affected population. Future work will include the analysis and estimation of parameters within different zones and the use of stochastic elements to analyze different scenarios.

References

1. Asociación Colombiana de Ingeniería Sísmica (AIS): Estudio general de amenaza sísmica de colombia. Tech. rep., Asociación Colombiana de Ingeniería Sísmica (AIS) (2009)
2. Ayala-García, J.: Desastres naturales en colombia: un análisis regional. Tech. rep. (July 2023). https://doi.org/10.32468/dtseru.317, https://repositorio.banrep.gov.co/handle/20.500.12134/10669

3. Bayraktar, O.B., Günneç, D., Salman, F.S., Yücel, E.: Relief aid provision to en route refugees: multi-period mobile facility location with mobile demand. Eur. J. Oper. Res. **301**(2), 708–725 (2022). https://doi.org/10.1016/j.ejor.2021.11.011 , https://www.sciencedirect.com/science/article/pii/S0377221721009577

4. Büsing, C., Comis, M., Schmidt, E., Streicher, M.: Robust strategic planning for mobile medical units with steerable and unsteerable demands. Eur. J. Oper. Res. **295**(1), 34–50 (2021). https://doi.org/10.1016/j.ejor.2021.02.037, https://www.sciencedirect.com/science/article/pii/S0377221721001508

5. Carter, W.N.: Disaster Management A Disaster Manager's Handbook (2008). https://www.think-asia.org/bitstream/handle/11540/5035/disaster-management-handbook.pdf?sequence=1

6. Centre for Research on the Epidemiology of Disasters (CRED): 2023 disasters in numbers: A significant year of disaster impact. Tech. rep., Centre for Research on the Epidemiology of Disasters (CRED) (2024). https://files.emdat.be/reports/2023_EMDAT_report.pdf

7. Fondo de Prevención y Atención de Emergencias (FOPAE): Escenario de daños en bogotá por un sismo de la falla frontal de magnitud 7.0. Tech. rep., FOPAE (2011). http://www.sire.gov.co/documents/13276/69801/Escenario+sismo+Magnitud+7.0+de+la+Falla+Frontal.pdf/99bf1555-291d-4ae6-8e7e-3fb90437776e

8. Kara, B.Y., Rancourt, M.È.: Location problems in humanitarian supply chains. In: Laporte, G., Nickel, S., Saldanha da Gama, F. (eds.) Location Science, pp. 611–629. Springer, Cham (2019). https://doi.org/10.1007/978-3-030-32177-2_21

9. Lim, Z.H., Soo, Y.P., Loo, J.H.Y.: Clinical profiles of patients referred to an ear, nose and throat specialist clinic via community mobile hearing clinic in singapore. Proc. Singapore Healthcare **30**(4), 286–293 (2021). https://doi.org/10.1177/2010105820979322

10. Organización Panamericana de la Salud (OPS): Nota técnica sobre los requisitos mínimos de los equipos médicos de emergencia (emt) que responden a desastres y emergencias en las américas. Tech. rep. (2020). https://www.paho.org/es/documentos/nota-tecnica-sobre-requisitos-minimos-equipos-medicos-emergencia-emt-que-responden

11. Santa González, R., Cherkesly, M., Crainic, T.G., Ève Rancourt, M.: Multi-period location routing: an application to the planning of mobile clinic operations in iraq. Comput. Operat. Re. **159**, 106288 (2023). https://doi.org/10.1016/j.cor.2023.106288. https://www.sciencedirect.com/science/article/pii/S0305054823001521

12. Savaşer, S., Kara, B.: Mobile healthcare services in rural areas: an application with periodic location routing problem. OR Spectrum **44**, 875–910 (2022). https://doi.org/10.1007/s00291-022-00670-3

13. SDP: Secretaría Distrital de Planeación de Bogotá (2022). https://sdpbogota.maps.arcgis.com/apps/MapSeries/index.html?appid=cfaba9e14f3e46ea8f2ef143075bb17d, Accessed 27 June 2024

14. Secretaría Distrital de Integración Social: Lineamientos para el montaje de alojamientos temporales institucionales en caso de emergencias nivel 3 para el distrito capital. Tech. rep., Secretaría Distrital de Integración Social. https://www.sire.gov.co/documents/504649/508838/LINEAMIENTOS+PARA+EL+MONTAJE+DE+ALOJAMIENTOS.pdf/f4918e0f-22b3-43a8-9825-4039f787cc2b

15. SGC, GEM, Zapata, O.P., Let al.: Modelo nacional de amenaza sísmica para colombia. Tech. rep., Servicio Geológico Colombiano; Global Earthquake Model (2018). https://recordcenter.sgc.gov.co/default.aspx
16. UN General Assembly, UNDRR: Report of the open-ended intergovernmental expert working group on indicators and terminology relating to disaster risk reduction. Tech. Rep. 644, UN General Assembly, UNDRR (2016). https://www.undrr.org/quick/11605

Harmony Search Based Metaheuristic for the Index Tracking Problem

Julián Antonio Díaz Ayón[✉], María de Lourdes Sandoval Solis,
Rogelio González Velázquez, Maya Carrillo Ruiz, and Alfonso Garcés-Báez

Benemérita Universidad Autónoma de Puebla, Puebla 72570, Mexico
julian.diazayon@viep.com.mx,
{maria.sandoval,maya.carrillo,alfonso.garces}@correo.buap.mx

Abstract. The Index Tracking Problem involves the creation of an investment portfolio that accurately replicates the behavior of a market index. Being an NP-Hard optimization problem, it is well-suited for metaheuristic approaches. Drawing inspiration from the Harmony Search algorithm, the Harmony Search algorithm for Portfolio Optimization is presented. This algorithm addresses the problem's complex constraints by utilizing two search operators that effectively handle both the problem itself and the most difficult constraints, and it incorporates two population initialization strategies that aid in achieving convergence and can deal with problems of big size.

Keywords: portfolio optimization · operations research · metaheuristics · index tracking · harmoy search

1 Introduction

The Index Tracking Problem involves the creation of an investment portfolio that accurately replicates the behavior of a market index.

Since the ITP is an NP-Complete problem, a viable alternative for its solution is to employ metaheuristic algorithms. In this regard, this study proposes a metaheuristic algorithm inspired by the Harmony Search algorithm (HS) that can provide high-quality solutions at a low cost for the ITP.

The main objective of this study is to propose a metaheuristic algorithm capable of: (1) producing high-quality solutions at a low cost for the ITP; (2) dealing with some of the most challenging constraints of the ITP.

The rest of this study is organized as follows: Sect. 2 summarizes the related work on the ITP; Sect. 3 presents the necessary definitions and the mathematical formulation of the problem; Sect. 4 analyzes and discusses the proposed algorithm to solve the ITP, including its inspiration and how it handles the constraints; Sect. 5 presents the conclusions; and finally, the references.

J. C. Figueroa-García et al. (Eds.): WEA 2024, CCIS 2223, pp. 15–26, 2025.
https://doi.org/10.1007/978-3-031-74598-0_2

2   Related Work

Doering et al. [5] do an excellent job of synthesizing the state of the art in the use of metaheuristics for solving various portfolio optimization problems, including the Index Tracking Problem (ITP).

Next, we describe the most recent works on portfolio optimization, specifically focusing on the ITP.

The mean-variance model for portfolio selection proposed by Markowitz [9] marks the beginning of portfolio theory. The ITP is a modification of the portfolio optimization problem solved by Markowitz.

The simplest formulation of the ITP has several limitations that hinder its practical application. Therefore, various extensions and modifications that consider operational, administrative, or transaction cost constraints have been developed. Beasley et al. [3] develop a formulation that considers transaction costs and solves the ITP with an evolutionary algorithm. Derigs and Nickel [4] consider transaction costs and other complex constraints, proposing a two-phase simulated annealing approach to solve the ITP.

Several authors have used genetic algorithms (GA) to solve the ITP, both in pure and hybrid forms. Torrubiano and Suárez [11] propose a hybrid algorithm that combines GA with a deterministic quadratic programming solver. Strub and Trautmann [14] employ a GA to solve the ITP, where the fitness of each individual is determined using quadratic programming. Garcia et al. [6] compare the performance between GA and the taboo search algorithm (TS), concluding that TS is more efficient than GA in tackling the ITP.

Due to its efficiency, modified or hybrid versions of the differential evolution algorithm (DE) have been applied to solve the ITP, yielding good results. Krink et al. [8] use a hybrid algorithm that combines DE with combinatorial search. Scozzari et al. [12] present a mixed-integer quadratic programming formulation that complies with the UCITS rules[1], and propose a hybrid algorithm that combines DE with a quadratic programming solver to solve it.

Other metaheuristics have also been employed to solve the ITP. Affolter et al. [1] use several modified versions of the invasive weed algorithm (IWO), but could not obtain better solutions than previous results. Silva et al. [13] utilize the adaptive random greedy search (GRASP) procedure, obtaining solutions of the same quality in less time than those obtained with hybrid CPLEX and GA.

3   Problem Formulation

In this section, the mathematical formulation of the problem is presented. This formulation is based on the one introduced in [2,10], with some modifications.

---

[1] The UCITS regulation specifies the asset classes in which a fund can invest, the way investments are linked to these asset classes, and the valuations that can be made in a fund.

3.1   Definitions

Suppose that the price of a market index I and the N instruments that compose it are observed over time periods $t = 0, 1, \ldots, T$.

Definition 1. *Let v_{it} be the value (price) of asset i at time t. Then, the continuously compounded return or logarithmic return of asset i at time t is:*

$$r_{it} = \log \left(\frac{v_{it}}{v_{it-1}} \right). \tag{1}$$

Definition 2. *Let I_t be the price of the index at time t. Then, the continuously compounded return or logarithmic return of the index at time t is:*

$$R_t^I = \log \left(\frac{I_t}{I_{t-1}} \right). \tag{2}$$

Definition 3. *Let X_i be the number of units of the asset in the portfolio $\mathcal{P}$ at time T. Let H be the cash added or withdrawn at time T. Then, the total value of $\mathcal{P}$ at time T is*

$$C = \sum_{i=1}^{N} v_{iT} X_i + H. \tag{3}$$

Definition 4. *Let $\mathcal{P}$ be a portfolio of N assets. Then, for all $i = 1, \ldots, N$, the following are defined:*

X_i is the number of units of asset i in portfolio $\mathcal{P}$.

$\varepsilon_i \in \mathbb{R}^+$ is the minimum proportion of $\mathcal{P}$ that must be held in asset i if the asset is present.

$\delta_i \in \mathbb{R}^+$ is the maximum proportion of $\mathcal{P}$ that should be held in asset i if the asset is present.

$f_i^b \in \mathbb{R}^+$ is the proportional transaction cost associated with buying one unit of asset i at time T, such that buying one unit of asset i at time T incurs a cost of $f_i^b v_{iT}$.

$f_i^s \in \mathbb{R}^+$ is the proportional transaction cost associated with selling one unit of asset i at time T, such that selling one unit of asset i at time T incurs a cost of $f_i^s v_{iT}$.

$F_i^b \in \mathbb{R}^+$ is the fixed cost of buying one unit of asset i at time T.

$F_i^s \in \mathbb{R}^+$ is the fixed cost of selling one unit of asset i at time T.

$M_i^b \in \mathbb{Z}^+$ is the maximum number of units of asset i that can be bought at time T, if it is decided to buy asset i.

$M_i^s \in \mathbb{Z}^+$ is the maximum number of units of asset i that can be sold at time T, if it is decided to sell asset i.

$\gamma \in [0, 1]$ is the limit on the proportion of C that can be consumed as transaction costs.

Definition 5. *Let X_i be the number of units of asset i in the portfolio $\mathcal{P}$. Let C be the total value of $\mathcal{P}$ at time T. Let v_{iT} be the price of asset i at time T. Then the weight*

$$w_i = \frac{X_i v_{iT}}{C}, \quad i = 1, \ldots, N \tag{4}$$

is the proportion of the value C of $\mathcal{P}$ assigned to asset i.

A portfolio $\mathcal{P}$ is completely determined by its weight vector $\mathbf{w} = (w_1, w_2, \ldots, w_N)$.

Definition 6. *Let $\mathcal{P}$ be a portfolio of N assets. Let w_i be the weight of asset i. Let r_{it} be the logarithmic return of asset i at time t. Then, the logarithmic return of $\mathcal{P}$ at time t is*

$$R_t^{\mathbf{w}} = \sum_{i=1}^{N} w_i r_{it}. \tag{5}$$

When solving the ITP, one can either construct a portfolio from scratch or, more commonly, already have a portfolio $\mathcal{P}$ in place and aim to update its weights to achieve better performance. By updating $\mathcal{P}$, an updated portfolio $\mathcal{P}_a$ is obtained. During this process, assets in $\mathcal{P}$ are bought and sold. To calculate transaction costs and other relevant quantities that appear in the problem's constraints, it is helpful to express them in terms of the following auxiliary variables, which are computed from $\mathbf{w}$.

Definition 7. *Let $\mathcal{P}$ be a portfolio of N assets. Let $\mathcal{P}_a$ be the updated portfolio. Then, $\forall i = 1, \ldots, N$:*

$x_i \in \mathbb{R}^+$ *is the number of units of asset i that are chosen to have in the new portfolio $\mathcal{P}_a$.*

$$z_i = \begin{cases} 1, & x_i > 0, \\ 0, & x_i = 0. \end{cases}$$

$y_i^b \in \mathbb{R}^+$ *the number of units of asset i that are bought at time T.*
$y_i^s \in \mathbb{R}^+$ *is the number of units of asset i that are sold at time T.*

$$\alpha_i^b = \begin{cases} 1, & \text{if at least one unit of asset i is bought at time T,} \\ 0, & \text{otherwise.} \end{cases}$$

$$\alpha_i^s = \begin{cases} 1, & \text{if at least one unit of asset i is sold at time T,} \\ 0, & \text{otherwise.} \end{cases}$$

Due to the large amounts of money involved, we can consider $x_i, y_i^b, y_i^s \in \mathbb{R}^+, \forall i = 1, 2, \ldots, N$.

The way to calculate x_i from w_i, $\forall i = 1, 2, \ldots, N$, is through the equation:

$$x_i = \frac{w_i C}{v_{iT}}. \tag{6}$$

3.2   Index Tracking Problem

Now we describe the decision variables, constraints, and objective function of the ITP.

Decision Variables. The decision variables of the ITP are the weights of the weight vector $\mathbf{w} = (w_1, w_2, \ldots, w_N)$.

Restrictions. The restrictions considered for the ITP are:
    Las restricciones consideradas para el ITP son:

$$\sum_{i=1}^{N} w_i = 1 \tag{7}$$

$$\sum_{i=1}^{N} z_i = K \tag{8}$$

$$\varepsilon_i z_i \leq w_i \leq \delta_i z_i, \qquad i = 1, \ldots, N \tag{9}$$

$$x_i = X_i + y_i^b - y_i^s, \qquad i = 1, \ldots, N \tag{10}$$

$$\alpha_i^b + \alpha_i^s \leq 1, \qquad i = 1, \ldots, N \tag{11}$$

$$y_i^b \leq M_i^b \alpha_i^b, \qquad i = 1, \ldots, N \tag{12}$$

$$y_i^s \leq \min[M_i^s, X_i] \alpha_i^s, \qquad i = 1, \ldots, N \tag{13}$$

$$\sum_{i=1}^{N} v_{iT} x_i = C \tag{14}$$

$$\sum_{i=1}^{N} \left(f_i^b v_{iT} y_i^b + f_i^s v_{iT} y_i^s + F_i^b \alpha_i^b + F_i^s \alpha_i^s \right) \leq \gamma C \tag{15}$$

$$y_i^b, y_i^s, x_i \geq 0, \qquad i = 1, \ldots, N \tag{16}$$

$$\alpha_i^b, \alpha_i^s, z_i \in \{0, 1\}, \qquad i = 1, \ldots, N \tag{17}$$

Equation 7 ensures that the sum of weights w_i equals 1 (consistency constraint).

Equation (8) ensures that there are only K assets in the new portfolio $\mathcal{P}_a$ (cardinality constraint).

Equation (9) ensures that if asset i is not in $\mathcal{P}_a$, then $x_i = 0$; it also ensures that if asset i is in $\mathcal{P}_a$, then the number of units of asset i remains within the allowed limits.

Equation (10) expresses the number of units of asset i in $\mathcal{P}_a$, that is, we have X_i units, buy y_i^b and sell y_i^s, resulting in x_i units.

Equation (11) makes it impossible to buy and sell units of asset i at the same time if we decide to change the units of that asset; that is, we have three options: buy, sell, or not modify the current number of units X_i.

Equation (12) ensures that the number of units we buy of asset i does not exceed the maximum allowed M_i^b, if we are going to buy at least one unit of that asset. That is, this equation forces $y_i^b = 0$ if $\alpha_i^b = 0$, and $y_i^b \leq M_i^b$ if $\alpha_i^b = 1$.

Equation (13) ensures that the number of units we sell of asset i is not greater than the minimum between: the minimum allowed M_i^s or the number of units X_i present, if we are going to sell at least one unit of that asset. That is, this equation forces $y_i^s = 0$ if $\alpha_i^s = 0$, and $y_i^s \leq \min(M_i^s, X_i)$ if $\alpha_i^s = 1$.

Equation (14) ensures that the value of the new portfolio $\mathcal{P}_a$ at time T is equal to the value of the initial portfolio $\mathcal{P}$ plus the change in cash.

Equation (15) limits the total transaction cost not to exceed the amount of γC.

Equation (16) establishes that integer variables are greater than or equal to 0.

Equation (17) establishes that binary variables take the value 0 or 1.

Objective Function

Definition 8. *The average of the absolute differences between the portfolio $\mathcal{P}$ and the index I is defined as:*

$$TE = \frac{\left(\sum_{t=1}^{T} |R_t^{\mathbf{w}} - R_t^{I}|^{\beta}\right)^{1/\beta}}{T} \tag{18}$$

where $\beta \geq 1 \wedge; \beta \in \mathbb{Z}$.

The ITP consists of minimizing the above objective function subject to the considered constraints.

4 Algorithms

In this section, the proposed algorithm for solving the ITP is presented. It is inspired by the harmony search algorithm proposed by Geem et al. in 2001 [7].

4.1 Harmony Search for Portfolio Optimization

Taking inspiration from the original HS algorithm, a modified version of HS is proposed to solve the ITP, called Harmony Search for Portfolio Optimization (HSPO). Algorithm 1 shows the pseudocode for HSPO.

Initialization. The initial population is generated (line 2). The step size α is initialized to 1 (line 3).

Algorithm 1. Harmony Search for Portfolio Optimization

Require: Number of iterations $niter$ and probability of performing exploitation mutation $hmpa$.

1:
2: Generate the initial population $population$.
3: $\alpha \leftarrow 1$
4: **for** $iter$ in $1 : niter$ **do**
5:
6:     Randomly choose a $candidate$ from $population$.
7:
8:     **if** $rand() < hmpa$ **then**
9:         $candidate \leftarrow$ EXPLOITATIONMUTATION$(candidate, \alpha)$
10:     **else**
11:         $candidate \leftarrow$ EXPLORATIONMUTATION$(candidate)$
12:     **end if**
13:
14:     **if** $candidate$ is better than the worst element in $population$. **then**
15:         Replace the worst element in $population$ with $candidate$.
16:     **end if**
17:
18:     $\alpha \leftarrow 1 - (iter - 1)/niter$
19: **end for**
20:
21: **return** Best element in $population$.

Main Body. The main body of the algorithm is developed in lines 4–19. The loop ends when the stopping criterion is met, in this case, the maximum number of iterations. In each iteration, a solution called $candidate$ is randomly chosen from the population called $population$ (line 6).

A random number is generated with a uniform distribution in the range $[0, 1]$ (line 8). If the previous random number is less than $hmpa$, an exploitation mutation is performed on $candidate$ using the function EXPLOITATIONMUTATION (line 9). Otherwise, an exploration mutation is performed on $candidate$ using the function EXPLORATIONMUTATION (line 11).

If $candidate$ is better than the worst solution in the population, then the worst solution in the population is replaced by $candidate$ (lines 14–16).

Finally, the step size α is reduced according to the chosen rule (line 18).

Postprocessing. The algorithm ends by delivering the best solution in the population (line 21).

Exploitation Operator. Algorithm 2 shows the pseudocode of the EXPLOITATIONMUTATION function. This function is responsible for performing exploitation or intensification of solutions.

The EXPLOITATIONMUTATION function takes as parameters a solution w, the step size α, and the limits ε and δ. Two integers i and j are chosen such that

$w[i] > 0$ and $w[j] > 0$ (lines 1-2). u is assigned the product of the step size α and a random number with a uniform distribution in the range $[0, \min(w[i] - \varepsilon, \delta - w[j])]$ (line 4). Using the term $\min(w[i] - \varepsilon, \delta - w[j])$ as the upper limit of the uniform distribution aims to directly satisfy constraint 9, which improves the efficiency of the algorithm. α is reduced with each iteration, so u takes increasingly smaller values, allowing for a finer search around promising regions. The amount u is added to $w[j]$ and subtracted from $w[i]$ (lines 6–7). The modified solution is returned (line 9).

Additionally, EXPLOITATIONMUTATION has a powerful advantage, and that is that all the solutions it delivers always satisfy the constraints.

$$\sum_{i=1}^{N} w_i = 1 \tag{19}$$

$$\sum_{i=1}^{N} z_i = K \tag{20}$$

$$\varepsilon_i \leq w_i \leq \delta_i. \tag{21}$$

Due to the fact that it adds to one asset what is subtracted from another, the guaranteed satisfaction of the above constraints is one of the most important reasons to perform exploitation in this way.

Algorithm 2. EXPLOITATIONMUTATION

Require: Weight vector w, step size α, limits ε and δ.
1: Choose i such that $w[i] > 0$.
2: Choose j such that $w[j] > 0$
3:
4: $u \leftarrow \alpha \cdot rand(0, \min(w[i] - \varepsilon, \delta - w[j]))$
5:
6: $w[j] \leftarrow w[j] + u$
7: $w[i] \leftarrow w[i] - u$
8:
9: **return** w

Exploration Operator. Algorithm 3 shows the pseudocode of the function EXPLORATIONMUTATION. This function is responsible for performing exploration or diversification of solutions.

The EXPLORATIONMUTATION function takes a solution w as a parameter. Two integers i and j are chosen such that $w[i] > 0$ and $w[j] == 0$ (lines 1–2). Then, the value of $w[i]$ is assigned to $w[j]$ and $w[i]$ is assigned the value 0 (lines 4–5). The modified solution is returned (line 7).

EXPLORATIONMUTATION also satisfies the constraints (19), (20), and (21). This is because it swaps the values of a weight equal to zero and a weight greater than zero. Therefore, similar to EXPLORATIONMUTATION, it is an effective way of conducting the search.

Algorithm 3. EXPLORATIONMUTATION

Require: Weight vector w.
 1: Choose i such that $w[i] > 0$
 2: Choose j such that $w[j] == 0$
 3: $w[j] \leftarrow w[i]$
 4: $w[i] \leftarrow 0$
 5:
 6: **return** w

The reason for performing exploitation and exploration with the functions EXPLOITATIONMUTATION and EXPLORATIONMUTATION, is that they produce solutions that always satisfy the constraints $\sum_{i=1}^{N} w_i = 1$ and $\sum_{i=1}^{N} z_i = K$, which are generally difficult to satisfy. EXPLOITATIONMUTATION adds to one weight what it subtracts from another, and EXPLORATIONMUTATION exchanges the value of a weight greater than zero with the value of a weight equal to zero. The inspiration for the EXPLOITATIONMUTATION and EXPLORATIONMUTATION operators comes from [2], where a version of SA with a similar, simpler operator is implemented.

4.2 Population Initialization

The initial population plays an important role in the performance of HSPO. Starting with a completely random population of solutions is not a good idea because, given an initial weight vector w_0, combined with the constraints that limit transaction costs, the optimal solution for a certain instance of ITP is relatively "close" to w_0. In other words, a proper construction of the initial population can improve the performance of HSPO.

The initial population is constructed using two distinct strategies for each half. The first half is constructed by starting with the initial weight vector w_0 and performing mutations according to the function MUTATION, which is a combination of EXPLOITATIONMUTATION and EXPLORATIONMUTATION. Algorithm 4 shows the pseudocode for the MUTATION function.

The MUTATION function takes as input a weight vector w and the limits ε and δ, chooses two random integers i and j, such that $w[i] > 0$ and $w[j] \geq 0$ (line 1). If $w[j] == 0$, it assigns $w[j]$ the value of $w[i]$, just like in the exploration operator (lines 3–5). Otherwise, it generates a random number u with a uniform distribution in the range $[0, \min(w[i] - \varepsilon, \delta - w[j])]$, adds it to $w[j]$ and subtracts it from $w[i]$ (lines 7–9), just like the exploitation function does. Finally, it returns the weight vector w (line 12).

The second half of the initial population is constructed by creating a weight vector w_b such that: $w_b[i] = 1/K \iff w_0[i] \geq 0$; and $w_b[i] = 0 \iff w_0[i] = 0$. Starting from w_b, perturbations are made using MUTATION to create new solutions.

The reason for following the above strategy for the second half is that the parameters ε and δ not only restrict the minimum and maximum weight of each asset but also the size K of the tracking portfolio. For example, in the experiments, values of $\varepsilon = 0.01$ and $\delta = 1$ are chosen, which make the maximum value of $K = 100 = 1/0.01$ in the tracking portfolio. As $\delta = 1$, there is a minimum value of $K = 1 = 1/1$. So, for large values of K, the optimal solution for an ITP instance could be"close" to w_b.

Algorithm 4. MUTATION

Require: Weight vector w and limits ε and δ.
1: Choose i, j such that $w[i] > 0$ and $w[j] \geq 0$.
2:
3: **if** $w[j] == 0$ **then**
4:     $w[j] \leftarrow w[i]$
5:     $w[i] \leftarrow 0$
6: **else**
7:     $u \leftarrow rand(0, \min(w[i] - \varepsilon, \delta - w[j]))$
8:     $w[j] \leftarrow w[j] + u$
9:     $w[i] \leftarrow w[i] - u$
10: **end if**
11:
12: **return** w

4.3   Dealing with All the Constraints

The ITP is a constrained optimization problem. HSPO's mutation operators are designed in such a way that they can help deal with the most difficult constraints of the ITP, but not all of them. Specifically, HSPO does not have a mechanism that deals with all the constraints of ITP. Therefore, some constraint-handling technique must be employed. There are several constraint-handling methods for *constrained optimization problems*, such as the *penalty method* [15].

5   Conclusions

Constructing an investment portfolio is generally a complex task. In principle, there are two types of strategies for building an investment portfolio: (1) active strategies and (2) passive strategies. One of these passive strategies involves creating a portfolio that replicates the behavior of a market index. This is known as the Index Tracking Problem (ITP). The ITP is an NP-Complete optimization problem, making it convenient to employ metaheuristic optimization techniques.

Taking inspiration from the Harmony Search algorithm, we present the Harmonic Search for Portfolio Optimization (HSPO) algorithm. The ITP involves complex constraints that make the search for its optimal solution challenging. HSPO utilizes two search operators that are particularly effective in addressing the ITP and certain constraints directly and it employs two population initialization strategies to facilitate convergence.

As part of future work, it is of interest to explore and compare the behavior of HSPO with mathematical programming software packages. Additionally, there is scope for enhancing the efficiency of the algorithm itself and its operators through further improvements and refinements.

References

1. Affolter, K., Hanne, T., Schweizer, D., Dornberger, R.: Invasive weed optimization for solving index tracking problems. Soft Comput. **20**(9, SI), 3393–3401 (2016). https://doi.org/10.1007/s00500-015-1799-x, 1st International Conference on Soft Computing and Machine Intelligence (ISCMI), New Delhi, INDIA, 2014
2. Arratia, A.: Computational Finance An Introductory Course with R. Atlantis Studies in Computational Finance and Financial Engineering, Atlantis Press (2014)
3. Beasley, J., Meade, N., Chang, T.: An evolutionary heuristic for the index tracking problem. European J. Operat. Res. **148**(3), 621–643 (2003). https://doi.org/10.1016/S0377-2217(02)00425-3
4. Derigs, U., Nickel, N.: On a local-search heuristic for a class of tracking error minimization problems in portfolio management. Annals Operat. Res. **131**(1-4), 45–77 (2004). https://doi.org/10.1023/B:ANOR.0000039512.98833.5a
5. Doering, J., Kizys, R., Juan, A.A., Fito, A., Polat, O.: Metaheuristics for rich portfolio optimisation and risk management: current state and future trends. Operat. Res. Perspect. **6** (2019). https://doi.org/10.1016/j.orp.2019.100121
6. Garcia, F., Guijarro, F., Oliver, J.: Index tracking optimization with cardinality constraint: a performance comparison of genetic algorithms and tabu search heuristics. Neural Comput. Appli. **30**(8), 2625–2641 (2018). https://doi.org/10.1007/s00521-017-2882-2
7. Geem, Z., Kim, J., Loganathan, G.: A new heuristic optimization algorithm: harmony search. Simulation **76**(2), 60–68 (2001). https://doi.org/10.1177/003754970107600201
8. Krink, T., Mittnik, S., Paterlini, S.: Differential evolution and combinatorial search for constrained index-tracking. Annals Operat. Res. **172**(1), 153–176 (2009). https://doi.org/10.1007/s10479-009-0552-1
9. Markowitz, H.: Portfolio selection*. J. Financ. **7**(1), 77–91 (1952). https://doi.org/10.1111/j.1540-6261.1952.tb01525.x, https://onlinelibrary.wiley.com/doi/abs/10.1111/j.1540-6261.1952.tb01525.x
10. Mezali, H., Beasley, J.E.: Index tracking with fixed and variable transaction costs. Optimizat. Lett. **8**(1), 61–80 (2014). https://doi.org/10.1007/s11590-012-0534-0
11. Ruiz-Torrubiano, R., Suarez, A.: A hybrid optimization approach to index tracking. Annals Operat. Res. **166**(1), 57–71 (2009). https://doi.org/10.1007/s10479-008-0404-4, symposium on Applied Mathematical Programming and Modeling (APMOD 2006), Madrid, SPAIN, JUN 18-21, 2006

12. Scozzari, A., Tardella, F., Paterlini, S., Krink, T.: Exact and heuristic approaches for the index tracking problem with ucits constraints. Annals Operat. Res. **205**(1), 235–250 (2013). https://doi.org/10.1007/s10479-012-1207-1
13. Silva, J.C.S., Silva, D.F.d.L., de Almeida Filho, A.T.: An enhanced grasp approach for the index tracking problem. Inter. Trans. Operat. Res. (2022). https://doi.org/10.1111/itor.13163
14. Strub, O., Trautmann, N.: A genetic algorithm for the ucits-constrained index-tracking problem. In: 2017 Ieee Congress On Evolutionary Computation (CEC), pp. 822–829. IEEE Congress on Evolutionary Computation, IEEE; IEEE Computat Intelligence Soc; Univ Pais Vasco; CEC (2017), iEEE Congress on Evolutionary Computation (CEC), Spain, 05-08 Jun (2017)
15. Yang, X.S.: Nature-Inspired Optimization Algorithms. Elsevier (2014)

Chaotic Binary Fox Optimizer for Solving Set Covering Problem

Felipe Cisternas-Caneo[1(✉)] [iD], Broderick Crawford[1] [iD], Ricardo Soto[1] [iD],
José Barrera-García[1] [iD], Marcelo Becerra-Rozas[1] [iD], and Giovanni Giachetti[2] [iD]

[1] Pontificia Universidad Católica de Valparaíso, Valparaíso, Chile
{felipe.cisternas.c, marcelo.becerra.r}@mail.pucv.cl,
{broderick.crawford, ricardo.soto, jose.barrera}@pucv.cl
[2] Universidad Andres Bello, Santiago, Chile
giovanni.giachetti@unab.cl

Abstract. In this paper, we binarize a novel algorithm called the Fox Optimizer using a two-step technique and test its performance against the Set Covering Problem. Additionally, we explore the incorporation of chaotic maps into the binarization process. To benchmark the binary Fox Optimizer, we compare it with two well-known and documented metaheuristics: Particle Swarm Optimization and Grey Wolf Optimizer. Each algorithm is tested with standard, sine chaotic, elitist, and elitist sine chaotic binarization rules. Our findings demonstrate that elitist configurations, especially when combined with sine chaotic binarization, consistently yield superior results, providing robust and reliable performance in obtaining high-quality solutions. Conversely, standard binarization configurations exhibit enhanced convergence capabilities, proving effective for problems with rapid convergence requirements or lower complexity. This study highlights the importance of aligning algorithm configurations with specific problem characteristics to optimize performance in practical applications.

Keywords: Fox Optimizer · Combinatorial Problems · Binarization Schemes · Chaotic Maps · Metaheuristics

1 Introduction

Optimization problems are increasingly common in the real world. Within optimization problems, we find combinatorial optimization problems where the decision variables are categorical, such as binary, and the optimization process lies in finding the best possible combination. The difficulty of solving these problems grows exponentially as we increase the number of decision variables. In particular, the search space of a binary combinatorial problem is 2^n, where n represents the number of decision variables. Among the various optimization algorithms that have been proposed in the literature [24], metaheuristics have emerged as a particularly promising approach.

© The Author(s), under exclusive license to Springer Nature Switzerland AG 2025
J. C. Figueroa-García et al. (Eds.): WEA 2024, CCIS 2223, pp. 27–38, 2025.
https://doi.org/10.1007/978-3-031-74598-0_3

The study of metaheuristics has grown in recent years, with hybridizations emerging as the current trend. There exist hybridizations between metaheuristics such as those proposed in [1,21], as well as approaches where machine learning techniques enhance metaheuristics [5,17]. Other approaches utilize chaos theory to modify the stochastic behavior of metaheuristics [2,14].

Stochastic behavior is the main component of metaheuristics. In recent years, there has been an interest in controlling these stochastic components and seeing their impact on the metaheuristic performance [6].

In reviewing the different metaheuristics existing in the literature [20], we can observe that most of them are designed to solve continuous problems; therefore, to solve binary combinatorial problems, it is necessary to binarize them. According to the literature [4,9], there are different ways to binarize metaheuristics, among which the two-step technique stands out. This binarization process is carried out in two steps: (1) applying a transfer function and (2) applying a binarization rule. In a recent study [8], we can see that a modification was made to the binarization rule by incorporating chaotic maps.

In the present work, we solved a classic combinatorial problems: the Set Covering Problem. We have used Fox Optimizer [19] to experiment as it is a newly developed metaheuristic for solving continuous optimization problems. The No Free Lunch Theorem [12] motivates us to try it in binary combinatorial problems.

A summary of the content structure of the following sections: Sect. 2 presents the application of chaotic maps in metaheuristics. Section 3 shows us the definition of Fox Optimizer, Sect. 4 shows us the definition of Binary Fox Optimizer, Sect. 5 shows us the definition of Chaotic Binary Fox Optimizer, Sect. 6 shows the experimental results with a convergence and execution time analysis to end with Sect. 7 with the conclusions of the work.

2   Chaotic Maps Into Metaheuristics

Hybridization between metaheuristics and chaotic maps can be classified into 4 categories:

- **Initialization:** Chaotic maps can be an alternative to random solution generation for metaheuristics, as they can generate initial solutions or populations. The chaotic dynamics facilitate the dissemination of the initial solutions throughout the search space, thereby promoting exploration [3,7,16,26].
- **Mutation:** Chaotic maps can perturb or mutate solutions. By utilizing chaotic behavior as a means of randomness, the metaheuristic algorithm can generate diverse and unpredictable variations within the solutions, thus facilitating exploration [2,25].
- **Local Search:** Chaotic maps can guide the local search process in metaheuristics. The incorporation of chaotic dynamics into the local search phase enables the algorithm to circumvent local optima and explore diverse regions of the solution space. [10,13,18,27].

– **Parameter Adaptation:** Chaotic maps can be utilized to adapt the parameters of the metaheuristics algorithm dynamically. The chaotic behavior can help in adjusting parameters such as mutation rate, crossover probabilities, or step sizes, enhancing the adaptability of algorithm during the optimization process [11, 14, 15].

Existing works primarily integrate chaotic maps to adjust metaheuristics parameters, with the objective of achieving a balance between exploration and exploitation.

3   Fox Optimizer

The FOX algorithm is inspired by the foraging behavior of foxes presented in [19]. It conceptualizes foxes hunting in snowy environments where they rely on subtle sensory cues to locate and capture prey. The algorithm translates this behavior into a mathematical model where the solution to an optimization problem improves iteratively in a way analogous to a fox closing in on its prey.

The algorithm begins with initializing a population of foxes, each representing a potential solution to the optimization problem. The main loop of the algorithm simulates the hunting process, where each fox adjusts its position in the search space to approach the optimal solution ($Best$). This process comprises two main phases: exploration and exploitation. To balance these two phases, a condition employing a random variable with a probability of 50% is used to determine whether the algorithm will engage in exploration or exploitation. Algorithm 1 shows the general behavior of the Fox Optimizer.

In the exploration phase, foxes randomly wander the search space according to the best position of the fox found so far. This randomness allows the algorithm to explore a wide range of potential solutions, avoiding local optima and providing a diverse solution base for the exploitation phase. This is conceptually similar to a fox scanning a broad area to detect signs of prey. This phase is evident between lines 17 and 20 of Algorithm 1.

In the exploitation phase, the fox can jump and catch its prey. This condition is linked to a variable p that fluctuates within a $[0, 1]$ range, consistent with the original work. As the value of p changes with each iteration, we must calculate the fox's new position after the jump made to approach or catch the prey. This phase is evident between lines 9 and 17 of Algorithm 1.

Algorithm 1. Fox Optimizer

    Input: The population $X = \{X_1, X_2, ..., X_i\}$
    Output: The updated population $X' = \{X'_1, X'_2, ..., X'_i\}$ and $Best$

1: Initialize random population X
2: Evaluate the objective function of each individual in the population X
3: Identify the best individual in the population ($Best$)
4: **for** *iteration* (t) **do**
5:     Initialize MinT, Jump and a

Algorithm 1. *Cont.* Fox Optimizer

6:	**for** *solution* (i) **do**
7:	r ← rand(0,1)
8:	p ← rand(0,1)
9:	**if** $r \geq 0.5$ **then** ▷ Exploitation Phase
10:	**if** $p \geq 0.18$ **then**
11:	Calculate $Dist\_Fox\_Prey$ and $Jump$
12:	$X_i^t = Dist\_Fox\_Prey \cdot Jump \cdot c_1$
13:	**else if** $p < 0.18$ **then**
14:	Calculate $Dist\_Fox\_Prey$ and $Jump$
15:	$X_i^t = Dist\_Fox\_Prey \cdot Jump \cdot c_2$
16:	**end if**
17:	**else** ▷ Exploration Phase
18:	Find MinT
19:	$X_i^t = Best \cdot \text{rand}\,(1, dimension) \cdot MinT \cdot a$
20:	**end if**
21:	**end for**
22:	Evaluate the objective function of each individual in the population X
23:	Update *Best*
24:	**end for**
25:	**return** the updated population X' where *Best* is the best result

4   Binary Fox Optimizer

Like many metaheuristics developed in the literature [20], Fox Optimizer is designed to solve continuous optimization problems. Consequently, when attempting to solve a binary combinatorial optimization problem, it is not advisable to incorporate a binarization process of the solutions. Therefore,

In the literature [4], we can highlight the two-step technique as the most used technique to binarize continuous metaheuristics. The binarization process, as its name indicates, consists of two steps. In the first step, we transfer the continuous solutions to a continuous number within the range [0,1] using a transfer function. In the second step, we apply a binarization rule to that transferred number, and as a result, we obtain a one and a zero. For more information related to transfer functions and binarization rules, you can consult [4,9].

Algorithm 2 shows the addition of binarization to Fox Optimizer. Specifically, we add only two lines. The first refers to line 1, where we generate the initial solutions randomly and with binary values. The second one refers to line 22, where we apply the two-step technique once all the solutions are perturbed according to the equations of motion of Fox Optimizer.

5   Chaotic Binary Fox Optimizer

As we have observed in Sect. 2, there are different ways to use chaotic maps within metaheuristics. Specifically, we have seen that the use of chaotic maps lies in modifying the stochastic metaheuristic behavior.

Algorithm 2. Binary Fox Optimizer

Input: The population $X = \{X_1, X_2, ..., X_i\}$
Output: The updated population $X' = \{X'_1, X'_2, ..., X'_i\}$ and $Best$

1: **Initialize binary random population X**
2: Evaluate the objective function of each individual in the population X
3: Identify the best individual in the population ($Best$)
4: **for** *iteration* (t) **do**
5:     Initialize MinT, Jump and a
6:     **for** *solution* (i) **do**
7:         r $\leftarrow$ rand(0,1)
8:         p $\leftarrow$ rand(0,1)
9:         **if** $r \geq 0.5$ **then**   ▷ Exploitation Phase
10:            **if** $p \geq 0.18$ **then**
11:                Calculate $Dist\_Fox\_Prey$ and $Jump$
12:                $X_i^t = Dist\_Fox\_Prey \cdot Jump \cdot c_1$
13:            **else if** $p < 0.18$ **then**
14:                Calculate $Dist\_Fox\_Prey$ and $Jump$
15:                $X_i^t = Dist\_Fox\_Prey \cdot Jump \cdot c_2$
16:            **end if**
17:        **else**   ▷ Exploration Phase
18:            Find MinT
19:            $X_i^t = Best \cdot \text{rand}\,(1, dimension) \cdot MinT \cdot a$
20:        **end if**
21:     **end for**
22:     **Binarization of X by two step technique**
23:     Evaluate the objective function of each individual in the population X
24:     Update $Best$
25: **end for**
26: **return** the updated population X' where $Best$ is the best result

---

Within this context, we have modified the binarization process by incorporating chaotic maps [8]. Specifically, we have modified the binarization defined in [4,9] that has a random number with a uniform distribution within the range [0,1]. This random number is replaced by a number obtained from a chaotic map.

Algorithm 3 shows the general behavior of Binary Fox Optimizer with the addition of chaotic maps. The difference with Algorithm 2 lies in lines 2 and 23. Line 2 refers to the initialization of the chaotic map to be used in the optimization process, while line 23 refers to the chaotic binarization process using a chaotic map.

6   Experimental Results

This section exhaustively analyzes the performances of various metaheuristic optimization algorithms utilizing different binarization strategies across a series of complex optimization problems. Three fundamental algorithms were analyzed:

Algorithm 3. Chaotic Binary Fox Optimizer

    Input: The population $X = \{X_1, X_2, ..., X_i\}$
    Output: The updated population $X' = \{X'_1, X'_2, ..., X'_i\}$ and *Best*

1: Initialize binary random population X
2: **Initialize the chaotic maps**
3: Evaluate the objective function of each individual in the population X
4: Identify the best individual in the population (*Best*)
5: **for** *iteration* (*t*) **do**
6:     Initialize MinT, Jump and a
7:     **for** *solution* (*i*) **do**
8:         r ← rand(0,1)
9:         p ← rand(0,1)
10:        **if** $r \geq 0.5$ **then**   ▷ Exploitation Phase
11:           **if** $p \geq 0.18$ **then**
12:               Calculate $Dist\_Fox\_Prey$ and $Jump$
13:               $X_i^t = Dist\_Fox\_Prey \cdot Jump \cdot c_1$
14:           **else if** $p < 0.18$ **then**
15:               Calculate $Dist\_Fox\_Prey$ and $Jump$
16:               $X_i^t = Dist\_Fox\_Prey \cdot Jump \cdot c_2$
17:           **end if**
18:        **else**   ▷ Exploration Phase
19:           Find MinT
20:           $X_i^t = Best \cdot \mathrm{rand}\,(1, dimension) \cdot MinT \cdot a$
21:        **end if**
22:     **end for**
23:     **Binarization of X using a chaotic number of a chaotic map**
24:     Evaluate the objective function of each individual in the population X
25:     Update *Best*
26: **end for**
27: **return** the updated population X' where *Best* is the best result

---

the Fox Optimizer Algorithm (FOX), Particle Swarm Optimization (PSO), and Grey Wolf Optimizer (GWO).

For each metaheuristic, we have used the S4 transfer function, which is detailed in [4] and four different binarization rules. The first of them corresponds to the standard binarization rule(STD), the second corresponds to the standard binarization rule with chaotic map (STD_SINE), the third corresponds to the elitist binarization rule (ELIT), and the fourth corresponds to the elitist binarization rule with chaotic map (ELIT_SINE). The chaotic map we have used is the sine chaotic map. All these binarization rules are detailed in [8].

6.1 Set Covering Problem

The Set Covering Problem (SCP) is a well-known combinatorial optimization problem that arises in various practical applications. SCP is NP-hard, which means that finding an optimal solution for large problem instances is computationally challenging.

If we consider a zero-one matrix $A = (a_{i,j})$ of size $n \times m$, a column j is said to cover a row i if $a_{i,j} = 1$. Each column j is associated with a non-negative real cost c_j. Let $I = 1, ..., n$ and $J = 1, ..., m$ represent the sets of rows and columns, respectively. The objective of the SCP is to find a subset $S \subset J$ with the minimum total cost, such that each row $i \in I$ is covered by at least one column $j \in J$.

$$\text{Minimize} \quad \sum_{j \in J} c_j x_j$$

$$\text{subject to}$$

$$\sum_{j \in J} a_{ij} x_j \geq 1, \quad \forall i \in I \tag{1}$$

$$x_j \in \{0, 1\}, \quad \forall j \in J$$

SCP is a problem that can be represented by binary values. Let $x_j \in 0, 1$, $\forall j \in 1, .., m$. In this binary representation, $x_j = 1$ if column j belongs to the feasible solution. In the case of our algorithm, each particle represents a potential binary solution.

6.2 Results Obtained

The results observed in the Tables (1, 2) revealed that the FOX-ELIT and FOX-ELIT_SINE variants consistently showed superior performance in terms of achieving the lowest values in standard deviation and relative percentage difference (RPD) metrics, suggesting greater accuracy and robustness. PSO's adaptability was evident in its relatively stable performance across the variants, with a tendency toward better outcomes in ELIT configurations, particularly in more complex problems.

In the problems scpb1 and scpnrf (Table 2), the ELIT configurations, especially with SINE binarization, proved to be the most effective, achieving not only the best individual values but also consistently low averages and minimal deviations. In less complex issues, the SINE and STD variants of FOX and GWO provided excellent outcomes. However, in more challenging scenarios, PSO with its STD version excelled, demonstrating the capability of this algorithm to effectively handle increasing complexity.

6.3 Convergence Analysis

Figure 1 shows the convergence of the algorithms used in the experimentation. For all figures, the x-axis refers to the iterations, and the y-axis refers to the best fitness obtained in each iteration. We have chosen to place the scpb1 instance randomly since, for all instances, we can observe similar behavior.

Figure 1 illustrates a noteworthy phenomenon. When the elitist binarization rule is applied, the three metaheuristics with and without chaotic maps exhibit accelerated convergence in the initial iterations. This suggests that the elitist binarization rule prioritizes the exploration of the search space.

Table 1. Results for SCP-41 to SCP-61

experiment	scp41 (429.0)				scp51 (253.0)				scp61 (138.0)			
	Best	Avg.	Dev-std	RPD	Best	Avg.	Dev-std	RPD	Best	Avg.	Dev-std	RPD
FOX-STD	20877.0	21616.23	308.9	4938.75	44801.0	45798.61	370.86	18002.22	21151.0	21591.39	214.88	15545.93
FOX-STD_SINE	21524.0	23083.94	366.16	5280.87	46642.0	48459.45	641.25	19053.93	22320.0	23172.29	346.77	16691.51
FOX-ELIT_SINE	**431.0**	**434.35**	**1.99**	**1.25**	266.0	267.26	0.51	5.64	141.0	142.65	1.84	3.37
FOX-ELIT	433.0	433.9	1.67	1.14	**257.0**	**267.03**	**1.91**	**5.55**	**138.0**	**142.97**	**2.07**	**3.6**
PSO-STD	22099.0	23086.94	338.8	5281.57	46266.0	48076.58	710.21	18902.6	22041.0	23001.97	325.27	16568.09
PSO-STD_SINE	22241.0	23244.77	442.37	5318.36	45508.0	48206.45	757.82	18953.93	21741.0	23370.0	507.43	16834.78
PSO-ELIT_SINE	433.0	434.16	1.82	1.2	256.0	267.06	2.08	5.56	141.0	142.61	1.75	3.34
PSO-ELIT	433.0	433.03	0.18	0.94	267.0	267.45	0.66	5.71	141.0	143.13	1.76	3.72
GWO-STD	22082.0	23121.26	438.07	5289.57	45717.0	48064.23	942.59	18897.72	22625.0	23295.35	333.38	16780.69
GWO-STD_SINE	22438.0	23362.71	468.52	5345.85	45888.0	48186.42	765.38	18946.02	22448.0	23414.29	378.88	16866.88
GWO-ELIT_SINE	**431.0**	**434.35**	**1.99**	**1.25**	261.0	267.13	1.24	5.58	141.0	142.52	1.81	3.27
GWO-ELIT	433.0	433.65	1.47	1.08	267.0	267.48	0.56	5.72	141.0	143.0	1.74	3.62

Table 2. Results for SCP-B1 to SCP-NRF1

experiment	scpb1 (69.0)				scpnrf1 (14.0)			
	Best	Avg.	Dev-std	RPD	Best	Avg.	Dev-std	RPD
FOX-STD	69150.0	70191.48	410.15	101626.79	115228.0	117030.52	612.62	835832.26
FOX-STD_SINE	68933.0	72946.71	1132.01	105619.87	118140.0	120663.71	1035.95	861783.64
FOX-ELIT_SINE	**69.0**	**69.45**	**0.8**	**0.65**	**14.0**	**14.06**	**0.25**	**0.46**
FOX-ELIT	**69.0**	**69.42**	**0.79**	**0.61**	**14.0**	**14.0**	**0.0**	**0.0**
PSO-STD	70431.0	72838.19	824.45	105462.6	118511.0	120892.81	968.12	863420.05
PSO-STD_SINE	71834.0	73080.06	699.59	105813.14	117880.0	120984.39	1044.06	864074.19
PSO-ELIT_SINE	**69.0**	**69.48**	**0.84**	**0.7**	**14.0**	**14.03**	**0.18**	**0.23**
PSO-ELIT	**69.0**	**69.52**	**0.76**	**0.75**	**14.0**	**14.03**	**0.18**	**0.23**
GWO-STD	71759.0	73164.84	758.57	105936.0	117934.0	120999.48	1037.68	864182.03
GWO-STD_SINE	71159.0	72871.45	776.74	105510.8	117207.0	120739.29	1307.68	862323.5
GWO-ELIT_SINE	**69.0**	**69.77**	**0.83**	**1.12**	**14.0**	**14.06**	**0.25**	**0.46**
GWO-ELIT	**69.0**	**69.32**	**0.69**	**0.47**	**14.0**	**14.0**	**0.0**	**0.0**

The standard binary classification rule exhibits a markedly different behaviour when applied in combination with a chaotic map. Figuref 1a show that the three metaheuristics used demonstrate minimal or no improvement in over the iterations. In other words, the standard binarization rule encourages the exploration of the search space. We can complement this observation with the results presented in Tables 1 and 2.

6.4   Times Analysis

Figure 2 shows the time required for each metaheuristic to execute each iteration of the optimization process. For all Figures, the x-axis refers to the iterations, while the y-axis refers to the time in seconds required for iteration execution. We have chosen the scpb1 instance again to analyze the time when its choice was random since all the instances have similar behavior.

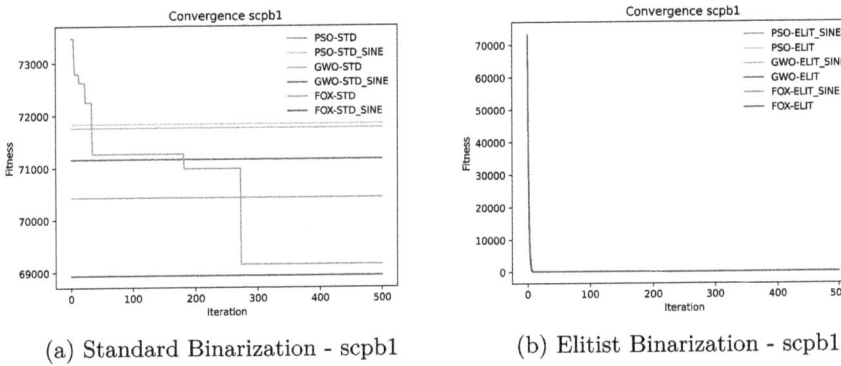

(a) Standard Binarization - scpb1   (b) Elitist Binarization - scpb1

Fig. 1. Algorithmic convergence for scp41 and scpb1 instances

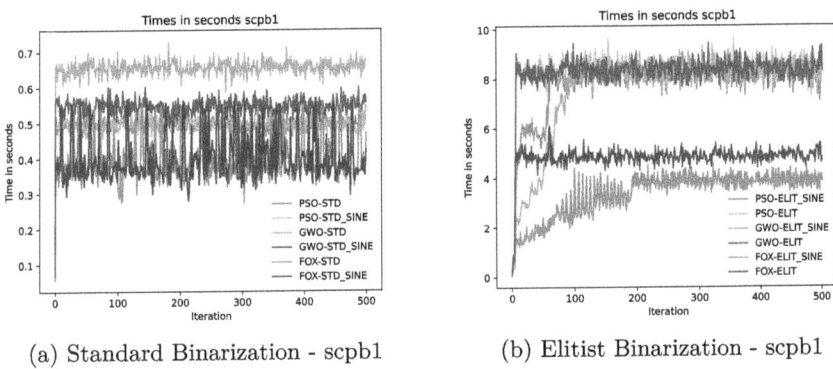

(a) Standard Binarization - scpb1   (b) Elitist Binarization - scpb1

Fig. 2. Time per iteration for scp41 and scpb1 instance (Color figure online)

Figure 2 presents remarkable findings. First, all three metaheuristics with and without chaotic map execute an iteration much faster when using the standard binarization rule over the elite binarization rule.

Secondly, Fox Optimizer executes its iterations faster than PSO and GWO in its binary and chaotic binary versions. We can see this in Figs. 2a and 2b, but it is more clearly presented in Fig. 2b.

Finally, using chaotic maps in the binarization rule helps to reduce the execution times of metaheuristics. This phenomenon is presented in Fig. 2a and Fig. 2b. Figure 2a depicts GWO with the standard binarization rule in green, whereas GWO with the standard chaotic binarization rule is presented in red. The time taken by GWO without a chaotic map to complete each iteration is between 0.6 and 0.7 s, while with the chaotic map, it is between 0.5 and 0.6 s.

On the other hand, Fig. 1b shows that the three metaheuristics with chaotic map in their first iterations are faster than the versions without chaotic map.

The main factor that differentiates execution times is the repair process used when confronted with an infeasible solution. The repair strategy proposed in our work in [22,23], has been applied in this context.

7 Conclusion

In the present work, we have demonstrated how easy is to binarize continuous metaheuristics using the two-step technique and chaotic maps. Furthermore, we have experimentally shown that Fox Optimizer, in its binary versions with and without chaotic maps, has competitive results against metaheuristics widely studied in the literature, such as Particle Swarm Optimization and Grey Wolf Optimizer.

The ELIT configurations tended to provide the best optimal results, underscoring the effectiveness of ELIT binarization in obtaining solutions that are closely aligned with the global optimum. In contrast, the STD configurations with and without chaotic map exhibited a lack of convergence across multiple runs, suggesting a high degree of efficiency in exploring the search space. The low values observed in the standard deviation and RPD metrics in the ELIT configurations with and without chaotic map reflect greater stability and consistency of the algorithm, which are desirable characteristics in practical applications where predictability is crucial.

The choice between different binarization algorithm and configuration should be guided by the specific characteristics of the optimization problem and the desired performance criteria. ELIT configurations, particularly when combined with the SINE chaotic map, tend to offer robust and reliable performance, which is ideal for obtaining high-quality solutions. For problems with fast convergence requirements or lower complexity, STD configurations may be sufficient. These findings highlight the importance of considering algorithm configuration and problem characteristics in optimizing strategies.

Acknowledgements. Felipe Cisternas-Caneo is supported by the National Agency for Research and Development (ANID)/ Scholarship Program/DOCTORADO NACIONAL/2023-21230203. Jose Barrera-García is supported by National Agency for Research and Development (ANID)/Scholarship Program/DOCTORADO NACIONAL/2024-21242516. Marcelo Becerra-Rozas is supported by National Agency for Research and Development (ANID)/ Scholarship Program/DOCTORADO NACIONAL/2021-21210740.

References

1. Abdel-Basset, M., Sallam, K.M., Mohamed, R., Elgendi, I., Munasinghe, K., Elkomy, O.M.: An improved binary grey-wolf optimizer with simulated annealing for feature selection. IEEE Access **9**, 139792–139822 (2021)
2. Agrawal, P., Ganesh, T., Mohamed, A.W.: Chaotic gaining sharing knowledge-based optimization algorithm: an improved metaheuristic algorithm for feature selection. Soft. Comput. **25**(14), 9505–9528 (2021)
3. Agrawal, U., Rohatgi, V., Katarya, R.: Normalized mutual information-based equilibrium optimizer with chaotic maps for wrapper-filter feature selection. Expert Syst. Appl. **207**, 118107 (2022)
4. Becerra-Rozas, M., et al.: Continuous metaheuristics for binary optimization problems: an updated systematic literature review. Mathematics **11**(1), 129 (2022)
5. Becerra-Rozas, M., Lemus-Romani, J., Cisternas-Caneo, F., Crawford, B., Soto, R., García, J.: Swarm-inspired computing to solve binary optimization problems: a backward q-learning binarization scheme selector. Mathematics **10**(24), 4776 (2022)
6. Chih, M.: Stochastic stability analysis of particle swarm optimization with pseudo random number assignment strategy. Eur. J. Oper. Res. **305**(2), 562–593 (2023)
7. Chou, J.-S., Truong, D.-N.: Multiobjective forensic-based investigation algorithm for solving structural design problems. Autom. Constr. **134**, 104084 (2022)
8. Cisternas-Caneo, F., Crawford, B., Soto, R., Giachetti, G., Paz, Á., Fritz, A.P.: Chaotic binarization schemes for solving combinatorial optimization problems using continuous metaheuristics. Mathematics **12**(2), 262 (2024)
9. Crawford, B., Soto, R., Astorga, G., García, J., Castro, C., Paredes, F.: Putting continuous metaheuristics to work in binary search spaces. Complexity **2017** (2017)
10. Gao, S., Yang, Yu., Wang, Y., Wang, J., Cheng, J., Zhou, M.C.: Chaotic local search-based differential evolution algorithms for optimization. IEEE Trans. Systems Man Cybernet. Syst. **51**(6), 3954–3967 (2021)
11. Hegazy, A.E., Makhlouf, M.A., El-Tawel, G.S.: Feature selection using chaotic salp swarm algorithm for data classification. Arab. J. Sci. Eng. **44**, 3801–3816 (2019)
12. Ho, Y.-C., Pepyne, D.L.: Simple explanation of the no-free-lunch theorem and its implications. J. Optimizat. Theory Appli. **115**(3), 549–570 (2002)
13. Hussien, A.G., Amin, M.: A self-adaptive harris hawks optimization algorithm with opposition-based learning and chaotic local search strategy for global optimization and feature selection. Inter. J. Mach. Learn. Cybernet., 1–28 (2022)
14. Ibrahim, A.M., Tawhid, M.A.: Chaotic electromagnetic field optimization. Artifi. Intell. Rev., 1–42 (2022)
15. Jalali, S.M.J., Ahmadian, M., Ahmadian, S., Hedjam, R., Khosravi, A., Nahavandi, S.: X-ray image based covid-19 detection using evolutionary deep learning approach. Expert Syst. Appl. **201**, 116942 (2022)
16. Khosravi, H., Amiri, B., Yazdanjue, N., Babaiyan, V.: An improved group teaching optimization algorithm based on local search and chaotic map for feature selection in high-dimensional data. Expert Syst. Appl. **204**, 117493 (2022)
17. Lemus-Romani, J., et al.: A novel learning-based binarization scheme selector for swarm algorithms solving combinatorial problems. Mathematics **9**(22) (2021)
18. Li, X.-D., Wang, J.-S., Hao, W.-K., Zhang, M., Wang, M.: Chaotic arithmetic optimization algorithm. Appli. Intell., 1–40 (2022)
19. Mohammed, H., Rashid, T.: Fox: a fox-inspired optimization algorithm. Appl. Intell. **53**(1), 1030–1050 (2023)

20. Rajwar, K., Deep, K., Das, S.: An exhaustive review of the metaheuristic algorithms for search and optimization: taxonomy, applications, and open challenges. Artifi. Intell. Rev., 1–71 (2023)
21. Seyyedabbasi, A.: Woascalf: a new hybrid whale optimization algorithm based on sine cosine algorithm and levy flight to solve global optimization problems. Adv. Eng. Softw. **173**, 103272 (2022)
22. Soto, R., et al.: Solving the non-unicost set covering problem by using cuckoo search and black hole optimization. Nat. Comput. **16**, 213–229 (2017)
23. Soto, R., et al.: Adaptive black hole algorithm for solving the set covering problem. Math. Problems Eng. **2018** (2018)
24. Talbi, E.G.: Metaheuristics: from design to implementation. John Wiley & Sons (2009)
25. Wang, R., Hao, K., Chen, L., Wang, T., Jiang, C.: A novel hybrid particle swarm optimization using adaptive strategy. Inf. Sci. **579**, 231–250 (2021)
26. Yang, H., et al.: An intelligent metaphor-free spatial information sampling algorithm for balancing exploitation and exploration. Knowl.-Based Syst. **250**, 109081 (2022)
27. Zhang, X., et al.: Gaussian mutational chaotic fruit fly-built optimization and feature selection. Expert Syst. Appli. **141**, 112976 (2020)

Optimal Selection of Distributed Generation Projects in Power Distribution Systems: A Genetic Algorithm Approach with DIgSILENT PowerFactory Integration

Alejandro Serna[ID], Oscar Gómez(✉)[ID], and Victor Vélez[ID]

University Tecnológica de Pereira, Pereira, Colombia
{jaider.serna,jr,victorvelez}@utp.edu.co

Abstract. In modern power distribution systems, the integration of distributed generation (DG) projects is crucial for enhancing system efficiency, safety, and sustainability. However, the optimal selection of DG projects amid various technical, economic, and operational constraints remains challenging. Previous research has focused on optimal placement and sizing of DG, but the realities faced by distribution system operators (DSOs) often involve evaluating predetermined project proposals. This paper introduces a novel approach for the optimal selection of DG projects in power distribution systems using a genetic algorithm (GA) framework integrated with DIgSILENT PowerFactory. The proposed methodology employs a GA to maximize system performance by considering factors such as voltage regulation, line loadability, power losses, and the direction of power flow while adhering to system constraints. The integration with DIgSILENT PowerFactory enables realistic simulation through unbalanced power flow analysis and evaluation of candidate DG projects within the distribution system context. The approach is implemented using DIgSILENT's built-in programming language, facilitating direct utilization of utility databases and intricate modeling of power system elements. A case study on a real Colombian utility's distribution feeder demonstrates the effectiveness of the proposed approach. The method achieved a 70.79% reduction in power losses, a 66.57% decrease in maximum line loadability, and voltage profile improvements of up to 7.5% at critical buses, while ensuring no reverse power flow towards the substation. This research contributes to advancing power system optimization by providing DSOs with a practical tool for assessing and selecting DG projects that enhance system performance while mitigating potential negative impacts. The integration with DIgSILENT PowerFactory ensures applicability in real-world scenarios. Future work may explore incorporating additional objectives such as reliability indices and economic factors, and revisiting the constraint on reverse power flow as distribution systems evolve.

J. C. Figueroa-García et al. (Eds.): WEA 2024, CCIS 2223, pp. 39–50, 2025.
https://doi.org/10.1007/978-3-031-74598-0_4

Keywords: Distributed generation · Power distribution system ·
Genetic algorithm · DIgSILENT PowerFactory

1 Introduction

Power distribution systems (PDS) serve as the crucial interface between the transmission system, and end-users. These systems comprise a complex arrangement of substations, transformers, overhead lines, underground cables, and distribution feeders designed to deliver electricity reliably, and efficiently to homes, businesses, and industries. PDS operate at lower voltage levels compared to transmission systems, and are characterized by radial configurations. Effective management, and operation of PDS are essential to ensure voltage regulation, power quality, and system stability while accommodating the integration of distributed energy resources such as distributed generation (DG), energy storage, and demand response technologies. Consequently, there is a growing interest in developing advanced tools, and methodologies to optimize distribution system planning, operation, and control, with a focus on enhancing system performance, resilience, and sustainability. Particularly, the increased use of distributed generation alters power flows within PDSs, and may require changes in an electric power system's operation, and commercial, and regulatory arrangements [1]. These small-scale generation units, often based on renewable energy sources like solar photovoltaic, wind turbines, and micro turbines, offer several advantages over centralized generation, such as reduced transmission losses, enhanced grid resilience, and increased energy efficiency. Additionally, DG systems contribute to the integration of renewable energy into the grid, thereby supporting efforts to mitigate climate change, and reduce greenhouse gas emissions. As a result, researchers are actively exploring methods to optimize the planning, operation, and integration of DG systems within existing PDS.

Traditionally, the location of DG in PDS has been considered flexible, with the understanding that such generation can be installed at any node within the system, regardless of its size. Most of the literature focuses on finding the optimal placement, and sizing of DG in PDS using various methods, often heuristics or metaheuristics. For example, in [2], a hybrid genetic particle swarm optimization method is proposed to minimize active, and reactive losses, and improve voltage regulation by determining the optimal locations of DGs. [3] improves power losses, and voltage profiles using an improved particle swarm optimization based methodology to allocate, and size the necessary DG units. Addressing the classical problem of optimal location, and sizing of DGs in radial distribution systems, [4] presents a mixed-integer nonlinear programming model. To reduce losses in distribution systems, [5] utilizes both the Grasshopper Optimization Algorithm, and Cuckoo Search technique to optimize DG location, and size. [6] introduces Single, and Multi-objective Harris Hawks Optimization algorithms for determining optimal DG placement in radial distribution systems. In [7], a high-convergence optimization technique for optimal DG placement in distribution systems is proposed to reduce power losses, improve voltage profiles, and enhance voltage stability index. Analytical expressions for optimal

DG allocation are provided in [8]. Convex models are explored in [9] considering a risk-constrained optimization model. [10] suggests an Enhanced Artificial Ecosystem-based Optimization approach for optimal DG allocation. In [11], authors implement a hybrid Grey Wolf Optimizer to minimize power losses, and improve voltage profiles by identifying optimal DG locations in PDS. [12] proposes a wild horse optimization technique for DG planning. Genetic Algorithm (GA) implementation in [13] addresses optimal DG allocation in radial distribution systems considering uncertainties in load, and generation. A multi-objective optimization approach in [14] identifies the best DG unit locations. [15] suggests a particle swarm optimization metaheuristic for optimal DG placement. In [16], authors present a mixed integer linear programming approach for solving optimal sizing, and allocation of DGs of different technologies in radial distribution systems.

While numerous studies have focused on optimal placement and sizing of DG units, they often overlook the practical reality DSOs frequently face which is evaluating predetermined project proposals rather than having complete freedom in DG placement. In practice, DG projects are usually proposed by external agents, such as investors, who consider various local conditions like energy resource availability, spatial constraints, licensing requirements, and economic factors. Consequently, DSOs must assess project viability and select DG projects to maximize benefits and mitigate potential negative impacts on the distribution system, particularly in scenarios of high DG penetration. The motivation for this research stems from these growing challenges faced by DSOs in integrating DG projects into existing PDS. This gap between academic research and industry practice necessitates a new approach. Our contribution addresses this need by developing a novel methodology that enables DSOs to optimally select from a set of proposed DG projects. By integrating a GA with DIgSILENT PowerFactory, we provide a practical tool that considers real-world constraints such as unbalanced power flow and the prevention of reverse power flow towards substations. This approach not only enhances system performance in terms of power losses, voltage regulation, and line loadability but also aligns with the operational realities of DSOs. Furthermore, our integration with industry-standard software facilitates the direct application of this method in real-world scenarios, bridging the gap between theoretical optimization and practical implementation.

This paper introduces a novel approach for the optimal selection of DG projects among several available projects in the PDS. GAs integrated with DIgSILENT PowerFactory are employed for this purpose, enabling realistic simulation when evaluating the candidate DG projects. Realistic simulation refers to the process of modeling and analyzing PDS in a way that closely approximates real-world conditions and operational constraints. Specifically, it involves conducting unbalanced power flow analysis, which accounts for the inherent imbalances in three-phase distribution systems. This approach considers factors such as varying loads across phases, different conductor configurations, and the presence of both single-phase and three-phase components. By using industry-standard software like DIgSILENT PowerFactory, which allows for detailed modeling of power system elements and direct utilization of utility databases, our simulations capture the complexities and nuances of actual distribution networks. This level of detail ensures that the results obtained from our optimization process are applicable and valuable in real-world scenarios faced by Distribution System Operators. The aim is to maximize system benefits while minimizing total power losses, lines loadability and voltage deviation, all while adhering to distribution system constraints. In this way, the DSO can decide to allow or deny connection requests for generation projects, considering the impact these projects will have on the system.

Conventional PDS are primarily designed for unidirectional power flow, typically utilizing non-bidirectional over-current relays (either inverse or definite time), reclosers, and switch fuses in their protection systems. Therefore, these devices lack the capability to account for flow direction and may fail when DG contributes to a fault. The introduction of DG can result in reverse power flows, which radial networks' protection systems may not adequately handle. Such reverse power flow towards the substation could compromise the effectiveness of these protection systems, potentially leading to safety and operational issues. Additionally, reverse power flow poses challenges for voltage regulation, power quality, and system stability, as these systems are not designed to accommodate bidirectional power flow. Preventing reverse power flow simplifies the management and control of the distribution system, aligning with its intended unidirectional operation. From the perspective of a DSO, limiting the integration of DG to prevent reverse power flow represents a practical and conservative approach. This approach ensures that existing infrastructure and protection systems remain effective while minimizing the need for extensive upgrades or modifications to accommodate bidirectional power flows.

Therefore, this paper proposes prohibiting changes in the direction of power flow, particularly any power flow directed towards the substation, thus restricting the optimization problem. However, it is important to note that as the penetration of DG increases, distribution systems may need to adapt and incorporate advanced protection schemes, control strategies, and infrastructure upgrades to accommodate bidirectional power flows safely and efficiently. This constraint may need to be relaxed or revisited in the future as distribution systems evolve to become more capable of handling reverse power flows.

The selection of the DIgSILENT software for this study was based on its built-in programming language, enabling the evaluation of numerous unbalanced power flows with low computational demands. Moreover, it facilitates the direct utilization of the utility database, and intricate modeling of power system elements, eliminating the necessity for external programming interfaces to apply the optimization algorithm. Consequently, this reduces the overall computational time required for the optimization approach.

The paper is organized as follows: Sect. 2 presents the proposed methodology. Section 3 presents the results obtained on a real distribution system. Finally, conclusions are outlined at the end of the paper.

2   Proposed Methodology

Let's consider a PDS, depicted in Fig. 1. This PDS comprises nine nodes, with four of them housing DG projects.

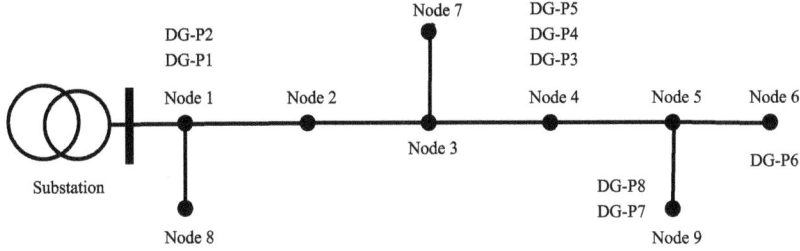

Fig. 1. Power distribution system with DG projects.

The objective of the methodology is to optimally select the DG Projects ($DG-Pn$) that enhance the performance of the PDS. It's important to note that a single node can host more than one DG project. A GA is employed to select the optimal set of projects. GA is an optimization method that emulates the principles of natural selection, and evolution. Its fundamental concept involves creating a population of potential problem solutions, and iteratively applying genetic operations such as selection, crossover, and mutation to progressively enhance the population towards improved solutions. These genetic operators were implemented using the DIgSILENT Programming Language (DPL).

2.1   Mathematical Model and Fitness Function

Mathematical model considers several factors related to an unbalanced power flow, including technical losses, voltage deviation, line loadability, voltage violations, and power flow towards the substation. In essence, the GA evaluates each individual (set of DG projects) to assess their impact on technical losses, nodal voltages, and operational constraints. The fitness function, represented as Ff, quantifies the overall quality of an individual. Mathematical model is defined as follows:

$$\text{Minimize } Ff = k_1 \sum_{\forall ij \in \Omega_l} R_{ij}\, I_{ij}^2 + k_2 \sum_{i=1}^{Nb} \|\overline{V} - V_i\| + k_3 \sum_{\forall ij \in \Omega_l} (\%LL_{ij}) \quad (1)$$

Subject to:

$$P_{ki} - \sum_{\forall ij \in \Omega_{li}} P_{ij} + P_i^s + \sum_{g \in \Omega_g} P_{ic,g}^{dg} = P_i^d; \quad \forall i \in \Omega_b \tag{2}$$

$$Q_{ki} - \sum_{\forall ij \in \Omega_{li}} Q_{ij} + Q_i^s + \sum_{g \in \Omega_g} Q_{ic,g}^{dg} = Q_i^d; \quad \forall i \in \Omega_b \tag{3}$$

$$V_i^2 - 2\left(R_{ij}P_{ij} + X_{ij}Q_{ij}\right) - Z_{ij}^2 I_{ij}^2 - V_j^2 = 0; \quad \forall\, ij \in \Omega_l \tag{4}$$

$$0 \le S_{ij} \le \overline{S}_{ij} \quad \forall\, ij \in \Omega_l \tag{5}$$

$$\underline{V}_i \le V_i \le \overline{V}_i; \quad \forall i \in \Omega_b \tag{6}$$

$$P_{ki} \ge 0; \quad \forall ki \in \Omega_l \tag{7}$$

$$Q_{ki} \ge 0; \quad \forall ki \in \Omega_l \tag{8}$$

The fitness function, given by Eq. (1), consists of minimizing the active power losses (first term), voltage deviation (second term), and system loadability (third term). In this equation, k_1, k_2, and k_3 are weight factors for the different objectives; Ω_l is the set of lines; R_{ij} and I_{ij} are the resistance and current of line ij, respectively; N_b is the number of buses; $\overline{V}$ is the voltage upper limit; V_i is the voltage of bus i; and finally, $\%LL_{ij}$ is the loadability of line ij in percent.

The optimization model is constrained by active and reactive power balances at each bus, given by (2) and (3), respectively. P_{ki} and Q_{ki} are the active and reactive power flows in line ki, while P_{ij} and Q_{ij} represent active and reactive power flows in line ij that belongs to the set Ω_{li} (set of lines outgoing from i). $P_{ic,g}^{dg}$ and $Q_{ic,g}^{dg}$ represent the active and reactive power injected by the DG unit at candidate bus ic. P_i^s and Q_i^s represent the active and reactive power supplied by the substation at bus i. P_i^d and Q_i^d are the active and reactive power demands at bus i. Equation (4) considers the voltage drop across each line ij. Voltage magnitudes are determined using the power flow through the line and its electrical parameters (R_{ij} and X_{ij}, which are the resistance and reactance of the line ij). The authors in [17] suggested eliminating the voltage angle to derive Equation (4). In this case, V_i represents the voltage magnitude at bus i and Z_{ij} is the impedance of line ij. Constraints (5) and (6) limit the power flow through line ij, and voltage at bus i, respectively. Here, $\overline{V}i$ and $\underline{V}i$ are the upper and lower voltage limits at bus i, while $\overline{S}_{ij}$ is the upper power flow limit of line ij. Finally, constraints (7) and (8) ensure the direction of power flow goes from the substation towards the load, avoiding reverse power flows.

Note that the proposed model must be considered for each phase, and it does not aim to minimize the cost of installing DG, as traditionally is done in other research. Instead, it focuses on minimizing technical losses, enhancing line loadability, and improving the voltage profile by selecting the optimal number of DG projects. This approach ensures that the selected projects provide the greatest benefit to the system, accomplish the system constraints and avoiding power flow towards substation. In this way, the DSO can decide to allow or deny connection requests for generation projects, considering the impact these projects will have on the system.

2.2   Encoding

The problem statement is represented using a vector with n columns, where n denotes the number of DG projects. This problem statement imply identifying DG projects that should be selected by the DSO to ensure the feasibility, and optimization of the PDS. Each column in the vector corresponds to a DG project, with binary digits indicating its consideration: a value of 1 signifies selection, while 0 denotes that the DG project will not be considered. This representation is illustrated in Fig. 2.

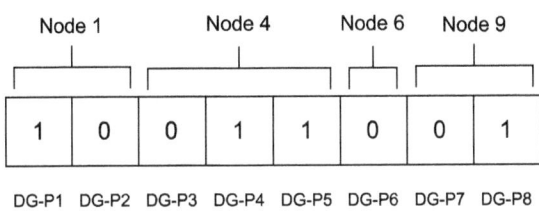

Fig. 2. Genetic algorithm individual encoding.

Utilizing this vector, the GA can efficiently identify the optimal set of DG projects. The algorithm achieves this by iteratively selecting DG projects based on the binary values within the vector. By doing so, it systematically explores different combinations of projects to determine the most beneficial configuration for enhancing the performance of the PDS.

The population in the GA is comprised of a collection of these vectors, each of which serves as a representation of an individual within the population.

2.3   Initial Population

The population of individuals (potential solutions) is randomly generated. First, the number of individuals in the population is decided. This parameter affects the genetic diversity and the computational resources required. Then, for each individual in the population, values of 0 or 1 are generated for each column in the vector. This random value assignment process is repeated for the total number of individuals specified by the population size. After the population is generated, each individual is evaluated using an unbalanced load flow; the individual with the best fitness function is saved and is called the incumbent solution.

2.4   Selection

The selection procedure involves two tournaments. In each tournament, two individuals are randomly chosen from the population, and the one with the superior fitness function is selected for reproduction. Individuals with higher fitness function values have a higher chance of being selected. At the end, two individuals will be selected for the crossover process.

2.5   Crossover

After the selection process, single-point crossover is performed to combine the genetic information of two selected individuals and generate two new offspring (see Fig. 3). The selection and crossover processes are repeated as many times as necessary to replace the entire population.

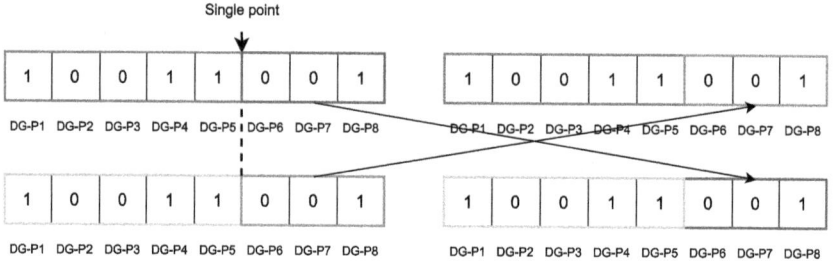

Fig. 3. Single-point crossover.

2.6   Mutation

The simple mutation operator is used to introduce random changes into the genetic information of an individual. This mutation is performed on the entire population by randomly selecting a gene, which represent a DG project. When a gene is selected, its value is checked to see if it is currently selected (1) or ignored (0). If it is selected (value = 1), it is changed to ignored (value = 0). Conversely, if the DG project is currently ignored (value = 0), it is changed to selected (value = 1).

2.7   Re-insertion

The goal is to ensure that the GA continues to explore new solutions while retaining the best solutions found so far. Therefore, the best solution (incumbent solution) is reinserted into the population if its fitness function value is better than that of any current population member. If its fitness function value is worse, it is not reinserted.

2.8   Stopping Criteria

The algorithm stops when it reaches a maximum number of generations, or when the fitness function fails to improve after a predefined number of iterations.

2.9   Pseudo-code

For a better illustration of the proposed GA, its pseudo code is given as follows.

$individualsNumber \leftarrow N$
$iterations \leftarrow Iter$
$nonImprovementIterations \leftarrow NN$
Create initial population
Evaluate population
Save and report Incumbent
$a \leftarrow 1$
while $a \leq iterations$ & $nonImprovementIterations \leq NN$ **do**
    Select parents
    Recombine parents and generate offspring
    Mutate offspring
    for $b \leftarrow 1, individualsNumber$ **do**
        Evaluate offspring
    end for
    Get NewIncumbent
    $incumbentIsBetter \leftarrow$ Compare Incumbent and NewIncumbent
    if $incumbentIsBetter = True$ **then**
        Save and report Incumbent
    else
        Reinsert Incumbent
    end if
    $a \leftarrow a + 1$
end while

---

3   Study Case and Results

The proposed methodology has been applied to a feeder within a Colombian utility's PDS, demonstrating its practical applicability. This feeder comprises 148 branches and 170 buses, the latter due to the presence of protection devices, and operates at a voltage level of 13.2 kV. With a peak feeder demand of 2.56 MW and 1.02 MVar, an unbalanced load flow analysis was conducted. The most heavily loaded distribution line exhibits loadability percentages of $FB = 56.93\%$, $FB = 81.92\%$, and $FC = 71.73\%$; it corresponds to the line going out of the substation. Minimum voltage levels on the feeder are recorded as $FB = 0.894\ p.u.$ and $FC = 0.893\ p.u.$; these correspond to the last bus of the feeder, which

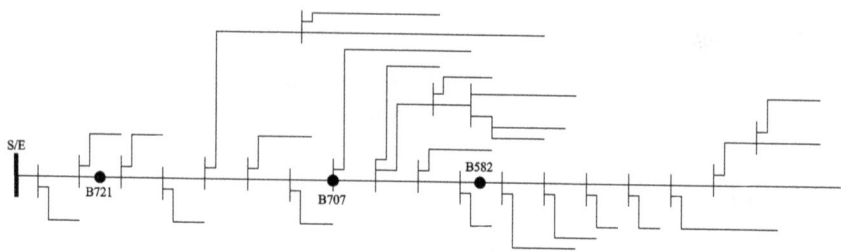

Fig. 4. Test feeder.

only has phases B and C (unbalanced power system). The system's active power loss is calculated at 160.2 kW. Figure 4 illustrates the reduced base topology of the test system.

It will be considered eleven DG projects. Table 1 displays the buses and sizes of the DG projects under consideration. These projects are proposed to be installed at the buses marked with a black circle in Fig. 4. As can be seen, several DG projects can be considered in the same bus.

Table 1. DG projects under consideration.

Bus	B721	B721	B721	B707	B707	B707	B707	B582	B582	B582	B582
Size [kW]	200	200	400	500	500	400	400	1000	500	500	400
f.p.	1.0	1.0	1.0	1.0	1.0	1.0	1.0	1.0	1.0	1.0	1.0

After executing the proposed GA in DIgSILENT PowerFactory, the algorithm selected the DG projects presented in Table 2. The algorithm selects the maximum number of DG projects to enhance system operation while adhering to operational constraints. Additionally, it ensures that power flow towards the substation is avoided.

Table 2. DG projects selected.

Bus	B721	B721	B707	B707	B582	B582
Size [kW]	200	400	500	400	500	400
f.p.	1.0	1.0	1.0	1.0	1.0	1.0

Using the set of DG projects determined by this methodology, the distribution feeder experiences active power losses of 46.78 kW. Also, it achieves maximum line loadabilities of $FA = 24.53\%$, $FB = 27.38\%$, and $FC = 28.96\%$ at the substation exit, along with minimum voltage levels of $FB = 0.9615\ p.u.$ and $FC = 0.9601\ p.u.$ at the last bus of the feeder, which only has phases B and C.

After the optimal selection of DG projects, there is a reduction in power losses by 70.79%. Additionally, the feeder and its corresponding buses experience improved voltages. Specifically, the bus with the minimum voltage sees an increase of 7.55% in phase B and 7.51% in phase C. Finally, the line loadability of the most heavily loaded line is reduced by 66.57%.

4 Conclusions

The integration of distributed generation projects into power distribution systems requires careful evaluation and selection to maximize system benefits while adhering to operational constraints. This study introduces a novel genetic algorithm approach integrated with DIgSILENT PowerFactory for the optimal selection of distributed generation projects within power distribution systems. Unlike existing approaches that primarily focus on the optimal placement and sizing of distributed generators, the proposed methodology emphasizes the selection of distributed generation projects suggested by external agents, thereby reflecting practical scenarios encountered by distribution system operators.

The case study results validate the effectiveness of this approach, demonstrating significant improvements in system performance metrics such as power losses, voltage regulation, and line loadability. The effectiveness is demonstrated by achieving a 70.79% reduction in power losses, a 66.57% decrease in maximum line loadability, and voltage profile improvements of up to 7.5% at the critical bus. By integrating with the widely-used DIgSILENT PowerFactory software, this research facilitates realistic simulations (unbalanced power flow) and streamlines the optimization process, thereby contributing to improved decision-making in distributed generation investment planning for electric utilities.

The constraint prohibiting changes in the direction of power flow, particularly any flow directed towards the substation, needs to be relaxed or revisited in the future as distribution systems evolve to become more capable of handling reverse power flows. Additionally, future work may explore the incorporation of additional objectives and constraints, such as reliability indices, stability indices and economic factors, to further enhance the applicability of this approach in real-world distribution system planning and operation.

References

1. Bell, K., Gill, S.: Delivering a highly distributed electricity system: technical, regulatory, and policy challenges. Energy Policy **113**, 765-777 (2018). https://www.sciencedirect.com/science/article/pii/S0301421517307851
2. Pesaran H.A.M., Nazari-Heris, M., Mohammadi-Ivatloo, B., Seyedi, H.: A hybrid genetic particle swarm optimization for distributed generation allocation in power distribution networks. Energy **209**, 118218 (2020). https://www.sciencedirect.com/science/article/pii/S0360544220313256
3. Werkie, Y., Kefale, H.: Optimal allocation of multiple distributed generation units in power distribution networks for voltage profile improvement, and power losses minimization. Cogent Eng. **9**, 2091668 (2022)

4. Montoya, O., Gil-González, W. & Grisales-Noreña, L.: An exact MINLP model for optimal location, and sizing of DGs in distribution networks: a general algebraic modeling system approach. Ain Shams Eng. J. **11**, 409-418 (2020). https://www.sciencedirect.com/science/article/pii/S2090447919301200

5. Suresh, M., Edward, J.: A hybrid algorithm based optimal placement of DG units for loss reduction in the distribution system. Appli. Soft Comput. **91**, 106191 (2020). https://www.sciencedirect.com/science/article/pii/S1568494620301319

6. Selim, A., Kamel, S., Alghamdi, A., Jurado, F.: Optimal placement of DGs in distribution system using an improved harris hawks optimizer based on single-, and multi-objective approaches. IEEE Access **8**, 52815–52829 (2020)

7. Rayes Ahmad Lone, S., Anees, A.: An improved analytical technique: optimal location, and sizing of distributed generation for distribution systems. Int. J. Green Energy **21**, 682–700 (2024)

8. Mahmoud, K., Yorino, N., Ahmed, A.: Optimal Distributed Generation Allocation in Distribution Systems for Loss Minimization. IEEE Trans. Power Syst. **31**, 960–969 (2016)

9. Akbari, M., et al.: Convex Models For Optimal Utility-based DG Allocation In Radial Distribution Systems. IEEE Syst. J. **12**, 3497–3508 (2018)

10. Eid, A., Kamel, S., Korashy, A., Khurshaid, T.: An enhanced artificial ecosystem-based optimization for optimal allocation of multiple distributed generations. IEEE Access **8**, 178493–178513 (2020)

11. Sanjay, R., Jayabarathi, T., Raghunathan, T., Ramesh, V., Mithulananthan, N.: Optimal allocation of distributed generation using hybrid grey wolf optimizer. IEEE Access **5**, 14807–14818 (2017)

12. Ali, M., Kamel, S., Hassan, M., Tostado-Véliz, M. & Zawbaa, H. An improved wild horse optimization algorithm for reliability based optimal DG planning of radial distribution networks. Energy Rep. **8**, 582-604 (2022). https://www.sciencedirect.com/science/article/pii/S235248472101461X

13. Ganguly, S., Samajpati, D.: Distributed generation allocation on radial distribution networks under uncertainties of load, and generation using genetic algorithm Sustainable Energy. IEEE Trans. **6**, 688–697 (2015)

14. Ali, A., Keerio, M., Laghari, J.: Optimal site, and size of distributed generation allocation in radial distribution network using multi-objective optimization. J. Modern Power Syst. Clean Energy **9**, 404–415 (2021)

15. Elkadeem, M., Abd Elaziz, M., Ullah, Z., Wang, S., Sharshir, S.: Optimal planning of renewable energy-integrated distribution system considering uncertainties. IEEE Access **7**, 164887-164907 (2019)

16. Rueda-Medina, A., Franco, J., Rider, M., Padilha-Feltrin, A., Romero, R.A.: mixed-integer linear programming approach for optimal type, size, and allocation of distributed generation in radial distribution systems. Electric Power Syst. Res. **97**, 133-143 (2013). https://www.sciencedirect.com/science/article/pii/S0378779612003616

17. Cespedes, R.: New method for the analysis of distribution networks. IEEE Trans. Power Delivery **5**, 391-396 (1990)

Location Model of Rural Centers as Logistical Support of the Agri-Food Supply Chain in the Sabanas Subregion, Department of Sucre

Gean Pablo Mendoza-Ortega[(✉)] [iD], M. Torregroza-Angélica[iD],
Laura Vanessa Sierra-Canchila[iD], and Erika Johana Ramírez-Ocampo[iD]

Corporación Universitaria del Caribe—CECAR, Sincelejo, Colombia
{gean.mendoza,angelica.torregroza,laura.cierra,
erika.ramirez}@cecar.edu.co

Abstract. Agri-food supply chains (ASC) focus on stakeholders with the objective of providing access to essential inputs, processing primary products, marketing and distributing the products to end consumers. In this context, it is proposed to design a model for locating rural centers that serves as logistical support for the yam agri-food supply chain. This location model for hubs aims to plan the distribution in the agri-food supply chain of yams in the Sabanas Subregion of the Department of Sucre, Colombia. Additionally, the use of the Hub Location Problem is considered, which is addressed as a mixed integer linear programming model. To this end, assumptions have been adopted that will allow obtaining results that maximize the profits of the warehouses (hubs). These results have been obtained through the use of GAMS software, solved with the CPLEX Solver. According to the results obtained, the optimal location for the opening of two strategic hubs has been identified. These distribution centers not only help reduce logistics costs, but also optimize delivery times, thus strengthening the supply chain.

Keywords: Yam · Hub´s · optimization

1 Introduction

The state of food security and nutrition in the world has deteriorated over time. Differences in the impact of the pandemic and recovery, combined with the limited coverage and duration of social protection measures, have contributed to widening inequalities, creating further obstacles to the 2030 goal of zero hunger [1]. In departments of the Caribbean and Pacific Region, food insecurity had an increase that exceeds 40%, where Guajira, Sucre, Córdoba, Cesar and Chocó reflect a prevalence that exceeds the national average, showing Sucre with a figure of 63% of food safety [2]. Furthermore, in the plan and strategic agreement of Science, Technology and Innovation [3] Sucre finds the agricultural and agroindustrial sector as one of the most important focuses. Likewise, the Department has an economy based on livestock, social services and the agricultural sector, where you can see climatic diversity, sectors rich in water, but with major problems with drainage, thus needing better infrastructure to seek better industrialization [4].

© The Author(s), under exclusive license to Springer Nature Switzerland AG 2025
J. C. Figueroa-García et al. (Eds.): WEA 2024, CCIS 2223, pp. 51–62, 2025.
https://doi.org/10.1007/978-3-031-74598-0_5

On the other hand, in supply chain management it has a link with agricultural products. In this sense, the management of supply chains for agricultural products has gained importance in the last decade, for which the concept of agri-food supply chains has been adopted. Which is responsible for producing and distributing an agricultural product [5]. Some factors such as climate change, product quality, management of perishable products, food security and life cycle, changing demand and prices, crop yield, crop production management, among other factors, make the agri-food supply chain more difficult [6]. With the aforementioned, [7] proposes that an alternative to minimize the negative impacts on productivity is to promote the coordination and cooperation of direct and indirect actors.

Due to the aforementioned factors, such as the poor management of waste that is generated by inadequate planning and management within the yam agri-food supply chain, logistics management for these foods is very important, since good planning and management It will allow them to reach their points of sale correctly and said waste can be reduced [8]. Previously, different productive activities were mentioned; One of them is agriculture, with different crops such as bananas, rice, cassava and yams. This last crop has wide use both locally and nationally; However, inadequate logistics management can be identified, which influences the well-being and food security of the population [9].

According to [10], the correct location of the facilities allows support for the logistics management of the agri-food supply chain, since it provides better performance. In addition, they create a competitive advantage that generates a series of strategic decisionmaking, which leads to a reduction in transportation costs and in turn mitigation of environmental impacts. For its part [11], states that research that is focused on location models for rural collection centers is increasing, because this type of problems are increasing, which generate great losses, both for the farmer as for the consumer. For this reason, we seek to solve these location problems in the yam agri-food supply chain (ASC) through the Hub Location Problem (HLP), which seeks to determine the locations that each hub (rural collection centers) must have, while assigning the different supply and demand points and the determination of routes, to obtain cost minimization [12]. Due to what was stated above, more tools are needed to help decision-making for the location models of rural centers, in order to contribute to the agri-food supply chain (ASC) and thus strengthen distribution methods that can avoid greater waste of these foods, for which we seek to design a model for locating rural centers as logistical support for the agrifood supply chain of yams, for the Sabanas Subregion in the Department of Sucre.

2 Literature Review

Supply chain optimization for perishable products has been a topic of great interest in recent literature. Various studies have addressed this problem from different approaches, providing innovative models and practical solutions to improve the efficiency and sustainability of supply chains.

For example, in their research on a multi-objective sustainable scheduling problem [13] presented a comprehensive model for the location of centers in the perishable food supply chain. This model, designed for fruits, vegetables, dairy and other time-sensitive products, optimizes the network in three dimensions: costs, responsiveness and environmental conservation. Using multi-objective mixed linear programming and the non-dominant sorting genetic algorithm II (NSGA-II), they were able to identify central nodes and allocate vehicles efficiently, improving both transportation costs and the freshness and quality of the food delivered, in addition to reducing carbon emissions.

Similarly [14] developed a model for the bagasse-based bioethanol supply chain in Iran, using a multi-objective mixed-integer linear programming approach. Its methodology allowed us to determine the location and capacity of the facilities, the ideal transportation, the flow of materials and the planning of production in different periods. They compared the results using the Pareto chart and highlighted the importance of shifting freight from road to rail to reduce CO_2 emissions, despite the higher initial cost.

Meanwhile [15] focused on supply uncertainty and greenhouse gas emissions in a robust intermodal transportation model for food grains. This model, which employs discrete, nonlinear, and mixed-integer optimization, was tested with hybrid metaheuristics for large and small data sets, demonstrating high solution quality and good computational times.

In the context of perishable products with different storage needs [16] used mixed integer linear programming in GAMS to design a bio-objective model. This model managed to identify the location of hubs, assign customers to distribution centers and vehicles, and optimize the sequence of deliveries. The results showed that improving the quality of the delivered product increased the total cost of the system.

In Spain [17] investigated the impact of perishability in the agri-food supply chain, developing a mixed integer linear programming model for multiple products. Their study revealed that considering perishability improves the economic performance of ASC, especially for products with short shelf lives.

In Colombia [18] proposed a competitive hub location model for the fresh food supply chain. This model considered that farmers can choose between hubs and consumption centers, optimizing the quantities delivered and reducing transportation costs and CO_2 emissions. The results indicated that the implementation of hubs is profitable, with a net benefit of $951,000 per hub.

Finally, in the Department of Sucre [19] applied a scenario-based model for the cassava supply chain, using mixed integer programming (MIP) and CPLEX Solver integrated into GAMS. This approach resulted in a significant reduction in distribution costs, highlighting the efficiency of the model in a low computational time.

In summary, the literature shows an evolution in the approaches and techniques used to optimize the supply chain of perishable products. From mixed linear programming and genetic algorithms to robust models and consideration of perishability, each study provides valuable strategies and solutions that can be adapted and applied in different contexts and regions to improve the efficiency, sustainability and profitability of supply chains. Supply. Comparing these studies, there is a trend towards the integration of multiple objectives and the use of advanced optimization techniques, reflecting an increasingly deep and sophisticated understanding of the challenges and opportunities in managing perishable supply chains.

3 Model Description

Next, a hub location model will be shown, which seeks to plan distribution in the agri-food supply chain of yam in the Sabanas Subregion of the Department of Sucre. To develop this model, some assumptions were adopted that are described below: I. Multiple types of products, including Creole yam, diamond and hawthorn II. The location of the producers, the consumption centers and the location of the hubs are known III. Production and transportation costs are known IV. Three different types of vehicles will be considered, one for transport from the producers to the centers and two for the trip from the hubs to the consumption centers, where the model will be in charge of choosing which of the two vehicles to use V. The flow of products between hubs is not allowed. SAW. Producers can be assigned to multiple hubs VII Symbol. The quantity sent from the hubs cannot be greater than the demand from the consumption centers. The sets, parameters and decision variables that will be used in the formulation of the model will be detailed below (Tables 1, 2 and 3).

Table 1. Model Sets

Symbol	Definition
$i \in I$	Set of producers ($i = 1,2,3, ..., I$)
$f \in F$	Set of products ($f = 1,2,3, ..., F$)
$q \in Q$	Set of potential warehouses ($q = 1,2,3, ..., Q$)
$h \in H$	Set of consumption centers ($h = 1,2,3, ..., H$)
$v \in V$	Set of vehicles ($v = 1,2,3,..., V$)

The first Eq. (1) is the objective function of the proposed model, which aims to maximize the profits of the warehouses (hubs). Additionally, we find the model's restrictions, where restriction (Eq. 2) indicates that the flow of product f from producer i to hub q does not exceed the capacity of producer i for product f.. (Eq. 3) indicates that the flow of product f through hub q to consumption center h in vehicle v does not exceed the demand of consumption center h for product f. Eq. (4) indicates a flow balance restriction that ensures consistency in the flow of products along the chain; it establishes that the amount of product f sent from producer i to hub q is equal to the amount of product f sent from hub q to consumption center h in vehicle v. Equations (4) and (5) are the restrictions that guarantee the maximum and minimum occupancy levels by vehicle type. Equation (6) is the opening restriction that will limit the number of warehouses to be opened; the sixth restriction (Eq. 8) gives viability to the generation of fixed costs in the open hubs. Equations (8), (9), and (10) are the non-negativity restrictions, and restriction (12) is for the admissible binary values for the decision variables.

$$MaxZ = \sum_{q \in Q} \sum_{h \in H} \sum_{f \in F} \sum_{v \in V} Pv_{fh} X2_{qhfv} - \left(\sum_{i \in I} \sum_{q \in Q} \sum_{h \in H} \sum_{f \in F} \sum_{v \in V} \frac{Costprod}{R_f} X1_{iqf}\right.$$
$$+ \sum_{i \in I} \sum_{q \in Q} \sum_{f \in F} (CostVh * D1_{iq}) X1_{iqf} + \sum_{q \in Q} \sum_{h \in H} \sum_{f \in F} \sum_{v \in V} (Cv_v * D2_{qh}) X2_{qhfv} \qquad (1)$$
$$\left. + \sum_{q \in Q} CFA_q Y_q\right)$$

Table 2. Model Parameters

Symbol	Definition
g_{if}	Maximum capacity of producer i for product f
D_{hf}	Demand from the consumption center, for product f
$Costprod$	Fixed production cost, associated with the planting and crop assistance requirements for product f in COP /Hectare
$D1_{iq}$	Distance from producer i to warehouse q in km
$D2qh$	Distance from the warehouse q to the consumption center h in km
$CostVh$	Cost of transportation of product f per Ton from producers i, to the warehouse, in COP
CFA_q	Fixed cost for opening a warehouse in COP
C_v	Cost per Km/Ton per vehicle
M_q	Maximum number of warehouses allowed to open
$Pvfh$	Sales price of product f of each consumption center h
R_f	Crop yield

Table 3. Model Decision Variables

Symbol	Definition
$X1_{iqf}$	Represents the flow of product f from the producer to the warehouse, in Tons
$X2_{fq}hv$	Represents the flow of the product f from the warehouse to the consumption centers, in the vehicle v, in Tons
$Truckfqhv$	Number of trucks v to be sent from warehouse q to consumption center h with product f
Y_q	Binary variable that determines whether the warehouse type is opened (1) or not (0) and triggers the corresponding fixed cost
$Y1qh$	Binary variable that determines that the warehouse is assigned to serve the consumption center

Subject to:

$$\sum_{q \in q} X1_{iqf} \leq g_{if}, \forall i \in I, \forall f \in F \tag{2}$$

$$\sum_{v \in V} X2_{qfhv} \leq D_{hf} Y1_{qh}, \forall f \in F, \forall q \in Q \forall h \in H \tag{3}$$

$$\sum_{i \in I} \sum_{f \in F} X1_{iqf} = \sum_{f \in F} \sum_{h \in H} \sum_{v \in V} X2_{fqhv}, \forall q \in Q \tag{4}$$

$$X2_{fqhv} \leq CAPV_v * Truck_{fqhv}, \forall f \in F, \forall q \in Q, \forall h \in H, v \in V \tag{5}$$

$$X2_{fqhv} \geq CAPV_v * (Truck_{fqhv} - (1 + Min_v), \forall f \in F, \forall q \in Q, \forall h \in H, v \in V) \quad (6)$$

$$Y1_{qh} \leq M_q, \forall h \in H, \forall q \in Q \quad (7)$$

$$Y1_{qh} = Y_q, \forall q \in Q, h \in H \quad (8)$$

$$X1_{iqf} \geq 0, \forall i \in I, \forall q \in Q, \forall f \in F, \forall v \in V \quad (9)$$

$$X2_{ihfv} \geq 0, \forall i \in I, \forall h \in H, \forall f \in F, \forall v \in V \quad (10)$$

$$Truck_{fqhv} \geq 0, \forall i \in I, \forall h \in H, \forall f \in F, \forall v \in V \quad (11)$$

$$Y_q, Y1_{qh} \in \{0, 1\}, \forall q \in Q, \forall h \in H \quad (12)$$

4 Description of the Case Study

The cultivation of yams in Colombia is of great economic and social importance due to its role as a source of basic food, generator of employment and engine of rural development. Yam (*Dioscorea spp.*) is a tuberous plant widely cultivated in various regions of the country, where its production contributes significantly to food security and the livelihood of numerous peasant families [20]. This is a tropical type of plant and maintains normal development, where temperatures between 25 °C and 30 °C are required [21]. In the Department of Sucre, different types of yams are produced, but for this research 3 varieties are taken into account: Criollo, Espino and Diamante, these being contributors of great economic value to the country, due to their demand and the large quantity planted [22].

In this sense [23], states that the cultivation of yams in Colombia not only provides food rich in carbohydrates and essential nutrients, but also promotes the diversification of agriculture, increases resilience against adverse climatic conditions and promotes the conservation of the agricultural biodiversity. Furthermore, yams are an important source of income for farmers, both locally and in national and international markets.

For the year 2022, in Colombia a total of 16 Departments were identified where yam production was carried out, covering a set of 129 municipalities dedicated to this crop [24]. Where the Departments with the highest production were, in the period from 2019 to 2022, Córdoba, Bolívar, Sucre, Antioquia and Chocó, as seen in Fig. 1. Sucre stood out as the third largest producer of yams nationwide, which which reflects its significant contribution to the country's economy [25]. The recognition of yam cultivation as an important economic potential is reflected in the internal productivity and competitiveness agenda of the Department of Sucre. This Department is geographically divided into five Subregions, with the Sabanas Subregion standing out as the main focus of this research. This Subregion covers nine municipalities, among which are Sincé, El Roble, San Pedro, Sampués, Los Palmitos, Buenavista, Corozal, San Juan de Betulia and Galeras. However, the municipality of Galeras is not considered in this study due to the absence of registered yam producers in that locality. Instead, the city of Sincelejo is included due to its relevance as an administrative and economic center of the region.

It is expected that the future of the Department and the performance of root and tuber agriculture will improve the socioeconomic conditions of producers in the Sabanas Sub-region. During the analysis, comparative advantages were evident in terms of production levels, which are influenced by the agricultural occupation of the population, the fertility and quality of the soil, as well as the extent of savannas and croplands. Furthermore, the rich agricultural cultural tradition and the suitability of the soils for the cultivation of cassava and yam contribute to strengthening the position of this Subregion in the agricultural sector [26].

According to what was reported in the database [24], in the period 2019–2022, the year that had the highest cropyield (ton/ha) was 2020 with 9.85%, compared to 2022, which had a lower yield of 8.98% hectares per ton, as seen in Fig. 2.

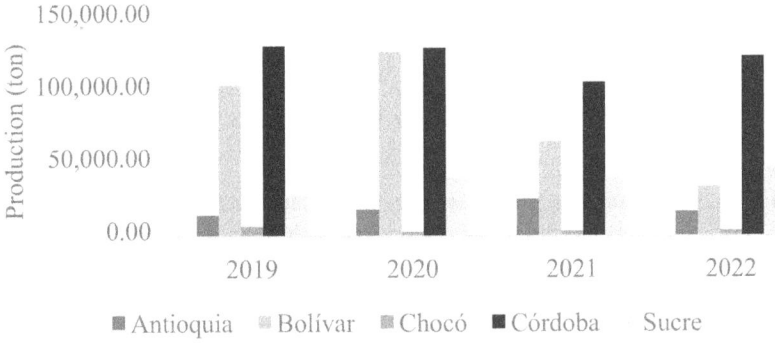

Fig. 1. Yam production by department in Colombia, 2019 – 2022.

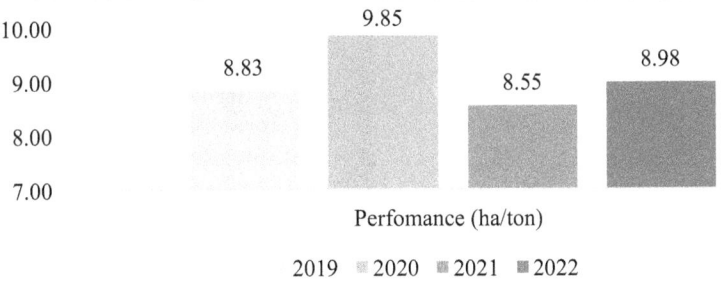

Fig. 2. Yam production by department in Colombia, 2019 – 2022.

The yam agri-food supply chain for this Subregion is integrated as follows: suppliers (natural or legal person who provides fertilizers, packaging, among other inputs that are considered essential for the yam production process), producer (person natural or legal that provides the site where the yam production is carried out), collection centers where the product is sought to be consolidated and marketed to consumption centers, be it the wholesale market (that which carries out wholesale commercial operations), retailers (municipalities where retail sales are located) and exporters who are in charge of taking the product abroad [27]. It should be taken into account that it is the producer's decision whether he decides to send the product to the associations or sends it directly to the consumption centers (Fig. 3).

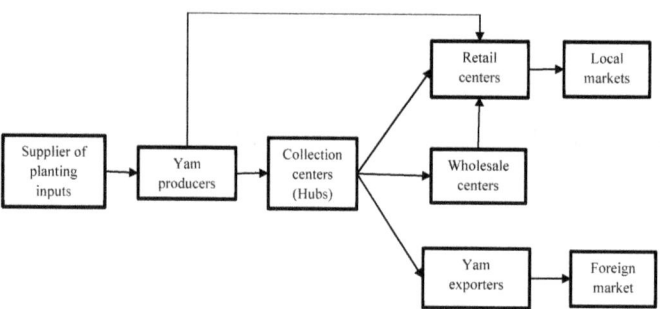

Fig. 3. Yam agri-food chain in the Sabanas Subregion

In this study, 173 yam producers are registered. These data were obtained from the survey of yam producers and processors carried out within the framework of this research. Figure 4(a) shows the geographical location of the 179 municipalities that are part of the Sabanas Subregion of the Department of Sucre. In the case of wholesale consumption centers, the following cities were considered: Sincelejo, Montería, Cartagena (Bazurto), Barranquilla (Granabastos and Barranquillita).

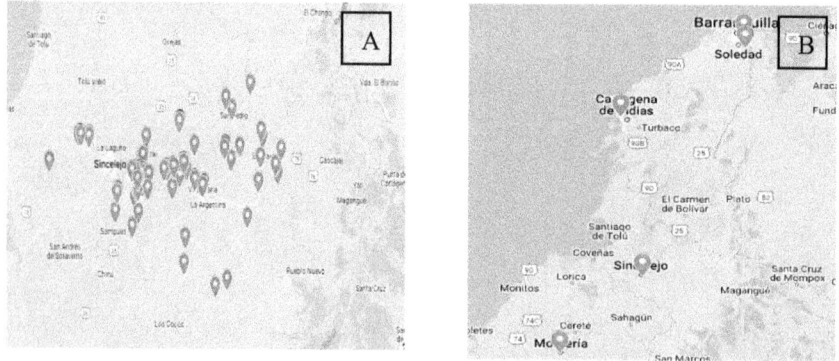

Fig. 4. (A) Geographic location of yam producers in the Sabanas Subregion and (B) wholesale consumption centers.

5 Computational Results

The proposed model was implemented using the GAMS software together with the CPLEX Solver, on a computer equipped with a 2.2 GHz Intel Core i5-5200U processor and 8 GB of RAM, running the Windows 10 Professional operating system. In this model, 179 yam producers were examined $i \in I$, located in the Sabanas Subregion of the Department of Sucre, considering three varieties of yam: hawthorn, diamond and criollo. In addition, the feasibility of locating eight potential hubs (Q) in the municipalities of San Juan de Betulia, Buenavista, Corozal, El Roble, Los Palmitos, Sincé, San Pedro and Sampués was evaluated.

As a strategic decision, the opening of a maximum of three warehouses was proposed, which would supply the five consumption centers. The parameters and variables presented for the solution of the model include production costs, transportation costs, availability of area to cultivate for producers, demand and sales prices managed by consumption centers.

According to the results obtained, the opening of three (3) strategic hubs was identified. These distribution centers not only reduced logistics costs, but also optimized delivery times, thus strengthening the supply chain. The selection of these locations was based on proximity to the main producers and market demand, achieving an optimal balance between costs and efficiency, having an expected profit of $7,092,932,970 COP or a best possible solution of $7,123,790,923 COP. This value, obtained after 789 iterations, with a relative GAP of 0.004351%, highlights the precision and robustness of the model. The calculation time of 0.3 s reflects the efficiency of the optimization process. Furthermore, as shown in Fig. 5, the model shows the axes that should be opened: San Juan de Betulia (a), Corozal (b) and Sincé (c).

Fig. 5. Open hub location

In this context, it is established that the capacities of the warehouses are determined by the amount of product that passes through them. The minimum capacity that must be established in the warehouses is defined according to the quantity of product distributed and the capacity of the selected vehicle. The implementation of the location model proved to be highly adaptable to changes in demand and variations in supply, allowing the distribution network to be dynamically adjusted and respond effectively to market fluctuations. This ensured the continuity of operations and customer satisfaction, thus consolidating the success of the implemented strategy.

On the other hand, from the results obtained from the model it can be said that the most shipped yam variety corresponds to the diamond yam, with a total of 199.8 tons per week. It is followed by the hawthorn yam, with 106.6 tons per week, and finally the Creole yam, with a total of 155 tons per week. Furthermore, it is important to keep in mind that of the 179 producers in total, 63 send the different varieties to hub 7, while 62 of the producers send to hub 3, and the remaining 54 producers send to hub 1.

The proposed model to optimize the yam supply chain in the Sabanas Subregion of the Department of Sucre introduces significant innovations in relation to the existing literature on the optimization of supply chains of perishable products. Unlike previous studies that generally focus on the optimization of logistics networks at a theoretical level, this model is distinguished by its specific focus on the strategic location of distribution centers. It proposes the strategic opening of up to three warehouses in key locations such as San Juan de Betulia, Corozal and Sincé. This strategy not only reduces logistics costs, but also improves delivery times by being close to the main producers and local market demand.

In terms of methodology, the model uses mixed integer linear programming (MIP), a technique recognized for its ability to efficiently solve complex combinatorial problems such as hub location and resource allocation in distribution networks. This methodological choice allows us to capture the geographical and logistical particularities of the Department of Sucre, such as local production and transportation costs, as well as the specific capacities of the available vehicles. This ensures that the model is precisely tuned to the economic and operational conditions of the region, which is crucial for the long-term effectiveness and sustainability of the yam supply chain.

Furthermore, the model demonstrates a unique ability to dynamically adapt to changes in demand and variations in supply of yam. This dynamic responsiveness ensures continuity of operations and customer satisfaction, aspects that are not always addressed in equal depth in previous studies that could have focused on static models. Together, these characteristics position the model as a powerful tool to improve the efficiency and profitability of the supply chain of perishable products in the specific local context of the Department of Sucre, thus contributing to the sustainable development and economic success of the region.

6   Conclusions

The results obtained with the application of the location model in GAMS have been crucial to support strategic decisions in supply chain management. Identifying the optimal locations for two strategic centers has meant important progress in reducing logistics costs, improving delivery times and comprehensively strengthening the supply chain. The careful selection of these locations was based on their proximity to both major producers and market demand, achieving an ideal balance between operating costs and distribution efficiency. This resulted in a total of $7,123,790,923 COP after 789 iterations, with an impressive margin of relative error of 0.004351%, and a calculation time of just 0.3 s. To reinforce and maintain the effectiveness of the model, it is recommended to establish a system of continuous data analysis that allows the effectiveness of strategic locations to be periodically evaluated. This approach will allow for proactive adjustments in response to the changing dynamics of the operating environment. The scalability and flexibility of the model are also essential for its long-term sustainability, considering possible changes in the distribution network or the introduction of new product varieties. In addition, it is suggested to explore the integration of emerging technologies such as the Internet of Things (IoT) and artificial intelligence (AI) to improve the operational efficiency and predictive capacity of the model.

References

1. Organización de las Naciones Unidas para la Alimentación y la Agricultura, El estado de la seguridad alimentaria y la nutrición en el mundo 2020. FAO, IFAD, UNICEF, WFP and WHO (2020). https://doi.org/10.4060/ca9692es
2. Escobar, J.P.: La inseguridad alimentaria en Colombia alcanzó a 15,5 millones de personas," Infobae (2023) https://www.infobae.com/colombia/2023/02/17/la-inseguridad-alimentaria-en-colombia-alcanzo-a-155-millones-de-personas/#:~:text=Este%20porcentaje%20representa%2015.5%20millones%20de%20personas.&text=En%20departamentos%20de%20la%20Regi%C3%B3n,seguido%20por%20Sucre%20(63%25) Accessed 28 Mar. 2023
3. Colciencias, "paed-sucre2016 (2016). https://minciencias.gov.co/sites/default/files/upload/paginas/paed-sucre2016.pdf . Accessed 28 Mar 2023
4. Aguilera Díaz, M.M., et al.: La Economia Del Departamento De Sucre: Ganadería Y Sector Público (2005). www.banrep.gov.co
5. Aramyan, L., Van Kooten, O., Oude Lansink, A., Ondersteijn, C.: Performance Indicators In Agri-Food Production Chains (2006)
6. Seuring, S., Müller, M.: From a literature review to a conceptual framework for sustainable supply chain management. J. Clean. Prod. 16(15), 1699–1710 (2008). https://doi.org/10.1016/j.jclepro.2008.04.020
7. Vianchá Sánchez, Z.H.: Models and configurations of supply chains in perishable goods, Ingeniería y Desarrollo 32(1), 138–154 (2014). https://doi.org/10.14482/inde.32.1.4577
8. Fernando, S., Judith, C., Gabriel, V.: Logística humanitaria: Un enfoque del suministro desde las cadenas agroalimentarias. Informacion Tecnologica 25(4), 43–50 (2014). https://doi.org/10.4067/S0718-07642014000400007
9. Aranza, Y. C. R.: El cultivo de ñame en el Caribe colombiano (2012"). https://doi.org/10.32468/dtseru.168
10. Andrea, L., Coronado, S.: Modelo De Localización De Instalaciones Capacitado Para La Cadena Frutícola Colombiana (2015). https://repository.udistrital.edu.co/handle/11349/3038, Accessed 28 Mar 2023
11. David, M., Leal, M., García, M.Á.: Centro de acopio y capacitación tecnológica para el agro en la región de Lengupá (2015)
12. Kayışoğlu, B., Akgün, İ.: Multiple allocation tree of hubs location problem for non-complete networks. Comput Oper Res. 136, 105478 (2021). https://doi.org/10.1016/j.cor.2021.105478
13. Musavi, M.M., Bozorgi-Amiri, A.: A multi-objective sustainable hub location-scheduling problem for perishable food supply chain. Comput. Ind. Eng. 113, 766–778 (2017). https://doi.org/10.1016/j.cie.2017.07.039
14. Saadati, M., Hosseininezhad, S.J.: Designing a hub location model in a bagasse-based bioethanol supply chain network in Iran (case study: Iran sugar industry). Biomass Bioenergy 122, 238–256 (2019). https://doi.org/10.1016/j.biombioe.2019.01.013

15. Maiyar, L.M., Thakkar, J.J.: Robust optimisation of sustainable food grain transportation with uncertain supply and intentional disruptions. Int. J. Prod. Res. **58**(18), 5651–5675 (2020). https://doi.org/10.1080/00207543.2019.1656836
16. Golestani, M., Moosavirad, S.H., Asadi, Y., Biglari, S.: A Multi-Objective Green Hub Location Problem with Multi Item-Multi Temperature Joint Distribution for Perishable Products in Cold Supply Chain. Sustain Prod Consum **27**, 1183–1194 (2021). https://doi.org/10.1016/j.spc.2021.02.026
17. Esteso, A., Alemany, M.M.E., Ortiz, Á.: Impact of product perishability on agri-food supply chains design. Appl. Math. Model. **96**, 20–38 (2021). https://doi.org/10.1016/j.apm.2021.02.027
18. Mejía, G., Granados-Rivera, D., Jarrín, J.A., Castellanos, A., Mayorquín, N., Molano, E.: Strategic supply chain planning for food hubs in central colombia: An approach for sustainable food supply and distribution. Applied Sciences (Switzerland) **11**(4), 1–22 (2021). https://doi.org/10.3390/app11041792
19. Mendoza-Ortega, G.P., Soto, M., Ruiz-Meza, J., Salgado, R., Torregroza, A.: Scenario-Based Model for the Location of Multiple Uncapacitated Facilities: Case Study in an Agro-Food Supply Chain. In: Figueroa-García, J.C., Díaz-Gutierrez, Y., Gaona-García, E.E., OrjuelaCañón, A.D. (eds.) Applied Computer Sciences in Engineering, pp. 386–398. Springer International Publishing, Cham (2021)
20. Mandal, R.: Tropical Root and Tuber Crops. Agrobotanical Publisher (1993)
21. Onwueme, I.C.: Sett weight effects on time of tuber formation, and on tuber yield characteristics, in water yam (Dioscorea alata L.). J. Agric. 317–319 (1978)
22. Fundacion Semana, "Ruta Montes de María (2009). http://www.rutamontesdemaria.com/sites/default/files/2016-05/CARACTERIZACION%20DE%20LAS%20CADENAS%20PRODUCTIVAS%2 0DE%20MMa.pdf, Accessed 07 Apr 2023
23. Reina Aranza, Y.: El cultivo del ñame en el caribe colombiano. Cartagena (2013). https://www.banrep.gov.co/sites/default/files/publicaciones/archivos/dtser_168.pdf
24. Agronet, "Reporte: Comparativo de Área, Producción, Rendimiento y Participación Departamental por Cultivo. Agronet. https://www.agronet.gov.co/estadistica/Paginas/home.aspx?cod=3, Accessed 13 Dec 2023
25. Reina-Aranza, Y.C.: El cultivo de ñame en el Caribe colombiano, Bogotá, Colombia (Jun 2012). https://doi.org/10.32468/dtseru.168

Optimization Models for the Development of the Agricultural Sector in Rural Territories

Germán Andrés Méndez[1] (ID) and Carolina Suárez Roldán[1,2](✉) (ID)

[1] Universidad Distrital Francisco José de Caldas, Bogotá, Colombia
csuarezr@udistrital.edu.co
[2] Universidad Cooperativa de Colombia, Bogotá, Colombia
carolina.suarez@campusucc.edu.co

Abstract. Rural development faces major challenges related to infrastructure, youth migration, employment shortages, and food security. Agriculture is a dynamic sector that is crucial in addressing these challenges. In this context, this work conducted a theoretical review of the optimization techniques used and the information available in a specific case study. From the above, two techniques were selected, linear programming and stochastic linear programming, to efficiently solve this problem. Four models were proposed to define the number of hectares to be planted for the crops i in the municipalities j, considering food security conditions and some limiting factors in each territory. The results indicate that the amount of food and income produced in the municipalities is significantly lower than that obtained with the proposed models; the tons of food produced represent 15% of the amount projected with the linear programming model and do not account for 1% of the income generated by said model. Likewise, it is observed that the third model, which has two stochastic parameters, yields better results regarding the number of hectares planted, the tons of food produced, and the income generated in comparison with the second model, which only defines one parameter. In conclusion, these optimization models allow analyzing municipalities' participation and diversification in relation to food production in the region, and their results are better that those of current empirical decisions.

Keywords: linear programming · stochastic programming · agriculture sector · food sustainability

1 Introduction

Over the years, a lag has been observed in the development of rural areas when compared to urban ones, partly due to political and economic processes that have prioritized urban development over time [1]. Consequently, governmental actors are committed to balancing equality in the access to resources and opportunities in rural territories, aiming to reduce disparities and highlighting rural spaces' importance and potential in contributing to balanced development. For instance, during the global COVID-19 pandemic, rural territories played a fundamental role in supplying food to the population [2].

J. C. Figueroa-García et al. (Eds.): WEA 2024, CCIS 2223, pp. 63–75, 2025.
https://doi.org/10.1007/978-3-031-74598-0_6

Likewise, the concept of *rural development* has evolved in response to the new conditions of economic, social, and environmental progress, which necessitate changes in both rural families and the activities they engage in. However, the objective of the concept remains the same: to improve the well-being of rural populations [7]. In the same way, [8] defines rural development as a process where activities in rural areas are balanced and self-sustaining with respect to economic, social, and environmental components. Similarly, in [9], abundant literature on the new paradigm of rural development is identified, contributing to current dynamics in rural territories. However, the authors acknowledge that the concept of *rural development* is ambiguous and poorly defined. Based on the above, the authors understand that rural development involves improving the living and work conditions of rural areas while respecting their social, cultural, and environmental values. In other words, rural development positively contributes to the quality of life of the population and its territory.

Similarly, it is worth mentioning that, in the last three decades, there has been a marked decline in the global population living in rural areas. Moreover, in the last decade, it has been evident that less than half of the world's population resides in rural areas, with a 43% decrease in rural population recorded in 2021. Additionally, projections indicate an unfavorable scenario, as this figure is expected to increase in the coming decade [10]. There is an urgent need to undertake efforts to activate economic, social, and environmental development in rural territories, aiming to tackle poverty, hunger, unemployment, and deficits in public services, among other challenges. Consequently, establishing long-, medium-, and short-term strategies is crucial to advancing towards achieving the Sustainable Development Goals (SDGs), which provide conditions to encourage the return of the population to rural areas [11]. In light of the above, it is recognized that the SDGs consider the three fundamental dimensions of sustainable development, corresponding to social, environmental, and economic aspects. Some of the SDGs are more pressing, given the urgency of the needs in rural regions, particularly regarding the availability of resources, which makes the rural population vulnerable [12].

The objective of the second SDG, *i.e.*, Zero Hunger, is to create a world free of hunger, in which access to adequate food can be ensured for all [13]. In contrast, food insecurity implies limited access to or insufficient quality of food, leading to malnutrition and hunger [14]. In Colombia, "54% of the population suffers from food insecurity (in concrete numbers, 27 million people), and more than half a million children and people suffer from chronic malnutrition" [15]. Given the above, agro-industrial production on an international scale has been identified as a predatory practice that does not favor balanced development, since its use of resources is excessive and increases malnutrition and food insecurity in some countries [14]. Consequently, there is a need to strengthen local production and consumption, making it necessary to improve family production by means of sustainable and innovative practices [14]. This research aims to guide decision-making with regard to the area of each crop type to be planted while considering the nutritional conditions that are part of food security, in addition to limiting factors such as land availability and demand.

Among the challenges posed by rural development, the most important one is moving towards sustainable production in the agriculture sector [16], reducing territories' food insecurity levels. Consequently, in the field of optimization, linear programming has particularly been recognized as a useful technique to guide decision-making. In this vein, [17] formulates a model to solve agricultural planning problems, whose constraints are related scarce or limiting resources such as the planted area (ha), water, labor, and the capital available for planting. Likewise, the objective function is generally defined to maximize the net income. In [18], a linear programming (LP) model is defined for the mixing problem in food preparation for the livestock sector, with the minimization of the total cost of food as the objective function, considering nutritional requirements according to the growth stages of the animals. An extension of LP known as mixed integer linear programming (MILP) has also been employed, wherein some of the variables are integers. For example, [19] elaborates an integer linear programming model (ILPM) that aids in deciding on the number of raw materials to be purchased for food preparation.

Likewise, another optimization technique known as *stochastic programming* has been identified. This technique is employed when some of the functions' parameters are random variables, with linear stochastic programming (LPS) being one of the most widely studied approaches [20]. Therefore, two types of stochastic programing have been identified: active and passive. The first type is employed when decision-making considers the variables before all the random events occur. On the other hand, the second approach waits for the variables to take values in order to indicate potential solutions [21]. In light of the above, active stochastic programming is regarded as a set of potential occurrences or scenarios that random variables may assume. In the same way, in establishing the objective function, expected values and penalizations are defined. This allows reducing deviations with respect to the expected value [21].

In this sense, SLP allows representing uncertainty in the demand of products, in the prices of inputs, and in production costs, among others, contemplating the external effects that generate a set of possible results in the stochastic parameters. In [22], a stochastic linear programming model SLPM is presented and solved with the scenario technique. This model optimizes the profit of the agricultural supply chain, in which some parameters are uncertain (*e.g.*, demand, price, and cost). Similarly, [23] presents a two-stage, fixed-resource SLPM for the tactical planning of soybean supply chains from the shipper's perspective. Finally, in [24], a two-stage mixed integer programming stochastic model is presented, which maximizes the economic and environmental benefits of food and biofuel production while calculating uncertain parameters such as yield and pricing.

Based on the above, the following question arises: *Are optimization techniques viable to guide decision-making towards balanced development in the rural agricultural sector?* This paper consists of three sections. The first section is the introduction, which outlines the context of the object of study. The second section explains the methods used in this work, and the third one presents and discusses the results obtained, ending with some concluding remarks.

2   Methods and Materials

The methodology presented in Fig. 1 was employed in this research, which consists of six stages.

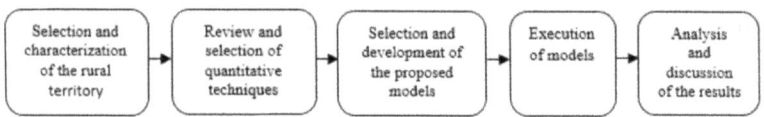

Fig. 1. Research methodology

2.1 Selection and Characterization of the Rural Territory

The administrative-political division of Colombia consists of 32 departments, which are led by governors. These departments are further divided into 1097 municipalities, each managed by a mayor. Additionally, there are 20 departmental *corregimientos* [districts] and the Special District of Bogotá, which is also the Capital of the Republic [25]. Based on the above, the Department of Tolima was selected as the geographical area of interest for this research, as it falls under the project titled *Proposal of a methodology for the sustainable development of economic activities in rural territories of Colombia using intelligent models* [Propuesta de una metodología para el desarrollo sostenible de las actividades económicas en los territorios rurales de Colombia a partir de modelos de inteligencia].

Tolima has a great diversity of soils and climates, which makes it highly important due to its natural richness. It is politically and administratively divided into 47 municipalities and stands out for having all thermal floors. Moreover, it is characterized by its strategic geographic location in the center of the country, amidst the triangle of major centers, where 80% percent of the national consumption is concentrated. The department offers a significant supply of raw materials for the industry, both in agriculture and mining, and its vast biodiversity has demonstrated potential for the development of 48 production chains in various sectors such as agriculture, cement, poultry, coffee, textiles, and garments [26]. It is also relevant that the departments of Antioquia, Valle del Cauca, Tolima, Cundinamarca, Meta, and Nariño account for 48.2% of the total agricultural production in the surveyed rural areas. Therefore, food security in Tolima must focus on 397 200 ha, which, according to studies by the Agustín Codazzi Geographic Institute, have the best soils for cultivation. These productive hectares encompass 12.9% of the department's territory. With this figure, Tolima ranks 11th out of 32 among the territories with the highest number of suitable hectares for crop development [27].

2.2 Review and Selection of Quantitative Techniques

Other applications of LP include the division of land for different types of crops in order to increase the overall benefit of growers, the management and distribution of crop water over time, and the allocation of routes in the transportation of agricultural products to minimize the total transportation costs [19]. Similarly, LP techniques belong to the family of quantitative tools within the field of operations research (OR). This is why the review by [28] addresses 33 types of applications related to forest exploitation and management in strategic, tactical, and operational planning. These applications encompass fire management, conservation, land use, and environmental concerns. This also encompasses the management of uncertainty through stochastic programming (SP), multi-objective programming (MO), goal programming (GP), hierarchical planning, and multi-attribute techniques, among others.

On the other hand, [29] describes a wide range of problems in the agricultural sector for different agro-logistic chains, such as vegetables, sugarcane, fruits, vegetables, maize, or livestock (cattle, swine, or fishery). In this vein, studies have shown the use of LP and its variants, such as mixed integer programming (MIP), MO, GP, and other methods, including simulation (SIM) and others like risk analysis (RA), forecasting (FOR), data envelopment analysis (DEA), multicriteria analytic hierarchy processes (AHP), stochastic programming (SP), and the Markov decision process (MDP). These applications were developed in Europe, Australia, Africa, and America.

Based on the above, two techniques were selected: LP and SP. These are summarized in Table 1. The objective function and constraints of the LP model are linear, and all variables are positive. The structure of the SP model [30] aims to solve planning problems under conditions of risk or uncertainty. A general approach to addressing these models is by assuming modifications to the original model with the transformations shown in Model II.

Table 1. Linear and stochastic programming models

Model I (LP)	Model II (SP)
$MaxZ = \overline{C}\overline{X}$	$MaxZ = \tilde{C}\overline{X}$
$\overline{A}\overline{X} \leq \overline{B}$	$\tilde{A}\overline{X} \leq \tilde{B}$
$\overline{X} \geq 0$	$\overline{X} \geq 0$

Z: Objective function (maximizing or minimizing a function Z) corresponding to a decision, *e.g.*, income or utility.

$\overline{X}$: Column vector representing the activity levels or generally the decision variables.

$\overline{C}$: Row vector representing the coefficients of the objective function.

$\overline{B}$: Column vector representing the availability of resources, known as the *right-hand side vector*.

$\overline{A}$: Matrix of technological coefficients representing the resource requirements.

Model II simply reflects the extent to which the cost vectors $\overline{C}$ can be regarded as random variables and hence be transformed into $\tilde{C}$. This can also occur with the matrix of technological coefficients $\tilde{A}$ and the resource vector $\tilde{B}$. . These modifications can be considered to be random variables (rvs) and, as such, they can reflect the expected value of a probability density function corresponding to each component of the linear model.

2.3 Selection and Development of the Proposed Models

One factor that was considered in the selection of the models was the availability of information, which is why the models formulated for the case study are LP and SP. The information used for development was obtained from two official sources: the National Administrative Department of Statistics (DANE), with historical data on food prices; and

Table 2. Proposed LP model

Table 3. SP model for $\tilde{R}_{ij}$

Model
$$Max\ F(X) = \sum_{i=1}^{m} \sum_{j=1}^{p} \overline{PV}_j\, \overline{R}_{ij}\overline{X}_{ij}$$
$$\sum_{j=1}^{p} \overline{X}_{ij} \le \overline{AD}_i \quad \forall\, i = 1\cdots 47$$
$$\sum_{i=1}^{m} \overline{R}_{ij}\overline{X}_{ij} \ge \overline{TP}_j \quad \forall\, j = 1\cdots 80$$
$$\overline{X}_{ij} \ge 0$$

Model I
$$Max\ F(X) = \sum_{i=1}^{m} \sum_{j=1}^{p} \overline{PV}_j\, \tilde{R}_{ij}\overline{X}_{ij}$$
$$\sum_{j=1}^{p} \overline{X}_{ij} \le \overline{AD}_i \quad \forall\, i = 1\cdots 47$$
$$\sum_{i=1}^{m} \tilde{R}_{ij}\overline{X}_{ij} \ge \overline{TP}_j \quad \forall\, j = 1\cdots 80$$
$$\overline{X}_{ij} \ge 0$$

the TerriData database of the National Planning Department (DNP). It is important to mention that the TerriData database contains over 800 simple and composite indicators, aggregated in terms of the municipalities, departments, capitals, and major cities of Colombia. These indicators are classified into 16 dimensions. However, not all of the information was available in the databases, and the number of dimensions or themes varied depending on the consulted territorial entity [31].

The first proposed model is shown in Table 2. It aims to optimize the expected income from the hectares to be produced by each crop in each municipality. This is based on real information from the base year of analysis.

$\overline{X}_{ij}$: The number of hectares to be cultivated for type-j crop in a type-i municipality.

$\overline{PV}_j$: : The estimated selling price (per ton) in the logistic chain of crop j.

$\overline{R}_{ij}$: The actual yield of crop j in tons per cultivated hectare in municipality i.

$\tilde{R}_{ij}$ is the expected yield (in tons) of crop j per hectare planted in municipality i.

$\overline{AD}_i$: The utilized area in ha for municipality i.

$\overline{TP}_j$: The actual production of crop j in tons.

The purpose of this first model is to compare the produced quantity of different crops against the optimal quantity produced in each municipality (Table 2), assuming that the limiting factors are the amount of available land, equal to the land used for crop cultivation in 2018, and that at least the tons of food reported for the year of analysis must be produced.

The second model (SP) is used in the expected yield coefficient of the objective function, which is why a probability density function (PDF) is defined. Therefore, in the estimation of the PDF, the possibility of planting other types of crops is considered, given the history of the collected data. Additionally, the expected value for the selling price of new types of crop must be estimated (Table 3).

This model enables the potential cultivation and production of new crops, thus bolstering food security. The third model utilizes identical constraints, but the availability of planting areas in each municipality is stochastically estimated using a PDF based on the collected data (Table 4).

Table 4. SP model for $\tilde{R}_{ij}$ and $\widetilde{AD}_i$

Table 5. SP model for $\tilde{R}_{ij}$ and $\widetilde{AD}_i$ with nutritional requirements (NR)

Model II

$$Max\, F(X) = \sum_{i=1}^{m} \sum_{j=1}^{p} \overline{PV}_j \tilde{R}_{ij} \bar{X}_{ij}$$

$$\sum_{j=1}^{p} \bar{X}_{ij} \leq \widetilde{AD}_i \quad \forall i = 1 \cdots 47$$

$$\sum_{i=1}^{m} \tilde{R}_{ij} \bar{X}_{ij} \geq \overline{TP}_j \quad \forall j = 1 \cdots 80$$

$$\bar{X}_{ij} \geq 0$$

Model III

$$Max\, F(X) = \sum_{i=1}^{m} \sum_{j=1}^{p} \overline{PV}_j \tilde{R}_{ij} \bar{X}_{ij}$$

$$\sum_{j=1}^{p} \bar{X}_{ij} \leq \widetilde{AD}_i \quad \forall i = 1 \cdots 47$$

$$\sum_{i=1}^{m} \tilde{R}_{ij} \bar{X}_{ij} \geq \overline{TP}_j \quad \forall j = 1 \cdots 80$$

$$\sum_{i=1}^{m} \widetilde{R}_{ij} \bar{I}_{jk} \bar{X}_{ij} \geq RI_k \quad \forall j = 1 \cdots 80$$

$$\bar{X}_{ij} \geq 0$$

In line with the Zero Hunger SDG, increasing agricultural productivity and moving towards sustainable food production is indispensable for mitigating hunger risks worldwide. Therefore, the fourth model incorporates constraints related to food sustainability, which are based on the nutritional requirements set forth by the Colombian Institute of Family Welfare (ICBF) (Table 5). The ICBF establishes an official dietary plan for the Colombian population, considering specific age groups and, in some cases, gender. The age groups are as follows: group 1 consists of boys and girls aged two to five; group 2 includes boys and girls between six and nine years old; group 3 includes both genders between 10 and 13 years old; group 4 comprises males aged 14–17; group 5 includes females aged 14–17 years; group 6 is composed of males aged 18–59; group 7 includes females aged 18–59; and group 8 includes males and females aged 60 or more.

Similarly, foods are categorized into four major food groups: group I consists of cereals, roots, tubers, bananas, and their derivatives; group II includes fruits and vegetables; group III represents milk and dairy products (which are not considered in this case, as they are not agricultural products); and group IV encompasses meats, eggs, dry legumes, nuts, and seeds. Consequently, a special unit called *exchange* is established. This measure represents a specific quantity of food that provides a similar contribution of energy or nutrients within the same group, allowing for replacement or interchangeability [32].

2.4 Executing the Mathematical Models

The models, as mentioned above, are based on the 47 municipalities of Tolima and encompass the 80 main crops that the department has established over the past 13 years. To develop our proposal, the Open Solver software [33] was employed, and information from TerriData was used to estimate the planted hectares and crop yields of each municipality, as well as to obtain food data sheets.

Model Data Estimation

The price estimation process involved the use of data from the food markets in the eight major cities of the Agricultural Supply and Price Information System (SIPSA) for the base year 2018. For the objective function coefficient $\overline{PV}_j$, , a random variable (rv) was assumed to follow a uniform distribution. Likewise, a triangularly distributed rv was defined for the expected yield of crop j per ha planted in municipality i, which was denoted as $\tilde{R}_{ij}$. This estimation was based on a dataset spanning 13 years of statistical information, which includes pessimistic, most probable, and optimistic yield values.

As per the purpose of the model, the available planting area in the municipalities $(\widetilde{AD}_i)$ was validated with regard to the ha cultivated in these geographical spaces, as this information is of interest for analyzing the distribution of each crop type defined by the models. These data were estimated from a 13-year dataset. Therefore, the independence of the data from each other and over time was verified, and a random variable was estimated which follows a triangular PDF with the optimistic (highest) value, the most probable (median) value, and the pessimistic (lowest value).

As part of the food security constraints, the necessary annual exchange quantity for various food groups was estimated. Equation (1) was employed to estimate the annual exchange amount for food group k across the m age groups of the population. With these results, Eq. (2) was applied to derive the data input for the model, representing the total annual exchange amount for food group k.

$$IA_{km} = P_m \times 365 \times Id_{km} \tag{1}$$

$$IA_k = IA_{k1} + IA_{k2} + IA_{k3} + ... + IA_{k8} \tag{2}$$

where:

IA_{km}: number of annual exchanges for food group k in each age group m of the population.

P_m: population in age group m.

Id_{km}: number of daily exchanges for food group k according to age group m in the population.

IA_k: number of annual exchanges for food group k.

Each of the first three models defined 3760 decision variables and 127 constraints (Tables 2–4). In the fourth model, three additional constraints were introduced, derived from the nutritional exchange requirements of groups I, II, and IV.

3   Results and Discussion

Table 6 presents the main results of the proposed models. The rows correspond to the different models, with the *current model* representing the actual statistical figures and the columns displaying the results of the objective function and constraints. Consequently, in the current model, the results obtained in 2018 regarding the food and income produced in the municipalities are significantly lower than those of the LP, SP-1, SP-2, and SP-3 models. Hence, there is a need for information allowing for the analysis and projection of different scenarios according to the region's requirements.

Table 6. Results of the different models

Model	Hectares planted	Tons of food produced	Income in USD	% IC-G1	% IC-G2	% IC-G4
Current Model	78 096	90 206	95 829	9	9	29
LP	78 096	588 576	23 211 323	7	10	12
SP-1	78 096	6 134 651	23 517 531	3	19	60
SP-2	156 140	10 472 430	35 431 411	5	42	96
SP-3	156 140	2 066 829	5 672 373	40	52	100

% IC-G is the fulfillment index of a food group measured in exchanges.

Furthermore, it was observed that the number of planted hectares in the first three models corresponds to 50% of the planted area in the SP-2 and SP-3 models, representing a considerably low percentage given Colombia's food and nutritional insecurity, where half of the households face difficulties in accessing a balanced diet [34]. Considering the context, it is essential to mention the challenges faced by farmers in accessing more land, seeking financial support for the cultivation process, implementing technology in their practices, and establishing sales channels to ensure the profitability of the harvest, among other issues [35]. Likewise, it is important to note that the number of deterministic or stochastic parameters influences the results of the optimization models. The first three models use deterministic values for available area, whereas the last two models define a stochastic parameter that considers uncertainty.

Similarly, the current model and the LP model use the same number of cultivated hectares, but with significantly different results in terms of food production and income in the municipalities. In other words, the tons of food produced in the current model represent only 15% of those reported by the LP model, which is why the income of the current model falls 1% short compared to that of the LP model. Furthermore, Fig. 2 shows the number of crop types that generate a level of production equal to or greater than 500 tons. The current model exhibits the smallest number of crop types, since other varieties or types are not profitable.

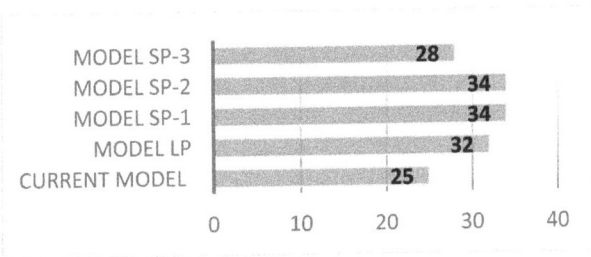

Fig. 2. Number of crop types in the proposed models

It was also observed that, in the current model, crops such as coffee, avocado, beans, cocoa, plantain, cotton, soursop, corn, and mango account for 80% of the total sales. On the other hand, in the LP model, coffee cultivation represents more than 80% of the food sales, followed by cocoa. Consequently, the cultivated area and prices are factors that determine the behavior of crop types in the region. Based on the above, the LP model shows better results compared to the current model (Table 6), but it does not provide an appropriate response to the need for crop diversification and the requirements for food security in the region, as proposed in the final model.

Similarly, coffee cultivation accounts for 80% of the food product sales in SP-1, whereas, in SP-2, 80% is primarily attributed to coffee, followed by cocoa. Table 6 shows that Model-SP2, which exhibits stochastic parameters, yields better results regarding the number of hectares planted, the tons of food produced, and the income generated when compared to Model SP-1. In the same way, according to Table 6, the food exchange constraints of groups I and II are not met due to insufficient land resources. This necessitates an increase in crop cultivation to enhance the exchange between these groups. Furthermore, it is recognized that there are crop types that are not cultivated in the region and have no demand from the population. In other words, the demand for crop types influences the fulfillment of food exchanges, which in turn enables a balanced diet in the region. Additionally, as previously mentioned, coffee cultivation represents over 80% of the sales, which partly explains the reduction in the number of crop types (Fig. 2), since 48% of the food production corresponds to this type of crop.

The percentage of compliance (% IC-G) with food exchange in the food groups was calculated from the results of the first four models. There is a lower compliance rate compared to the data obtained from SP-3, as this model integrates food security constraints that correspond to the exchange of food groups. SP-2 outperforms SP-3 in terms of both food production and income, but its nutritional performance is lower. With respect to the former, SP-3 exhibits differences of 35, 10, and 4% in the compliance with the exchanges of groups I, II, and IV, respectively. Likewise, the income of SP-3 is equivalent to 16% of the income of SP-2, which is a significant difference. This can be explained by the nutritional requirement constraints considered in SP-3, as it optimizes income while considering the nutritional needs of the population, compensating for the economic aspect with the social one.

4 Conclusions

It is the responsibility of governments, productive sectors, academics, and society as a whole to provide ideas and solutions that reduce the world's food insecurity. Therefore, the agricultural sector is a fundamental link to increase the production and quality of food. However, this sector faces important challenges, highlighting the need to move towards sustainable production that seeks to balance environmental, social, and economic components. Consequently, it is necessary to generate more reliable information in this regard, so that tools can be developed or applied to project scenarios and guide decision-making.

As per the literature on agricultural and agribusiness development, multiple modeling exercises have been conducted, employing various techniques. LP stands out as one of the most common techniques. Although this approach is deterministic, it has limited capabilities in representing uncertainty, which can be corrected by incorporating random variables in certain components of the model via a technique known as *stochastic programming*. In this case, income parameters were integrated by including the expected yield, which represents the number of tons produced per ha for different crops and across municipalities. This variability was also incorporated in both the selling prices of agricultural products and the cultivable land prices of each municipality. This enhanced the models' representation and allowed for a more accurate depiction of real-world agricultural systems.

The exercise conducted in this work was proposed for a Colombian region that is attractive due to its wide variety of climates and soil qualities, allowing for the cultivation of multiple types of crops, both transitory and permanent, and a broad range of yields. These proposed models represent important conditions that must be considered when deciding on the area (ha) and crop types to be planted in territories. It is evident that these models guide decision-making towards a balanced development in the agricultural sector. A reference year was established in the information collection phase and employed as input data for the models. Next, the results of the case study were analyzed, observing that the decisions made in the studied territories (productive farms) have not been appropriate. This assessment shows that farmers' decisions are partially based on the crop types they have traditionally grown, highlighting the need to apply knowledge that contributes to crop planning and management in order to diversify and improve yields, as these conditions contribute to the nation's food security. This improvement is not only related to merely economic objectives, but also to environmental and social ones.

However, these models highlight what is already known: the existing contradictions between different objectives in achieving sustainable development. If more natural resources are employed, there may be a greater economic benefit and an even more effective reduction in malnutrition and hunger. However, this goes against sustainability. Similar contradictions arise when producing a portfolio to reduce food insecurity, which may not necessarily guarantee a better level of economic remuneration. It is possible that, with multi-objective programming or meta-programming techniques, these contradictions can be balanced. This, however, requires sufficient and reliable information, which is lacking in the case of Colombia.

Declaration of Conflicting Interests.   The authors declare no potential conflicts of interest with respect to the research, authorship, and/or publication of this article.

References

1. Muñoz, L.V.: Poverty and rural underdevelopment in Colombia. An analysis from the urban bias theory. Estudios Políticos (54), 59–81 (2019) https://doi.org/10.17533/udea.espo.n54a04
2. Hidalgo, F.: Frente a La Pandemia: Potencialidades de la Ruralidad y las Agriculturas Campesinas. Boletín Académico "Sociología y Política Hoy" **4**(4), 103–13 (2020)
3. Santos, J.L., Martínez, T.C., Díaz, J.G.: Nueva Ruralidad y Dinámicas de Proximidad en el Desarrollo Territorial de Sistemas Agroalimentarios Localizados. Estudios Rurales **6**(10), 1–25 (2017). https://doi.org/10.48160/22504001er10.330

4. Castellano-Álvarez, F.J., Castro-Serrano, J., Durán-Sánchez, A.: El Concepto de Medio Rural: Dificultades y Perspectivas. Espacios **40**(14), 16 (2019)
5. Márquez, D.: Bases Metodológicas del Desarrollo Rural. Ediciones Akal. España (2002)
6. Samper, C.C.: Estrategias de Desarrollo Rural En La UE: Definición de Espacio Rural, Ruralidad y Desarrollo Rural (2013)
7. Souza, R.P.: O Desenvolvimento Rural no Estado do Rio de Janeiro a partir de Uma Análise Multidimensional. RESR **57**(01), 109–126 (2019). https://doi.org/10.22533/at.ed.3522214123
8. Quintana, J., Cazorla, A., Merino, J.: Desarrollo Rural en la Unión Europea: Modelos de Participación Social. Ministerio de Agricultura, Pesca y Alimentación, Madrid (1999)
9. Guinjoan, E., Badia, A., Tulla, A.: Noves Ruralitats i Desenvolupament Rural. Estat de la Qüestió i Aplicació d'un Nou Mètode d'anàlisi a Catalunya: La Rural Web. Documents d'Anàlisi Geogràfica **62**(3), 503–530 (2016). https://doi.org/10.5565/rev/dag.366
10. Gutiérrez, E., Moral B, E., and Ramos, R.: Tendencias Recientes de la Población en las Áreas Rurales y Urbanas de España. Documentos Ocasionales No.2027 (2020)
11. Liendo, R.: Desafío Boliviano: El Cumplimiento de Los Objetivos de Desarrollo Sostenible desde el Sistema Agroalimentario Campesino Indígena. LAJED 13–34 (2021). https://doi.org/10.35319/lajed.20210458
12. Hidalgo Capitán, A., Cubillo Guevara, A.P.: Good Living Goals an Alternative Proposal to the Sustainable Development Goals. Ibe-roamerican Journal of Development Studies **8**(1), 6–57 (2019). https://doi.org/10.26754/ojs_ried/ijds.354
13. Organización de las Naciones Unidas. (n.d.). *2 Hambre Cero - Objetivos de Desarrollo Sostenible.* https://www.un.org/sustainabledevelopment/es/hunger/
14. Acosta, A.R., Garbardella, A.D., Olaya, E., Trotta, M.E.V., Coxshall, W.: Diagnóstico situacional de seguridad alimentaria en Argentina, Brazil, Colombia e Inglaterra post Covid-19. Revista Katálysis **25**(3), 539–550 (2022). https://doi.org/10.1590/1982-0259.2022.e86289
15. DANE. Departamento Administrativo Nacional de Estadísticas. (2022). *Gran Encuesta Integrada de Hogares (GEIH)*
16. López-Rodríguez, C.E., Urrego Tunjuelo, C.Urrego Tunjuelo, A.R.: Methodological proposal for the adoption of good practices in sustainable agriculture aimed at colombian producers. Produccion y Limpia, *18*(1), 99–117 (2023). https://doi.org/10.22507/pml.v18n1a7
17. Sofi, N.A., Ahmed, A., Ahmad, N., Bhat, B.A.: Decision Making in Agriculture: A Linear Programming Approach. Int. J. Modern Math. Sci **13**(2), 160–169 (2015)
18. Alotaibi, A., Nadeem, F.: A review of applications of linear programming to optimize agricultural solutions. Int. J. Inf. Eng. Electron. Bus. **13**(2), 11–21 (2021). https://doi.org/10.5815/ijieeb.2021.02.02
19. Saxena, P., Khanna, N.: Formulation and computation of animal feed mix: optimization by combination of mathematical programming. Adv. Intell. Syst. Comput. **337**, 621–622 (2015). https://doi.org/10.1007/978-3-319-13728-5
20. Ramos, A., Cerisola, S.: Optimización Estocástica. Universidad Pontificia ICAI ICADE Comillas (2016)
21. Escobar, J., Rivas, D.: Modelos de Optimización Estocástica en la Generación Térmica de Energía Eléctrica. Universidad de el Salvador (2013)
22. Gharye Mirzaei, M., Gholami, S., Rahmani, D.: A mathematical model for the optimization of agricultural supply chain under uncertain environmental and financial conditions: the case study of fresh date fruit. Environ. Dev. Sustain. (Issue 0123456789) (2023). https://doi.org/10.1007/s10668-023-03503-7
23. dos Reis, S.A., Leal, J.E., Thomé, A.M.T.: A two-stage stochastic linear programming model for tactical planning in the soybean supply chain. Logistics **7**(3), 1–26 (2023). https://doi.org/10.3390/logistics7030049

24. Cobuloglu, H.I., Büyüktahtakın, E.: A two-stage stochastic mixed-integer programming approach to the competition of biofuel and food production. Comput. Ind. Eng. **107**(November), 251–263 (2017). https://doi.org/10.1016/j.cie.2017.02.017
25. DANE. División Político-Administrativa de Colombia (2007). https://www.dane.gov.co/files/investigaciones/divipola/olddivipola2007.pdf
26. Rivera, J.Q.: Actividades Económicas en el Departamento Tolima, Colombia: Afectaciones a partir de la Pandemia por COVID-19. SUMMA. Revista Disciplinaria En Ciencias Económicas y Sociales **4**(2), 1–10 (2022). https://doi.org/10.47666/summa.4.2.7
27. IGAC. Tolima, uno de los Departamentos con mayor potencial agrícola en Colombia (2024)
28. Rönnqvist, M., et al.: Operations research challenges in forestry: 33 open problems. Ann. Oper. Res. **232**(1), 11–40 (2015). https://doi.org/10.1007/s10479-015-1907-4
29. Plá-Aragonés, L.: Handbook of Operations Research in Agriculture and the Agri-Food Industry. Springer. New York (2015). https://doi.org/10.1007/978-1-4939-2483-7
30. Kall, P., Wallace, S.: Stochastic Programming, 1st edn. Wiley (1994)
31. DNP. Conceptos Básicos para un mejor Uso de Terridata, Colombia (2019). https://doi.org/10.2307/j.ctvpv50c0.5
32. ICBF, and FAO. Guías Alimentarias basadas en Alimentos para la Población Colombiana, Segunda Edición, Taller Creativo de Aleida Sánchez B. Ltda (2020)
33. Mason, A.: OpenSolver - an open-source add-in to solve linear and integer progammes in excel. In: Klatte, D., Lüthi, H.-J., Schmedders, K. (eds.) Operations Research Proceedings, pp. 401–406. Springer, Heidelberg (2012). https://doi.org/10.1007/978-3-642-29210-1_64
34. Camargo, C., Tarazona, M.: Análisis de la Implementación de Política de Seguridad Alimentaria y Nutricional en el Municipio de Armero-Guayabal Tolima, con Base en el Determinante de Disponibilidad de Alimentos. Tesis de Maestría. Universidad Jorge Tadeo Lozano (2020)
35. DNP. El Campo Colombiano: Un Camino Hacia El Bienestar y La Paz. Tomo I. Nuevas Edi. Bogotá – Colombia (2015)

Index Tracking Based on Norm-Constraints and Regularization

Carlos Andres Zapata Quimbayo$^{(\boxtimes)}$ ⓘ and John Freddy Moreno Trujillo ⓘ

Universidad Externado de Colombia, Bogotá, Colombia
{carlosa.zapata,jhon.moreno}@uexternado.edu.co

Abstract. This paper presents the implementation of two methods for sparse index tracking of the US Nasdaq 100 index. The proposed methods employ a regularization approach based on a non-convex cardinality constraint approximation of the ℓ_p-norm to identify the optimal asset weights of the tracking portfolio. The results demonstrate that the ℓ_0-norm-constrained sparse tracking portfolio is computationally efficient and exhibits a notable reduction in tracking errors during the out-of-sample testing periods. Furthermore, we present an empirical comparison of the results of performance measures with those of traditional constrained strategies using norm constraints for index tracking.

Keywords: Index Tracking · Norm-Constrained Optimization · Regularization Methods

1 Introduction

Index tracking (IT) is a strategy that is employed with the objective of replicating the performance of a market index (a benchmark), thereby minimizing the tracking error (TE). This approach allows investors to achieve returns that are equivalent to those of the benchmark index. This strategy involves the construction of a portfolio comprising a smaller number of assets that is designed to track or replicate the index. The objective is to achieve a result that is comparable to that of the underlying stock index while using a smaller number of stocks. This approach will result in a reduction of transaction costs, while also avoiding the necessity of holding very small or illiquid positions and facilitating the management of the portfolio [3].

The imposition of a constraint on the number of assets in the index tracking portfolio gives rise to an approach, known as sparse IT, which involves cardinality constraints [4]. This is achieved by directly constraining the quantity of assets within the tracking portfolio. However, this approach resulted in an NP-hard constrained optimization problem due to the non-differentiability and non-convexity of the search space [5, 6]. Furthermore, the implementation of this approach is computationally expensive, particularly in high-dimensional environments [3, 4]. Moreover, the sparse index tracking formulation requires the prior specification of the maximum number of selected assets, which is frequently impractical.

© The Author(s), under exclusive license to Springer Nature Switzerland AG 2025
J. C. Figueroa-García et al. (Eds.): WEA 2024, CCIS 2223, pp. 76–83, 2025.
https://doi.org/10.1007/978-3-031-74598-0_7

A common approach is to transform the optimization problem with the cardinality constraint into a mixed integer programming problem, as outlined in [6]. Its implementation is feasible only when the problem size is relatively small. However, as the problem size increases, computing the exact solution to such a problem may become time-consuming or even infeasible [3]. As an alternative approach, heuristic algorithms, including genetic algorithms, have been proposed to hurry up the solution of the cardinality constraint [7, 8]. However, these heuristic search algorithms are unable to guarantee the optimality of the solution, especially when the dimension is relatively large.

Alternative approaches have been proposed that are more computationally efficient. In order to simplify the solution process, some functions were employed in order to approximate the nonconvex cardinality constraint, as suggested [3] and [9]. [9] proposed the use of the ℓ_p-norm constraint, as a variation of the cardinality constraint. Meanwhile, in Benidis et al. [3], a logarithm-based function was employed to approximate the cardinality constraint, resulting in the derivation of a rapid and efficient algorithm for high-dimensional index tracking. Similarly, a feasible solution can be achieved by employing a regularization model to generate sparse IT portfolios through high-dimensional regression analysis. In this field, regularization techniques such as the least absolute shrinkage and selection operator (LASSO) have been employed. For further details, see [4, 10], and [11].

The recent literature has focused on the application of machine learning (ML) techniques to address the computational challenges associated with these problems. For example, [10] employed the LASSO method with short sales constraints achieving a minimum TE. [12, 13] employed the ℓ_2-norm to identify optimal solutions for generalizing the principal component analysis (PCA) for indexing and portfolio selection. It is important to note, however, that this method does have some notable limitations, as outlined in [3] and [14]. In particular, [3] and [14] demonstrated that the penalty associated with the LASSO method is unable to reduce the weights of many portfolios to zero. Furthermore, when total investment and short-selling constraints are considered, the LASSO method is inadequate for obtaining sparse index tracking.

To extend the applications of the methods for sparse index tracking, this paper implements a regularization LASSO approach based on a nonconvex cardinality constraint approximation of the ℓ_0-norm and norm-constrained optimization. The empirical results indicate that the proposed method is computationally efficient and demonstrates competitive out-of-sample results. The paper is organized as follows. Section 2 presents the main approaches to the sparse IT problem based on the general convex constraints, nonconvex constraints, and different tracking error functions. Section 3 presents numerical applications. Finally, the paper concludes in Sect. 4.

2   Index Tracking Models and Sparse Portfolios

The classical index tracking approach represents the regression problem in a least squares framework with tracking errors computed from a sample of historical data, as stated by Jorion [2] and van Montfort et al. [15]. Moreover, this problem is transformed into a convex quadratic optimization model, in which the TE between index returns and asset returns are minimized in order to construct equity-tracking portfolios [3]. Initially, Roll

[1] and Jorion [2] formulated a quadratic optimization problem for the TE, following an equivalent formulation to the Markowitz problem, which consists of minimizing the portfolio variance. Markowitz [16]17, developed an optimal solution for the selection of a portfolio of risky assets. The Markowitz formulation considers two inputs of the model: the expected return of assets (μ) and the covariances (Σ), under the assumption that the returns follow a normal distribution. Thus, a portfolio of n risky assets with expected return $E(R_P) = w'\mu = \mu_p$ and variance $\sigma_P^2 = w'\Sigma\,w$, where $\mu \in \mathbb{R}^{n\times 1}$ is the vector of expected returns, $\Sigma \in \mathbb{R}^{n\times n}$ is the covariance matrix, and $w \in \mathbb{R}^{n\times 1}$ is the vector of weights. The optimization problem is a quadratic programming (QP) problem and is solved by minimizing σ_P^2 for a given level of expected return (μ_p) depicted by:

$$\min_{\{w\}}\{w'\Sigma\,w\} \text{ s.t.} \begin{cases} w'\mu = \mu_p \\ w'1 = 1 \end{cases} \tag{1}$$

where, $1 \in \mathbb{R}^{n\times 1}$ is a vector of ones. In this context, Roll [1] proposed a TE minimization problem for a specified level of active return, which represents the difference between the return of the portfolio and the benchmark,

$$\min_{\{x\}}\{x'\Sigma\,x\} \text{ s.t.} \begin{cases} (x + 2q)'\Sigma x \leq 0 \\ x'1 = 0 \end{cases} \tag{2}$$

where, x represents the difference in the portfolio weights of the tracking and the index. The constraint $(x + 2q)'\Sigma\,x \leq 0$ is equivalent to $\sigma_p^2 \leq \sigma_b^2$. Then, Jorion [2] extended Roll's model by imposing additional constraints on the optimization problem. The author proposed that the objective function should be to maximize the active return for a given TE, while constraining the variance of the portfolio to be the same as the variance of the benchmark, that is, $\sigma_p^2 = \sigma_b^2$.

$$\max_{\{x\}}\{x'\mu\} \text{ s.t.} \begin{cases} \sigma_p^2 \leq \sigma_b^2 \\ x'1 = 0 \end{cases} \tag{3}$$

This classical index tracking approach represents the problem in a least squares framework with tracking errors computed using a sample of historical data [2, 3]. This problem can be formulated as a convex quadratic optimization model in which the TE between index returns and asset returns are minimized in order to construct indexed portfolios, but with a smaller number of stocks [15]. Consequently, IT consists of mimicking the performance of the market index with a reduced number of assets, thereby giving rise to the sparse IT approach. One of the most prevalent methodologies for achieving this objective is to impose a cardinality constraint on the tracking portfolio [3, 9]. In this context, an additional cardinality constraint $k \leq K_{max}$ can be introduced, indicating the maximum number of assets that may be used to track the index. Then, the cardinality constraint $k \leq K_{max}$ is imposed, and 0–1 mixed integer programming can be applied. If the number of 0–1 variables is relatively small, the exact solution to the optimization problem can be obtained using numerical solvers. However, if the number of integer variables is very large, the exact solution to such a problem represents a high-dimensional computational problem or even proves to be impossible. Therefore, the regularization method should be extended by high-dimensional regression analysis. The sparse IT problem can be considered analogous to a related issue in signal processing, namely compressed sensing. Benidis et al. [3] stated that signal processing methodologies that rely on the LASSO, which approximates the ℓ_0-norm constraint by a ℓ_1-norm constraint, are applicable to the sparse IT problem.

Following to DeMiguel et al. [18] and Brodie et al. [19], Ridge and LASSO regression, respectively, are implemented to minimize the regularization terms $\|w\|_2$ and $\|w\|_1$, in addition to the sum of squared errors. Imposing the cardinality constraint in the TE optimization results in the implicit imposition of tighter upper bounds on the non-convex ℓ_p-norm, such that $\|w\|_p \leq K_{max}^{(1/p)-1}$. In this case, p < 1, and the parameter K_{max} quantifies the sparsity of the portfolio. Consequently, the TE problem may also be formulated by replacing the cardinality constraint with a constraint that sets an upper bound on the ℓ_p-norm.

$$\min_{\{x\}}\{x'\Sigma\,x\} + \lambda\|w\|_p \text{ s.t.} x'1 = 0 \tag{4}$$

In this context, Benidis et al. [3] proposed a sparse IT problem formulated as a constrained ℓ_0-norm regression. In that sense, the vector of the sparse IT portfolio weights, w, represents the optimal solution to the optimization problem, which aims to minimize a TE measure, $f(r_b - Xw)$, where r_b are the returns of the index we are tracking, and X are the returns of the assets. The function, denoted by $f()$, represents the loss function whereas the constraints encompass full investment, no short sales, and the cardinality constraint, which can be expressed as a maximum value for the cardinality $\|w\|_0 \leq K_{max}$. However, this method requires two steps for its implementation. They suggest an approach that unifies these two steps, directly penalizing the cardinality of the tracking portfolio. The ℓ_1-norm constraint was reformulated as an ℓ_0-norm penalty integrated into the TE measure, as follows:

$$\min_{\{w\}}\|r_b - Xw\|_2^2 + \lambda\|w\|_0 \text{ s.t.} \begin{cases} w'1 = 1 \\ w \geq 0 \end{cases} \tag{5}$$

where, $\lambda \geq 0$ is a parameter that controls the sparsity of the portfolio. Benidis et al. [3] demonstrated that sparse portfolios can be obtained for larger values of λ. They employed the majorization-minimization framework to derive an algorithm based on the first-order Taylor expansion to obtain a linear approximation for the IT problem. In their application, they proposed several measures of TE, one of them is the empirical tracking error (ETE):

$$ETE = \frac{1}{T}\|r_b - Xw\|_2^2 \tag{6}$$

where, T is data sample size. ETE is convex and differentiable as follows:

$$\nabla ETE = -\frac{2}{T}X'(r_b - Xw) \tag{7}$$

The gradient ∇ETE is $\beta-$ Lipschitz continuous where $\beta = 2/T\lambda 1(X'X)$ and $\lambda 1(\cdot)$ denotes the maximum eigenvalue of $(\cdot)$.

3   Numerical Application

3.1   Data

In this study we implemented the sparse IT approach for the Nasdaq 100 Index (NDX) and its constituents. The total analysis period is defined as the period between January 2020 to December 2023. The total duration of the dataset is 1,008 days, and the data was obtained from the Yahoo Finance API. The daily adjusted closing prices of 86 stocks of the index are used for the analysis. The remaining stocks were excluded from the analysis as they lacked complete information for the specified period or were included in the index during the same period.

3.2   Strategy

The proposed sparse index tracking strategy for the NDX index based on the regularized LASSO method (LASSO) and convex norm-constrained optimization (CVX) was implemented. Furthermore, the NDX index was settled as the target, and experiments were conducted to assess the efficacy of the proposed models in tracking the cumulative returns of the original NDX index. Python was employed for data processing and the implementation of strategies using the CVXPY library, which includes the Splitting Conic Solver (SCS) for the CVX and MOSEK for LASSO. The designed experiments are implemented using a sliding window method (see Fig. 1). The sliding window method was employed to train the proposed models over a one-year period, with the testing period set to one month.

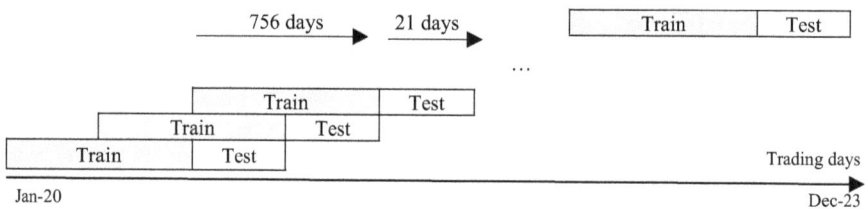

Fig. 1. Rolling training and testing windows.

Accordingly, the rebalancing of the portfolios is conducted on a monthly basis via the sliding window technique. In each instance of rebalancing, the models are trained over the course of the test period. To illustrate, the initial in-sample training period spanned from January 2020 to December 2022, encompassing the inaugural in-sample period of 756 observations and the subsequent 21 out-of-sample trading days. Then, the in-sample window is moved onward by 21 days, and a new optimal tracking portfolio is determined using a window of 756 observations and again held unchanged for the next 21 out-of-sample days, and the process is repeated. In that sense, sparse tracking portfolios are revised monthly, as we indicate in algorithm 1. Additionally, we proved the strategy considering different number of selected assets to identify a threshold until the stability of the algorithm is achieved, that is, identifying its small changes in the data only slightly change the results. Finaly, we define the penalty parameter λ following to Yen [21], who showed that the optimal λ can be specified as a function of the sample size T.

Algorithm 1: Norm-constrained and LASSO algorithms

1: Input: n, y, X, λ
2:   Initialize $w^o \in \mathcal{W}$
3:   For iteration $i = 0,1,2,\ldots$
4:        Calculate $\nabla f(w^i)$
5:        Solve the non-convex problems using CVX and MOSEK
6:        Found the optimal portfolio
7.   End for
8. Output: Portfolio weight vectors w^k

3.3   Empirical Results for NDX Index

The empirical analysis started with a comparison of the cardinality for LASSO and the norm-constrained approaches. Initially, using a sliding window strategy was employed, as previously described, to compare the performance of both methods regarding the training and testing periods, with a cardinality constraint of $n/2$ assets. Furthermore, we demonstrated that the cardinality constraint can be varied by considering all the tracking data, which included between 10 and 86 assets over the entire period. Figure 2 presents the results.

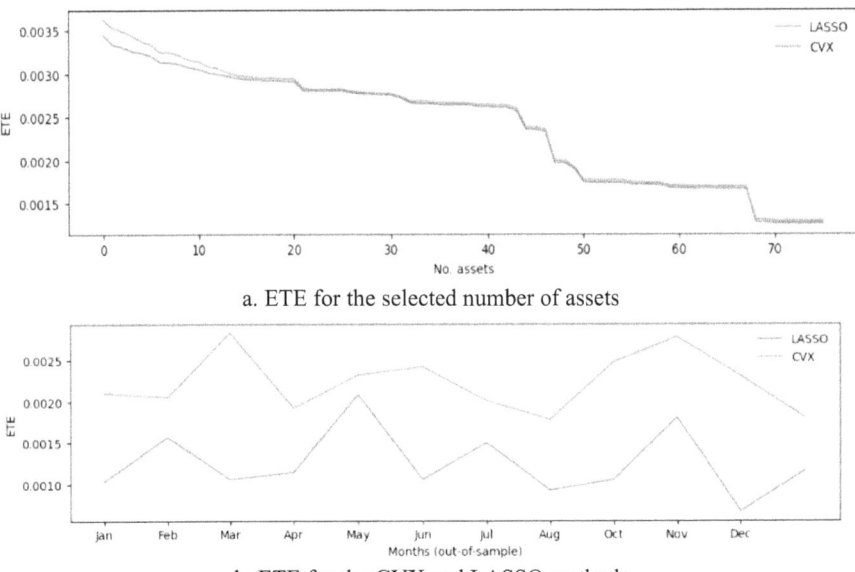

a. ETE for the selected number of assets

b. ETE for the CVX and LASSO methods

Fig. 2. ETE estimations and comparisons based on sliding testing windows.

The LASSO method initially demonstrated superior performance for the test period (the last year) as shown in Fig. 2b. For all out-of-sample test months, the ETE is lower, given that the cardinality constraint comprises in both cases $n/2$ assets. Moreover, as Fig. 1a shows, the ETE is also lower when few assets are used in the index tracking portfolio. Between 10 and 20 assets, the ETE of the LASSO method is lower. However, the two methods converge to the same result from this number of assets onwards.

Furthermore, Fig. 3 illustrates the in-sample performance of the cumulative return for the two tracking portfolios and for the NDX index. In this instance, only the initial in-sample period was considered. There, close tracking by the two methods, the CVX and LASSO, is observed.

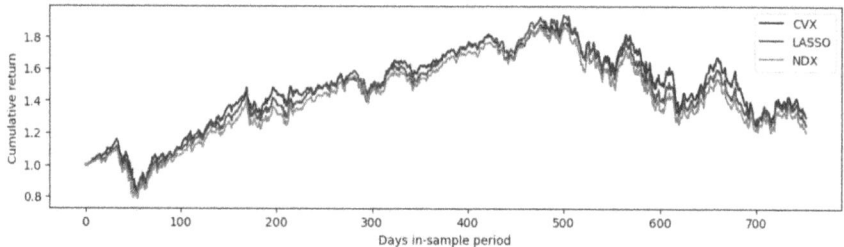

Fig. 3. Comparison of cumulative returns in the in-sample period.

4   Conclusions

The construction of tracking portfolios for sparse index tracking represents a challenging task due to the necessity of complex optimization algorithms. For example, the practical constraints that were introduced are complex and represent a high-dimensional problem. In this paper, two distinct methods were implemented, one based on regularized LASSO and the other one on norm-constrained algorithms. Although these methods satisfy the conditions for optimal tracking portfolios and generate sparse IT with low tracking errors in-sample and out-of-sample for the NDX index, they are not computationally efficient. This represents a challenge in the context of high-dimensional indices. For instance, in the case of an index containing more than 100 assets, the computational efficiency of the methods may be compromised. Consequently, it is necessary to explore alternative methods. Algorithms based on deep neural networks (DNN) may be considered as potential alternatives. Furthermore, there are other issues that have not been addressed in this paper that could be worthy of future research. On the other hand, it would be of interest to examine how the performance of norm-constrained portfolios could be enhanced when more sophisticated estimates for the covariance matrix are incorporated into the portfolio optimization problems, i.e. by applying regularized methods. Another illustrative example is the incorporation of transaction costs into the optimization problem.

Disclosure of Interests.   The authors have no competing interests to declare that are relevant to the content of this article.

References

1. Roll, R.: A mean/variance analysis of tracking error. J. Portfolio Manag. **18**(4), 13–22 (1992). https://doi.org/10.3905/jpm.1992.701922
2. Jorion, P.: Portfolio optimization with tracking-error constraints. Financ. Anal. J. **59**, 70–82 (2003). https://doi.org/10.2469/faj.v59.n5.2565
3. Benidis, K., Feng, Y., Palomar, D.: Sparse portfolios for high-dimensional financial index tracking. IEEE Trans. Signal Process. **66**(1), 155–170 (2017). https://doi.org/10.1109/TSP.2017.2762286
4. Shu, L., Shi, F., Tian, G.: High-dimensional index tracking based on the adaptive elastic net. Quant. Finan. **20**(9), 1513–1530 (2020). https://doi.org/10.1080/14697688.2020.1737328
5. Coleman, T.F., Li, Y., Henniger, J.: Minimizing tracking error while restricting the number of assets. J. Risk **8**(4), 33 (2006)
6. Takeda, A., Niranjan, M., Gotoh, J.Y., Kawahara, Y.: Simultaneous pursuit of out-of-sample performance and sparsity in index tracking portfolios. CMS **10**, 21–49 (2013). https://doi.org/10.1007/s10287-012-0158-y
7. Beasle, J., Meade, N., Chang, T.: An evolutionary heuristic for the index tracking problem. Eur. J. Oper. Res. **148**(3), 621–643 (2003). https://doi.org/10.1016/S0377-2217(02)00425-3
8. Strub, O., Baumann, P.: Optimal Construction and Rebalancing of Index-tracking Portfolios. Eur. J. Oper. Res. **264**(1), 370–387 (2018). https://doi.org/10.1016/j.ejor.2017.06.055
9. Fastrich, B., Paterlini, S., Winker, P.: Constructing optimal sparse portfolios using regularization methods. CMS **12**(2), 417–434 (2014). https://doi.org/10.1007/s10287-014-0227-5
10. Wu, L., Yang, Y., Liu, H.: Nonnegative-lasso and application in index tracking. Comput. Statis. Data Anal. **70**, 116–126 (2014). https://doi.org/10.1016/j.csda.2013.08.012
11. Wang, Y.J., Wu, L., Wu, L.: An integrative extraction approach for index-tracking portfolio construction and forecasting under a deep learning framework. J. Supercomput. **80**, 2047–2066 (2024). https://doi.org/10.1007/s11227-023-05538-z
12. Heaton, J.B., Polson, N.G., Witte, J.H.: Deep learning for finance: deep portfolios. Appl. Stochastic Mod. Bus. Ind. **33**, 3–12 (2017). https://doi.org/10.1002/asmb.2209
13. Ouyang, H., Zhang, X., Yan, H.: Index tracking based on deep neural network. Cogn. Syst. Res. **57**, 107–114 (2019). https://doi.org/10.1016/j.cogsys.2018.10.022
14. Zhang, C., Liang, S., Lyu, F., Fang, L.: Stock-index tracking optimization using auto-encoders. Front. Phys. **8**, 388 (2020). https://doi.org/10.3389/fphy.2020.00388
15. van Montfort, K., Visser, E., van Draat, L.F.: Index tracking by means of optimized sampling. J. Portf. Manag. **34**(2), 143 (2008)
16. Markowitz, H.: Portfolio selection. J. Fin. (7)1, 77–91 (1952)
17. Markowitz, H.: Portfolio Selection: Efficient Diversification of Investments. Yale University Press, New Haven (1959)
18. DeMiguel, V., Garlappi, L., Uppal, R.: Optimal versus naive diversification: how inefficient is the 1/N portfolio strategy? Rev. Fin. Stud. **22**, 1915–1953 (2009). https://doi.org/10.1093/rfs/hhm075
19. Brodie, J., Daubechies, I., De Mol, C., Giannone, D., Loris, I.: Sparse and stable Markowitz portfolios. PNAS **106**(30), 12267–12272 (2009). https://doi.org/10.1073/pnas.0904287106

Physical Benchmark for Evaluating Network Control Systems Under Cyber Attacks

Cristian Parada-Garcia[✉], Cristian Restrepo-Morales,
and Pablo S. Rivadeneira

Facultad de Minas, Universidad Nacional de Colombia, Grupo GITA,
Cra. 80 #, Medellín 65-224, Colombia
{cparada,crrestrepo,psrivade}@unal.edu.co

Abstract. This article describes the details of the configuration of a physical benchmark that is useful for assessing performance degradation of networked control systems (NCS) when exposed to cyber-attacks (for example, denial-of-service (DoS) attacks, deception attacks, man-in-the-middle (MiTM) attacks, and others, as stated in an NCS vulnerability taxonomy performed here), and explore countermeasures. The benchmark is a temperature control system controlled remotely through WIFI communication established in a private network under the UDP protocol. This is controlled here by an offset-free model predictive control. Two scenarios were visualized and tested, allowing input constraints, disturbances, mismatches, and DoS attacks. Experimental results are discussed, illustrating the potential use of this benchmark.

Keywords: Network control systems · Offset-free MPC · Kalman filter · Cyber vulnerabilities · Cyber attacks

1 Introduction

NCS are control systems whose system components, such as sensors, actuators, and controllers, are distributed and connected over a communication network. These are no longer systems connected solely by direct physical means, as is discussed in [7], showing the comparison of classical control systems and NCS.

With network control systems, cyber risks can be more common and have great implications for industrial processes. In [10], several cyber incidents caused in the last decade to industrial processes are mentioned and discussed, such as the famous Stuxnet case [3], the incident that occurred in 2015 in Ukraine, attacked by a Black Energy virus causing power outages, and the Flame malware that attacked industrial systems in the Middle East in 2012.

Knowing the vulnerabilities present in NCS, studies have analyzed different types of attacks and used tools to counteract their negative effects. Such is the case of [18], where a secure control is performed through Lyapunov compensation with a Luenberger observer in time-delay switch attacks (TDS). In [13], a

© The Author(s), under exclusive license to Springer Nature Switzerland AG 2025
J. C. Figueroa-García et al. (Eds.): WEA 2024, CCIS 2223, pp. 84–96, 2025.
https://doi.org/10.1007/978-3-031-74598-0_8

random switching controller is proposed to prevent system identification attacks in a MiTM scenario. It is also possible to have attack identification techniques that allow knowing when the system is being compromised and take action in time, as is the case in [12] where Gaussian white noise is introduced to detect the transfer function identified by the MiTM for data injection. On the other hand, actions can be implemented to create a much safer NCS environment, as shown in [10] with the design of control and IT security schemes, distributed detection and state estimation, and hybrid design in communication.

2   Bechmark Description and Configuration

The aim is to control a temperature plant built based on the well-known TCLAB [5]. The control system is implemented in MATLAB, and the communication is established via a WIFI network with UDP protocol similar to [1]. Figure 1 illustrates the control-loop system and device communication.

MATLAB uses Just-In-Time (JIT) compilation to speed up script programming, enhancing efficiency for network control applications due to its robust simulation environment, extensive libraries, and ease of hardware integration. This feature was implemented in the 2015 version and has continually improved in speed and performance efficiency [17].

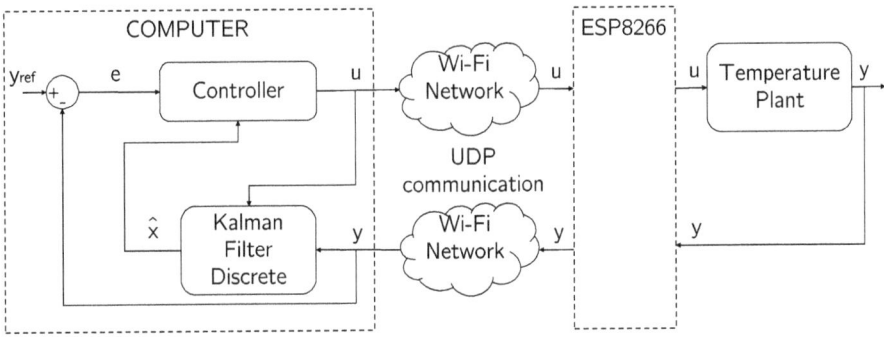

Fig. 1. Control scheme.

This temperature control plant is a thermal system that allows the application of control engineering systems in a real system. It consists of two transistors that provide temperature by activating the current flow when a voltage is applied to the gate pin. It heats up due to losses caused by the passage of electric current. Therefore, these transistors will be the heat source in the plant. It also consists of three TMP36 temperature sensors, which provide temperature data from the transistors and the ambient. The transistors also have heat sinks and a fan, allowing quick system cooling. Finally, a PCB integrates all the electronic components for operation, as shown in Fig. 2.

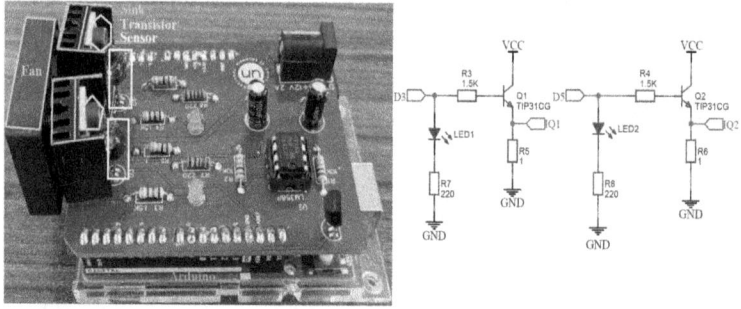

Fig. 2. Temperature control plant and its electronic circuit.

The NodeMCU ESP8266 module is used here to integrate communication via WIFI with the UDP protocol. It has one analog pin, which will collect data from the TMP36 temperature sensor. It also has GPIO pins to generate pulse-width modulation (PWM) output, enabling transistor and fan activation through duty cycles. Finally, the SAT wireless router WR5300N model will serve as an access point sustaining a local network for the device's communication.

2.1   Temperature Plant Model and Control Algorithms

The model under study contemplates three different thermal states for a transistor T_Q, a sensor T_S and a heat sink T_H. The model uses individual energy balances for each with specific heat transfer interactions. The temperature of each component is modeled using its own differential equation, capturing heat transfer through convection between components, with the environment T_A and from PWM input u. The model is summarized in the following equations

$$C_p m_Q \frac{dT_Q}{dt} = K_{QHS}(T_H - T_Q) + K_{QS}(T_S - T_Q) + K_{QA}(T_A - T_Q) + K_u u,$$

$$C_p m_S \frac{dT_S}{dt} = K_{QS}(T_Q - T_S) + K_{AS}(T_A - T_S), \tag{1}$$

$$C_H m_H \frac{dT_H}{dt} = K_{QHS}(T_Q - T_H) + K_{AHS}(T_A - T_H).$$

The thermal interactions between each component and its surroundings are performed using the total energy balance and Newton's law of cooling. Equation (1) can be written in the compact form $\dot{x}(t) = Ax(t) + Bu(t) + E$, where $x(t)$ represents the vector of temperatures for the transistor, sensor, and heat sink $[T_Q \ T_S \ T_H]'$. Here, $u(t)$ denotes the PWM input, and E encapsulates external influences such as ambient temperature. The matrix A contains the thermal interaction coefficients, and B the input influence coefficients. Furthermore, the output equation can be expressed as $y = Cx$, where y represents the sensor temperature T_s, with $C = [0 \ 1 \ 0]$ (Table 1).

The zero-order hold (ZOH) method with a sampling time of $T_s = 0.5$ seconds is used to discretize the system. The resulting discrete state-space system is

Table 1. Summary of parameters used in the multi-state thermal model.

Symbol	Description	Value
m_Q	Mass of the transistor	1.9517×10^{-3} [kg]
m_S	Mass of the sensor	7.8×10^{-4} [kg]
m_H	Mass of the heat sink	6×10^{-3} [kg]
C_p	Specific heat of the transistor/sensor	1900 [J/kg K]
C_H	Specific heat of the heat sink	880 [J/kg K]
K_{QHS}	Heat transfer coefficient transistor - heat sink	$1/35.7$ [W/K]
K_{QS}	Heat transfer coefficient transistor - sensor	$1/56.55$ [W/K]
K_{QA}	Heat transfer coefficient transistor - ambient	$1/62.5$ [W/K]
K_{AS}	Heat transfer coefficient sensor - ambient	$1/180$ [W/K]
K_{AHS}	Heat transfer coefficient heat sink - ambient	$1/14$ [W/K]
K_u	Power coefficient of input	0.059 [W/%dutty]

$x_{k+1} = A_d x_k + B_d u_k + E_d$ and $y_k = Cx_k$, where $A_d = e^{AT_s}$, $B_d = B_d = \int_0^{T_s} e^{Az} dz B$, and $E_d = \int_0^{T_s} e^{Az} dz E$.

The system analysis confirms that it is controllable and observable since their associated controllability and observability Kalman matrices have full rank. Furthermore, stability analysis of the system reveals that all eigenvalues of the matrix A are located in the left half of the complex plane, showing that the system is asymptotically stable.

The offset-free Model Predictive Control (MPC) is an advanced control technique that addresses reference tracking where mismatches and strong disturbances are present. The methodology uses a disturbance model and an observer framework to cope with these problems, as detailed in [8,11]. In this approach, the linear system is augmented with integral states $\hat{d}$, representing constant disturbances. The augmented system is described by $\hat{X}_{k+1} = A_{da}\hat{X}_k + B_{da}u_k + E_{da}$ and $\hat{y}_k = C_d\hat{x}_k + \tilde{C}_d\hat{d}_k$, where $\hat{X} = [\hat{x} \quad \hat{d}]'$ and the augmented matrices A_{da}, B_{da}, and E_{da} are defined as $A_{da} = \begin{bmatrix} A_d & \tilde{B}_d \\ 0 & I \end{bmatrix}$, $B_{da} = \begin{bmatrix} B_d \\ 0 \end{bmatrix}$, and $E_{da} = \begin{bmatrix} E_d \\ 0 \end{bmatrix}$, respectively. The disturbance model matrices $\tilde{B}_d$ and $\tilde{C}_d$ are selected to ensure that the rank condition $\text{rank}\left(\begin{bmatrix} A_d - I & \tilde{B}_d \\ C_d & \tilde{C}_d \end{bmatrix}\right) = n + n_d$ is satisfied, where n is the number of states and n_d is the number of added integral states.

This control technique optimizes a quadratic cost function over a prediction horizon, using the solution from the discrete state-space model in each sampling time and implementing the first element of the optimal control computed for the prediction horizon. The cost function penalizes quadratic deviations between the current temperature and the desired reference zone through scalar coefficients Q and S, as well as the control energy supplied to the process, adjusted by the scalar R.

$$\min_{\mathbf{U}, \bar{u}_t, \bar{x}_t} \sum_{j=0}^{H_p-1} \|x_{k+j} - \bar{x}_t\|_Q^2 + \|u_{k+j} - \bar{u}_t\|_R^2 + \|x_{k+H_p} - \bar{x}_t\|_S^2$$

$$\text{s.t.} \quad x_k = \hat{x}, \quad x_{k+j+1} = A_d x_{k+j} + B_d u_{k+j} + E_d + \tilde{B}_d d_k,$$
$$d_k = \hat{d}, \quad d_{k+j+1} = d_{k+j}, \tag{2}$$
$$u_{k+j} \in \mathcal{U}, \quad x_{k+j} \in \mathcal{X}, \quad j = 0, \cdots, H_{p-1},$$
$$u_{k+j} = u_{k+H_u-1}, \quad j = H_u, \ldots, H_p - 1,$$
$$\begin{bmatrix} A_d - I & B_d \\ C_d & 0 \end{bmatrix} \begin{bmatrix} \bar{x}_t \\ \bar{u}_t \end{bmatrix} = \begin{bmatrix} -\tilde{B}_d \hat{d} - E_d \\ r - \tilde{C}_d \hat{d} \end{bmatrix}.$$

The Eq. (2) represents a convex optimization problem and can be solved at each iteration using the interior-point algorithm through MATLAB. The first element of the optimal solution $\mathbf{U}^* = \{u_0, u_1, \cdots, u_{H_p-1}\}$ is sent to the plant.

The sets $\mathcal{U} = \{u \mid u_{min} \le u \le u_{max}, \Delta u_{min} \le u_{k+j} - u_{k+j-1} \le \Delta u_{max}\}$ and $\mathcal{X} = \{x \mid x_{min} \le x \le x_{max}\}$ define the operational constraints on the inputs and states, respectively. The parameters H_u and H_p denote the control and prediction horizons, respectively, while r correspond to the reference temperature.

Since the perturbation model requires an observer and not all states are measurable, the discrete-time Kalman estimator is included in the control problems formulation [14]. Given the system discrete dynamics of Eq. (1), we incorporate normally distributed process noise w_k with covariance Q_e in discrete-time, and normally distributed measurement noise v_k with covariance R_e in discrete-time. The system model incorporating these noises can be expressed as $X_{k+1} = A_{da} X_k + B_{da} u_k + E_{da} + w_k$ and $y_k = C_d x_k + \tilde{C}_d d_k + v_k$.

The Kalman estimator operates in two steps: prediction and update. The filter estimates the next state and error covariance in the prediction step based on the current estimates and system model. In the update step, the filter incorporates the new measurement to correct the estimates, which follows

$$\hat{X}_k^- = A_d \hat{X}_{k-1}^+ + B_d u_k, \quad P_k^- = A_d P_{k-1}^+ A_d' + Q_e, \quad K_k = P_k^- C_d' (C_d P_k^- C_d' + R_e)^{-1},$$
$$\hat{X}_k^+ = \hat{X}_k^- + K_k(y_k - C_d \hat{x}_k^-), \quad P_k^+ = (I - K_k C_d) P_k^-. \tag{3}$$

where $\hat{X}_k^-$ and $\hat{X}_k^+$ represent the a priori and a posteriori state estimates, respectively; P_k^- and P_k^+ denote the a priori and a posteriori error covariances; K_k is the Kalman gain matrix; and I is the identity matrix. Kalman filter it was selected for this study due to its simplicity and computational efficiency.

For the purpose of comparison, a discrete proportional state feedback control with feedforward compensation is designed using the standard pole-place problem. In this case, the control law is $u_k = Nr - P\hat{x}_k$, where N is the feedforward gain ensuring zero steady-state error, and P is the feedback gain adjusted to ensure a desired transient behavior.

2.2   Communication Configuration

As stated earlier, the control action computation will be done in MATLAB from a remote computer. The computer will send the control action data over the WiFi network, where the ESP8266 will receive the data. Based on the received information, it will execute the relevant control action towards the plant. Then, the same ESP8266 will retrieve the temperature values provided by the TMP36 sensors and send them back over the WiFi network to complete the control loop. Therefore, creating and configuring the WiFi network is essential for enabling communication between these devices, for which the SAT wireless router is used.

Once it is connected to the computer via Ethernet in the LAN ports of the router, the TCP/IP configuration of the computer's network must be established using the Local Area Connection properties in the computer. The Internet protocol version 4 (TCP/IPv4) must be selected there.

The default IP address to set up the SAT wireless router is *192.168.1.1*. After the initial setup, the quick settings for router/WISP/repeater mode will appear immediately, and you can choose any of these three options. Select the router option for this case, as it will create the network. Although Internet access will not be provided to the local area network, communication will be established. The network name for this study was *Redproyecto-01*. Channel 6 was chosen for the network, and the security encryption for the network password was of type *WPA2-personal* to improve the network's security with the password *123456789*. The default password for changing router settings is *admin*.

Once the network is created, you can connect the devices to it. When a device connects to the WiFi network, all devices receive an IP address to indicate which network they belong to. Typically, this IP address is dynamic. However, for this application, each connected device will be assigned a static IP address, ensuring no duplicate addresses exist. Therefore, the IP/mask addresses for the study devices were assigned as Router with *192.168.1.1/24*, ESP8266 with *192.198.1.2 /24*, and Computer with *192.168.1.3 /24*.

The User Datagram Protocol (UDP) was chosen to communicate devices in this work. UDP protocol provides unreliable transport of datagrams since it carries the necessary information for end-to-end communication. It does not introduce connection delays as it does not maintain any connection state and does not track sent data, unlike the TCP protocol, which provides reliable flow between applications by managing secure transport. However, TCP carries large amounts of information, affecting communication efficiency. Therefore, if speed is more important than security, UDP should be used [2].

The transport layer uses exclusive ports by UDP and TCP to redirect information to the required application. The command *netstat -a* displays all connections and listening ports for TCP and UDP.

For instance, the *Redproyecto-01* network uses the ports 137, 138, 1900, 5353, and 65027 associated with the IP address 192.168.1.3. This indicates that the computer within the network is using these ports. Therefore, it cannot be any of these when selecting the port since communication is impossible.

There is a wide range of available ports to use as long as they are not in use within the network. For this case, the available port 57098 was chosen and specified in the ESP8266 code. The port to be used for communication must also be specified in Matlab, in addition to being able to open sockets to allow the exchange of information. It is important to remember that ports act as the entry point to allow information access, while sockets transport the information to the application and enable the exchange of information.

In the ESP8266, the temperature provided by the sensor is read as an analog input. Therefore, the data is of a floating-point type after conversion. First, the voltage conversion is performed because the analog reading scales from 0 to 1023 due to the resolution of the ESP analog-to-digital converter. After this conversion, voltage values are obtained. Since the sensor provides an output of $10\,mV/^{\circ}C$ according to the TMP36 datasheet.

To send the data to MATLAB, it needs to be converted into a character array and specified that it contains floating-point data. Otherwise, the data would be rounded, resulting in a loss of sensor measurement accuracy. This is indicated by %2f" within the *snprintf* function in the ESP8266. This character array is then sent directly to MATLAB.

In MATLAB, the data is received in this character-type format. However, character data does not allow for operations or calculations. Therefore, this received data is converted to type double, which converts the data to bytes size to perform calculations with greater accuracy. After performing the relevant calculations for temperature control, the control action data (duty cycle) is sent. But before that, the data must be converted to a character type to be received in this format by the ESP8266. As mentioned earlier, the data sent from MATLAB are of character type. Therefore, when the ESP detects that information is being received via UDP, it reads the data from the character string and appends a zero to indicate when the string has ended. Then, this data is converted to floating-point type. Since Arduino handles a duty cycle in a range from 0 to 255, the value of the cycle is scaled to this range and entered into the *analogWrite* function on GPIO4 for control action.

3   Vulnerabilities and Attacks in Network Control Systems

Communication in NCS occurs through a network, so the usual channels through which information travels are from the controller to the actuator and from the sensor to the controller [4], which can be compromised by attackers, affecting communication and the system. To discuss security in NCS, three key factors of information flow in a control system mentioned in [16] must be addressed: confidentiality, integrity, and availability. When at least one of these three factors is compromised, it can be considered an attack on the NCS, which can mainly be classified into two types: DoS attacks and deception attacks [9,10].

Confidentiality entails sharing information only with authorized parties. Integrity involves protecting data from unauthorized modification and ensuring that information degradation does not occur. Finally, availability ensures continuous access to information [9]. With these definitions in mind, a possible taxonomy of attacks that undermine these three factors is proposed.

Denial-of-service (DoS) attacks are well-known for impacting the availability in Network Control Systems (NCS), interrupting information flow through significant data congestion, which can degrade control performance and potentially lead to a complete disruption of communication between devices. These attacks do not aim to acquire knowledge of the system but merely to disrupt it. Conversely, deception attacks stealthily infiltrate the system to monitor and sometimes manipulate information, affecting the NCS's integrity and confidentiality. Attackers may require detailed knowledge of the system to target specific process functions or just superficial knowledge to cause partial process disruptions. These tactics are summarized in an attack taxonomy that highlights how they undermine confidentiality, integrity, or availability of the system (Fig. 3).

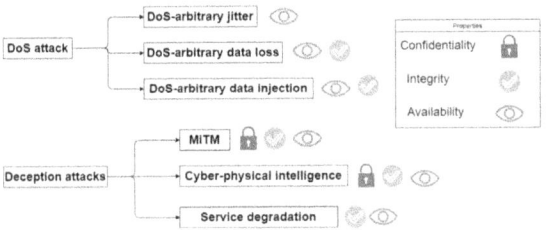

Fig. 3. Taxonomy of attacks on NCS and the properties that each attack violates.

In [15], it is noted that denial-of-service (DoS) attacks in Network Control Systems (NCS) can involve techniques to induce arbitrary communication delays or cause data loss. Moreover, arbitrary data injection can sabotage control information, expanding DoS attacks from mere disruption to severe system damage. Additionally, a variety of deception attacks, such as Cyber-physical Intelligence (CPI) attacks and system degradation tactics, are described. These attacks, though not always labeled as deception attacks, compromise the system's confidentiality and integrity and can impact availability. Among deception attacks, the Man-in-the-Middle (MiTM) attack is particularly significant as it underpins more complex strategies like replay attacks [6] and system identification attacks [13], which analyze information to reconstruct the system's operational model.

The vulnerabilities associated with the UDP protocol include: (i) **lack of encryption**, with data traveling in plain text; (ii) **no recovery of lost data** due to unresolved transmission errors; (iii) **no acknowledgment of successful data transfers**, resulting from the absence of a connection when sending datagrams; and (iv) **consecutive data sending**, lacking flow control or packet ordering. This last vulnerability can lead to UDP flooding, which involves sending messages to all ports-open or closed-thereby overwhelming the network, consuming excessive bandwidth, and potentially halting all communication by closing ports.

4   Results and Discussions

In this section, we present two scenarios to test the performance of the offset-free MPC strategy and the state feedback. The reference tracking capability was validated, considering disturbances, mismatches, and DoS cyberattacks, each applied at different times. In the second scenario, a strong DoS cyberattack occurs during the initial transient state, and after that, a constant disturbance is introduced during a second DoS cyberattack.

Throughout all experiments, the penalty weights for the offset-free MPC controller were set to $S = 1 \times 10^9 I_{3\times3}$, $Q = I_{3\times3}$, and $R = 1$ to ensure stability and improve the system's speed. The control horizon (H_u) and prediction horizon (H_p) were both set to 30 (equivalent to 15 s). The discrete Kalman filter built into the offset-free MPC system was always initialized with an estimated state $\hat{X}_0 = [T_a \quad T_a \quad T_a \quad 0]'$ and an initial a priori covariance error $P_0^+ = \text{diag}([5 \quad 0 \quad 10 \quad 100])$. The process noise covariance and measurement noise covariance were set to $Q_e = \text{diag}([0.1 \quad 0.1 \quad 1 \quad 0.0001])$ and $R_e = 1 \times 10^4$, respectively. The matrices $(\tilde{B}_d, \tilde{C}_d)$ associated with the inclusion of the perturbation model are $\tilde{B}_d = [1 \quad 1 \quad 2]'$ and $\tilde{C}_d = 1$, ensuring the system meets the detectability condition. The constraints on the input is given by $\mathcal{U} = \{u : 0 \le u \le 85, -8 \le u_{k+j} - u_{k+j-1} \le 8\}$.

The feedback gain matrix P of the state feedback was set to $P = [2.5 \quad 0.95 \quad 0.55]$, and the feedback gain N was set to ensure zero offset. In these tests, the discrete Kalman filter integrated with the P-controller inherits the characteristics of the previously described Kalman filter, except it does not estimate the perturbation state. The control action is forced to 0–85% of the duty cycle.

During the first 100 s of the first scenario (Fig. 4), the Kalman Filter is expected to converge to the actual system temperature. From this point, the sensor temperature set-point reference is fixed at 340°K. A constant disturbance is introduced between 500 and 1000 s, consisting of the fan activation. It is observed that the temperature estimated by the offset-free MPC captures the disturbance, resulting in an increase in the control action to compensate for this effect. In contrast, the temperature estimated with the state feedback controller barely changes, and the control action remains almost constant during this event. This is consistent since the state feedback cannot detect the disturbance since the compensation of mismatches is not robust. At 1000 s, the disturbance is deactivated, allowing the state feedback to follow the reference again, indicating its ability to reject non-constant disturbances. Between 1500 and 1800 s, a simple DoS cyberattack is introduced, disrupting the UDP communication between the control and estimation algorithm and the temperature plant. During this attack, the temperature received remains the last value sent from the plant, while the control action stays constant, preserving the last value sent from the computer. This attack was performed in the steady state, resulting in minimal change in the transistor temperature, indicating that the system is not significantly altered. Finally, at 2100 s, a parametric change of 20% in K_u is introduced. The state feedback controller loses its ability to control the system, whereas the offset-free

MPC control law adjusts to compensate for this effect, maintaining stability and performance.

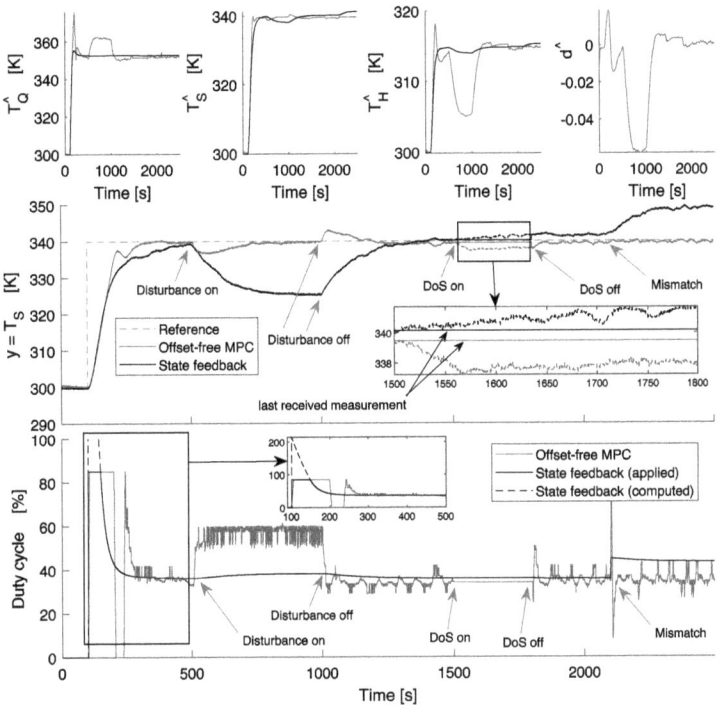

Fig. 4. Performance under disturbances, DoS attacks and mismatch.

In the second experiment (Fig. 5), several elements described earlier are combined to challenge the control strategies and observe potential adverse effects. Initially, the system was left uncontrolled for the first 100 s. After that, a new setpoint of 340°K was established for the sensor temperature and a DoS attack is introduced to assess the effect of such a disruption when the system is in a transient state. During the attack, as the UDP communication is lost and the duty cycle is at its maximum, the temperature rises, which could have damaged the system. However, once the DoS attack ends, the control law resumes the manipulation of the plant. The offset-free MPC strategy takes a bit longer to start correcting the overheating, as the temperature estimated by the Kalman Filter loses all physical coherence with the process and takes time to recover. Subsequently, at 800 s, another DoS attack is introduced, immediately followed by a constant disturbance. It is observed that the offset-free MPC control eventually recovers after the end of the DoS. However, the recovery would have been even quicker if the attack had not occurred. In contrast, the state feedback control fails to adequately compensate at any point, which could also lead to significant problems.

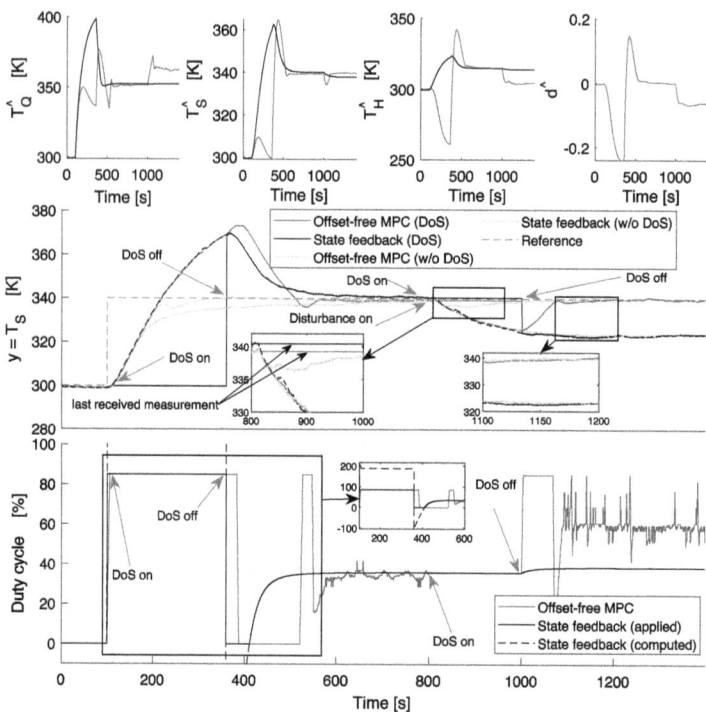

Fig. 5. Impact of DoS attacks. Note: "w/o" symbolizes "without".

The experiments reveal that attacks during transient states are particularly dangerous, as the output signal received by the controller freezes at the last measurement before the DoS attack, and the control action remains constant. This is problematic because, during transient states, the system will try to stabilize at a point different from the reference due to the control action and temperature measurement remaining fixed from the start of the attack. In contrast, DoS attacks during steady-state conditions have less impact, as in the absence of disturbances, this corresponds to an equilibrium for the discrete model associated with Eq. (1). Additionally, unexpected events occurring during an attack can exacerbate the situation, posing significant risks to both control strategies.

The performance indexes (ISE, IAE, ITAE) for each control strategy across the two scenarios demonstrate that the offset-free MPC outperforms the feedback P controller in all metrics, especially in scenarios involving disturbances and cyberattacks. In Fig. 4, the offset-free MPC achieves an ISE of 7.8×10^4, an IAE of 4.9×10^3, and an ITAE of 3.2×10^6, compared to the feedback P controller's ISE of 1.9×10^5, IAE of 1.5×10^4, and ITAE of 1.5×10^7. Similar trends are observed in Fig. 5, where the offset-free MPC maintains superior performance even during DoS attacks, highlighting its better overall performance and robustness.

5   Conclusions

A networked control system was implemented, allowing wireless communication between the Arduino ESP8266 IoT board and a computer to control the temperature of the TCLAB plant. This system constitutes a benchmark to assess controllers' performances under cyberattacks and evaluate countermeasures.

The results demonstrate that the offset-free MPC consistently outperforms the state feedback controller regarding tracking accuracy, disturbance rejection, and robustness to cyberattacks, which is expected. Applying DoS attacks during transient states and steady conditions shows how dangerous network vulnerabilities in NCS can be. The findings indicate that while both controllers can maintain performance under steady-state DoS attacks, transient-state attacks pose significant risks, potentially leading to undesired situations.

Despite the contributions, several open problems and potential areas for future research have been identified. Future work should explore advanced cybersecurity measures and adaptive control strategies to enhance resilience against more sophisticated cyberattacks. Also, could explore developing a noise model specific to this system. If necessary, alternative filters or state estimators that can handle nonlinear and non-Gaussian noise should be considered.

References

1. Chavoshi, H.R., Payam, O., Salasi, A.H., Khaloozadeh, H.: Robust control design of a nonlinear liquid-level networked control system: a comparative study between STR and Kharitonov analysis. Int. J. Dyn. Control 1–12 (2023)
2. Dye, M., McDonald, R., Rufi, A.: Network Kundamentals, CCNA Exploration Companion Guide. Cisco Press (2007)
3. Falliere, N., Murchu, L.O., Chien, E.: W32. stuxnet dossier. White paper, symantec corp., security response 5(6), 29 (2011)
4. Hespanha, J.P., Naghshtabrizi, P., Xu, Y.: A survey of recent results in networked control systems. Proc. IEEE 95(1), 138–162 (2007). https://doi.org/10.1109/JPROC.2006.887288
5. John D. Hedengren: Dynamics and control, temperature control lab (2024). http://apmonitor.com/pdc/index.php/Main/ArduinoTemperatureControl. Accessed 20 Mar 2024
6. Kedar Vadde Hulgesh, T.: Evaluation of cyber-attacks in networked control systems (2023)
7. Benítez-Pérez, H., Ortega-Arjona, J.L., Méndez-Monroy, P.E., Rubio-Acosta, E., Esquivel-Flores, O.A.: Introduction to networked control systems. In: Control Strategies and Co-Design of Networked Control Systems. MOST, vol. 13, pp. 1–23. Springer, Cham (2019). https://doi.org/10.1007/978-3-319-97044-8_1
8. Maeder, U., Borrelli, F., Morari, M.: Linear offset-free model predictive control. Automatica 45(10), 2214–2222 (2009)
9. Mousavinejad, S.E.: Cyber-Physical Attack Detection for Networked Control Systems. Ph.D. thesis, Griffith University (2020)
10. Pang, Z.H., et al.: Security of networked control systems subject to deception attacks: a survey. Int. J. Syst. Sci. 53(16), 3577–3598 (2022)

11. Pannocchia, G.: Offset-free tracking MPC: a tutorial review and comparison of different formulations. In: 2015 European control conference (ECC), pp. 527–532. IEEE (2015)
12. Oliveira de Sá, A., Casimiro, A., Machado, R.C., Carmo, L.F.D.C.: Identification of data injection attacks in networked control systems using noise impulse integration. Sensors **20**(3), 792 (2020)
13. de Sá, A.O., da Costa Carmo, L.F., Machado, R.C.: A controller design for mitigation of passive system identification attacks in networked control systems. J. Internet Serv. Appl. **9**, 1–19 (2018)
14. Simon, D.: Optimal state Estimation: Kalman, H Infinity, and Nonlinear Approaches. Wiley, Hoboken (2006)
15. de Sá, A.O., Carmo, L.F.R.D.C., Machado, R.C.S.: Covert attacks in cyber-physical control systems. IEEE Trans. Indust. Inform. **13**(4), 1641–1651 (2017). https://doi.org/10.1109/TII.2017.2676005
16. Teixeira, A., Sou, K.C., Sandberg, H., Johansson, K.H.: Secure control systems: a quantitative risk management approach. IEEE Control Syst. Mag. **35**(1), 24–45 (2015)
17. The MathWorks Inc.: Matlab performance (2024). https://la.mathworks.com/products/matlab/performance.html. Accessed 14 Jul 2024
18. Victorio, M., Sargolzaei, A., Khalghani, M.R.: A secure control design for networked control systems with linear dynamics under a time-delay switch attack. Electronics **10**(3), 322 (2021)

Exploring Oncolytic Measles Virotherapy for Cancer Tumor Reduction Using Linear MPC

Cristian Restrepo-Morales[1]([✉]), Anet J. N. Anelone[2], and Pablo S. Rivadeneira[1]

[1] Universidad Nacional de Colombia, Medellín, Colombia
{crrestrepo,psrivade}@unal.edu.co
[2] National University of Singapore, 12 Science Drive 2, Singapore, Singapore
anelone@nus.edu.sg

Abstract. Oncolytic virotherapy with measles represents a promising approach to combat cancer, often combined with other therapies to eradicate tumors. However, it faces many challenges, for instance, the toxic side effects that must be carefully managed during treatment, the optimal dose to apply, the determination time to extirpate the tumor, the monitoring system, and others. In this study, predictive control methodologies are employed based on the nonlinear system representing oncolytic virotherapy with measles. The objective is to present strategies for cancer treatment by either limiting the maximum dose per patient or bringing the tumor to a point where it can be surgically removed. This method utilizes system approximations at discrete time intervals for the model subsystems. To address the limitation of the maximum allowed injected virus dose, an additional state describing the total injected dose is incorporated. Simulations demonstrate dose optimization for tumor reduction, with successful therapy in up to 18 days. Moreover, careful dosing strategies maximize therapeutic efficacy while minimizing potential toxicity, underscoring the promising potential in achieving optimal treatment outcomes. These findings support the idea that feedback control has the potential to enhance robustness and toxicity reduction in oncolytic virotherapy.

Keywords: Virotherapy · Optimization · Model Predictive Control

1 Introduction

Oncolytic virus therapy offers a strategic cancer treatment by leveraging viruses' ability to target cancer cells. Despite its potential, challenges such as dose optimization and toxicity management persist, necessitating advanced control strategies. This study integrates MPC to refine dosing strategies, enhancing both safety and efficacy of oncolytic measles virotherapy. We build on previous experimental and mathematical models, aiming to optimize total administered doses, a key factor in mitigating side effects and improving patient outcomes.

© The Author(s), under exclusive license to Springer Nature Switzerland AG 2025
J. C. Figueroa-García et al. (Eds.): WEA 2024, CCIS 2223, pp. 97–109, 2025.
https://doi.org/10.1007/978-3-031-74598-0_9

Several studies have addressed this problem from different perspectives. The use of optimal optimization and control methods to adjust optimal doses at optimal times has been highlighted in the context of cancer immunotherapy and other treatment modalities. For example, [5] formulate the design of treatment protocols as an optimization problem, proposing an algorithm for its solution. In [6], it also points out the need to overcome the toxicity associated with traditional methods such as surgery and chemotherapy, highlighting the importance of immunotherapy and virotherapy. [10] discuss how the dose of pathogen included in a vaccine should be optimal to induce protective immunity without increasing costs or side effects. Finally, [4] reveals how optimization theory can maximize the benefits of virotherapy by optimally adjusting doses and administration times, highlighting the superiority of intermittent over continuous administration. [1] proposes an impulsive control strategy with state feedback, achieving effective tumor reduction and enabling efficient administration of personalized doses. On the other hand, [14] introduces a nonlinear control scheme that determines optimal doses for faster and more robust tumor reduction, even in the face of uncertainty in parameters and modeling [1,14].

This work is based on previous studies of experimental and mathematical models on oncolytic measles virotherapy. In this article, we aim to address the challenge of optimizing the total dose administered in cancer virotherapy by applying the Model Predictive Control (MPC) to the measles virus and the brief excision analysis. Traditional therapies often involve high levels of toxicity, creating a need for innovative approaches that can effectively limit tumor growth and minimize adverse effects. Leveraging the capabilities of MPC, we sought to dynamically adjust the dose of viral injections, optimizing therapeutic outcomes and mitigating potential toxicity. By formulating this problem as an optimization task and integrating it into a control framework, we aim to provide a pathway to improve the efficacy and safety of cancer virotherapy. Control analysis is performed in a system of ordinary differential equations (ODE) modeling oncolytic measles virotherapy for multiple myeloma xenografts cultured in mice [2,4,7].

2   Modeling of Oncolytic Measles Virotherapy

The dynamic interaction between tumor cells and the oncolytic virus is elucidated through a set of ODEs as given in [4]. These equations, summarized below, provide insights into the behavior of the system

$$
\begin{aligned}
Y' &= rY\left[1 - (Y+X)^{\epsilon}/K^{\epsilon}\right] - \kappa YV - \rho XY, \\
X' &= \kappa YV - \delta X, \\
V' &= \alpha X - \omega V - \kappa YV + u(t),
\end{aligned}
\tag{1}
$$

where $Y(t)$ denotes the quantity of uninfected tumor cells, $X(t)$ represents the quantity of infected cells, and $V(t)$ signifies the quantity of free virus particles. To facilitate analysis, tumor volume is converted into cell population assuming that $1\,\mathrm{mm}^3$ corresponds to 10^6 cells. Consequently, throughout our subsequent discussions, Y, X, and V are expressed in units of 10^6 cells. Additionally, time measurements are consistently expressed in terms of days. The growth dynamics of uninfected cells are modeled by the Bertalanffy-Richards equation, which is characterized by several parameters. These include r (day^{-1}), representing the effective growth rate constant, K (10^6 cells), indicating the maximum carrying capacity, and an exponent ϵ that shapes the sigmoidal growth curve. Additionally, parameters κ (per day per 10^6 cells or virions) and ρ (per day per 10^6 cells) describe the infection process of uninfected cells by the virus and the fusion-mediated infection of uninfected cells by infected ones, respectively. The effective death rate of infected cells is denoted by δ (day^{-1}), while ω (day^{-1}) represents the rate of clearance of free virus particles. Moreover, α (virions per day per cell) signifies the production rate of virions by infected cells. It is important to note that the model does not explicitly consider the effects of the immune response. However, certain aspects of the immune response can be approximated by the term δX as outlined in [2]. The model input, $u(t)$, encapsulates the delivery of viral particles at discrete time points τ_k, formulated as $u(t) = u(\tau_k)\delta(t - \tau_k)$. Here, $u(\tau_k)$ stands for the amplitude of the control action, while δ is the Dirac delta function. For simplicity, assuming that infected cells $X(t)$ can be discriminated in the measurement from uninfected cells $Y(t)$, we set the model output equal to uninfected cells, denoted by $Y(t)$.

In the absence of the input $u(t)$, the stability analysis of the system (1) has been previously conducted in [2]. Expanding upon this investigation to encompass the effect of the control action $u(t)$, it was discovered that the system exhibits three distinct equilibria, as summarized in Table 1. The derivation of the equilibria presented in the table involves setting the derivatives of model (1) to zero and solving the resulting algebraic system of equations with respect to the variables X, Y and V. Equilibrium 1 signifies complete tumor eradication or therapeutic success, while equilibrium 2 denotes therapeutic failure and equilibrium 3 represents a scenario of partial therapeutic efficacy, where both the tumor and the virus coexist.

Table 1. System Equilibria

Description	Equilibrium
Equilibrium 1	$Y_1 = 0$, $X_1 = 0$, $V_1 = 0$, $u_1 = 0$
Equilibrium 2	$Y_2 = K$, $X_2 = 0$, $V_2 = 0$, $u_2 = 0$
Equilibrium 3	$Y_3 = \delta\omega/[\kappa(\alpha - \delta)]$, $u_3 = 0$, $X_3 = c\left[1 - (X_3 + Y_3)^\varepsilon / K^\varepsilon\right]$, $V_3 = (\alpha - \delta)/(\omega X_3)$, $c = r\omega/[(\alpha - \delta)\kappa + \rho\omega]$.

2.1   Impulsive Representation of the Model

The model (1) of Oncolytic Virus Therapy (OVT) can be conceptualized as an Impulsive Continuous System (ICS) due to the periodic administration of the virus through injections at certain time intervals. Unlike continuous or discrete input scenarios, the impulsive approach provides a more accurate representation of the system dynamics, especially when the duration of each injection is significantly short compared to the sampling time. By defining the state vector as $x(t) = [Y(t) \quad X(t) \quad V(t)]^T$ and following a procedure similar to that of [14] the original nonlinear system (1) is reformulated as

$$\dot{x}(t) = f(x(t)), \quad x(0) = x_0, \quad t \neq \tau_k,$$
$$x\left(\tau_k^+\right) = x\left(\tau_k\right) + Bu\left(\tau_k\right), \quad t = \tau_k, \quad k \in \mathbb{N}, \qquad (2)$$
$$Y\left(\tau_k\right) = Cx\left(\tau_k\right), \quad t = \tau_k, \quad k \in \mathbb{N},$$

where $f(x)$ describes the behavior of the free system, $B = [0 \quad 0 \quad 1]^T$ represents the fixed matrix capturing the influence of viral injections at discrete time points τ_k, and $C = [1 \quad 0 \quad 0]$ serves as a matrix defining the output equation.

The nonlinear system (2) can be linearized around an equilibrium point x_e utilizing the Taylor series, resulting in

$$\dot{x}(t) = Ax(t), \quad x(0) = x_0, \quad t \neq \tau_k,$$
$$x\left(\tau_k^+\right) = x\left(\tau_k\right) + Bu\left(\tau_k\right), \quad t = \tau_k, \quad k \in \mathbb{N}, \qquad (3)$$
$$Y\left(\tau_k\right) = Cx\left(\tau_k\right), \quad t = \tau_k, \quad k \in \mathbb{N},$$

where $A = \left.\frac{df(x)}{dx}\right|_{x_e}$ is the corresponding Jacobian matrix.

Although tumor growth and therapy response are inherently nonlinear, we simplified cancer behavior to a linear system to apply linear model predictive control techniques and stability analysis.

Furthermore, the linearized system (3) can be described at times τ_k by

$$x_{k+1} = A_d x_k + B_d u_k, \qquad (4)$$

where $A_d = e^{AT_s}$, $B_d = e^{AT_s}B$, $x(0) = x(\tau_0)$, and T_s represents a fixed sampling time defined as $T_s = \tau_{k+1} - \tau_k$, after applying the impulsive discretization.

3   Estimation and Control Framework for Oncolytic Virus Therapy

This work aims to reduce or eliminate the total number of tumor cells in a period of time through a control strategy that calculates the optimal dose of injections. To achieve this, the controllability and observability of the system have been analyzed for each of the parameters used in [4], presented in Table 2.

Equilibrium state two is used for the control design. The parameters employed correspond to the three parameters described in Table 2, as the resulting model allowed satisfactory controller tuning through trial and error. The

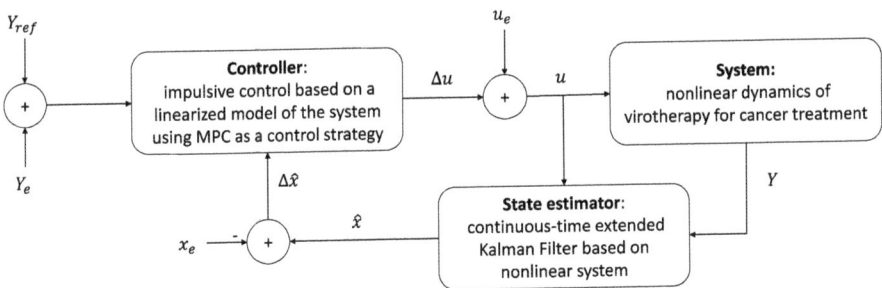

Fig. 1. Block diagram of oncolytic virus therapy with impulse control theory.

Table 2. Parameters

Description	α	δ	ω	ρ	κ	r	K	ϵ
Parameters 1	0.001	0.513	0.01	0.216	0.000958	0.2062	2139	1.649
Parameters 2	0.001	0.309	0.3	0.608	0.000448	0.2062	2139	1.649
Parameters 3	0.053	0.015	0.01	0.5	0.000958	0.2062	2139	1.649

other two parameter sets required very short time intervals between injections, which does not make much sense in this type of treatment.

The controllability of the system is assessed through the Kalman Matrix, which has full rank. Subsequently, the observability of the nonlinear system is examined using the approach outlined in [11]. After conducting the analysis, it was concluded that the rank of the nonlinear observability matrix is complete. Given the set of parameters three, and the fact that the linear system around equilibrium two is controllable and observable, it is justified to design an MPC control based on an observer for regulating the cancerous tumor.

Coupling the MPC control with a state estimator is necessary since the complete state is needed to calculate optimal virus doses. Therefore, the whole control scheme is shown in Fig. 1, where Y_e, u_e, and x_e are the equilibrium output, equilibrium input, and equilibrium state, respectively.

The developed methodology, although applied to a specific cancer type in this study, can be generalized to other tumors by adjusting model parameters and equilibrium points to match each tumor's characteristics.

3.1   The Discrete-Time Extended Kalman Filter

The manuscript deals with the acquisition of data represented by Y_{me}, which is gathered periodically. Moreover, inaccuracies in tumor volume measurements typically range from 0.5% to 10% [3,8].

Assume continuous-time process noise $w(t)$ follows a normal distribution with covariance Q_e, and discrete-time measurement noise v_k follows a normal distribution with covariance R_e. Consequently, the impulsive system is reformulated with these respective noise terms as follows

$$\dot{x}(t) = f(x(t), w(t)), \quad x(0) = x_0, \quad t \neq \tau_k,$$
$$x\left(\tau_k^+\right) = x\left(\tau_k\right) + B_u u\left(\tau_k\right), \quad t = \tau_k, \quad k \in \mathbb{N}, \tag{5}$$
$$Y_{\mathrm{me}}\left(\tau_k\right) = Cx\left(\tau_k\right) + v\left(\tau_k\right), \quad t = \tau_k, \quad k \in \mathbb{N}.$$

The methodology employs nonlinear dynamics for state estimation and error covariance propagation between measurements. Subsequently, the acquired measurement data at time points k are utilized to refine the estimation. Thus, the discrete extended Kalman filter (EKF), as outlined in [13], is employed.

$$\hat{x}_k = f(\hat{x}_{k-1}), \quad P_k = FP_{k-1}F' + Q_e, \quad K_k = P_k C'(CP_k C' + R_e)^{-1},$$
$$\hat{x}_k^+ = \hat{x}_k^- + K_k\left(Y_{\mathrm{me}} - C\hat{x}_k^-\right), \quad P_k^+ = (I - K_k C)P_k^-. \tag{6}$$

The initial step of the Extended Kalman Filter involves updating the state estimate $\hat{x}$ and error covariance P through temporal integration using the nonlinear model. Subsequently, the discrete-time equations update the posterior state and error covariance at time k using the Kalman gain matrix K and the measurement Y_{me}. It is noteworthy that the dynamics of the error covariance P rely on the matrix F, computed around the estimated point $\hat{x}_{k-1}^+$ at each iteration.

In this manuscript, the Kalman filter is used because it is well-established and widely implemented in many software packages. The study is theoretical and does not focus on real sensor data, which is why we assumed Gaussian noise.

3.2 Impulsive Linear Model Predictive Control

The initial step of the Extended Kalman Filter involves updating the state estimate $\hat{x}$ and error covariance P through temporal integration using the nonlinear model. Subsequently, the discrete-time equations update the posterior state and error covariance at time k using the Kalman gain matrix K and the measurement Y_{me}. It is noteworthy that the dynamics of the error covariance P rely on the matrix F, computed around the estimated point $\hat{x}_{k-1}^+$ at each iteration. The main objective is to decrease the total number of tumor cells Y below 1×10^{-6} cells through oncolytic virotherapy (OVT), to eradicate the tumor, or bring the size of the tumor $Y+X$ below 50×10^{-6} cells since in practical situations, doctors consider that after this point the tumor can be safely removed.

To accomplish this, we propose employing an MPC approach to determine the optimal sequence of injections. This strategy minimizes both the deviation between the system output and the target and the quantity of virus administered. Let $\mathbf{U}$ represent the input sequence $\mathbf{U} = \{u_k, u_{k+1}, \ldots, u_{k+H_p-1}\}$, and $\mathbf{x}$ denote the sequence of states $\mathbf{x} = \{x_k, x_{k+1}, \ldots, x_{k+H_p}\}$. The optimization problem to be solved at each time step k based on [9] can be formulated as follows

$$\min_{\mathbf{U},\mathbf{x}} \sum_{j=0}^{H_p-1} \|Y_{k+j} - Y_r\|_Q^2 + \|u_{k+j}\|_R^2 + \|Y_{k+H_p} - Y_r\|_S^2$$

$$\text{s.t.} \quad x_k = \hat{x}_k, \quad x_{k+j+1} = A_d x_{k+j} + B_d u_{k+j}, \tag{7}$$
$$Y_{k+j} = C x_{k+j}, \quad u_{k+j} \in \mathcal{U}$$
$$u_{k+j} = u_{k+H_u-1} = 0, \quad j = H_u, \ldots, H_p - 1.$$

Here, $\mathcal{U}$ stands for the input constraint set represented by $\mathcal{U} = \{u \,|\, u_{min} \leq u \leq u_{max}\}$. The optimal solution $\mathbf{U}^* = \{u_k^*, \ldots, u_{k+H_u-1}^*, 0, \ldots, 0\}$ consists of the optimal sequence, where the first element u_k^* is applied to. Notice that after H_u, the sequence is zero because the ideal treatment is with few injections.

Furthermore, the parameters H_u and H_p denote the control and prediction horizons, respectively. Matrices Q, R, and S are employed to penalize the output trajectory, energy, and final output of the system. Lastly, constants Y_r and u_r correspond to the reference output and reference input, respectively.

To introduce the limitation on the maximum total dose allowed per patient, the state space (4) is augmented by adding a state u_k^T that accounts for the cumulative dose that has been injected, that is $u_{k+1}^T = u_k^T + u_k$. Therefore, the augmented state space combining (4) and u^T is $\tilde{x}_{k+1} = A_a \tilde{x}_k + B_a u_k$, $Y_k = C_a \tilde{x}_k$ where $A_a = \begin{bmatrix} A_d & 0 \\ 0 & I \end{bmatrix}$, $B_a = \begin{bmatrix} B_d \\ I \end{bmatrix}$, $C_a = \begin{bmatrix} I & 0 & 0 & 0 \end{bmatrix}$. Consequently, the constraint is introduced as $u_{k+1}^T \leq u_{max}^T$. The formulation of the MPC (7) is reformulated as

$$\min_{\mathbf{U},\mathbf{x}} \sum_{j=0}^{H_p-1} \|Y_{k+j} - Y_r\|_Q^2 + \|u_{k+j}\|_R^2 + \|Y_{k+H_p} - Y_r\|_S^2$$

$$\text{s.t.} \quad x_k = \hat{x}_k, \quad x_{k+j+1} = A_a x_{k+j} + B_a u_{k+j}, \tag{8}$$

$$Y_{k+j} = C_a x_{k+j}, \quad u_{k+j} \in \mathcal{U}, \quad u_{k+j}^T \in \mathcal{U}^T,$$

$$u_{k+j} = u_{k+H_u-1} = 0, \quad j = H_u, \ldots, H_p - 1.$$

The set $\mathcal{U}^T$ represents the constraint on the maximum allowable dosage. Specifically, $\mathcal{U}^T = \{u^T \,|\, u^T \leq u_{max}^T\}$, where u^T denotes the cumulative dose administered to the patient, and u_{max}^T signifies the maximum allowable cumulative dose. This constraint is crucial for ensuring the safety and efficacy of the treatment regimen. It prevents excessive dosage that could lead to adverse effects or toxicity in the patient. The details of the impulsive MPC can be seen in [12].

Different simulation scenarios were considered, but in all of them the MPC is configured to reach the origin: (i) First, MPC formulations are explored without restrictions on the total virus dose, generating variations in the prediction horizon. For this scenario, the control law is set to zero once the tumor is eradicated. This analysis aims to understand how different combinations of these horizons influence treatment outcomes. (ii) MPC formulations are then investigated while introducing complete tumor removal $(Y + X)$, simulating scenarios where tumor excision and viral therapy are performed. In this situation, the control law is set to zero at the time the split is made. This addition to the model provides information on the effectiveness of combination therapies in achieving tumor eradication. (iii) Subsequently, the impact of variations in the sanction matrix Q is examined by setting the control law to zero when satisfactory therapy is achieved. By systematically modifying Q, the sensitivity of the controller to different aspects of the system dynamics can be evaluated. (iv) Finally, MPC formulations with restrictions on the total dose of virus available for tumor elimination are considered. In this simulation, the control law is forced to be zero at the time when successful therapy is achieved. This modification aims to optimize resource allocation while ensuring effective tumor management.

4   Results and Discussions

Initial experiments determined a daily sampling time, Ts = 1, as optimal, facilitating daily OVT injections and tumor measurements. This setup, while ideal in simulations, must consider practical aspects like patient tolerance and logistical feasibility for clinical application. Previous studies, including [1] and [14], have explored alternative treatment protocols for cancer with OVT, including injection schedules every two days. In all the following simulations, the initial plant conditions were set as $x_0 = [2000 \quad 0 \quad 0]^T$, and it was established that no virus injection would occur beyond horizon control.

First, the implementation of MPC (7) was performed without a maximum total dose constraint but with a minimum dose constraint at each sampling time $\mathcal{U} = u \geq 0$. The controller parameters are set in unity $Q = S = R = 1$. In this configuration, the control horizon was set to one day $H_u = 1$. Variations were made in the prediction horizon H_p. It was observed that treatment is accelerated with smaller prediction horizons, resulting in the elimination of cancer cells with higher doses injected. This finding corresponds well with the problem formulation since, for longer prediction horizons; the MPC determines that the application of high doses may not be necessary, predicting satisfactory treatment results even with smaller doses, which affects the speed of the treatment. The MPC-guided treatment strategy consistently administered calculated injection vectors for prediction horizons of $H_p = 2$, $H_p = 3$, and $H_p = 5$, maintaining respective values of 1.99, 1.44, and 1.03 (10^6 cells). Virus vectors were applied on day 1, with null injection vectors computed by the MPC for subsequent treatment days. Furthermore, when the prediction horizon is three days or less, the initial dose is sufficiently potent in achieving therapeutic success. However, in the absence of an elimination protocol such as excision or another mechanism, a resurgence of the virus was observed, leading to only a partially successful treatment outcome. The insights gleaned from these results are instrumental in pinpointing an optimal timing for transitioning to other, less complex therapies for tumor management. For a visual illustration of these findings, refer to vspace (Fig. 2).

In the context of the search for the global success of the therapy, a simulation is carried out that recreates the scenario of removal of the cellular tumor that has not yet been infected and infected cells; the simulation is presented in Fig. 3. The constraint on the input is given by $\mathcal{U} = u \geq 0$. The controller is tuned with the parameters: $H_p = 5$, $H_c = 1$ and $Q = S = R = 1$. The results of this simulation reveal a crucial finding: the lack of tumor regeneration after removal. This suggests that the excision of the tumor, along with the viral therapy procedure, effectively prevents tumor proliferation, representing a significant step toward therapeutic success. In this simulation the MPC calculated a single virus injection that was applied on the first day of treatment, the virus vector injected was

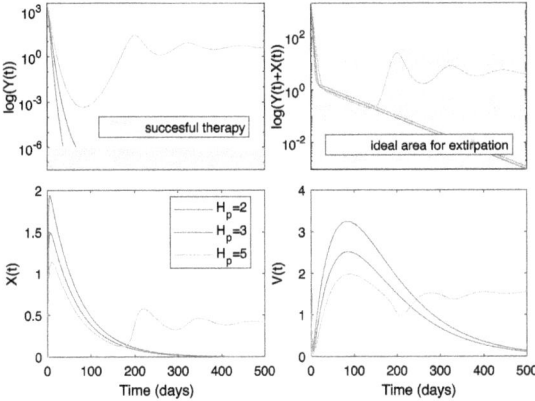

Fig. 2. Dynamic evolution of the OVT by varying the prediction horizon.

1.99 (10^6 cells). In addition, the body's immune response eliminates the cells infected by the treatment. This natural defense mechanism plays a fundamental role in eliminating residual cancer cells, further strengthening the effectiveness of the treatment.

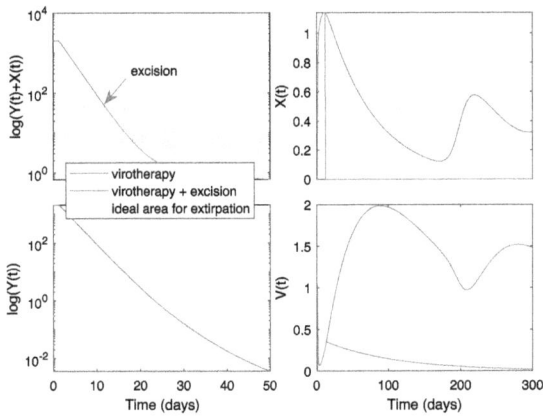

Fig. 3. Dynamic evolution of the excision of the tumor along with the viral therapy.

The above results set the control and prediction horizons to $H_u = 1$ and $H_p = 2$, respectively. The controller is tuned with the parameters according to formulation (7) in ($S = R = 1$), while the cost associated with the production transition (Q) varies by thousands. Case $Q = 1e3$ shows that the therapy reduced the duration of treatment by up to 18 days, representing a notable achievement in treating cancer by injecting a single vector of the virus of 3.8 (10^6 cells) throughout the treatment. While for the case $Q = 1$ and $Q = 1e - 3$ the viral load delivered throughout the therapy was 1.99 (10^6 cells) and 1.66 (10^6 cells), respectively for a single day. These results are shown in Fig. 4. Additionally, it is worth noting that this highlights the importance of controller tuning, which should be performed by an expert in both the subject matter and control theory.

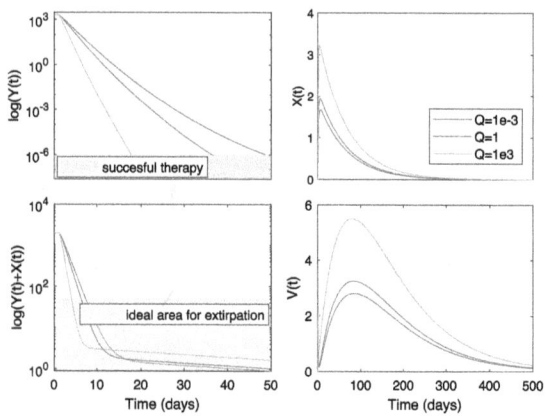

Fig. 4. Dynamic evolution of the OVT by adjusting the controller parameters.

Finally, a scenario is simulated to investigate the efficacy of MPC formulations in cancer therapy. In MPC formulation 1, constraints are defined by equation (7) as $\mathcal{U} = \{0 \leq u \leq 1.3\}$. For MPC formulation 2, constraints are formulated as shown in equation (8), subject to $\mathcal{U} = \{0 \leq u \leq 1.3\}$ and $\mathcal{U}^T = \{u^T \leq 2\}$. These constraints are designed to limit the maximum dose administered to the patient, considering safety and efficacy. Simulation conditions are meticulously set to ensure a fair comparison. In both cases, the controller is tuned with the parameters $S = R = 1$ and $Q = 1e3$, with control and prediction horizons set at one day and two days, respectively. It is crucial to emphasize that the augmented model remains controllable for the chosen set of parameters and equilibrium points. This ensures that the control system can effectively regulate the therapy process. The results, depicted in Fig. 5, demonstrate the therapeutic success of OVT in both scenarios. The Fig. 6 shows Despite achieving satisfactory results, it is noteworthy that the controller tuned with the formulation of (8) effectively satisfies the proposed constraints, limiting the total maximum dose administered. In contrast, the controller tuned with the formulation (7) does not consider the maximum available dose, potentially leading to increased toxicity. This observation not only reinforces the initial motivation described in the introduction regarding the importance of optimizing cancer treatment but also validates the effectiveness of the reformulated MPC approach (8) in mitigating toxicity risks while maintaining therapeutic efficacy.

This study implements a predictive control scheme based on a linearized model of oncolytic measles virotherapy, contrasting with reference [14], which

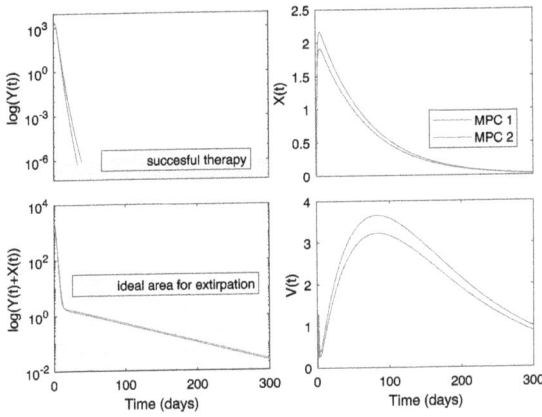

Fig. 5. Comparison of the dynamic evolution of therapy using MPC 1 and MPC 2.

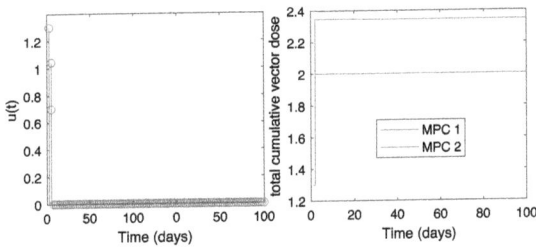

Fig. 6. Comparison of the viral vector applied using MPC 1 and MPC 2.

utilizes an impulsive nonlinear control approach for oncolytic adenovirus therapy. The results exhibit significant differences in dose adjustment and toxicity minimization. Unlike the reference, which adjusts doses with high initial intensities, this study optimizes doses throughout the treatment to achieve complete eradication with a conservative approach, thus reducing potential toxicity. Furthermore, this work introduces constraints on the maximum total allowable dose, enhancing control over treatment administration and preventing excessive toxicity, an aspect not addressed in [14].

5   Conclusion

One of the key contributions of this article is the utilization of the maximum permitted dose per patient as a constraint in the MPC framework. This approach mitigates toxicity and increases treatment options' availability, thereby improving patient safety and treatment accessibility. By incorporating such constraints, MPC-based virotherapy becomes more personalized and tailored to individual patient needs, leading to better treatment outcomes. Looking ahead, several avenues for future research emerge. Firstly, there is a need to formalize the

MPC framework with added state variables to optimize the maximum available dose. Furthermore, nonlinear MPC models to reduce the mismatch between predicted and actual treatment outcomes presents an exciting opportunity. By incorporating nonlinear dynamics into the control strategy, the system can better adapt to complex physiological variations, improving treatment precision and effectiveness. Another important direction for future work is the implementation of MPC with offset-free control to mitigate parametric uncertainty. By dynamically adjusting control inputs to compensate for uncertainties, the treatment process can become more robust and reliable, even in changing patient conditions.

In summary, this study has made significant contributions to the field of cancer treatment by integrating MPC into oncolytic virotherapy and tumor excision strategies. While promising results have been achieved, there remain ample opportunities for further research to optimize treatment efficacy, personalize therapy, and improve patient outcomes.

References

1. Anelone, A.J.N., Villa-Tamayo, M.F., Rivadeneira, P.S.: Oncolytic virus therapy benefits from control theory. Roy. Soc. Open Sci. **7**(7), 200473 (2020). https://doi.org/10.1098/rsos.200473
2. Bajzer, Ž, Carr, T., Josić, K., Russell, S.J., Dingli, D.: Modeling of cancer virotherapy with recombinant measles viruses. J. Theor. Biol. **252**(1), 109–122 (2008)
3. Barish, S., Ochs, M.F., Sontag, E.D., Gevertz, J.L.: Evaluating optimal therapy robustness by virtual expansion of a sample population, with a case study in cancer immunotherapy. Proc. Natl. Acad. Sci. **114**(31), E6277–E6286 (2017)
4. Biesecker, M., Kimn, J.H., Lu, H., Dingli, D., Bajzer, Ž: Optimization of virotherapy for cancer. Bull. Math. Biol. **72**, 469–489 (2010)
5. Cappuccio, A., Castiglione, F., Piccoli, B.: Determination of the optimal therapeutic protocols in cancer immunotherapy. Math. Biosci. **209**(1), 1–13 (2007)
6. Das, A., Sarmah, H.K., Bhattacharya, D., Dehingia, K., Hosseini, K.: Combination of virotherapy and chemotherapy with optimal control for combating cancer. Math. Comput. Simul. **194**, 460–488 (2022)
7. Dingli, D., et al.: Image-guided radiovirotherapy for multiple myeloma using a recombinant measles virus expressing the thyroidal sodium iodide symporter. Blood **103**(5), 1641–1646 (2004)
8. Feldman, J.P., Goldwasser, R., Mark, S., Schwartz, J., Orion, I.: A mathematical model for tumor volume evaluation using two-dimensions. J. Appl. Quant Methods **4**(4), 455–462 (2009)
9. Goodwin, G., Seron, M.M., De Doná, J.A.: Constrained Control and Estimation: An Optimisation Approach. Springer, Cham (2006). https://doi.org/10.1007/b138145
10. Handel, A., Li, Y., McKay, B., Pawelek, K.A., Zarnitsyna, V., Antia, R.: Exploring the impact of inoculum dose on host immunity and morbidity to inform model-based vaccine design. PLoS Comput. Biol. **14**(10), e1006505 (2018)
11. Kou, S.R., Elliott, D.L., Tarn, T.J.: Observability of nonlinear systems. Inf. Control **22**(1), 89–99 (1973)

12. Rivadeneira, P.S., Ferramosca, A., González, A.H.: Control strategies for non-zero set-point regulation of linear impulsive systems. IEEE Trans. Autom. Control **63**(9), 2994–3001 (2018)
13. Simons, D.: Optimal State Estimation, Kalman, H∞, and Nonlinear Approaches. Wiley-Interscience (2006)
14. Villa-Tamayo, M.F., Anelone, A.J.N., Rivadeneira, P.S.: Tumor reduction using oncolytic viruses under an impulsive nonlinear estimation and predictive control scheme. IEEE Control Syst. Lett. **5**(5), 1705–1710 (2021). https://doi.org/10.1109/LCSYS.2020.3043185

Dynamic Thermal Compensation in CNC Machining: Modeling a Linear Kalman Filter for Enhanced Positional Accuracy

Adalto de Farias[1]($\boxtimes$), Emeldo Rogelio Caballero Brochado[2],
Marcelo Otavio dos Santos[1], Nelson Wilson Paschoalinoto[1], Vanessa Seriacopi[1],
and Ed Claudio Bordinassi[1]

[1] Instituto Maua de Tecnologia, Praça Maua, 01, São Caetano do Sul, SP, Brazil
adalto.farias@maua.br
[2] Universidad Libre - Sede, Carrera 46 No. 48-170, Barranquilla, Colombia

Abstract. This work presents an application of a linear Kalman filter to control the effects of thermal expansion in a recirculating ball screw of a computer numerical control (CNC) machine, impacting the final position accuracy of the machining tool. Through the Kalman filter, the system's state ball screw position is estimated iteratively, allowing for real-time compensation of thermal variations, dilation, and positional inaccuracies on machining precision. The effectiveness of the proposed approach is demonstrated through experimental validation using a dataset comprising positional and temperatures measurements. The performance of the Kalman filter was evaluated through statistical analysis and for measurements taken during the heating cycle, the Y-axis exhibited R^2 of 0.913 and R^2_{adj} of 0.906, with an RMSE of 9.32 μm, indicating a good fit of the model to the data and acceptable precision of the estimates. For the X-axis under similar thermal conditions, higher values of R^2 and R^2_{adj} were obtained with a lower RMSE confirming the high accuracy of the estimates and the method.

Keywords: CNC machine · real-time control · Kalman filter · thermal error

1 Introduction

The reliability, accuracy in dimensioning and the quality of workpieces manufactured using CNC machining processes are influenced by machine errors, which can be determined based on geometric [1], thermal [2], and process factors, e.g. vibration [3]. In general, thermal errors can correspond to a parcel from 40 to 70% of the total error in machining, driving investigations into thermal error modeling and the implementation of real-time monitoring and compensation systems for these errors. In addition, machine tools manufacturers focus on reducing final heat in systems, promoting frictionless conditions in aerostatic/ hydrostatic spindle and slides, and/or applying material with low thermal expansion [4]. A recent review [4] highlighted that thermal errors in machine tools and workpieces arise from elastic thermal deformation due to various heat sources

J. C. Figueroa-García et al. (Eds.): WEA 2024, CCIS 2223, pp. 110–122, 2025.
https://doi.org/10.1007/978-3-031-74598-0_10

like conduction, convection, and radiation. They can be classified into categories such as internal sources (friction, ball screws, bearings, gears, motors) and external sources (room temperature and proximity to other machines), for instance.

Zimmermann et al. [5] evaluated the compensation of thermal errors in CNC 5-axis machines, used in milling operations of impellers. To achieve their objective of analyzing thermal errors based on ambient temperature variation, they considered 15 axis-specific thermal errors with different thermal loads. As a conclusion, the developed methodology of self-compensation of thermal errors allowed a reduction of up to 73% of root mean squared errors (RMSE), enhancing the precision for temperature variations of 10 °C. In a similar assessment and applying an analytical model, Cheng et al. [6] researched geometric and thermal errors in a CNC five-axis machine tool, considering the rotating axes and a disk-shaped workpiece with 12 grooves. In terms of thermal errors, heating and cooling cycles were defined, with probe measurements and modeling. The analytical model showed an agreement of 85.1%.

Concerning the recurrent neural network (RNN) and long short-term memory (LSTM) applications, an example of development in diamond turning was reported by Yeo et al. [7]. The authors developed a machine learning model to predict thermal errors and temperature distributions throughout the single-point diamond. Thermal error compensation was applied as a correction to the tool position control, via a piezoelectric actuator, focusing on minimizing surface waviness effects. It was found that the RMSE decreased from 43.1 nm in the uncompensated condition to 5.7 nm in the compensating condition.

Feng et al. [8] provided enhancements in the neural network approach focused on thermal errors of the spindle in a five-axis CNC machine tool using temperature transducers, proposing a particle swarm optimization (PSO) algorithm and radial basis function (RBF) neural network. The results indicated an improvement of around 10.5% compared to others neural networks currently employed. A similar methodology was employed by Farias et al. [9] in utilizing RBF to create an algorithm sufficiently simple and lightweight to be directly incorporated into the machine controller. The use of RBF for thermal error modeling also resulted in an improvement in positioning precision up to 77%. Huang et al. [10] reported a study focused on thermal errors of the ball screw feed axis, considering a CNC vertical machining center with a control using an embedded platform combining a defined limit and Kalman filtering methodology. The method was developed with identification, classification, pre-compensation, and post-modeling of dynamic loads applying a fitting of several thermal deformations acting over the positioning throughout the machining operations. As one of the main findings, the positioning accuracy in the X-axis of the feed system was improved by 53.11%.

The objective of this study was to investigate the use of a linear Kalman filter to assess and predict thermal errors in the Y-axis and X-axis ball screw spindle positioning of a three-axis CNC machine center. The aim is to simulate thermal error compensation to improve the final position accuracy of the machining tool.

2 Methods and Materials

The machine studied was a twenty-year-old milling center, a standard Romi Discovery 560, without linear scale. The main characteristics of this machine are CNC Siemens 810D; maximum speed 7,500 rpm; travel strokes: longitudinal stroke (X-axis) 560 mm; transverse stroke (Y-axis) 406 mm; vertical stroke (Z-axis) 508 mm; maximum axes speed: 20 m/min; table dimensions 840 × 360 mm; AC main motor 15/11 hp/kW; total installed power 20 kVA.

Firstly, the hot spots of machine were identified using a FLUKE VT02 thermographic camera. The machine tool was programmed to cycle run for 2 h, as this was the time necessary for the machine to reach a higher and constant temperature. The cycle used to warm the machine consisted in setting all three axes to move simultaneously and continually, at a constant speed of 12,000 mm/min for the axe's total strokes. Figure 1(a) presents an image of one of the axes bearings, the temperature was ~ 31 °C.

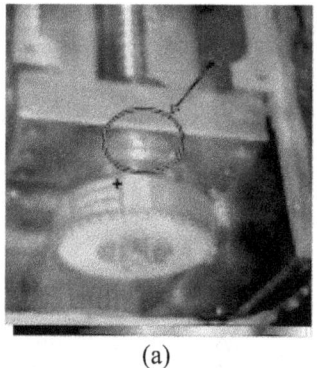   

(a)   (b)

Fig. 1. (a) Hot spot seen through the thermal camera, on the Y-axis of the machine.

Sensors were inserted on the hot spots, as Fig. 1(b) example, 2 for each axis (X and Y), at the bearing housing. A thin-film PT100 resistance temperature detectors (RTD) and the hardware SIMATIC S7–300 S PLC were used to acquire the measured temperatures. The PT100 RTD was fixed with aluminized adhesive, Fig. 1(b), for protection and to ensure its position. All the installation regions were protected from machining fluid and chips. The PT100 RTD installation scheme is shown in Fig. 2, where Fig. 2(a) presents the interior detail of the machine in the X-axis bearing region for the RDT assembling, and Fig. 2(b) temperature sensor assembly diagram.

A total of four RDTs were assembled with the nomenclature for the Y axis: RTD#1 bearing housing near to servomotor and #2 bearing housing opposite to servomotor; nomenclature for X-axis RTD#3 bearing housing near to servomotor and #4 bearing housing opposite to servomotor. The PLC module for acquisition of the PT100 RTD readings was installed at the electrical panel, providing the temperature to be accessed and evaluated directly from the CNC machine panel.

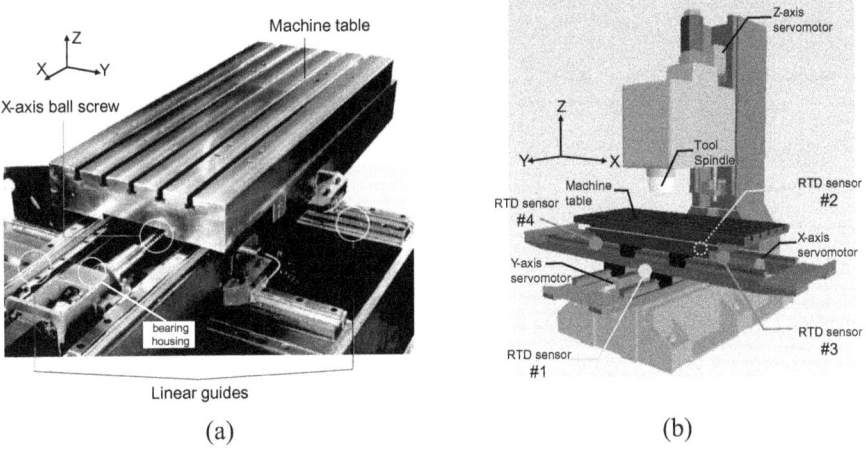

Fig. 2. (a) interior detail of the machine in the X-axis bearing, (b) RDT sensor diagram.

Figure 3(a) presents a general flowchart with all the steps involved in this work, for an initial understanding and to identify the different aspects that are necessary in the modeling of Kalman filter.

In Fig. 3(a) is possible to identify three important blocks to obtain valid results: i) Identify machine's hot spots to install temperature sensors, ii) Interferometric laser (IL) measurements of the coordinates positioning errors to create database for the Kalman filter implementation, and iii) Modeling and validation of the Kalman filter at machine´s Y axis and X axis.

The equipment used to perform the IL measurements was a RENISHAW XL-80 and a RENISHAW XC-80 compensator, Fig. 3(b). The measurements were made in several temperature conditions according to Fig. 4, after executing the cycle used to warm the machine for 2 h. The axis scan measurements were made every 25 mm along the total stroke of the axis. Once warmed, data were acquired at 10 points for each nominal position interval (25 mm intervals along the total stroke of the X and Y axes), five in the positive direction (+) of axis movement, and five in the negative direction (−), based on the forward and backward movements of the machine axis, Fig. 3(b).

As an example, Table 1 presents the sample relative positioning errors readings for the Y-axis at temperature ranges of 37.91–37.7 °C for RTD 1 (T1) and 38.3–37.88 °C for RTD 2 (T2) (readings 1 to 5). The relative difference are in micrometer, the experimental error was measured for each coordinate positioning of the Y-axis during the measurement with the IL in forward and backward direction. As an example, for the nominal positioning at the coordinate of 100.0000 mm, the machine presented an experimental positioning of 100.0341 mm in the first negative direction (backward movement to the origin coordinate 0 mm). The difference (error) between the nominal and experimental coordinates was + 34.1 μm, which will be utilized as an input reference for determining, through the Kalman filter method, the amount of error that needs to be corrected in the current axis positioning to achieve the nominal value requested by the CNC command during the movement.

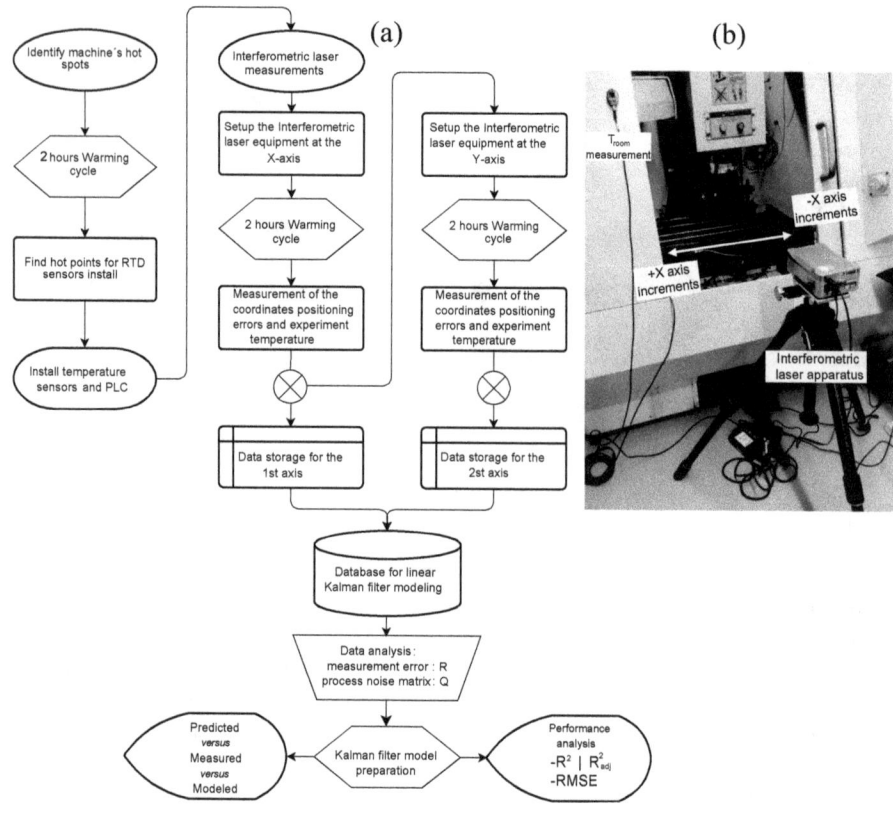

Fig. 3. (a) Flowchart of the methodology and experiments, (b) X-axis laser measurements.

Table 1. Measurements in the positioning of the Y-axis, last data readings #14.

nominal position [mm]	experimental relative errors readings on Y-axis [μm]									
	1st(−) Error	1st(+) Error	2nd(−) Error	2nd(+) Error	3rd(−) Error	3rd(+) Error	4th(−) Error	4th(+) Error	5th(−) Error	5th(+) Error
0	0.0	0.4	-0.6	1.4	0.6	2.2	1.0	2.9	2.2	4.4
25	9.3	9.6	8.9	10.1	10.2	10.3	9.7	10.4	10.3	11.7
50	12.4	12.3	12.6	13.0	13.5	12.9	13.5	13.1	14.9	14.7
75	28.9	27.9	28.2	28.4	28.5	27.9	29.0	28.9	29.7	28.7
100	34.1	35.1	33.9	34.5	33.1	35.1	33.8	34.7	34.1	35.2
125	41.6	40.2	40.8	39.9	40.2	39.9	40.5	40.4	39.7	39.8
150	48.8	47.5	47.3	47.3	47.5	46.6	47.3	47.3	47.3	47.2

(*continued*)

Table 1. (*continued*)

nominal position [mm]	experimental relative errors readings on Y-axis [μm]									
	1st(−) Error	1st(+) Error	2nd(−) Error	2nd(+) Error	3rd(−) Error	3rd(+) Error	4th(−) Error	4th(+) Error	5th(−) Error	5th(+) Error
175	62.1	62.0	60.6	61.4	60.2	60.7	60.1	60.3	59.4	60.7
200	59.3	60.6	59.8	59.5	59.4	58.9	58.8	59.0	58.0	58.4
225	73.0	73.6	72.6	71.6	71.5	71.0	71.0	70.3	70.4	70.2
250	81.1	81.6	79.7	80.0	77.2	78.8	77.8	78.4	77.0	77.5
275	87.0	87.7	85.4	86.6	83.6	85.5	82.8	84.0	83.0	83.3
300	88.7	87.2	87.2	86.2	86.3	85.1	85.5	84.0	84.0	83.8
325	104.0	103.9	102.8	103.8	101.1	102.0	100.4	100.5	99.6	99.9
350	102.7	102.7	100.7	100.9	99.3	99.9	97.6	98.3	96.8	97.6

Figure 4 shows the temperature at the time of measurement with the IL, which was manually started after each interval of warming. During the tests the room temperature (T_{room}), showed a stable behavior, therefore not interfering with the machine's natural cooling process. T_{room} was measured outside the machine's front door, Fig. 3(b).

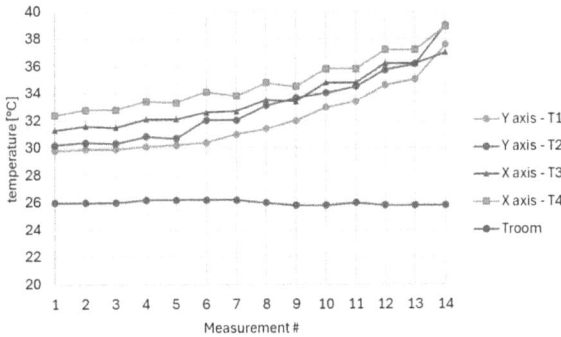

Fig. 4. Initial and final temperature ranges (°C) for each axis positioning measurement.

2.1 Kalman Filter Implementation

To implement a linear Kalman filter in the position controlling of the coordinate axes of a CNC machine, is necessary to define the fundamental equations and matrices of the model. For this model, a two-dimensional space (two-axis system) X and Y were considered. The equations of the Kalman filter in matrix form are divided into two main steps: prediction and update (or correction).

- State Extrapolation (prediction):

$$\hat{x}_{n+1,n} = F \cdot \hat{x}_{n,n} + Gu_n + w_n \tag{1}$$

$$P_{n+1,n} = F \cdot P_{n,n} \cdot F^T + Q \tag{2}$$

where $\hat{x}_{n+1,n}$, Eq. (1), is a predicted system state vector at time step $n + 1$, $\hat{x}_{n,n}$ is an estimated system state vector at time step n, composed by the current estimates of the axes and their velocities. The matrix u_n is a control variable or a measurable (deterministic) input to the system, w_n is a process noise or disturbance as an unmeasurable input that affects the state, F is a state transition matrix and G is a control matrix or input transition matrix (mapping control to state variables). In Eq. (2) $P_{n,n}$ is the squared uncertainty of an estimate (covariance matrix) of the current state, $P_{n+1,n}$ is the squared uncertainty of a prediction (covariance matrix) for the next state, F is the state transition matrix and Q is the process noise matrix.

- State update step:

$$K_n = P_{n,n-1} \cdot H^T \cdot (H \cdot P_{n,n-1} \cdot H^T + R_n)^{-1} \tag{3}$$

$$\hat{x}_{n,n} = \hat{x}_{n,n-1} + K_n \cdot (z_n - H \cdot \hat{x}_{n,n-1}) \tag{4}$$

$$P_{n,n} = (I - K_n \cdot H) \cdot P_{n,n-1} \tag{5}$$

In Eq. (3), K_n is the Kalman gain at time n, used to weigh between the predicted state estimates and the measurements (correction), $\hat{x}_{n,n}$, Eq. (4), is the updated state estimate at time n after incorporating the new measurement (state correction), R_n is the measurement error, H is the observation matrix, and $P_{n,n}$, Eq. (5), is the updated state error covariance at time n after incorporating the new measurement (covariance correction).

The identity matrix I have a 4x4 form, z_n is the measurement vector at time n in the form of Eq. (6), where z_{Xn} is the measurement of the position of axis X at time instant n, and z_{Yn} is the measurement of the position of axis Y at time instant n.

$$z_n = \begin{bmatrix} z_{Xn} \\ z_{Yn} \end{bmatrix} \tag{6}$$

These equations describe the iterative process of the Kalman filter, where the state estimate is continuously refined based on the model predictions and the new available measurements. The theoretical model of axis positioning considering the linear thermal expansion caused by temperature can be established based on Eq. (7).

$$x_{n+1} = x_n + \Delta t \cdot v \cdot (1 + 2 \cdot C_{\Delta l}) \tag{7}$$

where x_{n+1} is the next theoretical position of the axis in the time interval Δt when moving at a velocity v added to the linear thermal expansion caused by the temperature

$C_{\Delta l}$, according to Eq. (8), and α is the average coefficient of thermal expansion of steel $(1.3 \cdot 10^{-5}\ °C^{-1})$. The measured temperature $(T_{measured})$ was established as the average between the values read on the two bearing housings of the axis under study.

$$C_{\Delta l} = (T_{measured} - T_{room}) \cdot \alpha \tag{8}$$

This adjustment needs to be considered for the correct analysis of the phenomenon along with the Kalman filter by adding a control variable related to the current estimated system condition, Eq. (9) and the control matrix, Eq. (10) to the model. Equation (9) adds the temperature influence on the system.

$$u_n = \begin{bmatrix} C_{\Delta l} & C_{\Delta l} & 0 & 0 \\ 0 & 0 & 0 & 0 \\ 0 & 0 & C_{\Delta l} & C_{\Delta l} \\ 0 & 0 & 0 & 0 \end{bmatrix} \cdot \hat{x}_{n,n} \tag{9}$$

$$G = \begin{bmatrix} 1 & 0 & 0 & 0 \\ 0 & 1 & 0 & 0 \\ 0 & 0 & 1 & 0 \\ 0 & 0 & 0 & 1 \end{bmatrix} \tag{10}$$

The state transition matrix F has the form of Eq. (11), and the estimate of covariance matrix $P_{n,n}$ was established as the mean of the sum of squares from the maximum difference between the measured values, $z_{e,mx}$, and the nominal coordinate, z_{nom}, Eq. (12)

$$F = \begin{bmatrix} 1 & \Delta t & 0 & 0 \\ 0 & 1 & 0 & 0 \\ 0 & 0 & 1 & \Delta t \\ 0 & 0 & 0 & 1 \end{bmatrix} \tag{11}$$

$$P_{n,n} = \begin{bmatrix} 1 & 1 & 0 & 0 \\ 1 & 1 & 0 & 0 \\ 0 & 0 & 1 & 1 \\ 0 & 0 & 1 & 1 \end{bmatrix} \cdot \frac{\sum_i^n (z_{e,max} - z_{nom})^2}{n} \tag{12}$$

Figure 5 presents a flowchart of the Kalman filter algorithm, which consists of i) Initialization: Occurs once, providing initial system state and state variance; ii) Measurement: Yields measured system state and measurement variance; iii) State Update: Estimation of the current system state, utilizing measured value and variance, prior predicted state estimate, and its variance. Outputs include the Kalman gain, current system state estimate, and state estimate variance; iv) Prediction: Extrapolates current system state estimate and variance to the next state based on the system's dynamic model. In the first iteration, initialization serves as the Prior State. Prediction outputs become the Prior state estimate and variance in subsequent iterations.

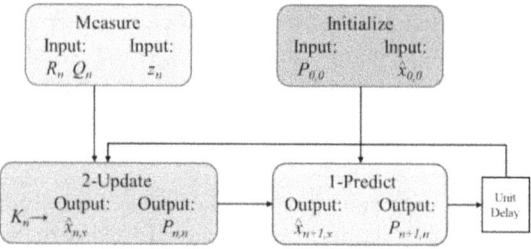

Fig. 5. Kalman filter algorithm.

3   Results and Discussion

For a better visualization of the filter model's performance, a numerical analysis was conducted with measurement #14, whose results are shown in Table 1, to serve as a reference in the discussions. Based on the measurements presented in Table 1, the measurement error R for the Y axis was established as the standard deviation of the 10 measurements taken for each nominal coordinate, Eq. (7). The process noise matrix Q for the Y axis was established as half the square of the maximum difference between the measured values ($z_{e,max}$) and the nominal values (z_{nom}) for each coordinate according to Eqs. (8) and (9).

$$R_Y^T = \begin{bmatrix} 1.5 & 0.76 & 0.89 & 0.55 & 0.68 & 0.57 & 0.55 & 0.86 & 0.73 & 1.19 & 1.63 & 1.79 & 1.63 & 1.73 & 2.1 \end{bmatrix} \tag{7}$$

$$Q = \frac{\left(z_{e,max} - z_{nom}\right)^2}{2} \tag{8}$$

$$Q_Y^T = [0.009 \; 0.07 \; 0.11 \; 0.44 \; 0.62 \; 0.87 \; 1.19 \; 1.93 \; 1.84 \; 2.71 \; 3.33 \; 3.85 \; 3.93 \; 5.41 \; 5.27] \cdot 10^{-3} \tag{9}$$

Table 2 displays predicted and current values from the linear Kalman filter for CNC machine axis position subjected to thermal expansion, alongside actual measurements. Theoretical values calculated from Eq. (7) serve as a reference for the thermal model, depicting an ideal thermal expansion scenario without additional interference. Discrepancies emerge between predicted/estimated values and actual measurements, indicating potential errors in the model. Nevertheless, initial proximity between predicted/estimated and actual values showcases the Kalman filter's potential for accurate anticipation of axis position. Anticipating the axis position error allows for its mitigation during the final movement of the axis, thus enhancing the accuracy of the system.

From Fig. 6, it's evident that the predictive estimates generally approximate the measured values, indicating the filter's effectiveness in predicting axis position based on previous readings. However, disparities arise at transition points or abrupt changes, suggesting the model's underestimation or overestimation of thermal expansion influence. Factors like inaccuracies in the thermal model or unaccounted variations in machine conditions, such as vibration and mechanical loosening, contribute to these discrepancies, and the self-adjustment capability of the Kalman filter allows for the incorporation of

Table 2. Result table for the Y axis measurement #14

Y axis position	Predicted	Measured	Current Estimate	Theoretical
[mm]	[μm]	[μm]	[μm]	[μm]
0	0.00	1.45	0.00	0.00
25	4.06	10.05	9.41	8.11
50	22.87	13.29	15.06	16.19
75	24.73	28.61	27.14	24.26
100	43.23	34.36	38.19	32.31
125	53.23	40.30	43.96	40.33
150	53.69	47.41	48.82	48.34
175	57.63	60.75	59.95	56.33
200	75.01	59.17	61.75	64.30
225	67.46	71.52	70.65	72.25
250	83.44	78.91	79.95	80.18
275	93.11	84.89	86.51	88.09
300	96.92	85.80	87.57	95.98
325	92.45	101.80	100.31	103.85
350	116.87	99.65	102.46	111.70

the influence of operational environment variance, resulting in more precise and reliable estimates of the axis position. The discrepancy between the predicted/estimated values and the actual measurements underscores the importance of continuous iteration and refinement of the Kalman filter gain and variances, as well as the need to consider additional factors that may influence the accuracy of position estimates in systems subject to thermal variations. The same procedure was done for the X axis, and the analysis of the results reveals a similar pattern to that observed for the Y axis. The predicted estimates generally exhibit a degree of alignment with the measured values, indicative of the filter's ability to track the axis position over time.

The variance analysis of the current state estimate yielded confidence intervals (CI: one σ) reflecting significant ranges in lower and upper limits for each data point. These intervals showed the uncertainty linked to linear Kalman filter estimates, influenced by factors like measurement noise and model inaccuracies. As axis position increases, intervals widen, suggesting heightened uncertainty away from the initial position due to error propagation over time or increased sensitivity to thermal expansion conditions.

However, all predicted values align within CI, alongside measurements and theoretical values, underscoring the filter's accuracy and robustness.

Measurements were also conducted prior to the heating cycle, with the Y-axis (Fig. 7) near the ambient temperature of 27.9 °C. It's important to consider that these measurements are less affected by thermal expansion but may be more prone to mechanical errors like vibration and potential loosening in bearings and ball screws. These factors

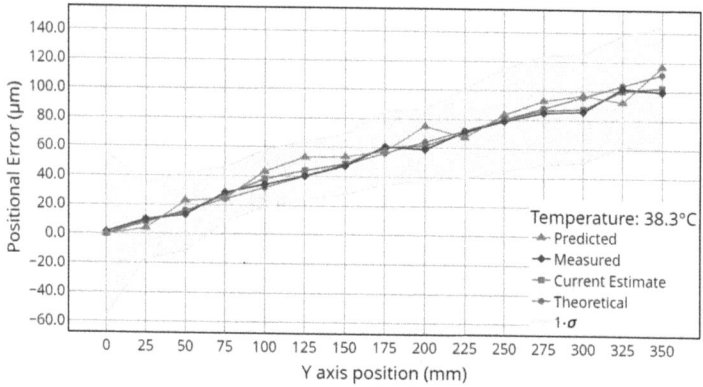

Fig. 6. Y-axis results comparison based on measurement #14.

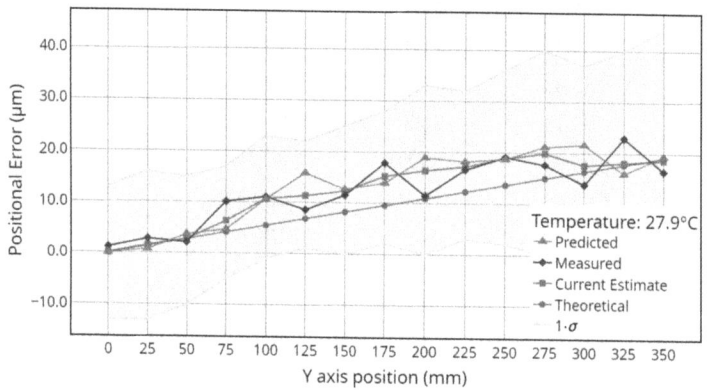

Fig. 7. Y-axis results comparison based on near room temperature measurement.

introduce uncertainty and inaccuracy in the measurements, affecting the linear Kalman filter's ability to predict axis positions accurately. In Fig. 7, the comparison reveals that the Kalman filter tends to align with measured values above the theoretical model around the middle position (175mm) of the Y axis, but closer to the extremities, it aligns more closely with the theoretical model. This alignment suggests the filter's ability to effectively track the axis position over time.

Figure 8 illustrates the comparison between measured value errors and the predicted Kalman filter value usage to simulate error compensation in Y-axis positioning for measurement #14 (refer to Table 2) to provide insights into potential improvements.

From Fig. 8, the model successfully reproduces the trends in the coordinates, albeit displaying disparities in absolute values. The thermal error compensation model, when applied for the length of Y-axis, exhibited a reduction in positioning error of up to approximately 90% at the axis stroke end. Comparable findings were observed for the X-axis. In accordance with the various results observed in the literature [5, 6, 10].

The performance of the Kalman filter was also evaluated using the coefficient of determination (R^2), adjusted coefficient of determination (R^2_{adj}), and Root Mean Square

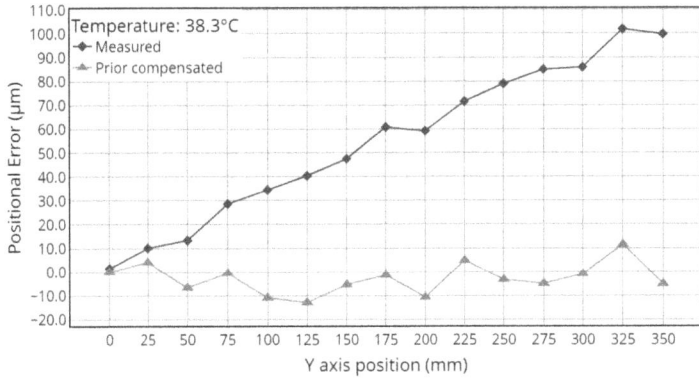

Fig. 8. Y-axis predicted error compensation simulation.

Error (RMSE). For the measurements taken on the Y-axis during the heating cycle (Table 2 and Fig. 6), a R^2 of 0.913 and an R^2_{adj} of 0.906 were observed, indicating a good ability of the model to explain the variability of the data. The RMSE presented a value of 9.32 μm suggesting an acceptable precision of the estimates in relation to the actual measurements, a reasonable value to be compared to [7]. For the measurements on the X-axis under the same thermal context, the values of R^2 0.986 and R^2_{adj} 0.985 were even higher, indicating an excellent fit of the model to the data. The corresponding RMSE of 5.28 μm confirms the high accuracy of the estimates for the X-axis for this condition, comparable to [7]. Near room temperature, a decrease in the Kalman filter's performance was noted. For the Y-axis (Fig. 7), with an R^2 of 0.512 and R^2_{adj} of 0.474, the model's ability to explain data variability is limited, implying reduced predictive capacity under conditions of lesser thermal influence. The RMSE of 3.56 μm still signifies reasonable estimation precision. At such temperatures, unaccounted source of variance may dominate the process, complicating the filter's adjustment during iteration. Upon analyzing results and mechanically inspecting the machine, slight loosening was observed in the nut of the recirculating ball screw drive. This variance is less evident during heating cycles, which induce thermal expansion, minimizing loosening.

4 Conclusion

The results from the Kalman filter modeling presented potential in predicting and compensating for thermal-induced errors in axis positioning. Despite some disparities between predicted and actual measurements, particularly at transition points, the filter generally aligns with measured values over time, indicating effectiveness in refining the model and providing more accurate estimates of axis position.

Evaluation of the Kalman filter's performance through statistical analysis revealed promising results. For measurements during the heating cycle, the Y-axis exhibited an R^2 of 0.913 and R^2_{adj} of 0.906, with an RMSE of 9.32 μm, indicating a good fit of the model to the data and acceptable precision of estimates. The X-axis, under similar thermal conditions, showed higher values of R^2 (0.986) and R^2_{adj} (0.985), with a lower RMSE of 5.28 μm, confirming the high accuracy of estimates.

However, at near-room temperature conditions, it is evident that the Kalman filter shows degradation in prediction accuracy when operating at temperatures close to ambient. This reduces result reliability, as evidenced by lower R^2 values for the Y-axis (0.512), likely due to a mechanical loosening observed in the nut of the recirculating ball screw drive. These challenges impacted the filter's predictive capacity, suggesting limited explanation of data variability by the model under such conditions.

Acknowledgments. This study was funded by Mauá Institute of Technology, São Caetano do Sul, SP, Brazil.

Disclosure of Interests. The authors have no competing interests to declare that are relevant to the content of this article.

References

1. Zhang, Z., Jiang, F., Luo, M., Wu, B., Zhang, D., Tang, K.: Geometric error measuring, modeling, and compensation for CNC machine tools: A review. Chinese J. Aeronaut. **37**(2), 163–198 (2024)
2. Ihlenfeldt, S.: 3rd International Conference on Thermal Issues in Machine Tools (ICTIMT2023) - Lecture Notes in Production Engineering. Springer, (2023)
3. Zhang, Z., et al.: Machining accuracy reliability evaluation of CNC machine tools based on the milling stability optimization. Int. J. Adv. Manuf. Technol. **124**(11–12), 4057–4074 (2023)
4. Gao, W., et al.: Machine tool calibration: Measurement, modeling, and compensation of machine tool errors. Int. J. Mach. Tools Manuf. **187** (2023)
5. Zimmermann, N., Müller, E., Lang, S., Mayr, J., Wegener, K.: Thermally compensated 5-axis machine tools evaluated with impeller machining tests. CIRP J. Manuf. Sci. Technol. **46**, 19–35 (2023)
6. Cheng, T., Xiang, S., Zhang, H., Yang, J.: New machining test for identifying geometric and thermal errors of rotary axes for five-axis machine tools. Meas. J. Int. Meas. Confed. **223**, 113748 (2023)
7. Yeo, W.J., et al.: Enhancement of optical surface quality based on real-time compensation of temperature-driven thermal errors in diamond turning. J. Manuf. Process. **110**, 424–433 (2024)
8. Feng, Z., Min, X., Jiang, W., Song, F., Li, X.: Study on thermal error modeling for CNC machine tools based on the improved radial basis function neural network. Appl. Sci. **13**(9) (2023)
9. Farias, A., dos Santos, M.O., Bordinassi, E.C.: Development of a thermal error compensation system for a CNC machine using a radial basis function neural network. J. Brazilian Soc. Mech. Sci. Eng. **44**(10), 1–21 (2022)
10. Huang, B., Xie, J., Liu, X., Yan, J., Liu, K., Yang, M.: Vertical machining center feed axis thermal error compensation strategy research. Appl. Sci. **13**(5) (2023)

Simulation

Simulation Model for the Strategic Analysis of a Cassava Starch Production Company: A Case Study

Gean Pablo Mendoza-Ortega$^{(\boxtimes)}$ (ID), Torregroza-Angélica M (ID),
Adriana Jaraba-Amaya (ID), Dina Marcela Mejía Gáspar (ID),
and Rolando López-Martínez (ID)

Corporación Universitaria del Caribe—CECAR, Sincelejo, Colombia
{gean.mendoza,angelica.torregroza,adriana.jaraba,dina.mejiag,
rolando.lopez}@cecar.edu.co

Abstract. This article presents a method to evaluate batch production scheduling in a cassava starch production company. The company uses specialized machinery to process cassava. The method is based on a study of the practical operations of the company and the production technologies used, including the construction of a simulation model. The simulation model reflects the technical aspects of the production process and the company's requirements. The simulation program FlexSim (from FlexSim Software Products, Inc.) was used in the experiments. The proposed method was evaluated using 12 possible scenarios. When comparing the simulated scenarios with the real data, it was concluded that there is an average percentage variation of 0.018%. These results highlight the effectiveness of advanced tools to optimize processes and improve efficiency in cassava starch production. The method was applied directly in a company to improve its performance; Furthermore, it is scalable and can be applied to problems of varying complexity and to production systems of different types and sizes, especially in small and medium-sized companies in the agri-food industries of the region.

Keywords: Production flow · FlexSim · Cassava starch · Process improvements

1 Introduction

Manufacturing has undergone significant evolution, transcending its conventional technical role in the production of goods [1]. Today it is recognized as a management activity of high strategic value that can play a prominent role in the global strategies of companies; This paradigm shift has driven the emergence of a specialized academic field, called manufacturing strategy or operations strategy [2].

Over the years, companies have faced many specific challenges arising from their operations. These challenges encompass various issues such as difficulties in logistics management, inefficiencies in production, obstacles in quality control, bottlenecks and complexities in supply chain management. These challenges impede the progress of companies and hinder their ability to achieve growth and profitability [3].

J. C. Figueroa-García et al. (Eds.): WEA 2024, CCIS 2223, pp. 125–137, 2025.
https://doi.org/10.1007/978-3-031-74598-0_11

Management as a multifaceted discipline plays a fundamental role in the success and sustainability of companies in various sectors. This involves a range of activities, including planning, organizing, leading and controlling, aimed at achieving organizational objectives efficiently [4].

According to Brenes [5], logistics is defined as the component of the supply chain management process that strategically coordinates and monitors the uninterrupted flow and storage of goods and services, both directly and reversely. The main objective of the logistics process is to satisfy customer needs in terms of quality by managing the flow of materials and information within companies.

There are different simulation tools that can help mitigate problems in companies. According to Céspedes [6], simulating is replicating the behavior of a process or system in the tangible world over a period. This process covers the documentation of the system and based on its analysis, the obtaining of analytical conclusions about the operational characteristics of the real system.

Discrete event simulation is the computational representation of systems that change over time through instantaneous changes in system variables; these changes occur at distinct points in time, where transitions and interactions are not continuous but occur at discrete intervals, which can be accurately represented with this method [7]. Three main components generally constitute a discrete event simulation model: input, process, and output. The number of vehicles arriving at a factory or the arrival of orders at a warehouse are examples of situations represented by discrete variables that assume integer values [8].

Continuous simulation systems, unlike discrete systems, assume uninterrupted variation of variables over time. For example, an airplane in motion with continuously changing speed and position is a typical continuous system [9]. In manufacturing and dynamic systems, continuous simulation is valuable for modeling real-time interactions and predicting the impact of different scenarios, making it a crucial tool for decision-making and process improvement [10, 11].

Although some systems can be considered continuous, continuous systems are those whose variables evolve non-stop over time [12]. In production systems there are continuous flow systems that are online manufacturing methods, these systems are based on the control and monitoring of the process, as well as continuous analysis and control techniques of the system to ensure the efficiency and quality of both the process and product [13] The responses of a system are tracked continuously during the simulation using "continuous simulation", which means that results are generated continuously throughout the simulation and not at predetermined intervals. This type of simulation is used for systems where the condition of the system changes over time, such as the water level in a dam or the movement of a plant [14].

For their part, Marmolejo, Santana and Granillo [15] describe that fluid simulation is used in a wide range of industrial procedures, including the operation of chemical plants and oil refineries. When designing a model for this specific type of system, it is essential to keep in mind that the state of the system components undergoes continuous modifications over time. However, most academic articles published in the field of simulation focus on the simulation of discrete events (those that alter at specific time intervals). Furthermore, not all simulated systems are necessarily completely continuous or discrete, but rather a combination of both, which some authors call hybrid or continuous-discrete change models.

In companies, it is necessary to have an effective tool for decision-making that allows the execution of experiments that are being carried out. Many companies currently choose to use simulation to adjust resources and processes without the need for interruptions in their production. Another case study carried out with the purpose of optimizing production capacity in a food company highlights the advantage of using simulation tools due to their optimal results, such that it was not necessary to stop real production during the different tests or simulated attempts [16].

In the automotive industry, companies can face various challenges that vary depending on the market to which they belong. However, by using simulation, it is possible to analyze these challenges efficiently thanks to the breadth of results it offers. For example, a company that manufactures crankcase covers has incorporated simulation using Flex Sim software to address its problems, such as the need to identify the optimal number of expensive machines, such as die-casting machines and vertical milling centers. This is due to the industry's budget constraints. In addition, they seek to optimize the distribution of operators and process stations to improve efficiency and reduce downtime in the manufacturing system [17].

Optimizing processes in the food industry is essential to achieve operational efficiency, product quality and regulatory compliance at optimal levels. Where currently it is required to be more competitive through the optimization of these processes, therefore, it is required to improve the use of resources that act in production [16].

Therefore, the applied case of the company specialized in the production and marketing of natural cassava starch and related products in Sucre, revolves around the inefficient management of the flow of materials and equipment within the production process. Cassava starch production plays a crucial role in the food industry, as cassava starch and flour are valuable ingredients used in a wide range of applications, including foods, pharmaceuticals, pulp and paper, and adhesives [18].

Natural cassava starch, a vital product for various industries, serves as a carbohydrate derived from the grinding of cassava, composed of amylose and amylopectin. This starch finds application in the industrial, food and pharmaceutical sectors, serving as an excipient, gelling agent, texturizer and water retainer [19].

The company's central problem revolves around the difficulties in reaching its theoretical production capacity of 200 tons of cassava starch per day, due to limitations in the production process and the supply chain. This situation is due to a combination of factors including inefficiency in tracking raw material inputs and equipment within the plant that can contribute to this production shortfall, leading to disruptions and reductions in operational efficiency. The lack of meticulous analysis to identify and address these bottlenecks has sometimes resulted in final product shortages, underscoring the importance of accurate demand estimation and effective management of productive resources to optimize company performance.

To propose improvement scenarios, a simulation model has been developed using specialized software tools such as FlexSim. The selection of a cassava starch producing company as a case study is especially appropriate, offering a unique opportunity to demonstrate the transformative impact that simulation models can have in the strategic analysis of industrial processes. This method allows us to precisely replicate the operation of the company's production system, ranging from the receipt of raw materials to the storage of final products. The comprehensive simulation of the process not only facilitates the identification and correction of bottlenecks, optimizing logistics management and aligning production with the real capabilities of the plant, but also allows solutions to be evaluated in a controlled environment, significantly reducing the risks associated with the implementation of changes in the real production process [15].

2   Literature Review

There are several production software available that are capable of simulating a company's production system [20]. These applications are designed to simulate various aspects of the supply chain, inventories and monitor dynamic process flows of activities and system, a notable example is the FlexSim software, which serves as a valuable tool to improve every scenario imaginable [21].

Recent research has shown that using simulation with FlexSim can generate significant impacts, such as a 43.92% reduction in wait times and an 88.93% increase in productivity. These results are concrete examples of the potential that simulation tools, specifically FlexSim, can have in complex operating environments. Furthermore, by understanding all the components involved in the implementation of this tool, a cost-benefit analysis was carried out which showed a difference of 43% compared to the estimated cost for the inventory area [22].

At the same time, there are other studies or scientific articles that focus on improving logistics production lines using FlexSim software. In one particular case, a military factory is described that modified its production approach, using FlexSim to optimize its four production lines, addressing problems related to productivity and costs in these lines, highlighting the importance of simulation by computer, throughout the study the urgency of increasing efficiency and reducing logistical expenses in production chains is being addressed. It is emphasized that only 10% of the time is spent in manufacturing and processing, while the remaining 90% is dedicated to storage, loading, waiting and transportation [23]. In this way, using computer simulation, improvements in efficiency, balance and cost reduction were finally obtained, which demonstrates the effectiveness of simulation in improving logistics production systems [23].

3   Simulation Model Building Assumptions

This work is based on the methodology proposed by [24], which provides a solid basis for understanding simulation and its application in decision-making in complex systems. Likewise, the FlexSim simulation software is used for model development. The productive process of a company dedicated to the production of native cassava starch was taken as an applied case. Firstly, the analysis was focused on all the elements involved in its production, from the acquisition of raw materials to the storage of the final product, which comprehensively address the characterization of the cassava starch production process. This includes collecting and analyzing historical data, creating a block diagram of the process, and statistical analysis of production using tools such as Statgraphic and R Studio.

Variables were considered: production capacity per day of the company, vehicle arrival time, tons of input input, tons of cassava starch, equipment capacity, storage utilization percentage, which are directly and indirectly throughout the simulation process of the continuous flow of the cassava starch production process.

In a second stage, a simulation model was created using the FlexSim software, which represents the behavior of the production process. To validate this model, following the methodology used, the optimal number of repetitions was initially determined using Eq. (1). A hypothesis test was then conducted by comparing the mean of the real data with the mean of the simulated data. In the event that the simulated problem is related to a process that is sought to be improved, it is essential that the model be tested under current operating conditions. This will provide us with behavior like what is actually observed in our process.

$$n = \left[\frac{\sigma Z_{\alpha/2}}{\in} \right]^2 \tag{1}$$

Once the model has been validated, the next step was the definition of the scenarios to be analyzed, which are directly related to pessimistic, optimistic and intermediate scenarios. In these, assumptions such as intermittency in the arrival of vehicles were evaluated, according to [25] the average yield of cassava in Sucre is 20 tons/ha.

Finally, strategies are evaluated to improve the flow of materials and input logistics, simulating different scenarios to analyze the system's response capacity to variations in market demand.

4 Results

4.1 Description of the Case Study

The cassava starch production process begins with the reception of transport trucks loaded with cassava. This stage begins with precise weighing on a truck scale, which incorporates detailed controls of weight, crop age and starch content. Unloading is carried out carefully, package by package, followed by dry cleaning using a vibrating screen that separates unwanted materials, such as shavings and mud, as well as part of the cassava cuticle.

Once cleaned, the yuccas are temporarily stored before undergoing a washing process in a specialized machine that uses jets of recirculated water to remove soil and impurities. Next, in two stages of cevaderas, the cassava roots in poor condition and any foreign elements present are removed. The crushed cassava then goes through two grinding stages, followed by a process of separation and extraction of starch from the bran using screens and jets of clean water.

The resulting starch slurry, which contains proteins, fats and some impurities, is subjected to a centrifugation, backwashing and storage process. To reduce humidity, centrifugal dehydrators are used that filter the slurry, removing as much water as possible. The remaining moisture is eliminated by Flash Dryer drying, achieving a native starch with a final moisture content between 12% and 13.5%. Finally, the dry starch is classified by sieving to eliminate coarse particles and the product is packaged using a conveyor belt, ready for subsequent storage and distribution. This exhaustive process ensures the quality and purity of cassava starch, ready for use in various industrial and food applications (Fig. 1).

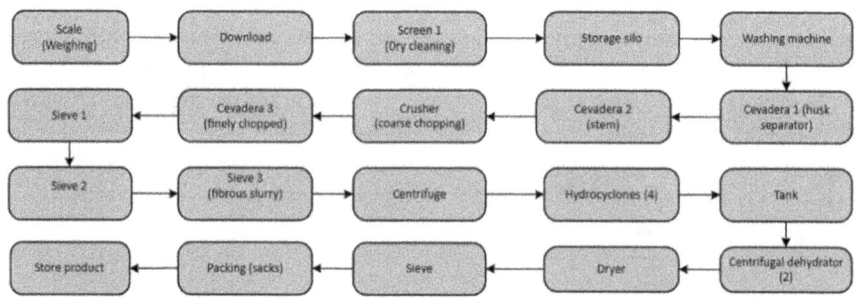

Fig. 1. Block diagram of cassava starch production process

4.2 Data Collection

Data collection and tabulation focused on the analysis of historical grinding records for the years 2020, 2021, and 2022. This detailed study involved a review of monthly operations, as well as an evaluation of productive and unproductive days associated with the mill. Cassava milling during the specified periods. To facilitate a more understandable and coherent analysis, we worked in units of tons of processed cassava, thus establishing a single functional unit for the study. In addition, the number of days worked each month was meticulously recorded, providing a clear view of operational continuity and variations in production capacity throughout the years analyzed.

The analysis of the quantities of cassava that can be processed per day reveals a distribution biased towards lower values, with an average production of 123.51 tons and a median of 152,724 tons (Fig. 2(a)). This difference suggests significant variability, supported by a standard deviation of 58.2074 tons and a range of 177.63 tons. This variability in production can be the result of several factors, such as fluctuations in raw materials, processing conditions, or machinery efficiency.

In Fig. 2(b), the statistical analysis of daily cassava starch production reveals a mean of 28.17 tons and a median of 33.17 tons, showing a bias towards low values. The standard deviation of 13.55 tons highlights significant dispersion, with productions ranging from 0 to 42.57 tons. The quartiles indicate a main concentration of production between 23.53 and 36.92 tons.

In Fig. 2(b), the statistical analysis of daily cassava starch production reveals a distribution skewed towards low values, with a mean of 28.17 tons and a median of 33.17 tons. The standard deviation of 13.55 tons highlights a considerable dispersion, evidencing productions that range from 0 to 42.57 tons. The quartiles show a main concentration of production between 23.53 and 36.92 tons, indicating the range where most of the daily production is concentrated. This detailed analysis provides a clear view of the distribution and variability of daily cassava starch production, essential aspects for effective production management and the identification of possible areas of improvement in the process. On the other hand, these findings are crucial to understanding the distribution of production volumes and can point out areas for improvement in the production process, as well as provide valuable information for production capacity planning.

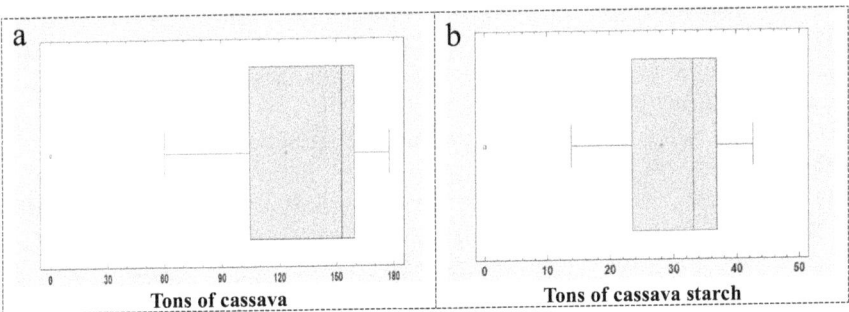

Fig. 2. Behavior of industrial cassava and cassava starch (2020 to 2022) and frequency histogram of the data.

Finally, regarding the number of packages of cassava starch in 25 kg presentations, the analysis presented in Fig. 3 reveals that the average production is 1126.92 packages, with an upper median of 1326.71 packages. This difference suggests a bias toward lower production values. The standard deviation of 542,046 packages indicates high variability in production. The production range goes from 0 to 1702.64 packages, with 50% of the data concentrated between 941.334 and 1476.99 packages.

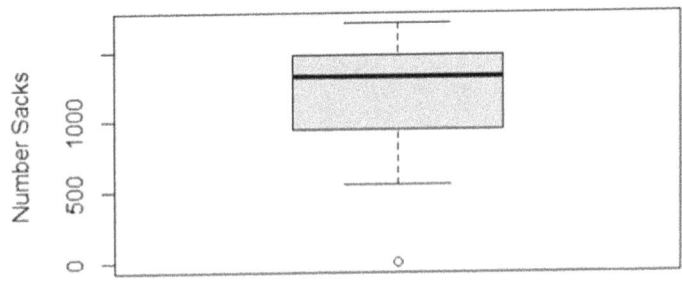

Fig. 3. Behavior of cassava starch bags from (2020 to 2022).

4.3   Model Coding

When evaluating the company's production system, it is crucial to initially understand the type of system being analyzed. During the code design phase for the system, it was identified that it operates both discretely and continuously. In the initial stage of the process, the system behaves discretely; However, it becomes a continuous process when the cassava begins to be processed. At the end of the process, it becomes discreet again by producing lumps of tons of starch.

With this understanding, it was decided to clearly define key locations within the system, such as processing areas and temporary warehouses. Additionally, machine capacity limitations and process flow were evaluated to ensure effective transformation from discrete to continuous units at the start, with input of raw material. Similarly, at the end of the process, the system converts units from fluid to solid form, allowing starch to be output in tons. After defining the locations, entities and other critical requirements, and considering the operational logic of the system, the process was coded. This code was developed considering the specific capabilities of the production area for the efficient production of cassava starch packages.

Understanding the type of system evaluated was essential for building the model. For the design, it was necessary to correctly model the entire simulation system and specify the capacity and operating time of each machine during a full 24-h workday. The model is composed of a discrete part and a fluid part. The discrete components include a source, 3 queues, 1 combiner, and a conveyor, while the fluid components are: 1 ItemToFluid, 3 fluid tanks ("FluidTank"), 18 fluid pipes ("FluidPipe"), 16 fluid processors ("FluidProcessor") and 1 "FluidToItem". The logical order and location of the machines is shown in Fig. 4.

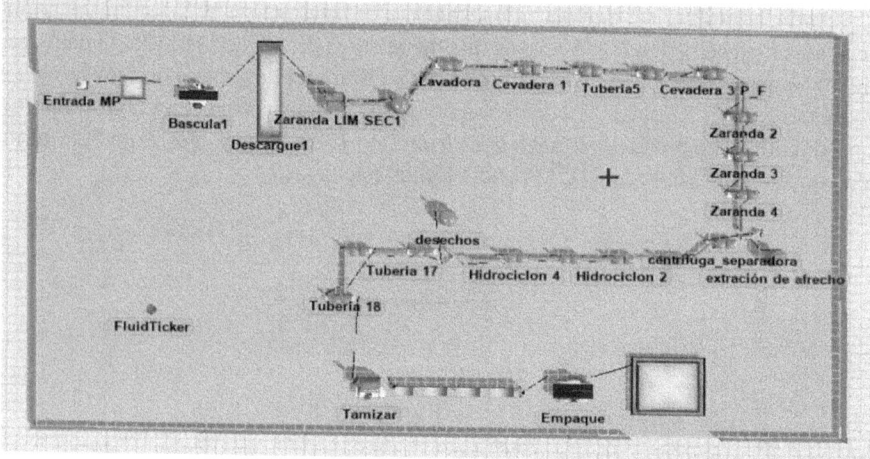

Fig. 4. Layout of the production process in FlexSim

The number of tons of cassava that enter the system is defined from the source or the source under the Arrival Schedule command, which establishes an arrival time of the raw material to the system in a total of 19 arrivals, with an arrival time of 720 min, so that a certain amount of cassava comes out in tons in a certain time. It was established that the flow element that represents the cassava in the discrete part is a box that simulates the raw material input process. For the starch generated, a shepere is used that reaches the sieving machine from the entire process in the fluid part of the model. In packaging, it is represented by a cylinder that simulates the combination of the starch generated and the individual packaging of 25 kg each.

4.4 System Validation

To determine the optimal number of replicates per run, initial calculations were performed using Eq. (1) with a 5% significance level. The results indicated that the optimal number of replicates was approximately 697, with a margin of error of 10%. Subsequently, a Z test was applied for the mean of two samples, using the historical data of the quantities of packages produced by the company and the simulated data. The Z value resulting from the test was -0.9, within the acceptance limits. This confirms the homogeneity in the dispersion of both data sets, since there is not enough evidence to reject the null hypothesis.

By carrying out 697 replications for each scenario, the confidence interval that validates the simulation model was obtained. The scenarios were established to observe the behavior of the system under different raw material input conditions, in order to determine the amount of starch obtained and, therefore, the number of 25 kg packages generated. Table 1 presents the confidence intervals calculated for each scenario, along with the standard deviation, and the minimum and maximum values of the data. This meticulous approach ensures rigorous validation of the model, providing a solid basis for decision-making in optimizing the cassava starch production process.

Table 1. Model Sets

Esc	Cassava per day (Tons)"	Mean (95% CI)			Standard scenario	Min.	Max.
1	80	800,90	<	802,44	5,96	788	812
2	90	880,70	<	882,27	6,03	867	894
3	100	1000,93	<	1002,71	6,85	983	1016
4	120	1201,28	<	1203,31	7,81	1181	1217
5	130	1281,00	<	1283,08	8,00	1260	1296
6	140	1401,15	<	1403,2	7,89	1376	1414
7	150	1480,518	<	1481,166	8,617	1453	1506
8	160	1600,407	<	1601,072	8,843	1573	1626
9	170	1681,13	<	1683,22	8,06	1658	1695
10	180	1801,08	<	1803,33	8,68	1777	1816
11	190	1881,58	<	1883,88	8,87	1858	1896
12	200	2001,82	<	2004,27	9,45	1976	2019

Figure 5 shows the behavior of the number of bags generated in each scenario, taking into account the minimum and maximum data established in Table 1. The figure presents a linear trend line with a coefficient of determination R^2 of 0.9938, indicating a precise fit to the data obtained. This value suggests that approximately 99.38% of the variability in the data can be explained by the linear trend model, which shows a relationship between the independent variable and the dependent variable.

In addition, an equation has been generated that allows forecasts to be made based on the data, where "y" represents the dependent variable. This equation offers a robust predictive tool for future scenarios based on current observations.

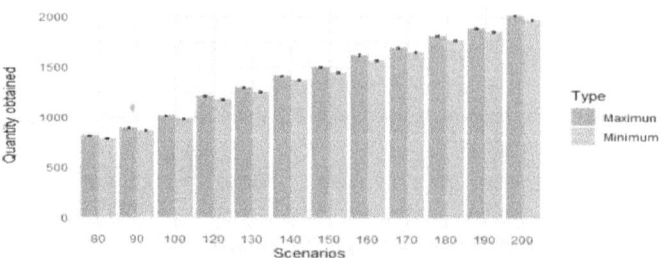

Fig. 5. Number of bags generated for the scenarios

In Fig. 6. The data and the experimental graph corresponding to scenarios 7 and 8 of 150 and 160 tons are shown. The results present a 95% confidence interval for all scenarios, which means that there is a 95% probability that the data provided, which simulate the number of bags generated from 150 and 160 tons, are within the established numerical range. The graphical interpretation of this scenario is shown in Fig. 5.

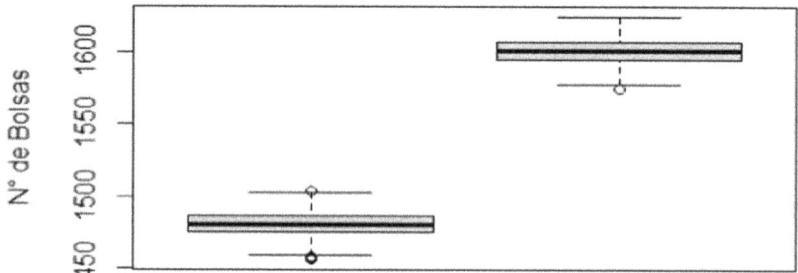

Fig. 6. BoxPlot diagram for the 150 and 160 Ton scenario

The experiment report for this scenario indicates that there is a mean of 1480.518 with a margin of error of 0.648, a median of 1483, a standard deviation of 8.617 and a minimum and maximum value of 1453 and 1506 respectively for the scenario of 150 tons. For 160 tons there is an average of 1600.407 with a margin of error of 0.665, median of 1601, standard deviation of 8.843, a minimum data of 1573 and a maximum of 1626. The data, as seen in Fig. 5, are within the confidence interval, suggesting that there is no significant evidence to affirm that the simulation model is not valid. Table 1 presents the confidence intervals calculated for each of the individual scenarios, along with the standard deviation, and the minimum and maximum data.

The 150-ton stage accurately simulates the company's material flow. According to recent research, the company has the capacity to process 52,000 tons of cassava per year, resulting in 13,000 tons of starch produced [21]. This means that they would process approximately 153 tons of cassava in a full 24-h day, generating a total of 38 tons of starch, equivalent to 1,512 bags in presentations of 25 kg each. Figure 7 shows the results of the experimentation, validating the proposed model.

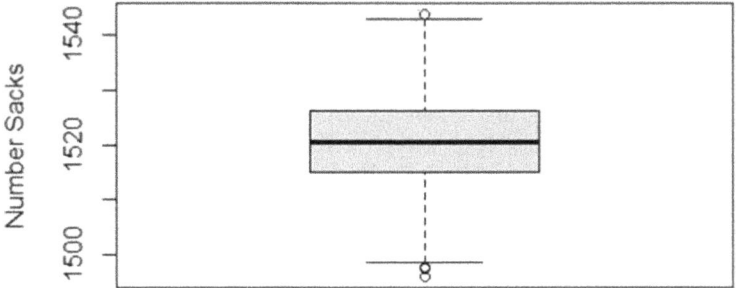

Fig. 7. BoxPlot diagram for the 153 Ton scenario

The experiment report for this scenario indicates that there is a mean of 1520.472 with a margin of error of 0.653, a median of 1521, a standard deviation of 8.689 and a minimum and maximum value of 1495 and 1546 respectively. Thus, it is confirmed that the 1512 bags generated in the real scenario are within the confidence interval of the minimum and maximum data presented in the experiment.

5 Conclusion

Manufacturing has moved from a conventional technical activity to a strategic management function. It is now recognized as a crucial component in companies' global strategies. This evolution has driven the creation of an academic field specialized in manufacturing or operations strategy. This suggests that companies are increasingly recognizing the importance of efficiently managing their production processes to achieve their strategic objectives and remain competitive.

Simulation is presented as a valuable tool to address challenges in the manufacturing industry. It allows the behavior of real production systems to be replicated, which facilitates the identification and correction of bottlenecks, the optimization of logistics management and the alignment of production with the real capacities of the plant. This has been shown in studies where the use of simulations has led to significant improvements in efficiency and productivity.

The importance and effectiveness of simulation is highlighted using tools such as Statgrafit, FlexSim and RStudio to address specific challenges in cassava starch production, as identified in the company. The analysis and statistical tests developed, focused on the number of 25 kg packages, demonstrate that the simulation model is an essential tool to predict the number of bags that will be produced from a certain amount of cassava in tons that enters the the system. When comparing the simulated scenarios with the real data, it is concluded that there is an average percentage variation of 0.018%. This result indicates that the simulated data closely approximates the real data, with a slight tendency to be higher. Therefore, the simulation model provides an accurate and reliable estimate to produce cassava starch in the company.

References

1. Adamides, E.D.: Linking operations strategy to the corporate strategy process: a practice perspective. Bus. Process. Manag. J. **21**(2), 267–287 (2015). https://doi.org/10.1108/BPMJ-07-2013-0107
2. Fazal, H., Muhammad, J., Zahoor, U.H.: Operational perspective of SMEs performance and competitive priorities practices: path analytic approach. Studies Business Economics **15**(1), 55–67 (2020). https://doi.org/10.2478/SBE-2020-0006
3. Analuisa, F.L.: Relationship of industry 4.0 technologies in business development. a literature review. May 2023. Available http://doi.org/10. Accessed 7 Oct 2023
4. Rojas, C.P., Pacheco, C.M., Niebles, L.D., Hernández, H.G., Niebles, W.A.: Cultura organizacional y estrategias para el manejo del cambio en PyMEs de la costa caribe colombiana Organizational culture and strategies for the management of change in SMEs of the Colombian Caribbean Coast. **41**(36), 2020. Available https://www.revistaespacios.com
5. Cornejo Gómez, D.: Análisis de la falta de control en el sistema de inventarios y logística de la empresa fármaco veterinaria s.a. favesa de la ciudad de guayaquil en el periodo 2010–2014. (2016)
6. Muñiz Edgar, S., et al.: diseño, analisis y evaluación de un proceso con la ayuda de la administración de operaciones (2015)
7. Fritzson, P.: Introduction to Modeling and Simulation of Technical and Physical Systems with Modelica (2012).https://doi.org/10.1002/9781118094259
8. Regaliza, J.C.P., Gual, J.C., Val, P.A.: Simulación como herramienta de ayuda para la toma de decisiones empresariales. Un caso práctico (2016)
9. Law, A.M.: Simulation modeling and analysis. McGraw-Hill Education (2015)
10. Miñan-Olivos, G.S., Cardoza-Sernaque, M.A., Cisneros-Hilario, C.B.: Tactical production planning. Simulation of data under uncertainty scenarios | Planificación táctica de la producción: Simulación de datos ante escenarios de incertidumbre. Rev. Venezolana de Gerencia **27**(8), 1213–1229 (2022). https://doi.org/10.52080/rvgluz.27.8.31
11. Fullana Belda, C., Grande, E.U.: los modelos de simulación: una herramienta multidisciplinar de investigación
12. Kofman, E.: Simulación de Sistemas Continuos. Notas de Clase
13. Tejeda, A.S.: Mejoras de lean manufacturing en los sistemas productivos. Cienc Soc, vol. Volumen XXXVI, pp. 278–279 (2011). Available: http://www.redalyc.org/articulo.oa?id=87019757005. Accessed 22 Oct 2023
14. Lara, J., et al.: Adsorción de plomo y cadmio en sistema continuo de lecho fijo sobre residuos de cacao. Revista ION **29**(2), 113–124 (2016). https://doi.org/10.18273/REVION.V29N2-2016009
15. Simón Marmolejo, Francisca Santana, Robles Rafael Granillo, Macías Víctor Manuel Piedra, and I. Mayorga, "La simulación con FlexSim, una fuente alternativa para la toma de decisiones en las operaciones de un sistema híbrido. enero-Científica, **17**(1), 39–49 (2013)
16. Vanessa, L., Ariza, P., Felizzola Jimenez, H.A.: Optimización de la capacidad de producción en una empresa de alimentos usando simulación de eventos discretos Optimizing production capacity in a food company using discrete event simulation (2020)
17. Chawla, S., Singari, R.M.: Modelling and simulation of crankcase cover manufacturing in the automobile industry. J. Sci. Ind. Res. (India) **82**(6), 597–602 (2023). https://doi.org/10.56042/jsir.v82i06.1816
18. Cobana, M.: Revista boliviana de química proceso de extracción de almidón de yuca por vía seca
19. "Almidones de Sucre - Almidón de Yuca." Available: https://almidonesdesucre.com.co/. Accessed 22 Oct 2023

20. Krynke, M.: Personnel management on the production line using the FlexSim simulation environment. Manufacturing Technol. **21**(5), 657–667 (2021). https://doi.org/10.21062/mft.2021.073
21. Ashish B Kanse and Ashish T Patil.:Manufacturing Plant LayoutOptimization Using Simulation (2020). Available www.ijisrt.com
22. García, S., Montenegro, D.: Implementation and evaluation of lean healthcare tools through the FlexSim simulator. In: Proceedings of the LACCEI international Multi-conference for Engineering, Education and Technology, Latin American and Caribbean Consortium of Engineering Institutions (2021). https://doi.org/10.18687/LACCEI2021.1.1.594
23. Dong, H., Wang, Z.; Logistics Production Lines Optimization Analysis Based on Flexsim (2017)
24. EduardoGarcía, D., Heriberto García Reyes, L.E.C.B.: Simulación y análisis de sistemas con ProModel, 2da Edición (2012)
25. Dr. J. C. R. Ing. Otto Vila Flórez.: El desafío de las cadenas de suministro Finanzas y Desarrollo (2022)
26. García Paternina, M., Cardona Arbeláez, A.A., García Mogollón, C.A.: Diagnóstico del manejo del afrecho de yuca en el departamento de Sucre. In: Innovación en la Región Caribe de Colombia: aportes teóricos y buenas prácticas, Editorial CECAR (2020). https://doi.org/10.21892/9789585547858.9

Experimental Results of a Cascade Control for Autonomous Attitude Tracking in a UAV with Actuator Compensation

Juan E. Ruiz$^{(\boxtimes)}$, Omendey Sanchez Alarcón, and Pablo S. Rivadeneira

Universidad Nacional de Colombia, Facultad de Minas, Grupo GITA,
80#65-224 Medellín, Colombia
{jruizz,omjsanchezal,psrivade}@unal.edu.co

Abstract. This paper presents a cascade control strategy for attitude tracking in unmanned aerial vehicles (UAVs), addressing external actuator disturbances. UAVs have become increasingly relevant in various fields, necessitating precise control strategies for enhanced performance. The study focuses on a quadcopter model and employs a PID-P cascade controller, incorporating an additional loop to account for battery dynamics and disturbances in the electronic speed controllers (ESC) and brushless DC motors (BLDC). The proposed control strategy aims to improve trajectory tracking, disturbance rejection, and robustness. The research includes the development of a specialized test platform that allows for safe and accurate implementation and telemetry of the control algorithms. The results demonstrate the efficacy of the cascade control with an auxiliary loop in achieving desired angular positions and velocities, highlighting significant performance improvements compared to traditional control methods.

Keywords: UAV · quadcopter · cascade control · PID-P controller · actuator disturbances · trajectory tracking · robust control

1 Introduction

Unmanned aerial vehicles (UAVs) have become increasingly relevant in various fields such as exploration, aerial search, precise spraying in agriculture, and aerial photography for topographic studies. These devices offer significant advantages over conventional helicopters or airplanes, including maneuverability, portability, control, and cost-effectiveness [1–3].

It is essential to continue researching and improving both the physical structure and navigation control systems of UAVs to enhance maneuverability, avoid collisions, and reduce costs from potential damages [4]. While simulations help in understanding control strategies, real UAV implementations in secure environments provide a more comprehensive understanding.

Direct implementation of control strategies in UAVs can be risky and potentially damaging, affecting costs and experimentation time [5]. Platforms that

© The Author(s), under exclusive license to Springer Nature Switzerland AG 2025
J. C. Figueroa-García et al. (Eds.): WEA 2024, CCIS 2223, pp. 138–149, 2025.
https://doi.org/10.1007/978-3-031-74598-0_12

allow safe testing of control algorithms, such as those by Eureka Dynamics and Quanser, are available but can be costly and limited in customization [6,7].

Research on UAVs spans various areas, including dynamic modeling, control algorithm design, and detection schemes [8]. Studies have developed control algorithms using sliding mode techniques for trajectory tracking and robustness, though these often overlook actuator dynamics and have high computational costs [9].

Detection systems, critical for UAV performance, have advanced significantly. Systems designed to provide reliable measurements despite noise and errors have shown promising results [10]. Research has also introduced adaptive formation control systems for multiple UAVs, enhancing cooperative task performance and collision avoidance [12,13].

Recent work on dynamic modeling of quadcopters using Newton-Euler equations and sliding mode control laws has demonstrated robustness and reliability, especially when using UWB sensors for position estimation in indoor environments [14].

This study proposes a classical control strategy for UAV attitude dynamics using a PID-P cascade controller and an additional loop considering battery dynamics. The paper is structured as follows: 1) Introduction; 2) Test platform; 3) UAV mathematical model; 4) Control strategy; 5) Implementation; 6) Results.

2   Testing Platform

With the growing interest in improving and optimizing drone performance, it has become crucial to examine how drones behave in different situations and to evaluate how they react when combined with various control strategies to manage their attitude, altitude, and automatic maneuvers [15]. This increased interest has generated a clear need in the academic and research fields to explore and apply various control techniques. The fundamental objective of this research is to comprehensively analyze drone performance and determine which controller design maximizes the system to achieve the desired behavior.

The literature on attitude control in drones identifies three main approaches to evaluating controller designs: trial and error [15–17], simulations [18,19], and the use of an external platform [20,21]. Trial and error offers realistic insight but can be costly and risky. Simulations are safer but may not consider all uncertainties. Using an external platform secures the drone but may involve additional unplanned modifications.

Considering the above, we propose to carry out the necessary tests using a specially designed test platform. This platform is based on a gyroscope-type mechanical device, with a quadcopter drone at its center to perform movements safely using its actuators. The structure will be equipped with encoder-type sensors on each gyroscope pivot to accurately measure angular position. In addition, the drone can be powered directly by a battery or through a power source. The platform allows the assembled drone to have a full 360° angular movement in all three spatial axes.

In addition, it facilitates telemetry of all system dynamic variables, including angular position, angular velocity, actuator dynamics, and supply voltage. Figure 1 shows the platform design.

Fig. 1. CAD model of the plataform used.

3   Dynamic Model

3.1   UAV Model

The UAV of interest, for which it is desired to define a dynamic model, is a multirotor with four engines. These engines are configured in what is known as "X" position, meaning that two of them are located at the front of the vehicle and the other two at the rear.

Understanding the relative orientation between bodies is fundamental to construct the mathematical representation of the UAV quadrotor, especially how it is aligned with respect to a stationary observer. This explanation is based on [22], taking into account the following considerations:

– The movement of the UAV is represented using Newton's equations, formulated concerning two distinct frames of reference: an inertial frame denoted as F^i and a non-inertial frame denoted as F_v.
– The forces exerted on the UAV are explained within the framework of the UAV's rigid body, identified as F^v.
– Onboard sensors, like accelerometers and gyroscopes, gather data relative to the UAV's rigid body because of their placement on the UAV.

– The testing setup provides the capability to measure spatial angles or the angles between F_i and F_v.

Taking into account the above, the following hypotheses are proposed for the modeling of the UAV:

– The UAV is considered a rigid body with six degrees of freedom (three spatial movements and three angular movements).
– The center of mass is located at the geometric center of the UAV.
– Aerodynamic effects are not considered.
– Flat Earth model and constant gravity.
– The model is planted like a phenomenological-based semi-physical models (PBSM) developed in continuous time.

To understand the dynamic behavior of the system, it is essential to analyze both its kinematics and dynamics. $[\dot{x}, \dot{y}, \dot{z}]^T \in \mathbb{R}^3$ is defined as the spatial velocity vector, and $[\dot{\phi}, \dot{\theta}, \dot{\psi}]^T \in \mathbb{R}^3$ as the angular velocity vector, both referred to the reference frame F_i. Additionally, $[\dot{u}, \dot{v}, \dot{w}]^T \in \mathbb{R}^3$ is defined as the spatial vector of accelerations, and $[\dot{p}, \dot{q}, \dot{r}]^T \in \mathbb{R}^3$ as the vector angular acceleration, both in the reference frame F_v [22]. These variables are considered as the system's states. $\{I_x, I_y, I_z, m, g\}$ represent constants of the model, the first three represent the moments of inertial about each spatial axis of the body, m is the total mass of the UAV and g the gravitational acceleration.

According to the above, the resulting UAV model after establishing and operating the force and torque balances, produces a set of 12 equations of state as described in [22]. Taking into account that the UAV under study is a rotary wing drone with four engines, which will be placed on the test platform suggested for this project, as specified in the previous section. Given the influence of this platform on the UAV behavior, it is expected that it will not exhibit translational dynamics. Consequently, the model is simplified to just the set of equations detailed in (1) describing the UAV attitude dynamics.

$$
\left.
\begin{aligned}
\dot{\phi} &= p + r \cos(\phi) \tan(\theta) + q \sin(\phi) \tan(\theta), & \dot{p} &= \frac{I_y - I_z}{I_x} rq + \frac{\tau_x}{I_x} \\
\dot{\theta} &= q \cos(\phi) - r \sin(\phi), & \dot{q} &= \frac{I_z - I_x}{I_y} pr + \frac{\tau_y}{I_y} \\
\dot{\psi} &= r \frac{\cos(\phi)}{\cos(\theta)} + q \frac{\sin(\phi)}{\cos(\theta)}, & \dot{r} &= \frac{I_x - I_y}{I_z} pq + \frac{\tau_z}{I_z}
\end{aligned}
\right\} \quad (1)
$$

3.2   Actuator Model

It works with a configuration of four actuators. The inputs τ_x, τ_y, τ_z, and f_t should be defined according to the quantity and distribution of these actuators or can be expressed the angular velocities of each of the actuators in terms of the torques τ_x, τ_y, τ_z, and the thrust force f_t, where Ω_i is the angular velocity of motor i, l is the distance between any motor and the geometric center of the UAV, d is the aerodynamic drag factor of the propeller, and b is the motor thrust factor, as is shown in Eq. (2).

$$\left.\begin{array}{ll} \Omega_1^2 = \dfrac{f_t}{4b} - \dfrac{\tau_x}{4bl} + \dfrac{\tau_y}{4bl} - \dfrac{\tau_z}{4d}, & \Omega_2^2 = \dfrac{f_t}{4b} - \dfrac{\tau_x}{4bl} - \dfrac{\tau_y}{4bl} + \dfrac{\tau_z}{4d} \\[2mm] \Omega_3^2 = \dfrac{f_t}{4b} + \dfrac{\tau_x}{4bl} - \dfrac{\tau_y}{4bl} - \dfrac{\tau_z}{4d}, & \Omega_4^2 = \dfrac{f_t}{4b} + \dfrac{\tau_x}{4bl} + \dfrac{\tau_y}{4bl} + \dfrac{\tau_z}{4d} \end{array}\right\} \quad (2)$$

Inputs to the UAV model include torques (τ_x, τ_y, τ_z) and thrust force (f_t), which directly affects the translational model. f_t is substituted by the body's equilibrium force ($f_t = mg$) due to platform influence. These inputs translate to angular velocities of quadcopter motors (Ω_1, Ω_2, Ω_3, Ω_4) via Eq. (2). Practically, ESC + BLDC sets generate these velocities from a PWM signal at 250 Hz. Under ideal conditions, the algebraic relationship between motor angular velocity square and corresponding PWM signal (experimentally determined) is expressed in Eq. (3).

$$U_{i[us]} = \frac{900}{1166400}\Omega_{i[rad/s]}^2 + 1100. \quad (3)$$

UAVs rely on batteries powering brushless motors (BLDC) for thrust. Battery discharge is assumed constant, but dynamics vary during charge/discharge [24]. Each battery behaves uniquely despite similar construction [24]. Hence, modeling the ESC + BLDC assembly is more effective, comprising:

- **Brushless DC motor (BLDC):** are widely used and implemented in the development of UAVs. They are responsible for generating rotary motion, which, through the propellers, generates the necessary thrust for the UAV's flight.
- **Electronic Speed Control (ESC):** is a set of electronic components designed to construct a three-phase power signal from a direct current power source, which will excite the BLDC.

The main objective of this research is to develop a model for the assembly. To demonstrate the influence of voltage and/or battery charge on the speed of the brushless motor, a constant duration pulse was applied to the ESC input, while the revolutions per minute (RPM) of the BLDC were measured using a velocity sensor along with battery voltage. The collected data underwent filtering with a 3rd-order Butterworth filter, revealing the dynamic characteristics of the system, as illustrated in Fig. 2.

In this scenario, the dynamics of the assembly system can be empirically represented as an input-output relationship using an autoregressive model with exogenous input (ARX model) [25]. This structure provides implementation advantages due to its simplicity, allowing for linear modeling of input-output effects and reducing impacts within real-time control algorithms. It is described by Eq. (4).

$$A(q)y(t) = B(q)u(t) + C(q)w(t) + e(t) \quad (4)$$

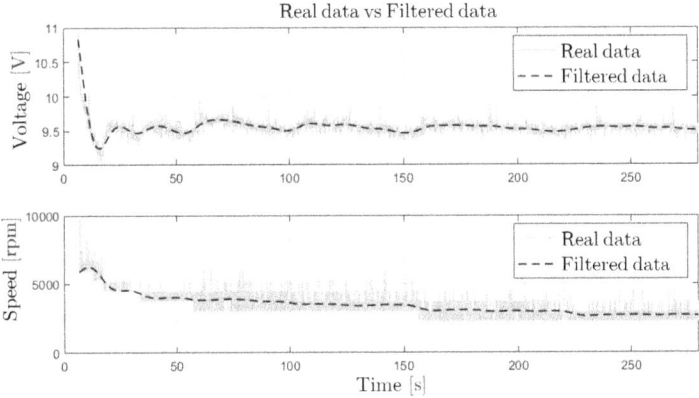

Fig. 2. Battery voltage and BLDC angular velocity dynamics after applying a step pulse to ESC.

when q is the right-shift operator, $y(t)$ is the speed of the brushless motor and the output, $u(t)$ is the duration of the input pulses of the ESC and the known input, $w(t)$ is the battery voltage and the non-manipulated input, $e(t)$ is the model residuals, and $A(q) = 1 + a_1 q^{-1} + \cdots + a_{n_a} q^{-n_a}$, $B(q) = b_1 q^{-1} + \cdots + b_{n_b} q^{-n_b}$, and $C(q) = c_1 q^{-1} + \cdots + c_{n_c} q^{-n_c}$ are the coefficients of the model.

The matrix form of (4) is $y(t) = \varphi^T(t)\theta$,

where $(\cdot)^T$ stands for the matrix transpose, θ is the parameter vector, and $\varphi(t)$ is the output and input matrix, which can be seen as

$$\varphi(t) = \begin{bmatrix} -y(t-1) & \cdots & -y(t-n_a) \\ u(t-1) & \cdots & u(t-n_b) \\ w(t-1) & \cdots & w(t-n_c) \end{bmatrix}, \tag{5}$$

$$\theta^T = \begin{bmatrix} a_1 \cdots a_{n_a} & b_1 \cdots b_{n_b} & c_1 \cdots c_{n_c} \end{bmatrix}. \tag{6}$$

For simplicity, it was assumed that the polynomials are first order, and then, a pseudorandom binary sequence (PRBS) was used to compute the unknown parameters of the model θ.

As the proposed model is linear with respect to the parameters, the least-square identification method was used to compute θ, resulting in the following values

$$\theta = \begin{bmatrix} -0.89 & 1526800 & 107.75 \end{bmatrix}^T. \tag{7}$$

Finally, the model of the actuator assembly expressed as a discrete transfer function with a time stamp of $4ms$ is show in Eq. (8).

$$Y(Z) = \frac{1526800 z^{-1}}{1 - 0.89 z^{-1}} U(z) + \frac{107.75 z^{-1}}{1 - 0.89 z^{-1}} W(z). \tag{8}$$

4   Control Algorithm

A PID-P cascade control algorithm for quadcopter drones consists of two main loops: an internal proportional controller for angular velocities and an external proportional-integral-derivative controller for spatial angles. This setup ensures precise regulation of the drone's attitude, maintaining stability against disturbances.

Additionally, a control loop monitors UAV battery charge by voltage. Positioned at the system's end, it generates a signal to counteract battery dynamics, ensuring optimal and safe flight.

The algorithm aims to maintain stable angular trajectory despite changes in battery charge, compensating for efficiency loss. Figure 3 depicts the algorithm's block diagram, where C_E, C_I, and C_B represent external, internal, and battery controller transfer functions, respectively, and $f(\tau_x, \tau_y, \tau_z, f_t)$ models Eq. (2) with $f_t = mg$.

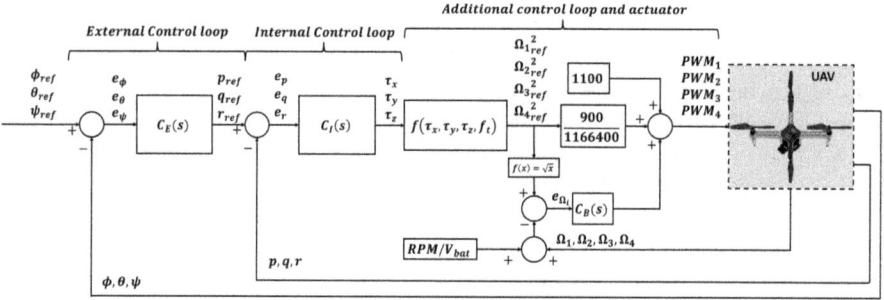

Fig. 3. Control algorithm block diagram.

4.1   Cascade Attitude Control

Typically, the design of such control algorithms is carried out in the Laplace domain [23]. The set of equations in (1) can be linearized using a first-order Taylor expansion approximation, resulting in the Eq. 9.

$$\left. \begin{array}{cc} \dfrac{\Phi}{P} = \dfrac{1}{s}, & \dfrac{P}{\tau_x} = \dfrac{1/I_x}{s}, \\[2mm] \dfrac{\Theta}{Q} = \dfrac{1}{s}, & \dfrac{Q}{\tau_y} = \dfrac{1/I_y}{s}, \\[2mm] \dfrac{\Psi}{R} = \dfrac{1}{s}, & \dfrac{R}{\tau_z} = \dfrac{1/I_z}{s}, \end{array} \right\} \tag{9}$$

The internal control governs UAV angular velocities (p, q, and r) in each spatial axis. According to Eq. (9), angular velocities relate to torque via

$\frac{V_{ang}}{\tau} = \frac{A}{s}$, where A represents the inverse of inertial momentum constant along axes. The inner loop employs proportional control ($C_I = K_{pI}$) to mimic first-order system behavior ($\frac{t_s}{4}s + 1$), targeting a settling time (t_s) of 0.2 s.

Similarly, the external loop employs PID control (Eq. (10)) with a low-pass filter in the derivative term (τ_d). Pole placement ensures second-order system behavior ($s^2 + 2\zeta\omega_n + \omega_n^2$), designed for a settling time close to 2 s and less than 15% overshoot, with $\zeta = 0.79$ and $\omega_n = 2.52$ respectively.

$$C_E = K_{pE} + K_{iE}\frac{1}{s} + K_{dE}\frac{s}{t_d s + 1} \tag{10}$$

Each of the variables to be controlled (ϕ, θ, and ψ) has its own control loop, as illustrated in Fig. 3. To regulate the angle ϕ, a proportional gain of $K_{pI,p} = 0.8$ is used in the internal control, while in the external control, the gains $K_{pE,\phi} = 7$, $K_{iE,\phi} = 800$, $K_{dE,\phi} = 0.1$, and a derivative time $\tau_{d,\phi} = 0.5$ are employed. To regulate the angle θ, a proportional gain of $K_{pI,q} = 0.6$ is used in the internal control, while in the external control, the gains $K_{pE,\theta} = 9$, $K_{iE,\theta} = 100$, $K_{dE,\theta} = 0.5$, and a derivative time $\tau_{d,\theta} = 0.5$ are employed. To regulate the angle ψ, a proportional gain of $K_{pI,r} = -0.6$ is used in the internal control, while in the external control, the gains $K_{pE,\psi} = 9$, $K_{iE,\psi} = 100$, $K_{dE,\psi} = 0.5$, and a derivative time $\tau_{d,\psi} = 0.5$ are employed.

4.2   PI Control for Actuator Disturbance Compensation

Naturally, the inputs to the UAV are the torques τ_x, τ_y, τ_z, and the thrust force f_t. These are translated into the angular velocities produced by the four motors of the quadcopter, Ω_1, Ω_2, Ω_3, and Ω_4, through the relationships shown in (2). In practical terms, these velocities are generated by the ESC + BLDC set from a given PWM signal at 250 Hz. Under ideal conditions and without disturbances, the algebraic relationship between the square of the angular velocity of the motors and the corresponding PWM signal (experimentally determined) is expressed as shown in Eq. (3).

Given that the state of charge of the battery and failures in the ESC or the BLDC motor can influence the final speed of the actuators (considered as permanent input disturbances), an auxiliary loop is proposed to compensate, if necessary, the angular velocity demanded by the PID-P control, as illustrated in Fig. 3.

The control strategy for this auxiliary feedback loop is a standard PI (proportional - integral) controller designed using the pole assignment method and Diophantine's equation according to [26], where $G(s) = \frac{B(s)}{A(s)}$ is the transfer function that establishes the relationship between the time of the PWM signal and the angular velocity of the motor in the Laplace domain, whore $B(s) = 4.037 \times 10^8$ and $A(s) = s + 28.26$, and $C(s) = \frac{P(s)}{L(s)}$ is the transfer function of the controller, where $P(s) = K_p s + K_i$ and $L(s) = s$. By operating these closed-loop transfer functions and equating their denominator to a desired polynomial of the form $p_d = s^2 + 80s + 2.3446$, constructed from a settling time of 1 s and a percentage overshoot of 1%, it is found that the controller gain values are $K_p = 1.2816 \times 10^{-17}$ and $K_i = 5.8078 \times 10^{-16}$.

5   Implementation

Using the developed test platform and a custom quadrotor UAV with 4 motors, the cascade control algorithm was implemented both alone and with an auxiliary loop. The system has all the necessary components to execute the control algorithm shown in Fig. 3 and perform real-time telemetry on each of its variables.

Figures 4 and 5 show the results obtained by implementing the cascade control strategy and its behavior with the auxiliary loop. Two tests were carried out: one with only the cascade control loop and another with the same control loop but adding an auxiliary loop compensation to each control action. In the implementation of the compensation with the auxiliary loop, it is activated after 5 s. To highlight the behavior of the auxiliary loop, a reference for the ψ angle was set at 0° throughout the data collection, and a reference change for the θ angle from 0^circ to 15^circ and then to -15^circ and finally back to 0^circ all at 15, 25 and 35 s respectively.

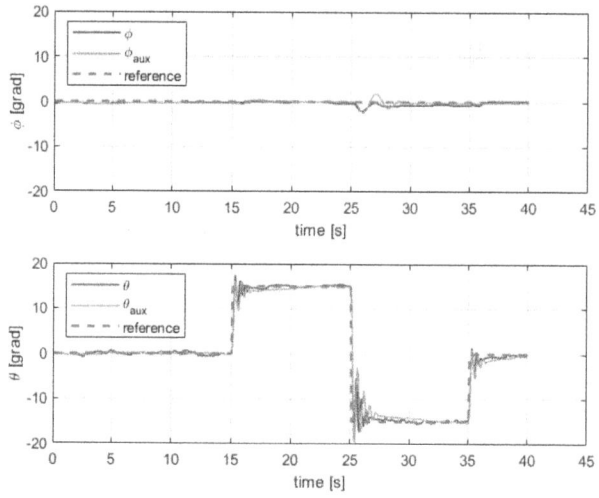

Fig. 4. Time trajectories obtained for the following states ϕ and θ.

The performance indices for the cascade control loop and the same control with an auxiliary loop exhibit notable differences. In the cascade control loop alone, the IAE is 258.6, ITAE is 6028.6, ISE is 1506.6, and ITSE is 37856.6. Conversely, with the addition of an auxiliary loop, the IAE increases to 338.76, ITAE to 8607.71, ISE to 2010.15, and ITSE to 51366.48. These results indicate that the auxiliary loop amplifies the performance indices, suggesting higher error

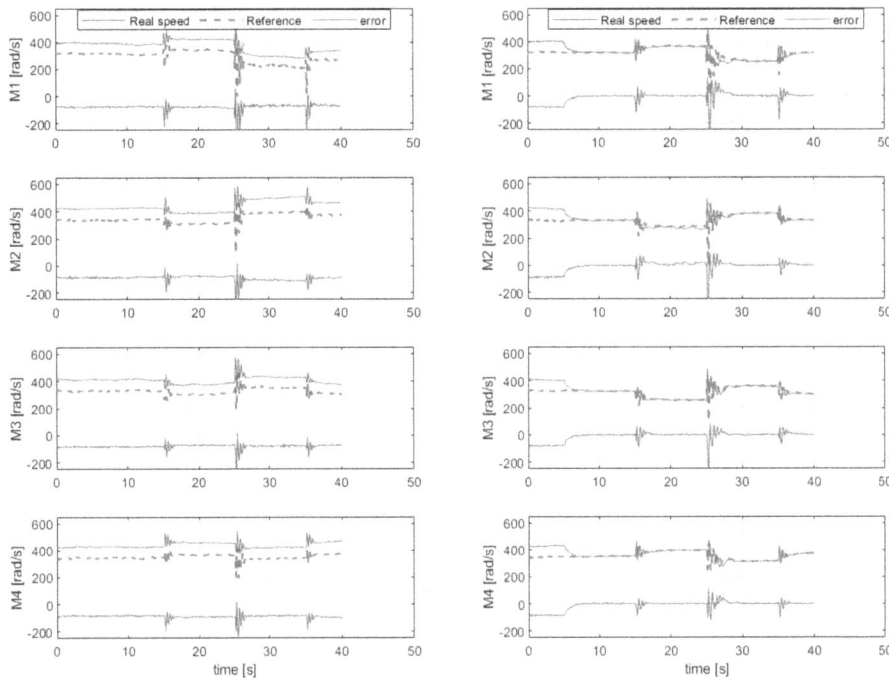

Fig. 5. Actuator dynamics, only with the cascade control loop (left) and with the auxiliary control loop (right).

magnitudes and their persistence over time. This suggests a potential decrease in control efficiency with the inclusion of the auxiliary loop. These performance indices are illustrated in Fig. 4, where oscillations become apparent during reference changes.

6   Conclusions

The figures demonstrate that cascade control alone (Fig. 4) effectively tracks the reference angles ϕ and θ with less error than auxiliary loop control. This approach also results in a more stable system response characterized by smaller oscillations and faster settling times.

The addition of the auxiliary loop leads to increased motor oscillations, particularly noticeable during reference changes for the θ angle. This indicates that the auxiliary loop adds complexity to the system dynamics, potentially reducing control efficiency. However, despite this, the desired control value is maintained, and improvements in auxiliary loop design could mitigate these challenges.

During testing, it was observed that the motors had to operate at slightly lower speeds than their initial settings in all cases. This discrepancy is rectified by incorporating the auxiliary loop, decreasing electrical energy consumption.

Although this adjustment slightly compromises control performance, it facilitates the attainment of desired values, showcasing a potential advantage in energy efficiency.

It is speculated that a decrease in electrical power availability, such as during battery discharge in real-world scenarios, may lead to a decline in the efficiency of the attitude control system. This could occur as the motors start decelerating, affecting the system's ability to maintain desired values. However, the auxiliary loop could mitigate this effect by adjusting the reference speed above the actual speed. In response, the auxiliary control action would increase the PWM value, compensating for these disturbances and aiding in sustaining performance.

Likewise, it is theorized that in case of any malfunction or damage to a component within the ESC + BLDC + propeller assembly during flight, the auxiliary loop could rectify such issues, ensuring UAV stability amidst such failures. Coupled with a failure detection algorithm, this setup could facilitate preemptive measures to address issues before they escalate, thereby averting system failure. These hypotheses are potential avenues for future exploration, leveraging experimentation with the developed technology.

References

1. Eslava-Pedraza, J., Martínez-Sarmiento, F. Soto-Vergel, A., Vera Rozo, E., Guevara-Ibarra, D.: Vehículos aéreos no tripulados como alternativa de solución a los retos de innovación en diferentes campos de aplicación: una revisión de la literatura," Investigación e Innovación en Ingenierías, vol. 9, no. 1, pp. 149-166 (2021). https://doi.org/10.17081/invinno.9.1.40174
2. Vergouw, B., Nagel, H., Bondt, G., Custers, B.: Drone technology: types, payloads, applications, frequency spectrum issues and future developments. In: The future of drone use: Opportunities and threats from ethical and legal perspectives, pp. 21–45 (2016)
3. Ayamga, M., Akaba, S., Nyaaba, A.A.: Multifaceted applicability of drones: a review. Technol. Forecast. Soc. Chang. **167**,120677 (2021). https://doi.org/10.1016/j.techfore.2021.120677
4. Puchalski, R., Giernacki, W.: UAV fault detection methods, state-of-the-art. Drones, **6**(11), 330 (2022). https://doi.org/10.3390/drones6110330
5. Mora Hincapie, L.F.: Análisis de riesgos asociados a la operación de drones ante un posible uso en la vigilancia privada. Undergraduate thesis, Universidad Tecnológica de Pereira, Pereira, Colombia (2016)
6. Eureka Dynamics. Eureka Dynamics Product Catalogue 2022 (2022)
7. Quasner, "Quasner Innovate Educate", Quasner. https://www.quanser.com/products/3-dof-hover/ Access 6 May 2024
8. Rinaldi, M., Primatesta, S., Guglieri, G.: A comparative study for control of quadrotor UAVs. Appl. Sci. **13**(6), 3464 (2023). https://www.mdpi.com/2076-3417/13/6/3464
9. Zheng, E.-H., Xiong, J.-J., Luo, J.-L.: Second order sliding mode control for a quadrotor UAV. ISA Trans. **53**(4), 1350–1356 (2014). https://doi.org/10.1016/j.isatra.2014.03.010

10. Leishman, R.C., MacDonald, J.C., Beard, R.W., McLain, T.W.: Quadrotors and accelerometers: state estimation with an improved dynamic model. IEEE Control Syst. **34**(1), 28–41 (2014). https://doi.org/10.1109/MCS.2013.2287362

11. Sabatini, A.M., Genovese, V.: A sensor fusion method for tracking vertical velocity and height based on inertial and barometric altimeter measurements. Sensors (Switzerland) **14**(8), 13324–13347 (2014). https://doi.org/10.3390/s140813324

12. Dydek, Z.T., Annaswamy, A.M., Lavretsky, E.: Adaptive control of quadrotor UAVs: a design trade study with flight evaluations. IEEE Trans. Control Syst. Technol. **21**(4), 1400–1406 (2013). https://doi.org/10.1109/TCST.2012.2200104

13. Dydek, Z.T., Annaswamy, A.M., Lavretsky, E.: Adaptive configuration control of multiple UAVs. Control Eng. Pract. **21**(8), 1043–1052 (2013). https://doi.org/10.1016/j.conengprac.2013.03.010

14. Xia, D., Cheng, L., Yao, Y.: A robust inner and outer loop control method for trajectory tracking of a quadrotor. Sensors (Switzerland) **17**(9), 2147 (2017). https://doi.org/10.3390/s17092147

15. Tanyeri, B., Ural Bayrak, Z., & Uçar, U. U. The experimental study of attitude stabilization control for programmable nano quadcopter. J. Aviat. **6**(1), 1-11 (2022). https://doi.org/10.30518/jav.1007737

16. Tang, B.: Attitude Control of a Quadrotor UAV: Experimental Implementation. Supervised by Dr. Abdelhamid Tayebi. Master's thesis. Thunder Bay, Ontario, Canada: Lakehead University, Sept (2022)

17. Darwito, P.A., Agustina, N.P.: Performance evaluation of a Sliding Mode Control-Kalman Filter-based mathematical model for altitude and attitude control in quadcopters. J. Intell. Syst. Control **2**(2), 70–81 (2023). DOhttps://doi.org/10.56578/jisc020202

18. Esmail, M.S., Merzban, M.H., Khalaf, A.A.M., Hamed, H.F.A., Hussein, A.I.: Attitude and altitude nonlinear control regulation of a quadcopter using quaternion representation. IEEE Access **10**, 5884-5894 (2022). https://doi.org/10.1109/ACCESS.2022.3141544

19. Karakaya, Ş.E., Goren, A.: Performance Comparison of PID and NARX Neural Network for Attitude Control of a Quadcopter UAV. J. Mater. Mechat. A **3**(1), 1–19 (2022). https://doi.org/10.55546/jmm.1010919

20. Dynamics, E.: Eureka Dynamics Product Catalogue 2023. 2023. Available https://eurekadynamics.com/product-catalog/. Accessed 09 May 2024

21. Quasner, "Quanser Innovate Educate. Available: https://www.quanser.com/products/3-dof-hover/. Accessed 09 May 2024

22. Sabatino, F.: Quadrotor control: modeling, nonlinear control design, and simulation. KTH Electrical Enginerring (2015)

23. Ogata, K.: Modern Control Engineering, 5th ed. Prentice Hall (2010)

24. PodhradskÃİ, M., Coopmans, C., Jensen, A.: Battery state-of-charge based altitude controller for small, low cost multirotor unmanned aerial vehicles. J. Intell. Robotic Syst. Theor. Appl. **74**(1-2), 193–207 (2014). https://doi.org/10.1007/s10846-013-9894-7

25. Ljung, L.: System identification: theory for the user. Prentice-Hall, Inc., USA, 1986, isbn: 0138816409

26. Goodwin, G.C., Graebe, S.F., Salgado, M.E.: Control System Design. Prentice Hall (2012)

Battery Life Estimation of a Solar-Electric Boat Based on Hybrid Simulation of Real-Life Operation Using Python-Based Algorithms

Santiago Gomez-Oviedo$^{(\boxtimes)}$, Alejandro Montoya, and Ricardo Mejía-Gutiérrez

School of Applied Sciences and Engineering, Universidad EAFIT, Carrera 49 No 7
Sur–50, Medellín, Colombia
{esgomezo,jmonto36,rmejiag}@eafit.edu.co

Abstract. This study aims to estimate the battery life of a solar-electric boat using Python-based algorithms, with a primary focus on predicting battery degradation during the boat's operation. Real-life operational data, including power consumption along a predetermined route and charging process information, were collected from the solar-electric boat. Laboratory experiments provided essential parameters of the battery cells. Leveraging this dataset, several Python-based algorithms were employed to simulate the expected battery life of the electric boat. The integration of real-world operational data and laboratory-derived cell parameters enhances the accuracy of the predictions, contributing valuable insights into the sustainable and efficient use of electric propulsion in waterway applications.

Keywords: Battery degradation · solar-electric boats · hybrid simulation · python-based algorithms

1 Introduction

In recent years, various electric boat solutions have been developed to mitigate CO_2 emissions [1–3]. Studies comparing the environmental impact over the lifespan of electric and gasoline-powered pump-out boats have consistently shown that electric boats produce fewer greenhouse gas emissions throughout their lifetime, especially when charged using renewable energy sources [4]. For example, a passenger boat could consume an average of 4 200 gallons of fuel annually, resulting in the generation of 38 tons of CO_2 during the same period [5]. This highlights the pressing need for transitioning to cleaner, electric alternatives to reduce the environmental impact of water transportation.

It is widely acknowledged that battery performance significantly influences the economic viability of electric boats [6]. Therefore, a comprehensive understanding of battery performance over the long term is crucial. While extensive research has been conducted on battery performance in electric vehicles, it is

J. C. Figueroa-García et al. (Eds.): WEA 2024, CCIS 2223, pp. 150–161, 2025.
https://doi.org/10.1007/978-3-031-74598-0_13

equally important to conduct similar studies in electric boats, given their distinct power demands and operational requirements. On the other hand, battery degradation tests are costly and time-consuming, especially for large format batteries [7]. Therefore, the research presented aims to develop a methodology to predict the battery degradation of a solar-electric boat based on single-cell experiments and data from real operations.

The data is derived from the operation of a solar-electric passenger transport boat, which is the result of a recent research project [8–15]. The cell under study is an 87.5 Ah NMC cell. Further details about the solar-electric boat will be presented in Sect. 4.

Battery degradation prediction is crucial for the efficient and reliable operation of lithium-ion batteries. Several studies have focused on developing accurate methods for estimating battery health and predicting remaining useful life (RUL) [16]. These studies emphasize the importance of prognostics in understanding battery energy/power degradation and predicting when battery performance will deteriorate [17]. Accurate prediction of state of health (SoH) and RUL is essential due to the unpredictability of battery degradation, informing users about potential replacements and preventing unexpected capacity fade [17].

This paper investigates the development and performance evaluation of a solar-electric boat's battery system. It begins with an overview of the research methodology, followed by detailed battery cell modeling techniques. The features of the solar-electric boat, including its design, components, and operational characteristics, are then discussed. A tailored battery model for the boat is developed and examined. The paper also covers the tests and data acquisition processes used to validate the battery system's performance. A long-term simulation of the boat's operation under various conditions is presented, with the results analyzed and discussed. The paper concludes by summarizing the findings and suggesting future research directions for solar-electric boat battery systems.

2 Methodology

The methodology illustrated in Fig. 1 was employed to predict the degradation of an electric boat battery. Initially, experimental procedures were conducted to acquire the discharge curve of a single cell and derive model parameters. These parameters were primarily based on the Shepherd model [18], which includes series resistance and capacity fade as variables that reflect the degradation of the cell over its usage. Subsequently, the real power demand of the electric boat was determined through autonomy tests, capturing current and voltage parameters during normal operation. Using the obtained parameters from a single cell and the power demand data, a comprehensive battery model was implemented using Python-based algorithms. Finally, a simulation of the boat's long-term operation, also implemented in Python, was conducted to predict battery degradation. The anticipated degradation is reflected in changes to the equivalent series resistance and battery capacity.

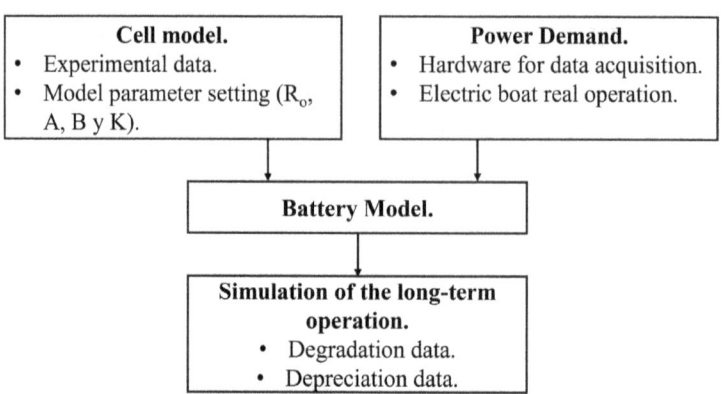

Fig. 1. Research Methodology

3   Battery Cell Modeling

The Shepherd model [18] has been extensively used for dynamic simulations of hybrid electric vehicles and battery energy storage systems, demonstrating its versatility and applicability in various domains [19,20]. The Shepherd model's simplicity and ability to accurately capture the dynamic behavior of batteries make it a popular choice for parameter identification and dynamic simulations, as it allows for the estimation of battery parameters from manufacturer datasheets without the need for extensive laboratory testing [21].

$$V_{cell} = V_0 - K\left(\frac{Q}{Q - it}\right)i - R_0 i + Ae^{-Bit} \qquad (1)$$

Parameters K, A, B, and R_o can be extracted from the discharge curve of a cell by identifying the exponential zone and nominal zone of the curve. Figure 2 depicts three distinct zones within the battery's discharge process. The initial zone, known as the exponential zone, follows an exponential discharge curve characterized by two key points: from the battery's full charge $(0, V_{full})$ to the point (Q_{exp}, V_{exp}). The subsequent zone, termed the nominal zone, extends from the conclusion of the exponential zone to the point (Q_{nom}, V_{nom}), displaying a relatively constant voltage.

Laboratory tests were performed to obtain the parameters K, A, B, and R_o. To achieve this, an electronic load was employed to demand constant currents from the cell. Temperature information was also recorded during these tests. Table 1 displays the parameters obtained from the experiments. Additionally, Fig. 2 presents the results obtained with the model. Dashed lines represent the experimental data, while dotted lines depict the discharge curve obtained with the model. There is a slight difference between the two curves, attributed to the model's effective performance.

Table 1. Shepherd model parameters

R_0 (mΩ)	V_0 (V)	K (Ω)	A (V)	B (1/Ah)
0.491	3.65	0.00035	0.58	0.057

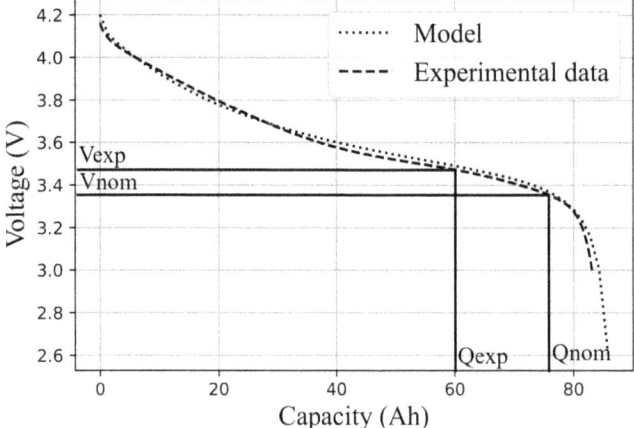

Fig. 2. Comparison of cell model results with laboratory test results

4   Features of the Electric Boat

The solar-electric boat under study is the culmination of a thorough research project that meticulously considered a conceptual design process to establish the boat's primary design requirements [8]. This process involved a detailed study of hydrodynamic performance across various hull geometries to determine the optimal design [9]. Furthermore, efforts were made to enhance the transmission and propulsion system of the boat through the utilization of Python-based software solutions [10–12]. Additionally, extensive studies were conducted to determine the optimal sizing and thermal management of the boat's batteries, necessitating the development of an efficient cooling system [13,14]. Lastly, meticulous planning was undertaken to establish test routes in diverse environments such as lakes and dams [15].

The solar-electric boat in Fig. 3 was designed for passenger transportation. It can transport up to 12 passengers. The main characteristics of the vessel are summarized in Table 2. Additionally, the solar-electric boat is equipped with a 6.6 kW onboard charging system complemented with a solar roof of 14 m^2 and 2.2 kWp. While the charging rate may be slow, it offers the advantage of being able to charge in areas lacking developed charging infrastructure or electric grids, a common scenario in various regions of Colombia.

Fig. 3. Solar-Electric Boat Under Study

Table 2. Technical specifications of the electric boat under test

Lenght	7.9 m
Width	2.15 m
Capacity	12 passengers
Total Weight	4.2 Ton
Power	110 kW
Cruising speed	45 km/h
Top Speed	61 km/h
Nominal Voltage	303 V
Battery capacity	117 kWh

5 Battery Model

The battery model plays a pivotal role in understanding the behavior and performance of electric vehicle batteries, serving as a fundamental tool for predictive analysis and optimization. In this section, we elucidate the development and application of a comprehensive battery model tailored for a solar-electric boat.

Battery modeling commences with the development of a comprehensive cell model. This model is replicated to match the specific configuration of the analyzed battery, which, in our case, comprises 4 cells in series and 83 cells in parallel. To enhance computational efficiency, we determine the equivalent voltage of each series module, considering factors such as internal resistance (R_0). This determination is facilitated by Eq. 2, where R_{eq} denotes the equivalent parallel resistance of each cell's parameter R_o.

$$V_{eq} = R_{eq1}(\frac{V_{n1}}{R_{n1}} + \frac{V_{n2}}{R_{n2}} + \frac{V_{n3}}{R_{n3}} + ... + \frac{V_{nn}}{R_{nn}}) \tag{2}$$

Finally, the sum of all V_{eq} and R_0 values yields an equivalent battery model featuring a dependent voltage source and a series resistance. Through the integration of advanced modeling techniques and empirical data, our battery model offers valuable insights into the performance characteristics and operational dynamics of the solar-electric boat's energy storage system.

5.1 Current Distribution

The development of a system of equations facilitates the simulation of each cell's behavior within the battery, enabling the determination of current flow when subjected to a load. This system relies on variables such as the number of cells in series and parallel, alongside the parameter R_0 for each cell. Figure 4b provides a visual representation of this system through a matrix, where each unknown value denotes the current across individual cells in response to the battery's power demand. Figure 4a depicts the arrangement of cells corresponding to the matrix in the example, showcasing an array of 2 series and 3 parallel cells.

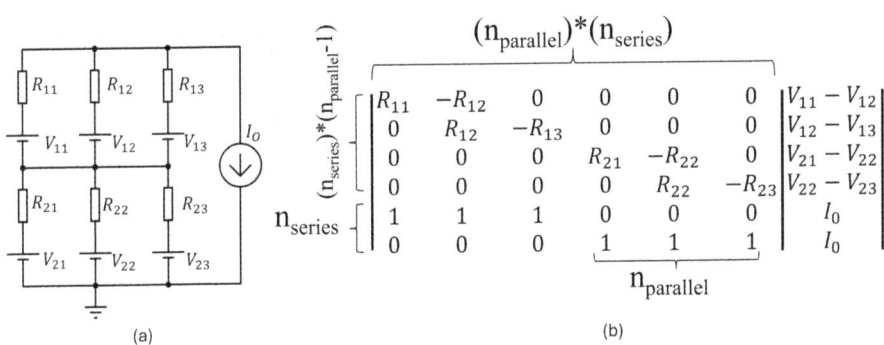

Fig. 4. Matrix for current distribution calculation

5.2 Battery Degradation

The degradation of the battery is evidenced by an increase in the parameter R_o and a decrease in the total capacity of the cell [22]. Equations 3 and 4 are used to compute these parameters, as they are functions dependent on the number of cycles of the cell (n). The total number of cycles is determined using the methodology proposed by Gundogdu and Gladwin [23], which has been applied by several authors [24,25], as shown in Fig. 5. The method is outlined as follows:

- The algorithm iterates through the historical State of Charge (SOC) data, acquired by simulating the solar-electric boat's operation over a specified duration. Initially, it assesses the change in battery SOC. According to the algorithm proposed in this paper, if the SOC change is positive, the battery is in a charging state; if negative, it is discharging; and if zero, the battery is at rest.
- Each positive and negative change in battery SOC is designated as "Up" and "Down" indexes, respectively. These indexes are aggregated in the second step, where the sum of all "Up" indexes constitutes the battery SOC charging dataset (SOCch), and the sum of all "Down" indexes forms the battery SOC discharging dataset (SOCdchg).
- In the third step, during simulation, each instance where SOCch and SOCdchg reach 100% signifies the completion of a battery charge and discharge cycle, respectively. These cycles are tallied independently. A complete battery cycle is computed as the average of charge and discharge cycles over the specified period.
- This algorithm is reiterated across the considered SOC data history, ultimately yielding a total cycle count upon completion.

The degradation factor (ε) ranges from 0 to 1 and is also influenced by the number of cycles of the cell. Furthermore, the influence of individual cell parameter discrepancies on the performance of series-parallel battery packs has been investigated, revealing that the internal resistance increased to 166.4% of the initial value when the capacity of the aged single cell decreased to 80% of the original [26]. Therefore, in this study, a cell is deemed to have reached its end of life (EOL) when its capacity falls below 80% of the original value. At this stage, the battery is considered unsuitable for electric vehicle applications [27].

$$R(n) = \begin{cases} R_{BOL} + \varepsilon(n)(R_{EOL} - R_{BOL}) \; if \;\; n/2 \neq 0 \\ \\ R_{BOL} \qquad\qquad\qquad\qquad\; otherwise \end{cases} \tag{3}$$

where:
   R_{BOL} is the Resistance in the beginning of life.
   R_{EOL} is the Resistance in the end of life.

$$Q(n) = \begin{cases} Q_{BOL} - \varepsilon(n)(Q_{BOL} - Q_{EOL}) \; if \;\; n/2 \neq 0 \\ \\ Q_{BOL} \qquad\qquad\qquad\qquad\; otherwise \end{cases} \tag{4}$$

where:
   R_{BOL} is the Resistance in the beginning of life.
   R_{EOL} is the Resistance in the end of life.

6   Simulation Development

The Simulation Development section provides a thorough overview of the essential components involved in implementing the simulation model. It details the

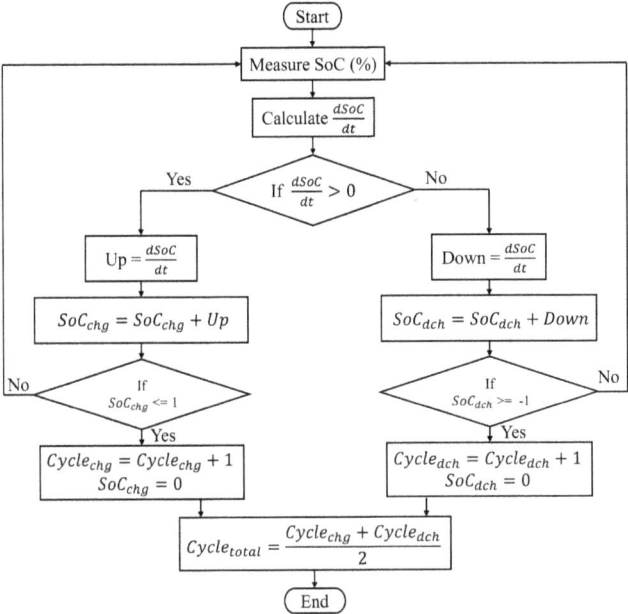

Fig. 5. Diagram illustrating a rapid method for estimating battery cycle counts [23, 28]

input data used, including the charging and discharging current profiles, battery configuration, and nominal characteristics of the cells under study. Additionally, it explores the data obtained from the simulation, with a particular emphasis on the battery's degradation and depreciation over time. By examining the input parameters and simulation results, valuable insights into the behavior and evolution of the battery system can be gained, aiding in informed decision-making and enhancing the understanding of battery dynamics in practical applications.

This section also introduces the specific parameters and objectives of the simulation, which aims to replicate the real operation of a solar-electric boat. The boat performs four trips daily at a constant speed of 40 km/h, with a total daily trip duration of 3 126 s. After each trip, the battery is fully recharged, and this operational pattern is repeated from Monday to Friday. Figure 6 presents the current profile demanded during these trips, derived from actual boat operations. This profile will serve as an input parameter for the simulation.

The simulated battery configuration is 83s4p, utilizing the specific cells discussed in previous sections. The simulation will focus on the increase in the parameter R_o of the cells and the overall capacity degradation. The process will continue until the battery capacity drops to 80% of its initial capacity [26], a threshold below which it is deemed unsuitable for electric vehicle applications. The objective is to determine the battery's degradation after one cycle and estimate the total operational lifespan of the boat in years. This information will be invaluable for boat owners considering investments in such electric solutions.

Figure 6 illustrates the voltage behavior during the first operation of a typical day for the solar-electric boat. The graph demonstrates the initial depth of discharge at the beginning of the day, showing the battery's state before the first trip. Throughout the operation, the voltage changes as the boat's energy demand fluctuates. By the end of the day, the figure shows the battery returning to a fully charged state, highlighting the daily charging cycle's effectiveness in maintaining battery performance. This pattern is crucial for understanding the battery's daily operational dynamics.

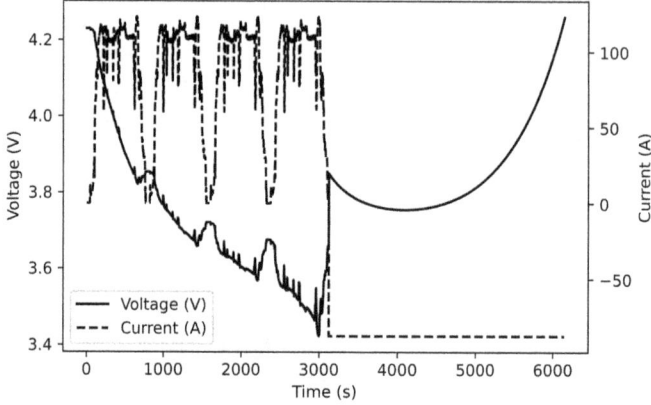

Fig. 6. Voltage behavior of a single cell during one day of operation

Figure 7(a) illustrates the changes in total capacity and series resistance of a single cell over the first 1 578 d of operation. The figure clearly shows an expected increase in resistance and a decrease in total capacity. Although the total capacity remains above 80% of the initial capacity at this point, the solar-electric boat can no longer complete the full trip but is still operational for shorter trips. The maximum capacity of a single cell is 73.5 Ah. At this stage, a decision must be made regarding the potential need to change the battery pack or adjust the operational schedule to maintain service levels. Consequently, the simulation continues with half of the daily trips. Fig. 7(b) shows that after 704 additional days, the cells reach a maximum total capacity of 80 Ah and a series resistance of 0.817 mΩ, indicating the end of their life for electric vehicle applications.

After running the entire simulation under the selected operating regime, the solar-electric boat is expected to operate for a total of 2 282 d. Considering only working days, this translates to approximately 8.7 years of operation, with 7.66 years at the full desired operation (four trips daily at a constant speed of 40 km/h, with a total daily trip duration of 3 126 s during business days) and the remaining time at half of the desired operation.

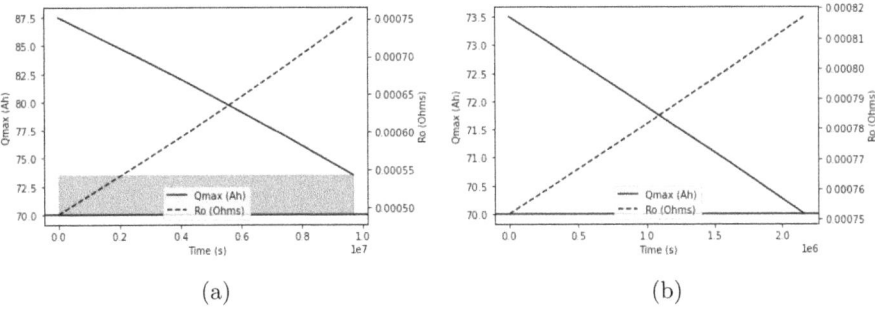

Fig. 7. Total capacity and series resistance changes of a single cell: (a) during the first 1578 d of operation, and (b) during the last 704 d

7   Conclusions and Further Research

The simulation estimates that the solar-electric boat can operate for up to 8.7 years, functioning at full capacity for 88% of the time and at half capacity for the remaining time. This information is crucial for investors to understand battery lifespan and boat performance, aiding in decisions about the number of boats to purchase, their operational use, and second-life applications for the batteries.

Future research should validate the model with real-world data from the boat's operation, incorporating variables such as temperature and real degradation data to improve accuracy and reliability. Integrating real-world degradation data of lithium-ion cells from lab and field studies, and analyzing capacity loss, impedance growth, and voltage decay, will refine the model. Comparing simulation results with long-term operational data from solar-electric boats will help validate the model. Additionally, considering temperature effects on cell degradation and conducting experimental validation through lab and field tests will further enhance the model's robustness and practical application.

Acknowledgement. The authors would like to thank Universidad EAFIT for supporting this research through the Research Assistantship grant from project 1111-11110102021.

References

1. Kurniawan, A.: A review of solar-powered boat development. IPTEK The J. Technol. Sci. **27**(1) (2016)
2. Gorter, T., Joore, P., Reinders, A., Van Houten, F.: Scenario-based simulation of PV boats in an early design stage. In: 2013 IEEE 39th Photovoltaic Specialists Conference (PVSC), pp. 0769–0774. IEEE (2013)
3. Barelli, L., et al.: Dynamic modeling of a hybrid propulsion system for tourist boat. Energies **11**(10), 2592 (2018)

4. Hemez, C., Chiu, J., Ryan, E.C., Sun, J., Dubrow, R., Pascucilla, M.: Environmental and health impacts of electric service vessels in the recreational boating industry. Water Pract. Technol. **15**(3), 781–796 (2020)

5. Moya, M., Martínez-Gómez, J., Urresta, E., Cordovez-Dammer, M.: Feature selection in energy consumption of solar catamaran INER 1 on galapagos Island. Energies **15**(8), 2761 (2022)

6. Tercan, Ş.H., Eid, B., Heidenreich, M., Kogler, K., Akyürek, Ö.: Financial and technical analyses of solar boats as a means of sustainable transportation. Sustain. Prod. Consumption **25**, 404–412 (2021)

7. Amini, M., Nazari, M.H., Hosseinian, S.H.: Optimal scheduling and cost-benefit analysis of lithium-ion batteries based on battery state of health. IEEE Access, **11**, 1359–1371 (2022)

8. Mira, J.D., et al.: Preliminary design tools applied to a solar powered vessel design: a south american river analysis. In: 2020 Fifteenth International Conference on Ecological Vehicles and Renewable Energies (EVER), pp. 1–9 (2020)

9. Giraldo-Pérez, E., Betancur, E., Osorio-Gómez, G.: Experimental and statistical analysis of the hydrodynamic performance of planing boats: a comparative study. Ocean Eng. **262**, 112227 (2022)

10. Gómez-Oviedo, S., Mejía-Gutiérrez, R.: An interactive tool for propeller selection according to electric motor exploration: an electric boat design case study. In: 2020 IEEE Transportation Electrification Conference & Expo (ITEC), pp. 147–151. IEEE (2020)

11. Mira, J.D., Mendoza, F., Betancur, E., Manrique, T., MejÃa-GutiÃrrez, R.: A propulsion system design methodology based on overall efficiency optimization for electrically powered vessels. IEEE Trans. Transp. Electrification **8**(1), 239–250 (2022)

12. Mira, J.-D., Gómez-Oviedo, S., Betancur, E., Mejía-Gutiérrez, R.: Preliminary sizing of a propulsion unit for an electrically-powered vessel using a screw propellers performance comparison tool. In: Figueroa-García, J.C., Garay-Rairán, F.S., Hernández-Pérez, G.J., Díaz-Gutierrez, Y. (eds.) WEA 2020. CCIS, vol. 1274, pp. 465–476. Springer, Cham (2020). https://doi.org/10.1007/978-3-030-61834-6_40

13. Giraldo-Pérez, E., Gaviria, G., Betancur, E., Osorio-Gómez, G., Mejía-Gutiérrez, R.: Influence of energy consumption on battery sizing of electric fluvial vessels: a Colombian case study. In: 2020 Fifteenth International Conference on Ecological Vehicles and Renewable Energies (EVER), pp. 1–8. IEEE (2020)

14. Bustamante-Castaño, S., Mejía-Gutiérrez, R.: Temperature performance simulation in a solar-electric vessel battery design. In: Workshop on Engineering Applications, pp. 366–378. Springer (2022). https://doi.org/10.1007/978-3-031-20611-5_30

15. Uribe, A., Calvache, M., Álvarez, C., Montoya, A.: Design of electric vessels test routes using image processing and optimization techniques. In: Workshop on Engineering Applications, pp. 243–253. Springer (2022). https://doi.org/10.1007/978-3-031-20611-5_21

16. Yang, J., Zou, L., Wei, Y., Yuan, P., Zhou, C.: Health status prediction of lithium battery based on lstm model with optimization algorithms. J. Phys. Conf. Ser. **2473**, 012020. IOP Publishing (2023)

17. Zhang, Y., Tang, Q., Zhang, Y., Wang, J., Stimming, U., Lee, A.A.: Identifying degradation patterns of lithium ion batteries from impedance spectroscopy using machine learning. Nature communications, **11**(1), 1706 (2020)

18. Shepherd, C.M.: Design of primary and secondary cells: II. an equation describing battery discharge. J. electrochem. soc. **112**(7), 657 (1965)
19. Moussa, S., Ghorbal, J.B.M.: Shepherd battery model parametrization for battery emulation in EV charging application. In: 2022 IEEE International Conference on Electrical Sciences and Technologies in Maghreb (CISTEM), vol. 4, pp. 1–6. IEEE (2022)
20. Campagna, N., et al.: Battery models for battery powered applications: a comparative study. Energies **13**(16), 4085 (2020)
21. Ferahtia, S., Djeroui, A., Rezk, H., Chouder, A., Houari, A., Machmoum, M.: Optimal parameter identification strategy applied to lithium-ion battery model. Int. J. Energy Res. **45**(11), 16741–16753 (2021)
22. Sandelic, M., Sangwongwanich, A., Blaabjerg, F.: Incremental degradation estimation method for online assessment of battery operation cost. IEEE Trans. Power Electron. **37**(10), 11497–11501 (2022)
23. Gundogdu, B., Gladwin, D.T.: A fast battery cycle counting method for grid-tied battery energy storage system subjected to microcycles. In: 2018 International Electrical Engineering Congress (iEECON), pp. 1–4. IEEE (2018)
24. Al-Ghussain, L., Ahmad, A.D., Abubaker, A.M., Hovi, K., Hassan, M.A., Annuk, A.: Techno-economic feasibility of hybrid pv/wind/battery/thermal storage trigeneration system: toward 100% energy independency and green hydrogen production. Energy Rep. **9**, 752–772 (2023)
25. Hokmabad, H.N., Husev, O., Belikov, J., Vinnikov, D., Petlenkov, E.: Energy storage and forecasting error impact analysis in photovoltaic equipped residential nano-grids. In: 2023 IEEE 17th International Conference on Compatibility, Power Electronics and Power Engineering (CPE-POWERENG), pp. 1–6. IEEE (2023)
26. Wang, Y., et al.: Impact of individual cell parameter difference on the performance of series-parallel battery packs. ACS Omega **8**(11), 10512–10524 (2023)
27. Xu, B., Oudalov, A., Ulbig, A., Andersson, G., Kirschen, D.S.: Modeling of lithium-ion battery degradation for cell life assessment. IEEE Trans. Smart Grid **9**(2), 1131–1140 (2016)
28. Cetinkaya, U., Bayındır, R. Avcı, E., Ayık, S.: Battery energy storage system sizing, lifetime and techno-economic evaluation for primary frequency control: a data-driven case study for turkey. Gazi Univ. J. Sci. Part C Des. Technol. **10**(2), 177–194 (2022)

Fuzzy PID Control Architectures for Continuous Industrial Processes: A Comparative Study

Jhon Edisson Rodriguez-Castellanos[1]([✉]), Jorge Eduardo Cote-Ballesteros[1],
and Victor Hugo Grisales-Palacios[2]

[1] Universidad ECCI, Bogotá, Colombia
jhrodriguezc@ecci.edu.co
[2] Universidad NACIONAL, Bogotá, Colombia

Abstract. Conventional PID controllers have been a practical solution when controlling linear processes, but their time response is degraded in many non-linear processes. Fuzzy control has non-linear capabilities that may improve the performance against industrial processes. This article presents a comparative analysis for tuning fuzzy architectures: Direct, Supervisor, and Parallel in order to provide guidance in design decision-making. A non-linear mathematical model and continuous stirred tank reactor process have been considered to assess reference tracking and disturbance rejection. Results show that the Parallel fuzzy logic controller presents a more consistent response in the temporal performance indexes.

Keywords: Fuzzy Control · Nonlinear Control · Direct Fuzzy Controller · Supervisor Fuzzy Controller · Parallel Fuzzy Controller

1 Introduction

Although the literature reports multiple alternatives for non-linear process behavior, the fuzzy approach can provide a simple strategy while PID architecture is maintained. The fuzzy logic controllers (FLC) are based on membership grades and rules, which depend on the error as conventional PID controllers. Thus, the FLC can apply a non-linear control action through their parameter's variation, which might be suitable for controlling non-linear processes. Therefore, FLC is likely to replace a conventional PID controller or improve its performance. Several FLC architectures have been proposed, such as Direct FLC, fuzzy supervisor, and Parallel FLC [1–4].

Direct Fuzzy Logic Control (FLC) operates within the feedback control loop, directly influencing the process based on rules and fuzzy inference mechanisms [5]. One tuning approach, outlined by [6], involves performance analysis to adjust scale factors, membership functions (MFs), and rule base parameters of a PI-FLC. Similarly, [7, 8] suggests considering both steady-state and transient behaviors for scale factors tuning based on trial and error methods. Theoretical analysis-based methodologies aim to establish equivalences between linear PID controllers and FLCs [9, 10]. [11] proposes an FLC PI+D scheme derived from a linear PI+D controller, using two fuzzy systems and five scale factors. Non-linear FLC tuning, as proposed by [12], transforms a linear

© The Author(s), under exclusive license to Springer Nature Switzerland AG 2025
J. C. Figueroa-García et al. (Eds.): WEA 2024, CCIS 2223, pp. 162–173, 2025.
https://doi.org/10.1007/978-3-031-74598-0_14

PID tuning controller into a fuzzy equivalent, the fine-tuning was carried out via trial and error. Additionally, [13] modifies the control surface of FLC by adjusting scale factors from a conventional two degrees of freedom PID controller, these approaches require stimulation or in-process tests for optimal parameter values.

The fuzzy supervisor combines a hierarchical combination of a linear PID controller and FLC, with FLC adjusting PID parameters online to achieve a desired system response at a specific operating point [5, 14]. Fuzzy gain scheduling supervisors (FGS) fall into two categories: first where rules dictate the time response features, such as settling time, and the other where pre-specified gains of local PID controllers are determined at various process operation points. Transition between these gains is governed by variables like error signal and its derivative or output and reference signals of the process [15]. Modifications to FGS include the supervision of local PID controllers tuned by IMC and λ factor variation for the local controller [4]. In the second category, FGS supervisors contain a rules-base based on pre-specified gains of the local PID controllers, calculated at several process operation points. For example, in the architecture proposed in [14], y and r are used as inputs to the FGS inference mechanism, while the output is the values of a PID controller tuned by IMC. Practical examples of FGS may be found in studies such as [16–19].

A parallel FLC controller integrates various control architectures by combining their individual contributions, using weighting factors based on system dynamics. Fuzzy controllers can be paired with traditional linear controllers or other schemes [20]. Combining fuzzy and linear controllers, such as PID, can enhance performance against industrial non-linear processes [21, 22]. For instance, [23] propose a parallel architecture to regulate molten aluminum temperature in an atomizing oven, requiring multiple simulation tests for behavior refinement. Meanwhile, [24] present a parallel architecture combining a direct fuzzy controller and a conventional PI controller to manage pressure and flow in a sprinkler irrigation station. This hybrid system employs a parameter α to gradually transition between the linear and fuzzy controllers, determined by a fuzzy system with inputs of absolute error values and their changes (Δe).

A comparative analysis of several architectures of the FLC is carried out in this work, considering metrics such as initial and structural considerations and performance measures, seeking to guide decision-making when selecting a fuzzy architecture. The non-linear mathematical model and Matlab CSTR model are used to apply each fuzzy architecture considered. Error performance has been measured through IAE and ITAE indexes on tracking control tasks for several operation points.

This article is organized as follows: Sect. 1 introduces different architectures of FLC PID controllers and presents the methodological approach for the tuning of the considered fuzzy PID controllers; Sect. 2 reveals the analysis of results through simulations applied to non-linear systems; and finally, Sect. 3 presents conclusions from the study cases considered.

2 Architectures of FLC

The versatility and computational efficiency of fuzzy inference systems (FIS) enable their integration into control applications, complementing traditional controllers like PID and PI. FLC PID architectures are categorized into Direct, Supervised, and

Parallel types. Various structures have been proposed for each, such as fuzzy proportional-derivative-plus-integral (FPD+I) [12], and modified hybrid proportional-integral-derivative (MHPID) [13] for Direct FLCs. Supervisory FLCs use inputs like error (e) and its derivative (de) or process reference (r) and output (y) (FGS(e, de) [15], other structures, depending on the reference (r) and the output (y) of the process (FGS(r,y)) [14]. Tuning methods involve process modeling and adjustment of fuzzy system scaling factors [25, 26]. Parallel FLCs combine controllers like PID with Direct FLCs or Supervisory FLCs [24]. This paper explores hybridization methods to integrate these approaches effectively.

2.1 Tuning Methodology

Direct FLC
For this work, the tuning methodology proposed in [26] will be considered, which consists of:

- Linear sub-models at several operating points

Obtain the linear submodels (transfer functions) at different operating points from the open-loop reaction curve of the process. Calculate the coefficient Kf, from Eq. (1), which relates to highest (Ks) and lowest (Ki) operating points:

$$K\_f = K\_i / K\_s \qquad (1)$$

- Obtaining Fuzzy Scale Gains

From PID gains of conventional PID controller, an equivalent FLC is provided through methodology proposed in [12, 13].

- Fine Tuning

Finally, the Kf parameter allows obtaining the final scaling gains for direct FLC, which will replace the conventional PID.

FLC Supervisor
Supervisor FLC Tuning methodology reported in [25] is considered as follows:

1. FGS - f(e, de)
Tuning: The first-level PID controller must be tuned by IMC. From these gains and (1) the variation ranges of the FLC supervisor are established for two cases:

- The response of the system takes more time to reach the set point.
- The response of the system presents an overshoot that increases.

2. FGS - f(y, r)
Identification of the models in the different operation points: empirical sub-models of process, through reaction curve tests.

- Tune local PID controller for the different operating points: build an off-line matrix that contains first-level PID controller gains.

- Create the Fuzzy System
- Tuning: The response must be overdamped. To assign values to weight factors wy and wr.

3. Parallel FLC

The aim is to generate a weighted control action between a conventional PID controller focused on transient responses and an FLC controller focused on non-linearities due to changes in operating points [24]. Thus, one way to make smooth transitions is through a fuzzy selector (fuzzy supervisor) based on e and Δe.

The control law for the parallel architecture can be written as follows:

$$UPC = \alpha\, UFLC + (1 - \alpha)\, UPID \tag{2}$$

The parameter α is a weight factor. This change is achieved by using a fuzzy system that presents as inputs the absolute values of e and Δe. Hence, the α parameter changes dynamically depending on the behavior of the closed-loop system. In Fig. 2, the behavior of α can be observed, in the transitory state, there is a small intervention of the fuzzy controller that increases until the closed-loop system reaches the stationary state, showing that both the error and the derivative of the error tend to zero. The tuning techniques considered for Parallel FLC architectures are:

1. FLC-PID by αSupervision

The following steps are considered for the construction of the parallel architecture:

- Design the Direct
- Design the conventional PID Controller.
- Design the fuzzy selector

2. FLC Direct-Supervisor FLC.

- Design the Direct FLC (FPD + I)
- Design the Supervisory FLC (FGS (e, de))
- Design the fuzzy selector according [26]

All these methods were obtained to develop a practical but effective tuning method applicable to an industrial environment. The determination of tuning values is supported by extensive computational tests considering performance measurements and time response analysis of the system. The following section illustrates the application of the methodology and its experimental results in a case study.

3   Results and Discussion

A non-linear mathematical model [14] and a Non-linear continuously stirred reaction tank (CSTR - Matlab) were used to assess the performance of the considered tuning methodologies of the different fuzzy architectures considered. Tasks of reference tracking and disturbances rejection will be tested. In order to analyze the controllers behavior, the following performance measurement criteria were used: Integral of absolute error (IAE), Integral of time due to absolute error (ITAE), IAU, and ITAU. For each system, a linear PID controller was tuned under the internal model control (IMC) technique [32].

3.1 Non-linear Model

A non-linear mathematical model parametrized between 0 and 1 has been considered, given by the following equation:

$$x(t) = \begin{bmatrix} x_2(t) \\ -0.25*x_1(t) - 0.70*x_2(t) + (4.75 - 4.50*x_1(t))*u(t) \end{bmatrix} \quad (3)$$

$$y(t) = x(t)$$

Figure 1 shows the reaction curve of the process due to step inputs.

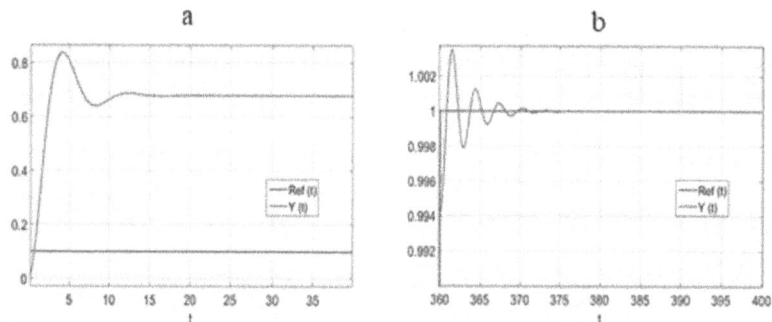

Fig. 1. System reaction curve. a) lower. b) upper.

The IMC PID controller tuning is Kp = 0.0295, Ti = 1.0016, and Td = 1.4302. With these pa-rameters and Kf, the fuzzy controllers, were tuned: FPD+I, MHPID, FGS – f (e, de). For FGS - f (y, r), the following matrices were considered:

$$\theta_{in} = P_y = P_y = [0.20.40.60.81]$$

$$\theta_{out} = \begin{bmatrix} K_{p1} & T_{i1} & T_{d1} \\ K_{p1} & T_{i2} & T_{d2} \\ \vdots & \vdots & \vdots \\ K_{pmy} & T_{imy} & T_{dmy} \end{bmatrix} = \begin{bmatrix} 0.0299 & 1.7270 & 1.4450 \\ 0.1350 & 5.4560 & 1.4436 \\ 0.2423 & 5.9000 & 1.4260 \\ 0.3579 & 4.6970 & 1.4260 \\ 0.4287 & 1.4600 & 1.4930 \end{bmatrix} \quad (4)$$

Figure 2 shows the time response of the different FLC architectures analyzed. The response of the PID IMC presents an overshoot in the lower part and steady-state degradation in the upper part, while the PID FLCs present a more consistent temporal performance, as Table 1 shows. ITAE values: FPD+I 95.3%, MHPID 86.6%, FGS–f(e, de) 95.1%, FGS–f(y, r) 85.4%, FLC-PID αFunc 95.06% and FLC Dir–Sup FLC 95.5%.

The control action of the different analyzed FLC architectures is presented in Table 1, in references tracking tasks, these signals were parameterized from 0 to 100, It can be seen that the response of the PID IMC has the lowest energy consumption against part of its time performance is reduced because it requires more time to reach the reference,

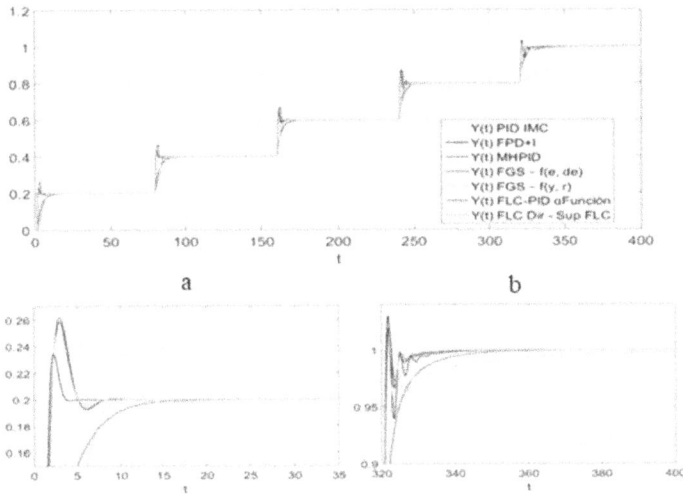

Fig. 2. Time response of controllers to variations of the reference (a) low point of operation (b) high point of operation

Table 1. Performance Measurements for reference variations

	Direct FLC		FLC Supervisory		FLC Parallel		PID IMC
	FPD+I	MHPID	FGS – f(e, de)	FGS – f(y, r)	FLC-PID αFunction	FLC Dir - Sup FLC	
IAE	1.15	3.151	0.971	3.372	1.221	1.078	14.71
ITAE	195.2	556.2	203.4	604.4	205.1	186.3	4158
IAU	2.50e4	2.47e4	2.49e4	2.45e4	2.50e4	2.505e4	2.233e4
ITAU	5.66e6	5.58e6	5.64e6	5.40e6	5.67e6	5.67e6	4.709e6

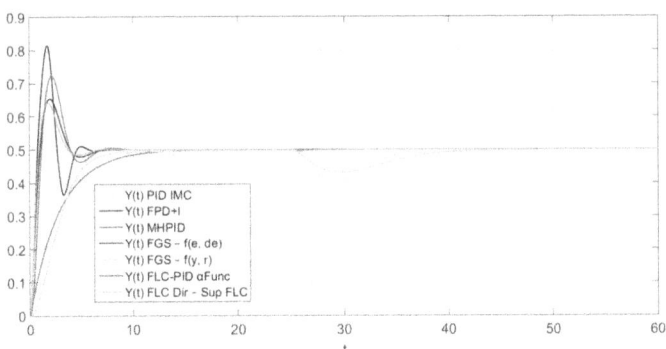

Fig. 3. Time response of controllers

while the FLC FGS-f (y, r), has the lowest energy consumption compared to the other FLC PID.

Figure 3 shows the time response of the analyzed FLC controllers in regulation tasks when introducing a step type disturbance at t = 25 s.

Table 2. Performance Measurements for disturbances

Controller	Measurements without disturbances until t = 50 s		Disturbance = 25 s	
	IAE	ITAE	IAE	ITAE
PID-IMC	1.72	5.457	2.397	27.01
FPD+I	0.5522	0.8951	0.5596	1.095
MHPID	1.445	4.188	1.451	4.362
FGS – f(e, de)	0.7266	1.224	0.7332	1.395
FGS – f(y, r)	1.413	3.675	2.029	23.76
FLC-PID αFunc	0.7826	1.418	0.7902	1.623
FLC Dir – Sup FLC	**0.4774**	**0.6854**	**0.4851**	**0.891**

The previous table shows that the best IAE and ITAE indexes, with or without disturbance, are presented by the FLC parallel, FLC Dir-Sup FLC. Additionally, the shortest settling time in contrast with moderate overshoot. While the FLC supervisor FGS - f(e, de) presents the lowest rise time (0,76 s) but the highest overshoot. It is observed that the FLCs make an almost immediate rejection of the disturbance, except for the FGS-f (y, r), which presents comparable performance indexes with the linear PID. The numerical evaluation of the time response and performance indexes is presented in Table 2.

3.2 Non-linear Model

A CSTR process model was considered, which converts a chemical matter A to a chemical matter B through an irreversible exothermic reaction of first order A → B. The model consists of 2 non-linear differential equations. The reactor temperature must be constant at a particular set point to maximize the transformation of the chemical matter A by regulating the temperature of the coolant in the jacket.

Reaction curve tests have been applied to CSTR through incremental reference changes of 10K. The whole range consists of 300K to 350K as can be seen in Fig. 4.

After the application of the tuning methodologies, the parameters obtained are shown in Table 3.

Figure 5 shows the time response of the different FLC architectures analyzed. The response of the PID IMC shows an increase in oscillations with the variation of the SP, while the FLCs reduce the overshoot and the low amplitude oscillations. Merit figures are obtained from Table 4 ITAE values: FPD+I 59.6%, MHPID 69.9%, FGS–f(e, de) 63.3%, FGS–f(y, r) 15.24%, FLC-PID αFunc 54.7% and FLC Dir–Sup FLC 57.5%.

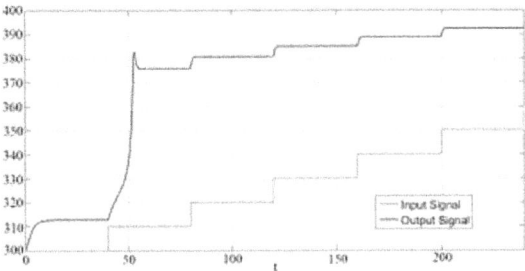

Fig. 4. System reaction curve.

Table 3. FLC Parameters

PIDIMC	Kl = 1.27	Ku = 0.47	Kf = 2.702	
	Kp = 14.2	Ti = 1.65	Td = 0.0025	
FPD+I	GE = 100	GCE = 0.12	GIE = 60.51	GU = 0.38
MHPID	GE = 1	GCE = 0.005	GU = 76.77	GCU = 23.22
FGS - f (e, de)	Kpmin = 14.2	Kpmax = 38.3	Kdmin = 0.035	Kdmax = 0.023

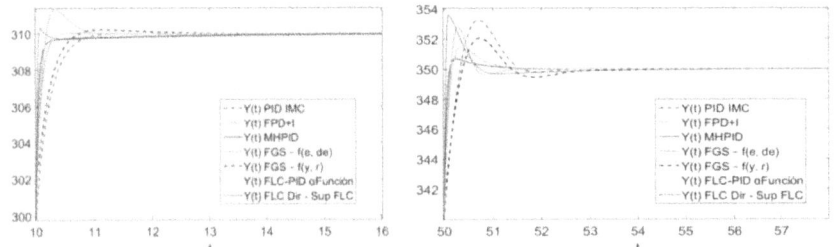

Fig. 5. Time response of FLCs to variations in the reference at the low point of operation and high point of operation.

Table 4. Performance Measurements for CSTR references tracking

	Direct FLC		FLC Supervisory		FLC Parallel		PID IMC
	FPD+I	MHPID	FGS – f(e, de)	FGS – f(y, r)	FLC-PID αFunción	FLC Dir - Sup FLC	
IAE	18.74	16.29	10.82	35.24	19.68	18.5	48.75
ITAE	247.8	184.6	247.4	562.7	277.9	260.5	614

Figure 6 shows the time response of the analyzed FLC controllers in regulation tasks when introducing a step type disturbance at t = 15 s.

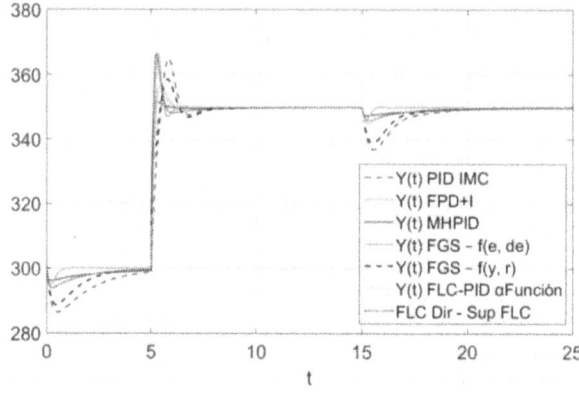

Fig. 6. Time response of the controllers to a step-type disturbance

It is observed that the FLCs make an almost immediate rejection of the disturbance, except for the FGS-f (y, r), which presents comparable performance indexes with the linear PID. The numerical evaluation of the time response and performance indexes is presented in Table 5.

Table 5. Performance Measurements for CSTR disturbances

Controller	Measurements without disturbances until t = 50 s		Disturbance = 25 s	
	IAE	ITAE	IAE	ITAE
PID-IMC	50.26	164.7	73.35	547.8
FPD+I	18.25	54.31	26.79	196.2
MHPID	14.2	51.82	22.35	196.9
FGS – f(e, de)	10.81	46.61	12.36	70.24
FGS – f(y, r)	33.71	112.4	50.58	388.2
FLC-PID αFunc	20.68	67.12	29.22	208.4
FLC Dir – Sup FLC	21.32	79.1	29.81	223.2

3.3 Designer Effort

From Table 6, it can be seen that direct FLCs present a simplicity at the time of their construction, which translates into a lower computational expense. However, the FLC parallel FLC Dir-Sup FLC presents the highest computational consumption due to the presence of three fuzzy systems, by the fuzzy supervisor, which requires MFs of output and proprietary defuzzification; despite this, it manages to obtain the best IAE and ITAE performance indexes in regulation tasks and the best ITAE index in tracking task.

Table 6. Designer Effort (Implementation Requirements)

Requirements	DIRECT FLC		SUPERVISED FLC		PARALLEL FLC	
	FPD+I	MHPID	FGS – f(e, de)	FGS – f(y, r)	FLC-PID αFunción	FLC Dir - Sup FLC
Models of the system	[2] In upper and lower operating points	[2] In upper and lower operating points	[2] In upper and lower operating points	Several models	[2] In upper and lower operating points	[2] In upper and lower operating points
Requires of a conventional PID	NO	NO	YES	YES	YES	NO
MFs for the inputs	3	2	7	It depends on the models	It depends on the direct FLC	It depends on the direct FLC and the Fuzzy Supervisor
MFs for the outputs	5	–	2			
Inference	Product	Product	Product	Product	Product	Product
Base of rules	Mamdani	Takagi-Sugeno	Mamdani	Mamdani	It depends on the direct FLC	It depends on the direct FLC and the Fuzzy Supervisor
Defuzzification	COG	Weighted Sum	Owner	COG		
Normalization	YES	YES	YES	NO	YES	YES
Number of fuzzy systems in the control architecture	1	1	3	2	2	It depends on the direct FLC and the Fuzzy Supervisor
Control architecture execution time	LOW	LOW	HIGH	LOW	LOW	HIGH

4   Conclusions

Regarding the architecture, it is possible to conclude that the techniques FPD+I, MHPID, FGS-f (e, de), FLC-PID by αSupervision and FLC Direct-Supervisor FLC require less intervention by the designer in the parameters tuning. While FGS – f (y, r) requires a more specific intervention by the designer, several tests must be done in simulation or the process so that the control performance is acceptable (establish the appropriate number of models).

In general, the three techniques present a better performance than a conventional PID, both in tasks of tracking references when operating at different points of operation or in the regulation tasks (rejection of disturbances). However, to provide these results, it is strictly necessary to normalize the inputs and outputs for all the techniques except the fuzzy supervisor FGS - f (y, r).

Depending on the nature of the process to be controlled, if it allows the presence of overshoots, the designer is suggested to use a direct fuzzy controller FPD+I due to the low complexity of implementation good indexes in tracking references and regulation tasks. To reach the reference in the shortest possible time at the expense of a more significant overshoot, it is suggested to implement an FGS - f (e, de) controller, but this involves a greater computational expense, if you do not have these limitations, it is suggested to implement an FLC Dir - Sup FLC which meets the above characteristics.

References

1. Hu, B.G., Mann, G.K.I., Gosine, R.G.: A systematic study of fuzzy PID controllers - function-based evaluation approach. IEEE Trans. Fuzzy Syst. (2001)
2. Ketata, R., De Geest, D., Titli, A.: Fuzzy controller: design, evaluation, parallel and hierarchial combination with a PID controller. Fuzzy Sets Syst. (1995)
3. Precup, R.E., Hellendoorn, H.: A survey on industrial applications of fuzzy control. Comput. Ind. **62**(3), 213–226 (2011)
4. Yesil, E., Guzelkaya, M., Eksin, I.: Fuzzy PID controllers: an overview. In: Third Triennial ETAI. International Conference on Applied Automatic Systems, Skopje, no. October, pp. 105–112 (2003)
5. Passino, K., Yurkovich, S.: Fuzzy Control: The Basics (1998)
6. Zheng, L.: A practical guide to tune of proportional and integral (PI) like fuzzy controllers (1992)
7. Li, H.X., Gatland, H.B.: A new methodology for designing a fuzzy logic controller. IEEE Trans. Syst. Man. Cybern. (1995)
8. Zeng, W., et al.: Core power control of a space nuclear reactor based on a nonlinear model and fuzzy-PID controller. Prog. Nucl. Energy **132**, 103564 (2020)
9. Chao, C.T., Sutarna, N., Chiou, J.S., Wang, C.J.: Equivalence between fuzzy PID controllers and conventional PID controllers. Appl. Sci. **7**(6), 513 (2017)
10. Chao, C.T., Sutarna, N., Chiou, J.S., Wang, C.J.: An optimal fuzzy PID controller design based on conventional PID control and nonlinear factors. Appl. Sci. **9**(6), 1224 (2019)
11. Misir, D., Malki, H.A., Chen, G.: Design and analysis of a fuzzy proportional-integral-derivative controller. Fuzzy Sets Syst. **79**, 297–314 (1996)
12. Jantzen, J.: Tuning of fuzzy PID controllers. Tech. Univ. Denmark, Dep. Autom. **871**(98-H), 1–22 (1998)
13. Escamilla-Ambrosio, P.J., Mort, N.: A novel design and tuning procedure for PID type fuzzy logic controllers. In: 2002 1st International IEEE Symposium (2002)
14. Viljamaa, P., Koivo, H.N.: Fuzzy logic in PID gain scheduling. In: Third European Congress on Fuzzy and Intelligent Technologies EUFIT 1995 (1995)
15. Zhao, Z.Y., Tomizuka, M., Isaka, S.: Fuzzy gain scheduling of PID controllers. IEEE Trans. Syst. Man Cybern. **23**(5), 1392–1398 (1993)

16. Babuška, R., Te Braake, H.A.B., Van Can, H.J.L., Krijgsman, A.J., Verbruggen, H.B.: Comparison of intelligent control schemes for real-time pressure control. Control Eng. Pract. (1996)
17. Ahmad, N., Ramli, R., Tajjudin, M., Tajjudin, S.: Comparison of the performance and Energy consumption between PID control and self-tuning FuzzyPID in compact hydro distillation process. In: IEEE International Conference on Automatic Control an Intelligent Systems (2018)
18. Tamayo, E., Zuluaga, C., Alvarez, H.: A fuzzy-evaluated gain scheduling approach for the PID control of a pressure plant. In: IEEE 4th Colombian Conference on Automatic Control as Key Support Industrial Productivity, CCAC 2019 - Proceedings (2019)
19. Zhu, Z., et al.: Fuzzy PID control of the three-degree-of-freedom parallel mechanism based on genetic algorithm. Appl. Sci. 12(21), 11128 (2022)
20. Baroud, Z., Benmiloud, M., Benalia, A., Ocampo-Martinez, C.: Novel hybrid fuzzy-PID control scheme for air supply in PEM fuel-cell-based systems. Int. J. Hydrogen Energy 42(15), 10435–10447 (2017)
21. Anitha, T., Gopu, G., Nagarajapandian, M., Devan, P.A.M.: Hybrid fuzzy PID controller for pressure process control application. In: 2019 IEEE Student Conference on Research and Development (SCOReD 2019), pp. 129–133 (2019)
22. Zeng, W., Jiang, Q., Xie, J., Yu, T.: A fuzzy-PID composite controller for core power control of liquid molten salt reactor. Ann. Nucl. Energy 139, 107234 (2020)
23. Zhang, Y., Shao, C.: Fuzzy-PID hybrid control for temperature of melted aluminum in atomization furnace. In: Sixth International Conference on Intelligent Systems Design and Applications, pp. 332–335 (2006)
24. Chakchouk, W., Zaafouri, A., Sallami, A.: Hybrid control of a station of irrigation by sprinkling: fuzzy supervisor approach. In: 2015 4th International Conference on Systems and Control, ICSC 2015 (2015)
25. Rodriguez-Castellanos, J.E., Grisales-Palacio, V.H.: A tuning proposal for fuzzy gain scheduling controllers for industrial continuous processes. In: 2018 IEEE 2nd Colombian Conference on Robotics and Automation, CCRA 2018 (2018)
26. Rodríguez-Castellanos, J.E., Grisales-Palacio, V.H., Cote-Ballesteros, J.E.: A tuning proposal for direct fuzzy PID controllers oriented to industrial continuous processes. IFAC-PapersOnLine (2018)

Applications

Design of a Right-Hand Rehabilitation Orthosis

Abigail P. Hernandez Morelo⬤, Juan F. Romano Parra⬤,
Christian M. Orozco Rios⬤, Natalia Rangel Franco(✉)⬤,
Malorys M. Elles Fang⬤, and Sonia H. Contreras-Ortiz⬤

Universidad Tecnológica de Bolívar, Km 1 Vía Turbaco, Cartagena, Colombia
nrangel@utb.edu.co

Abstract. This study presents a dynamic orthosis designed to support the therapies of patients with muscle stiffness in the hand through gripping and relaxation movements. The orthosis features a modular design with sections for the phalanges, palm, and forearm, enabling adjustments to fit different hand and arm sizes. It uses motors to generate hand movements and feedback sensors for precise position adjustments during therapy. Testing demonstrated its effectiveness and adaptability in different users. Future improvements include validating the device with professionals for clinical use.

Keywords: Orthosis · Assistive wearable device · Hand and wrist · Rehabilitation

1 Introduction

Stroke is a leading cause of disability and mortality in the Americas, with millions of cases occurring each year [9]. Among the various types of stroke, ischemic stroke represents about 85% of all cases [5]. This type of stroke results from a blockage in blood flow to a part of the brain, typically caused by a blood clot, leading to damage to brain cells due to a lack of oxygen [4]. Sequelae from ischemic stroke can include dysarthria, muscle stiffness, hypersomnia, cognitive deficits, and more [3].

Muscle stiffness is one of the most common sequelae, affecting between 30% and 80% of stroke survivors [2]. This stiffness primarily affects the extremities, such as the hands and wrists. Rehabilitation therapies designed to address muscle stiffness in the hands and wrists have demonstrated effectiveness in promoting recovery and increasing range of motion [7].

However, the issue of limited access to advanced rehabilitation technologies in Colombia is a significant one, with the costs involved often beyond the reach of most people. This underscores the urgent need for innovative, cost-effective solutions that can bridge this gap and improve the quality of life for those in need.

J. C. Figueroa-García et al. (Eds.): WEA 2024, CCIS 2223, pp. 177–187, 2025.
https://doi.org/10.1007/978-3-031-74598-0_15

The development of orthosis has been an evolution of the treatment of various medical conditions affecting the mobility and functionality of limbs. We have witnessed significant advances in orthotic technology throughout history, from the earliest rudimentary devices [8,11] to the sophisticated solutions of today. This continuous progress has sparked growing interest and relevance in the medical and scientific community, aiming to address patients' needs effectively. In this context, medical devices designed to treat conditions impacting the proper functioning of limbs, such as the hand, stand out.

Furthermore, the innovative use of 3D printing technology for manufacturing personalized hand orthoses [6,10,13,14] has been demonstrated. This technology offers numerous advantages in orthotic manufacturing, including the ability to produce highly customized devices tailored to the specific needs of each patient.

As for the development of orthotic control, various techniques and technologies have been explored. Notably, electromyography (EMG) sensors have been implemented. These sensors, which record muscle electrical activity and translate it into control signals for the orthosis, offer a unique and effective way to customize the design and operation of the orthosis, adapting to the individual needs of users.

This paper presents the development of an orthosis for the rehabilitation of the right hand designed in 3D that consists of 3 main parts (rings, palm and forearm) and that by means of sensors and actuators generates a passive movement that helps the recovery of patients.

2   Materials and Methods

Our device's purpose is to provide a dynamic and controlled tool that assists in hand and wrist rehabilitation therapies.

The requirements of the system are:

- Individual finger position control for grasping and relaxation movements.
- Anatomical shape for comfortable use during therapies.
- Adaptable Modular structure to different arm and hand sizes of patients within an average range of these sizes.
- Wireless Bluetooth connection for device control.

2.1   Mechanical Design

We created the 3D design of the orthosis using SolidEdge software. Based on the design provided by H Yoo et al. [14], we proposed several modifications to allow the device to be custom-fitted to various people within a specific range.

The orthosis consists of a modular structure separated into three main parts: phalanges, palmar-dorsal, and forearm (Fig. 1).

- **Phalanges ring design.** This structure supports the fingers for general movement through artificial tendons.

– **Palmar-dorsal.** This structure supports the palmar area, allows the locking of the wrist using two lateral fasteners, and provides a guide for the artificial tendons that transmit the movement of the motors to the fingers.

– **Forearm.** This is the structure where we placed the motors and printed circuit boards for controlling the device. It also includes guide rails for artificial tendons. We incorporated another type of rail specifically for engines to adjust the distance between the fingers, allowing the device to adapt for people with different measures.

In addition, the orthosis has two volar structures, which support the hand and arm and direct the rails through which the threads pass. The device uses a mechanism comprising motors that coil the artificial tendon and generate the force to activate the traction system. Simultaneously, the tendon retraction system efficiently pulls back the artificial tendon, enabling controlled extension and retraction according to user requirements. Together, these components form an integral unit designed for stroke patient rehabilitation, with the motor providing power and the retraction system ensuring smooth movement control. Additionally, the design incorporates feedback sensors that monitor the force and position of the tendon, allowing for precise adjustments and personalized adaptations during rehabilitation therapy.

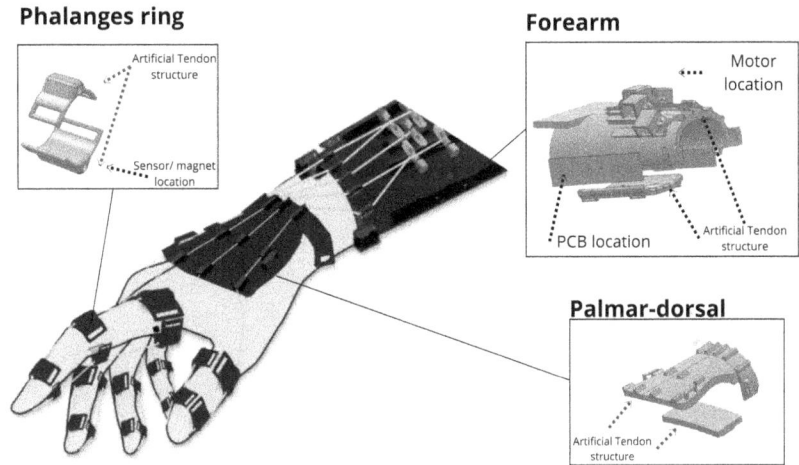

Fig. 1. Schematic design of the hand orthosis.

2.2 Materials

3D Prints. These rings were manufactured through 3D printing using polylactic acid (PLA) filament [12]. The forearm, palmar-dorsal design, along with its complements, was made of thermoplastic polyurethane (TPU) filament [12], which we adjusted with Velcro straps.

Sensors. We utilized five linear Hall effect sensors (SS49E) to measure the degree of flexion in a patient's fingers. These sensors have a linear output voltage that varies with the strength of the magnetic field, providing a proportional measurement of finger movement. We housed the sensors on the proximal phalangeal rings and the magnets on the middle phalangeal rings.

Actuators. We actuated the rings with nylon threads attached to winding drums driven by geared motors. The orthosis has *six geared motors*, each providing a torque of 2 Kg*cm and a rotational speed of 15 RPM (at 3 V).

2.3 Electronic Design

We located the motors and microcontrollers in the forearm section of the orthosis. We connected the motors to an *Arduino Nano ESP32*, which interfaced with a *Pro Mini 328P* module operating at 3.3 V/8 MHz.

An electronic circuit was designed for the orthosis function control system, integrating all components that would work together to perform the actions.

Four different printed circuit board models were designed and implemented, each defined by the components it integrates and its specific function.

The system consists of four interconnected boards (Fig. 2): the **Main Board**, housing the NANOESP32 module for controlling device movements and managing Bluetooth communication while instructing a **Secondary Board** equipped with a PRO MINI 328p module for additional motor signal generation; the **Motor Board**, incorporating the DVR8833 module to control up to two motors simultaneously via PWM signals received from the main board; and the **Sensor Board**, integrating hall sensors.

(a) Sensor, Main, Secondary

(b) PCB: Motors drivers

Fig. 2. Boards

2.4   Analysis and Calculations

Force Measurement

An analysis of the patient's forces was necessary to select the motors to develop the orthosis. Relevant literature was consulted, including studies on analyzing finger strength capacity using anthropometric and myoelectric measurements. In a previous study with 100 subjects, we found the mean grip strength for males to be 452.44 N, while for females, their mean was 288.91 N [1] (Fig. 3).

Motor Choice Calculations

(a) Artificial tendon hoist   (b) Measure winding drum

Fig. 3. Artificial tendon system - winding drum

Formulas for required engine power:

$$P = \frac{W}{t} = \frac{F \cdot d}{t} \tag{1}$$

$$T = 2\,\mathrm{Kg/cm} = 16.6\,\mathrm{N/cm}$$

$$F = r \cdot T \tag{2}$$

$$F = \frac{1}{2}cm \cdot \frac{19.6\,\mathrm{N}}{cm} = 39.2\,\mathrm{N}$$

where maximum power available from the motor is

$$P = \frac{39.2\,\mathrm{N} \cdot .2\,\mathrm{m}}{4\,\mathrm{s}} = 1.96\,\mathrm{W}$$

and the power required for a 3 kg grip is

$$F = 3\,\mathrm{kg} \cdot .8\,\mathrm{m/s}^2 = 29.4\,\mathrm{N}$$
$$P = \frac{29.4\,\mathrm{N} \cdot .2\,\mathrm{m}}{4\,\mathrm{s}} = 1.47\,\mathrm{W}$$

Control Strategy

Proportional control with hall effect sensor feedback is used to control finger position. In this strategy, a proportional response is obtained from the error determined by subtracting the deflection percentage from the setpoint value (Fig. 4).

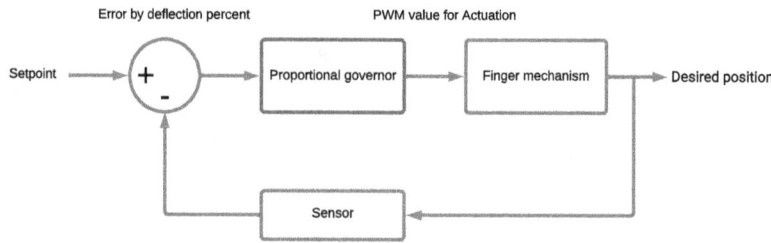

Fig. 4. Proportional control

The PWM output of the actuator is determined by the following formula

$$PWM = \frac{SP - MD}{100\%} \cdot 255(V_{dac}) \tag{3}$$

where:

- SP = Set Point
- MD = Measure Deflection
- V_{dac} = Value of the 100% DAC
- D_{min} : Minimum Deflection (Fig. 5a)
- D_{max} : Maximum Deflection (Fig. 5b)

Measurement of Deflection Percent
We obtained the deflection percentage by calibrating and normalizing the maximum and minimum values obtained from the flex sensor (Fig. 6).

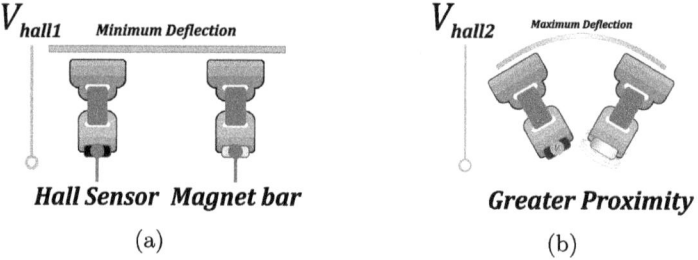

(a)   (b)

Fig. 5. Hall effect

Figure 7a shows the process for obtaining the maximum and minimum values for this normalization, and Fig. 7b shows a flowchart representing the implementation of the programming code in the device

Finally, we used the following formula to obtain the deflection percentage, which we implemented on the microcontroller to calculate the measurement.

$$PD = \frac{MD - D_{min}}{D_{max} - D_{min}} \cdot 100 \tag{4}$$

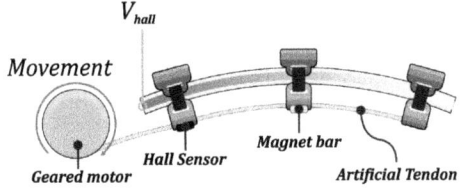

Fig. 6. Schematic of the implementation of the hall effect sensor in the prototype

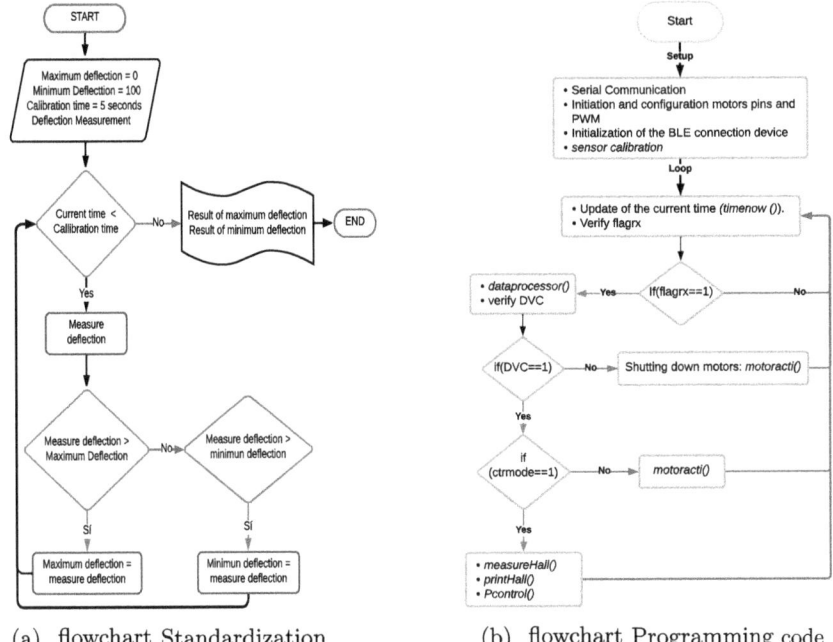

(a) flowchart Standardization   (b) flowchart Programming code

Fig. 7. The description is "Diagrams for system control analysis"

where:

- PD = Deflection Percentage
- MD = Measure Deflection
- D_{min} : Minimum Deflection (Fig. 5a)
- D_{max} : Maximum Deflection (Fig. 5b)

3   Results

3.1   Interface

We developed the interface using Java in the NetBeans environment. The main objective of this interface is to provide control over the movements of the orthosis, including the possibility of regulating the speed of the motors to adapt them to the specific needs of each patient. Also, a clear and precise visualization allows monitoring of the data coming from the sensors. It has two main panels: control and visualization. In the control panel are all the buttons containing each possible movement so far: Relaxation and grip of the hand and the opening and closing of each finger independently. As well as the buttons to start, stop, speed control, and turn on or off.

On the other hand, the display panel contains labels on which we located the hall sensors' data indicating each finger's position. Next to the label, we stated the desired position values. Finally, there is also a progress bar indicating the device battery percentage (Fig. 8).

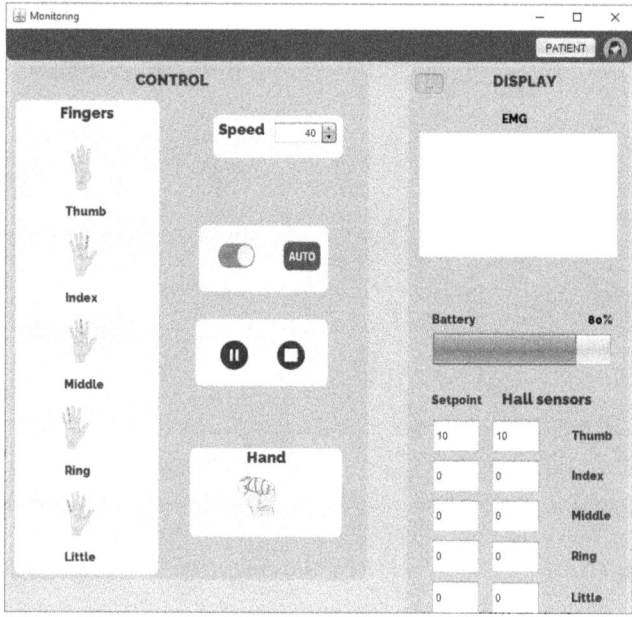

Fig. 8. Interface

3.2   Adaptability to Different User Sizes

The orthosis was designed and constructed with a modular and adjustable structure that allowed its use by people with different hand and arm sizes. The device adapted effectively to a small woman and a more prominent man during testing, demonstrating its versatility and adjustability. The range of sizes handled were:

– Finger diameter: [4.8–8] cm
– Forearm diameter: [19–24] cm

– Finger length: [5–10] cm

The orthosis was able to independently perform the movements of grasping and relaxing the fingers. We controlled these movements through an intuitive user interface connected wirelessly via Bluetooth (Fig. 9).

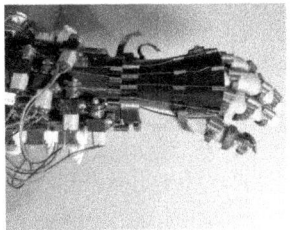
(a) subject 1: Woman - small size

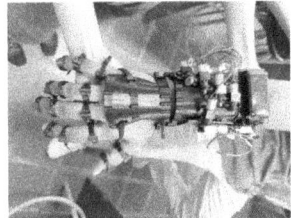
(b) Subject 2: Man - large size

Fig. 9. Results

After testing the orthosis, we placed it over a cloth glove to enhance patient comfort (Fig. 10).

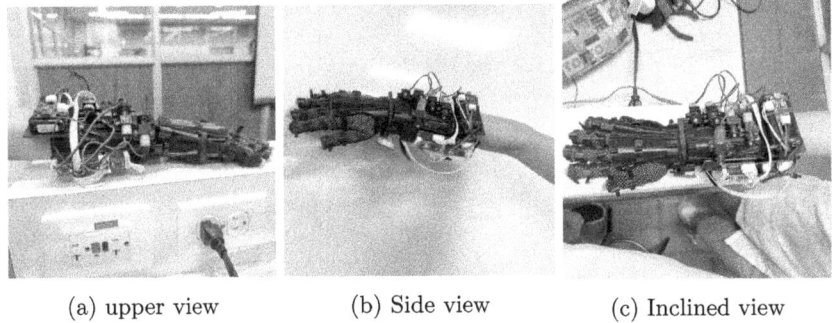

(a) upper view   (b) Side view   (c) Inclined view

Fig. 10. Result with glove

Besides of the two early items mentioned before, after test the functionality of the orthosis, we obtained as results:

– That the prototype requires approximately 7 min to be placed and requires assistance, as the user cannot independently done it.
– The device has a total weight of 397 g. Although this is relatively light, we recommend supporting the arm during therapy sessions for additional comfort.
– The voltage supplied by the battery was measured at 8.31 V, powering two microcontrollers, five motors, five sensors, and three H-bridges.
– With continuous use of the orthosis, the battery depletes to nearly half of its capacity in approximately 40 min. The battery charging time is about 30 min.

4   Conclusions

In this paper, we designed, developed, and tested a passive motion orthosis to support muscle stiffness therapies for stroke patients. We based the design and construction of the orthosis on research and standards for electronic and medical devices. Key components, including Hall sensors and magnets, were meticulously selected to control finger position by accurately measuring proximity and movement using magnetic properties. We operated the device via a wireless connection interface via Bluetooth.

During testing, this prototype demonstrated its effectiveness in performing the established movements and its ability to adapt to different people.

In future work, we proposed to improve the prototype by replacing TPU and PLA filaments with resin to increase the device's durability. Additionally, using smaller components to reduce its size and weight. Developing a mobile application could facilitate therapists' use of orthosis. Implementing another type of movement and making the device ambidextrous would further enhance its usability and range. Validate the device with professionals to prove its functionality and be able to test it with patients is also recommended.

Finally, it is necessary to validate the device with professionals to verify its functionality and be able to test it with patients.

Acknowledgments. We extend our gratitude to the Universidad Tecnológica de Bolívar for providing the facilities and data essential for the previous research and development of the prototype. We also thank all the professors for their valuable support in the design of the prototype.

Disclosure of Interests. The authors have no competing interests to declare relevant to this article's content.

References

1. Astin, A.D.: Finger force capability: measurement and prediction using anthropometric and myoelectric measures, December 1999. https://vtechworks.lib.vt.edu/handle/10919/30923
2. Hatem, S., et al.: Rehabilitation of motor function after stroke: a multiple systematic review focused on techniques to stimulate upper extremity recovery. Front. Hum. Neurosci. **10**, 442 (2016). https://doi.org/10.3389/fnhum.2016.00442
3. Hui, C., Tadi, P., Patti, L.: Ischemic Stroke, June 2022. https://www.ncbi.nlm.nih.gov/books/NBK499997/
4. Kuriakose, D., Xiao, Z.: Pathophysiology and treatment of stroke: present status and future perspectives. Int. J. Mol. Sci. **21**(20), 7609 (2020). https://doi.org/10.3390/ijms21207609
5. Madera, I.C.P.: Epidemiología de las enfermedades cerebrovasculares de origen extracraneal. Revista Cubana de Angiologîa y Cirugía Vascular **15**(2), 66–74 (2014). http://scielo.sld.cu/pdf/ang/v15n2/ang02214.pdf

6. Martins, H.V.P., et al.: Development of a robotic orthosis for fingers flexion motion by surface myoelectric control: open source prototype. Biomed. Signal Process. Control **85**, 105014 (2023). ISSN: 1746-8094, https://doi.org/10.1016/j.bspc.2023, https://www.sciencedirect.com/science/article/pii/S1746809423004470

7. McGrath, M., et al.: Evaluation of static progressive stretch for the treatment of wrist stiffness. J. Hand Surg. **33**(9), 1498–1504 (2008). https://doi.org/10.1016/j.jhsa.2008.05.018

8. Pylatiuk, C., et al.: Design of a flexible fluidic actuation system for a hybrid elbow orthosis. In: IEEE International Conference on Rehabilitation Robotics, June 2009. https://doi.org/10.1109/icorr.2009.5209540

9. Organización Panamericana de la Salud. La OMS revela las principales causas de muerte y discapacidad en el mundo: 2000–2019 (2020). https://www.paho.org/es/noticias/9-12-2020-oms-revela-principales-causas-muerte-discapacidad-mundo-2000-2019

10. Tóth, L., et al.: Developing an anti-spastic orthosis for daily home-use of stroke patients using smart memory alloys and 3D printing technologies. Mater. Des. **195**, 109029 (2020). https://doi.org/10.1016/j.matdes.2020.109029

11. Vitiello, N., et al.: Functional design of a powered elbow orthosis toward its clinical employment. IEEE/ASME Trans. Mechatron. **21**(4), 1880–1891 (2016). https://doi.org/10.1109/tmech.2016.2558646

12. What is Medical-Grade TPU-ICP DAS-Biomedical Polymers. https://bmp.icpdas.com/what-is-medical-grade-tpu/

13. Yeh, P.-C., Chen, C.-H., Chen, C.-S.: Using a 3D printed hand orthosis to improve three-jaw chuck hand function in individuals with cervical spinal cord injury: a feasibility study. IEEE Trans. Neural Syst. Rehabil. Eng. **31**, 2552–2559 (2023). https://doi.org/10.1109/tnsre.2023.3273300

14. Yoo, H.-J., et al.: Development of 3D-printed myoelectric hand orthosis for patients with spinal cord injury. J. Neuroeng. Rehabil. **16**(1), 162 (2019). https://doi.org/10.1186/s12984-019-0633-6

Detection of Broken Bars in Three-Phase Electric Motors Using Current and Vibration Signals

Gabriel Hoyos[ID] and J. L. Villa[(⊠)][ID]

Universidad Tecnologica de Bolivar, Bolivar, Colombia
{ghoyos,jvilla}@utb.edu.co

Abstract. The maintenance and diagnosis of failures in mechanical machines, especially in induction motors, represent critical and costly challenges. Rotor failures, such as breaks or fractures, are especially problematic and can affect operational safety and efficiency. To address these challenges, intelligent fault diagnosis has become vital, employing machine learning techniques such as KNN, SVM and decision trees to prevent failures in real time. Motor current signature analysis (MCSA) stands out as a non-intrusive diagnostic technique, complemented by signal processing such as FFT and wavelet. Alternatives to MCSA include vibration signal analysis, with accelerometers capturing data and classification techniques identifying rotor and bearing faults. In this paper, the CRISP-DM model was applied, including data preprocessing, Fourier analysis and Hamming window for current and vibration signals. Machine learning models such as Random Forest and SVM were trained and evaluated, reaching an average accuracy of 90% when combining current and vibration data.

Keywords: Current signal · Vibration signal · ML · Machine Learning · Detection · Motor

1 Introduction

Mechanical machines play a crucial role in a variety of industries, but their maintenance and fault diagnosis represent costly and fundamental challenges [18, 21]. Induction motors, widely used in industrial environments, are particularly susceptible to failure due to their exposure to adverse conditions and intense duty cycles.

Rotor failures, such as end ring breaks or fractures, are recurring problems in induction motors, causing serious malfunctions that can affect safety and operating efficiency [16]. These failures, initially localized, can spread and compromise the integrity of the motor, underscoring the importance of preventive maintenance.

Intelligent fault diagnosis emerges as a vital tool in predictive equipment maintenance, employing machine learning techniques such as KNN, SVM and

J. C. Figueroa-García et al. (Eds.): WEA 2024, CCIS 2223, pp. 188–199, 2025.
https://doi.org/10.1007/978-3-031-74598-0_16

decision trees to analyze real-time data and prevent breakdowns [3,20,22,25,29]. The effectiveness of these methods lies in their ability to provide accurate and timely diagnostics.

The key challenge in intelligent fault diagnosis lies in the training speed, accuracy and generalization of the model [4,17]. Ensemble learning methods, particularly effective with smaller data sets, offer greater accuracy and generalization capability [26,30].

The process begins with the collection of relevant data and its subsequent processing using feature engineering, which encompasses traditional methods. Although traditional methods are useful for simplifying models and improving accuracy, their dependence on specialized knowledge limits their applicability.

This paper is organized as follows, first we present a review of the literature, then in Sect. 3, we describe the methodology, then in Sect. 3.1, we present the main results.

2   Review of Literature

Motor Current Signature Analysis (MCSA) is a notable method utilized for evaluating the health of induction motors without the need for invasive procedures. This method involves examining the current waveform produced by the motor during normal operation and contrasting it with an established reference standard to identify possible deviations and faults. It is usually the first step in the fault diagnosis process, often combined with signal processing techniques such as Fast Fourier Transform (FFT) [10,14,19], wavelet [9,12,14] or Hilbert-Huang Transform [1,5,14]. However, it is important to note that MCSA can generate inaccurate results in situations of saturation, inter-bar currents or magnetic asymmetry [2].

The study conducted by Khechekhouche et al. [12] explored two signal processing methods within the framework of Motor Current Signature Analysis (MCSA) to identify inter-turn short circuits (ITSC) and voltage supply imbalances (UVS). Initially, a preliminary assessment was conducted employing the Fast Fourier Transform (FFT), succeeded by the discrete wavelet energy ratio (DWER) [14]. Conversely, Kompella et al. [13] utilized MCSA for the detection of bearing faults. They applied the Discrete Wavelet Transform (DWT) to mitigate noise, followed by the implementation of an adaptive filter (Wiener filter) for pre-fault component elimination, and ultimately estimated the fault using the Matrix Pencil Method (MPM) [14]. This same approach was used in [6] for various types of fault detection. In addition, [15] provided guidance for avoiding false fault detections based on MCSA, considering the relationship between different faults and strategies to address this problem. While Motor Current Signature Analysis (MCSA) is primarily utilized under stationary conditions, researchers have explored its application in non-stationary scenarios. For instance, Yassa et al. [27] investigated the detection of start-up time eccentricities by developing a model for the induction motor. Additionally, Antonino et al. [1,14] utilized novel transient-based models incorporating time-frequency transformations for diagnostic purposes.

Alternatives to MCSA have been explored, most notably the analysis of vibration signals. Accelerometers are employed for vibration data capture, and their proper placement is crucial for accurate results. The quote [10] suggested the use of vibration signals for rotor fault detection, supported by machine learning classification techniques. It is common to employ the Fast Fourier Transform (FFT) in the processing of [28] vibration signals. Track fracture in bearings can be identified using radial and axial accelerometers [23]. In bearing failure or imbalance situations, machine vibration can be measured through an antenna and subsequently analyzed using deep learning techniques [7]. The combination of vibration and stator current signals shows great potential for accurate classification of broken rotor bars [8].

3   Methodology

The methodology used for broken bus bar detection in induction motors is based on the CRISP-DM model (Fig. 1), which comprises six key stages. In the first stage, a comprehensive analysis is conducted to understand the business needs and objectives related to broken bar detection, including its impact on motor operation and associated risks. This sets the framework for the project and provides a clear understanding of the objectives to be achieved.

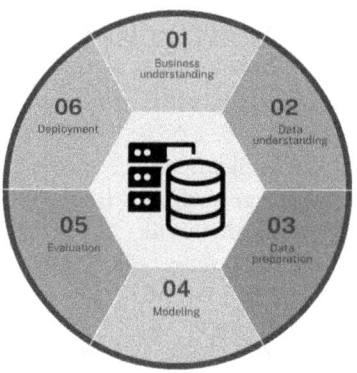

Fig. 1. Methodology CRISP-DM

In the second stage, we proceed to the exploration of data related to the operation of induction motors, focusing on variables relevant to the detection of broken bars, such as sensor signals and electrical and mechanical parameters. This data exploration is crucial to identify relevant features and establish a solid basis for further analysis.

The data set used in this project is obtained from a database hosted at IEEE, as documented by [24]. The database used includes electrical and mechanical signals from three-phase induction motors, covering load variations and different levels of rotor bar defects, with reference data without defects. Experiments were performed on a workbench with a WEG motor coupled to a DC machine simulating load torque. Currents were recorded using Hall effect sensors and other signals such as voltages and mechanical vibration velocities.

During data preparation, several tasks were carried out to ensure data quality and relevance to the modeling process. This included data cleaning, selection of relevant features, and their transformation for use in subsequent modeling. Specifically, features useful for broken bar detection were identified and extracted, and the stable part of the signal corresponding to the current and vibration cases was selected (Fig. 2).

The choice of the Fourier Transform and Hamming window in the current and vibration signal processing is justified for several reasons. The Fourier Transform allows to analyze signals in the frequency domain, which is crucial for understanding the signal energy distribution in different frequency components, especially in the context of broken bar detection in induction motors. The Hamming window is used to reduce the effect of discontinuities in the signal, thus improving frequency resolution and reducing noise in the resulting spectrum. This combination of techniques provides a more accurate representation of the frequency content of the signals, facilitating the detection of characteristic patterns associated with broken bars in induction motors.

During data preparation, several crucial tasks are performed to ensure data quality and relevance to the modeling process. This includes data cleaning, selection of relevant features and their transformation in order to adequately prepare them for use in modeling. Specifically, specific features that could be useful in broken bar detection are identified and extracted by taking records after an engine time-out and start-up process. The stable part of the signal corresponding to the current and vibration cases is selected, and a windowing of the signal is performed to delineate segments of interest. This approach ensures the consistency and representativeness of the data used, thus providing a solid basis for the study of broken bar detection.

The choice of the Fourier Transform and the Hamming window in current and vibration signal processing is justified for several reasons. The Fourier Transform allows to analyze signals in the frequency domain, which is crucial to understand the signal energy distribution in different frequency components, especially in the context of broken bar detection in induction motors. The Hamming window is used to reduce the effect of discontinuities in the signal, thus improving frequency resolution and reducing noise in the resulting spectrum. This combination of techniques provides a more accurate representation of the frequency content of the signals, facilitating the detection of characteristic patterns associated with broken bars in induction motors.

In the modeling phase, various classification models are built and evaluated to predict the presence of broken bars in induction motors. This includes selection of suitable algorithms, creation of training and test sets, parameter tuning and performance evaluation with metrics such as precision, accuracy, f1 and

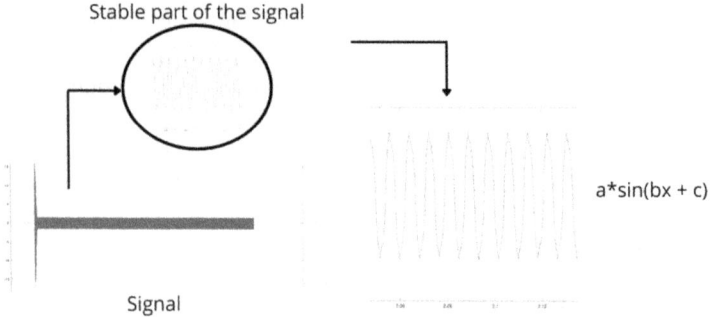

Stable part of the signal

Signal

a*sin(bx + c)

Fig. 2. Data Preprocessing

recall. This process determines the most effective models and whether they meet established business requirements.

In the final stage, the optimal classifier model is implemented in a real-time system that continuously monitors the induction motors. When a broken bar is detected, the system notifies operators by e-mail and suggests maintenance actions. The goal is to intervene without generating unscheduled outages, thus extending the life of the equipment [11].

3.1   Methodology to Classify Faults Using Current Signals

In the signal preprocessing phase, the stable part of the data, essential to ensure quality and consistency, is identified. This involves selecting segments that represent stable engine conditions, excluding noise and interference. Once this stable part is identified, the processing stage begins.

Processing. The initial analysis employs the Fourier Transform to examine the frequency domain behavior of the signals, essential for detecting variations associated with defects in the motor rods. Four fault scenarios are evaluated to understand how the signals vary in response to different levels of rod deterioration and to establish correlations between signal changes and defect severity.

Feature Extraction. The curve fitting technique extracts signal attributes for engine failures using a sine function $a*sin(bx+c)$. A DataFrame is split into 2048-row segments, and the $curve_fit$ function fits the sine function to each segment. The fitted parameters are stored as absolute values in a list. This process uses data from the time and currents columns and is repeated 400 times, once for each segment.

Extraction of Characteristics by Harmonics of the Signal. The Hamming window technique was applied together with the Fourier Transform to improve resolution and reduce noise in the signal spectrum. MATLAB's "findspeak" function was used to find local peaks in a data set. Mathematically, a peak in a data vector is a point where the data value is greater than its adjacent neighbors, indicative of engine faults, and a database enriched with these attributes was generated for the classification models. This strategy enabled accurate characterization of engine operating conditions and facilitated fault detection by the models.

Evaluation Measures. In this project, key evaluation measures are used to analyze the performance of machine learning models in induction motor fault classification. These measures include F1 Score, which combines accuracy and completeness to provide a balanced evaluation of the model; precision, which indicates the proportion of correctly classified positive samples; and recall, which measures the model's ability to correctly identify all positive samples. In addition, accuracy is used to assess the overall precision of the model, although it can be misleading in situations of sample class imbalance. These measures provide a complete picture of the model's performance in induction motor fault classification.

Training. The training stage in machine learning models for induction motor fault classification encompasses several crucial steps:

- Loading of current signals: Collection of current data and fault details.
- Creation of matrices for each fault: Organization of data into separate matrices by fault type.
- Extraction and assignment of new data: Use of curve fitting techniques to extract features from current signals.
- Matrix splicing: Combining individual matrices to feed the model.
- Descriptive and distribution analysis: Use of descriptive statistics and visualizations to understand the data.
- Identification and elimination of repeated data: Elimination of duplicates to avoid biases.
- Database partitioning: Separation into training and test sets.
- Review of evaluation measures: Calculation of metrics such as F1, Precision, Recall and Accuracy.
- Implementation of cross-validation techniques: Use of k-fold cross-validation to assess generalization.
- Identification of important features: Analysis of the importance of features to understand their influence on the model's ability to classify failures.

Model Parameters. Machine learning models used to classify induction motor failures are described:

- Random Forest: $n - stimators = 500$ and $random - state = 11$
- Decision Tree: $criterion =' entropy'$
- SVM: $StandardScaler(), SVC(gamma =' auto')$
- KNN: per default

3.2   Methodology to Classify Faults Using Vibration Signals

In the preprocessing of the vibration signal, a similar process was carried out was carried out in order to ensure the quality and consistency of the data prior to its analysis of the data prior to analysis.

Processing. Focuses on the initial analysis of the vibration signals in the frequency domain, using the Fourier Transform to decompose the signals and reveal the predominant frequencies. This analysis provides a detailed view of the frequency characteristics, facilitating early detection of engine problems.

Feature Extraction. The MATLAB function "findspeak" is used to identify significant peaks in the vibration signal, providing the position and amplitude of each peak. This tool allows an accurate analysis of key vibration characteristics, essential for fault diagnosis in induction motors.

3.3   Methodology to Classify Faults Using Current and Vibration Signals

In this stage, all the analysis previously performed is consolidated, which includes the application of Fourier Transforms to analyze current and vibration signals, as well as the extraction of relevant features from these signals. The main objective is to implement a comprehensive strategy to classify motor faults, taking advantage of the information obtained from both current and vibration signals and vibration signals.

4   Results

A confusion matrix is a table that evaluates the performance of classification models by showing true positives, true negatives, false positives, and false negatives (Fig. 3). Its main metrics are accuracy, recall, specificity, and F1 score. Analyzing these values helps identify the strengths and weaknesses of the model and adjust its performance. Artificial Intelligence models used in the classification of broken bars in three-phase induction motors using current and vibration signals are discussed, providing insight into how these metrics are applied in real-world scenarios.

4.1   Current Signal

In this section we applied k-fold cross-validation, a crucial technique in the evaluation of machine learning models. This strategy involves repeatedly splitting the data into training and test sets using k-folds, where each fold is used as a test set once and the rest as a training set. The choice of k, in this case ten, is essential and can influence the stability and reliability of the model evaluation, although the minimum and maximum values of k may vary depending on the algorithm and the context of the problem.

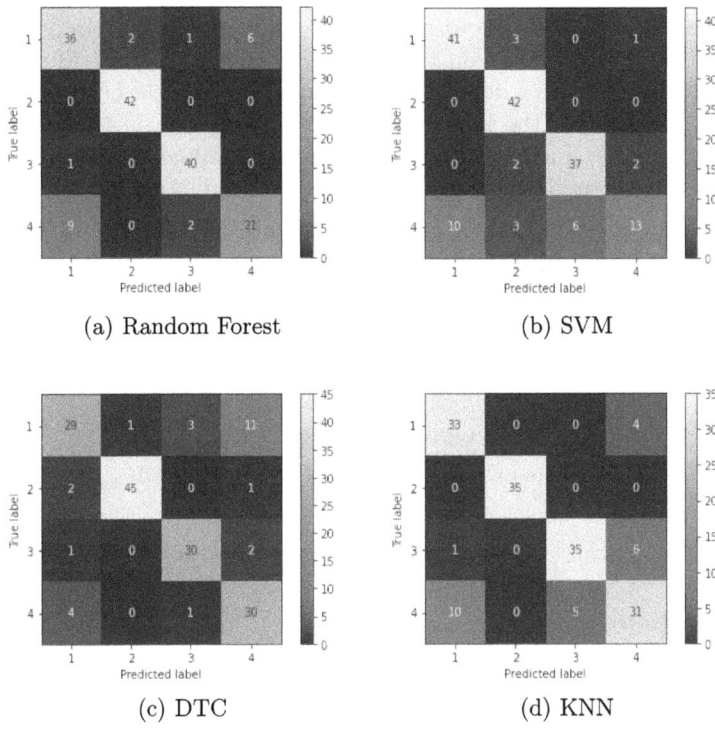

(a) Random Forest

(b) SVM

(c) DTC

(d) KNN

Fig. 3. Confusion matrix per model of current with cross validation

To demonstrate the importance of cross-validation in model evaluation, the confusion matrices corresponding to the Random Forest algorithms were presented, showing the results obtained for the lowest and highest accuracy (Github). These matrices provide a detailed view of the model performance in terms of its classification capabilities for each class, allowing a comprehensive evaluation of its performance in induction motor fault detection (Table 1).

Table 1. Results with cross-validated model evaluation models

Model	F1	Precision	Recall	Accuracy
Random Forest	0.85	0.85	0.86	0.85
SVM	0.79	0.82	0.80	0.83
Decision Tree Classifier	0.83	0.83	0.84	0.83
K Neighbors Classifier	0.84	0.84	0.84	0.83

4.2 Harmonic Current

In this section, we analyze the results of the study of current signals in relation to different harmonics, achieving an impressive accuracy of 95% (Table 2). This analysis provides us with a detailed understanding of how the current varies with frequency, highlighting the importance of each harmonic in the overall signal behavior (Github). Crucially, these findings provide valuable information to better understand the performance and health of the induction motor.

Table 2. Current results by harmonics

Model	F1	Precision	Recall	Accuracy
Random Forest	0.96	0.97	0.96	0.96
SVM	0.93	0.95	0.92	0.93
Decision Tree Classifier	0.93	0.93	0.93	0.93
K Neighbors Classifier	0.96	0.97	0.96	0.96

4.3 Vibration

In this section, the results of different classification models in induction motor fault detection are analyzed and discussed. The results show an average performance above 85%, indicating a significant ability to identify and classify faults accurately. It is important to note that, in this particular case, a cross-validation was not performed because the results obtained are high enough to be considered reliable and satisfactory.

Table 3 provides a detailed summary of the evaluation measures, including F1-score, precision, recall and overall accuracy, giving a complete overview of the performance of each model in terms of its ability to classify faults based on vibration signals.

4.4 Current and Vibration

In this section, the results obtained by merging the current and vibration databases (Github), yielded better percentages in all areas than separately,

Table 3. Vibration results

Model	F1	Precision	Recall	Accuracy
Random Forest	0.94	0.94	0.94	0.94
SVM	0.93	0.93	0.93	0.93
Decision Tree Classifier	0.88	0.88	0.88	0.88
K Neighbors Classifier	0.82	0.82	0.82	0.83

obtaining an average of 90% accuracy without cross-validation, as shown in Table 4.

Table 4. Current and vibration results

Model	F1	Precision	Recall	Accuracy
Random Forest	0.98	0.98	0.98	0.98
SVM	0.90	0.90	0.90	0.90
Decision Tree Classifier	0.89	0.89	0.89	0.90
K Neighbors Classifier	0.94	0.94	0.94	0.95

5   Conclusion

This research explored crucial aspects of prescriptive maintenance for three-phase electric motors, focusing on monitoring and detection systems and classifying broken bars using current and vibration signals. Maximum accuracies achieved were 86.9% for current by curve fitting, 96% for current by harmonics, 93% for vibration, and 98% for current and vibration coupling. High accuracy was attributed to data reprocessing and processing. Cross-validation was implemented for current data to mitigate overtraining biases, while higher quality data extraction methods were used for vibration. Differentiated pre-processing strategies addressed the specific characteristics of each signal, contributing to more accurate results in classifying broken bars in three-phase induction motors.

Models for classifying broken bars through vibration achieved over 89% accuracy on average, without needing cross-validation due to high accuracy. Random Forest stood out with 94% accuracy in this category. The combination of current and vibration data resulted in superior performance, achieving an average of 90% accuracy without cross-validation. Random Forest again led with 98% accuracy, followed by SVM, Decision Tree Classifier, and K Neighbors Classifier. This integration proved highly effective in improving predictive capability.

References

1. Antonino-Daviu, J.: Electrical monitoring under transient conditions: a new paradigm in electric motors predictive maintenance. Appl. Sci. **10**(17), 6137 (2020)
2. Bellini, A., et al.: Advances in diagnostic techniques for induction machines. IEEE Trans. Ind. Electron. **55**(12), 4109–4126 (2008)
3. Chen, Y., et al.: Acting as a decision maker: traffic-condition-aware ensemble learning for traffic flow prediction. IEEE Trans. Intell. Transp. Syst. **23**(4), 3190–3200 (2020)
4. Wen, C., Lü, F.: Review on deep learning based fault diagnosis **42**(1), 234–248 (2020)
5. Cherif, B.D.E., et al.: Machine-learning-based diagnosis of an inverter-fed induction motor. IEEE Latin Am. Trans. **20**(6), 901–911 (2022)
6. Deekshit, K.K.C., Rao, M.V.G., Rao, R.S.: Fault indexing parameter based fault detection in induction motor via MCSA with wiener filtering. Electr. Power Compon. Syst. **48**(19–20), 2048–2062 (2021)
7. Dutta, S., Basu, B., Talukdar, F.A.: Classification of induction motor fault and imbalance based on vibration signal using single antenna's reactive near field. IEEE Trans. Instrum. Measur. **70**, 1–9 (2021)
8. Peilun, F., et al.: Dynamic routing-based multimodal neural network for multisensory fault diagnosis of induction motor. J. Manuf. Syst. **55**, 264–272 (2020)
9. Gao, H., et al.: Feature extraction method of series arc fault occurred in three-phase motor with inverter circuit. IEEE Trans. Power Electron. **37**(9), 11164–11173 (2022)
10. Glowacz, A., et al.: Detection of deterioration of three-phase induction motor using vibration signals. Measur. Sci. Rev. **19**(6), 241–249 (2019)
11. Hoyos, G.: Detection of broken bars in three-phase motors by using curve fits and classification algorithms. In: IEEE ANDESCON, pp. 1–6. IEEE (2022)
12. Khechekhouche, A., et al.: Experimental diagnosis of interturns stator fault and unbalanced voltage supply in induction motor using MCSA and DWER. Periodicals Eng. Nat. Sci. **8**(3), 1202–1216 (2020)
13. Kompella, K.C.D., et al.: Robustification of fault detection algorithm in a three-phase induction motor using MCSA for various single and multiple faults. IET Electr. Power Appl. **15**(5), 593–615 (2021)
14. de Las Morenas, J., Moya-Fernández, F., López- Gómez, J.A.: The edge application of machine learning techniques for fault diagnosis in electrical machines. Sensors **23**(5), 2649 (2023)
15. Lee, S.B., et al.: Identification of false rotor fault indications produced by online MCSA for medium-voltage induction machines. IEEE Trans. Ind. Appl. **52**(1), 729–739 (2015)
16. Mehrjou, M.R., et al.: Rotor fault condition monitoring techniques for squirrel-cage induction machine–a review. Mech. Syst. Signal Process. **25**(8), 2827–2848 (2011)
17. Mian, Z., et al.: A literature review of fault diagnosis based on ensemble learning. Eng. Appl. Artif. Intell. **127**, 107357 (2024)
18. Misra, S., et al.: Fault detection in induction motor using time domain and spectral imaging-based transfer learning approach on vibration data. Sensors **22**(21), 8210 (2022)
19. Mustafa, M.O., et al.: Detecting broken rotor bars in induction motors with model-based support vector classifiers. Control Eng. Pract. **52**, 15–23 (2016)

20. Peng, D., et al.: Multibranch and multiscale CNN for fault diagnosis of wheelset bearings under strong noise and variable load condition. IEEE Trans. Ind. Inform. **16**(7), 4949–4960 (2020)
21. Sayyad, S., et al.: Data-driven remaining useful life estimation for milling process: sensors, algorithms, datasets, and future directions. IEEE Access **9**, 110255–110286 (2021)
22. Shi, Q., Zhang, H.: Fault diagnosis of an autonomous vehicle with an improved SVM algorithm subject to unbalanced datasets. IEEE Trans. Ind. Electron. **68**(7), 6248–6256 (2020)
23. Sudhakar, I., AdiNarayana, S., AnilPrakash, M.: Condition monitoring of a 3-ø induction motor by vibration spectrum analysis using Fft analyser-a case study. Mater. Today Proc. **4**(2), 1099–1105 (2017)
24. Treml, A.E., et al.: Experimental database for detecting and diagnosing rotor broken bar in a three-phase induction motor. In: IEEE DataPort (2020)
25. Xiong, J., et al.: An information fusion fault diagnosis method based on dimensionless indicators with static discounting factor and KNN. IEEE Sens. J. **16**(7), 2060–2069 (2015)
26. Xu, J.W., Yang, Y.: A survey of ensemble learning approaches. J. Yunnan Univ. (Nat. Sci. Ed.) **40**(6), 1082–1092 (2018)
27. Yassa, N., Rachek, M., Houassine, H.: Motor current signature analysis for the air gap eccentricity detection in the squirrel cage induction machines. Energy Procedia **162**, 251–262 (2019)
28. Zheng, X.: Eccentricity severity estimation of induction machines using a sparsity-driven regression model. In: IEEE Energy Conversion Congress and Exposition (ECCE), pp. 1–6. IEEE (2022)
29. Zhong, G., et al.: Bus travel time prediction based on ensemble learning methods. IEEE Intell. Transp. Syst. Mag. **14**(2), 174–189 (2020)
30. Zhou, Z.-H., Zhou, Z.-H.: Ensemble Learning. Springer, Cham (2021)

Setting-Up the Audiomoth Recorder for Wildlife Monitoring in the Rainforest

José López[1]([✉]) [iD], Claudia Isaza[1] [iD], David Luna-Naranjo[1] [iD],
Angela Sucerquia[2] [iD], Camilo Sanchez[1] [iD], and Juan Daza[1] [iD]

[1] Universidad de Antioquia UDEA, Calle 57 No. 63-108, Medellín, Colombia
josedavid@udea.edu.co
[2] Universidad EAFIT, Medellín, Colombia

Abstract. Ecoacoustics is a widely used wildlife passive monitoring discipline. Professional audio recorders offer robust casings able to resist adverse environmental conditions. However, the need of using clouds of recorders (for e.g. landscape level analyses) is obligating most researchers to migrate to low-cost devices, which unfortunately do not offer robust low-cost casings. In this work, we propose a home-made casing design and define a protocol of experiments for testing the recorder performance under real-life conditions. Specifically, we set-up an Audiomoth recorder for long-term wildlife monitoring in a Colombian rainforest and as a result, we find that it behaves similar to a professional SM4 recorder in terms of gain and dynamic range, and better in terms of soundscape information provided.

Keywords: Audiomoth · Ecoacoustics · Casing · Song Meter

1 Introduction

Passive-monitoring of biodiversity with audio recordings has become a standard technique to study wildlife [6,21,22]. It allows from characterizing specific species behavior [2,8,11,25] to finding environmental acoustic indicators when monitoring extensive geographic areas [14,15,23]. Several brands provide professional audio recorders with robust casings that protect them from the environment (such as the SongMeter –www.wildlifeacoustics.com or the Bioacoustic Recorder –www.frontierlabs.com.au) [3], as long-term monitoring requires fixing these devices for weeks/months in the wild. In our particular experience, we have used SongMeter recorders (SM2/4) for monitoring biodiversity in Colombia [2,5,7,19] and we have identified two main drawbacks: their price is prohibitive for large-scale studies of landscapes (approx. USD$1000 per device), and their microphones are not fully protected. About the latter issue, we have observed that insects (mainly fireants) eat their foam protector and the constant rain wets the microphones, rapidly (and permanently) degrading their gain (see Fig. 1).

J. C. Figueroa-García et al. (Eds.): WEA 2024, CCIS 2223, pp. 200–212, 2025.
https://doi.org/10.1007/978-3-031-74598-0_17

Fig. 1. Causes of deterioration of recorders exposed to real-life conditions.

The high-price problem has been tackled by several researchers who are developing low cost wildlife recorders [1,6,10,13,16,20,24], but the protection-to-elements issue remains because these devices do not include a proper case. Protecting audio recorders from the environment is not a widely studied issue because established companies offer excellent cases with their devices, and the use of low-cost recorders is still at its initial steps. Additionally, these devices are still mostly used under controlled conditions or short periods of time. But bad-casing in long-term wildlife monitoring could derive in loss of the device and its information.

Due to the success of the Audiomoth open-source recorder (approx. USD70) designed by Oxford University researchers [9,10,12], its developers initially proposed a simple casing [10] and recently a robust waterproof one (IPX7 https://www.openacousticdevices.info/case). However, its cost (close to the price of the recorder itself) is still too expensive for monitoring with hundreds of devices. Therefore, in this work we propose a set-up for the Audiomoth recorder (or any similar device) with a home-made low-cost alternative (less than USD$5 per case) that could be easily produced. We compare it (both in terms of audio quality and protection from the environment) with a SM4 recorder as a gold standard [17], and with two other commonly used options (a freezing bag and an aluminum paper bag). We test their:

i) audio quality under controlled conditions, ii) audio quality under real-life conditions (tested in a rainforest), and iii) long-term performance.

This paper is divided as follows. We start describing the proposed casing and experimental conditions for setting-up the device in the Materials and Methods section. Then, we present comparative results focusing on dynamic range and loss of gain; and we finish presenting our conclusions.

2   Materials and Methods

The set-up proposed here is intended for long-term (weeks/months) monitoring of wild-life either for species identification or acoustic-index analysis purposes. This set-up has two key components: building a low-cost casing able to keep the recorder dry and safe while guaranteeing good audio quality, and configuring the gain for an optimal recording

2.1   Recorders and Casing

We use a SoundMeter SM4 recorder (Wildlife Acoustics, Inc.) as gold standard. This recorder is sold in a sealed robust waterproof casing (See Fig. 3), it features stereo programmable recording, a sampling frequency of up to FS = 44.1 kHz, a linear response of up to 5 kHz, and quasi linear response of up to approx. 12 kHz (as reported in its datasheet https://www.wildlifeacoustics.com/resources/user-guides). Additionally, we selected the Audiomoth recorder (Open Acoustics research) as the low-cost alternative. It is open-source, mono, with a built-in microphone and a FS of up to 192 kHz. According to the developer, it showed a SNR of approx. 5 dB less than the SM2 (same microphone than the SM4; www.openacousticdevices.info/audio).

The main issues for performing passive recording in a rainforest are the rain, humidity, and animals (especially insects). The proposed casing for the Audiomoth consists of an hermetic plastic box for food (available at any store) with the next modifications (see Fig. 2): 1) the size of the recorder and the box must be similar; 2) drill a hole of 10 mm in the microphone position; 3) cut a hydrophonic speaker grille cloth and 4) glue it with acrylic waterproofing; 5) cut a foam to cover the recorder, 6) to fit the space within the box.

The Audiomoth developers suggest that a resealable freezing bag is enough for most outdoor recordings. Therefore, in preliminary tests we added some other possible casings for comparison purposes (freezing bag, aluminum paper bag, waterproof plastic bag for smartphone, and an hermetic plastic box for food without modifications). In all cases the built-in microphone was properly separated from the casings with dish-washing sponge and tape. We found that the sealed bag for smartphones and the plastic box significantly attenuated the gain, so we discarded them. The casing of the SM4 was not modified.

2.2   Experiments

We first tested the different casings under controlled conditions for having a loss of gain baseline and looking for reduced dynamic ranges. Then, we repeated this test under real-life conditions at a coastal-rainforest (Buenaventura, Chocó region in Colombia). Finally, we performed a long-term test under real-life conditions in two different rainforests (Antioquia region, Colombia).

For all experiments, the SM4 was configured at its maximum frequency sample of FS = 44.1 kHz. The audiomoth was configured at 48 kHz as they do not match on their available options. We used their own default gains (reported

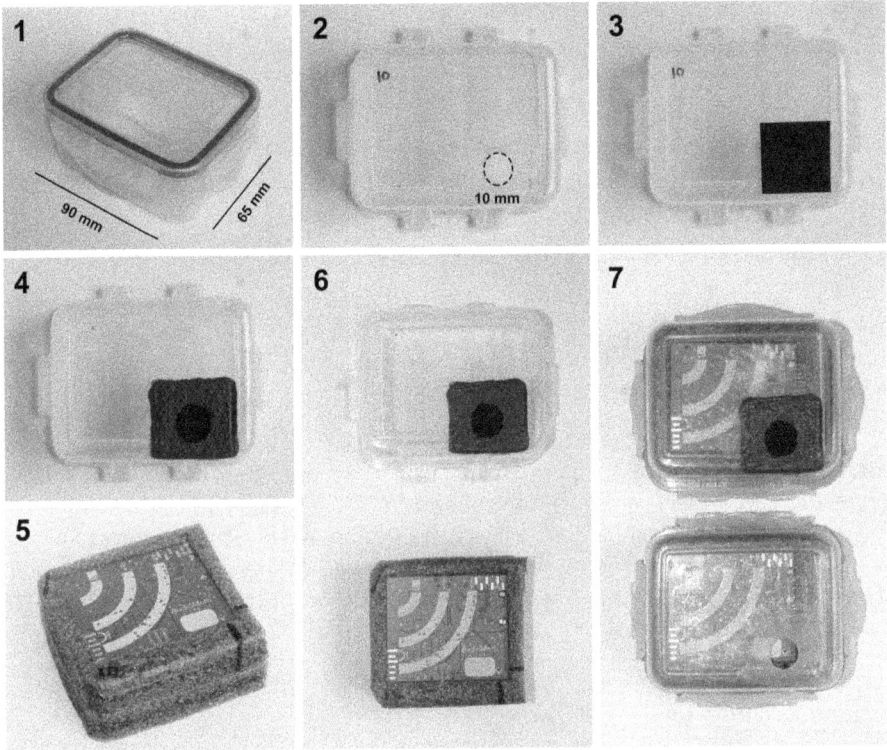

Fig. 2. Design of the proposed casing.

at 16 dB for the SM4, mid -unknown value- for the Audiomoth). For the initial experiments, we configured both devices for recording 1 min every 5 min in WAV format, with clock differences among devices of less than 2 s. For the long-term validation, we extended the recordings to 1 min every 19 min. In a preliminary test (not shown here), we tested three SM4 and ten Audiomoth devices, and verified that the gains within devices of each brand were similar between 20 Hz and 10 kHz.

Controlled Conditions. We started placing the recorders with casings shown in Table 1 in a silent room and played twice 30 s of music. The music was previously selected for having similar power in all frequencies up to 12 kHz (see Fig. 4). We discarded the use of synthetic generated signals (such as a chirp) because they do not show the typical complexity of sounds of a rainforest, so a good result with them would not be representative of the real-life issue. Additionally, in previous tests (not shown here) we found that the gain of the chirp or sinusoids provided by different types of speakers were not stable.

The post-hoc analyses consisted of averaging power spectrum plots from recordings. Then, correlation among spectra and mean level differences were

Table 1. List of recordings and casings used for testing.

Label	Recorder	Casing	FS	Gain
SM4	SM4	Default	48 kHz	Default (16 dB)
A1	Audiomoth	Without casing	48 kHz	(mid –Default)
A2	Audiomoth	Freezing bag	48 kHz	(mid –Default)
A3	Audiomoth	Aluminum bag	48 kHz	(mid –Default)
A4	Audiomoth	Proposed casing	48 kHz	(mid –Default)

computed. The two (stereo) channels of the SM4 were averaged for comparison purposes.

Real-Life Conditions. The next step consisted of determining the dynamic range and gain of the configurations shown in Table 1 under real-life conditions. For this purpose, we tested the devices in a Colombian tropical rainforest located at approx. 45 km from Buenaventura port. Figure 3 shows the actual placement of the devices. Post-hoc analyses are the same of the previous experiment.

Fig. 3. Positioning of the recorders for the experiment.

Gain Selection. The last step consists of determining the true gain levels of the Audiomoth recorder. This device can be configured with five levels but the developers do not provide information about gain differences. Therefore, we placed six devices (Five Audiomoth + one SM4) for 12 h in the same location (recording times: 6 pm–8 pm and 3:30 am–6:30 am), each Audiomoth with a different gain. Post-hoc analyses were the same of the two previous experiments.

Long-Term Recordings. To validate the proper function of the proposed casing, we placed an SM4 and an Audiomoth with the proposed casing in two different rainforests: Anorí, and Amalfi, in Antioquia region, one week each. With this, we expect to reduce the bias introduced by the acoustic landscape, as these are uncontrolled conditions and the recorders could show a different response in a different environment. The configurations of both recorders were the same ones of the first experiment, except for the duration of the recordings, which was 1 min acquired every 19 min, for a total of 3,532 recordings.

We used the Ecoacoustic Global Complexity Index (EGCI) [4] to compare the recordings. This index represents the state of an acoustic landscape, by taking into account the characteristics of the signal in both time and frequency domains. The EGCI index is based in the combination of three measures of information: Shannon entropy, Jensen-Shannon divergence, and generalized statistical complexity. It is represented in the HxC plane (entropy vs. complexity) and is used to study complex dynamic systems [18]. In this way, we characterized the recordings by including all the soundscape information.

We used the methodology described in [4] to calculate the EGCI index. Briefly, one computes the autocorrelation of each recording; then, a singular value decomposition is performed and a probability density function (PDF) of its histogram is obtained, from which the tree measures of information are computed. As a result, each recording provides a coordinate in the HxC plane. This index requires defining an initial parameter τ_{max} corresponding to the time lag. In our case, this parameter was fixed to $\tau_{max} = 256$, since this value allows speeding-up the calculations and delimiting points (recordings) in the minimum and maximum limits of generalized statistical complexity, as explained in [4].

To assess the statistical significance of the observed differences between recordings, we performed a Mann-Whitney U test. This non-parametric test was chosen to compare the entropy and complexity values of the recordings. This comprehensive statistical analysis provides a robust evaluation of the data, enhancing the reliability of our findings.

3 Results

3.1 Controlled Conditions

Figure 4 shows the power spectrum (limited to 20 Hz–12 kHz) with the casings of Table 1. The mean loss of gain with respect to the SM4 was 2.72 dB for the Audiomoth (A1), 3.62 dB and 7.17 dB for the freezing and aluminum bags, A2 and A3 respectively; and 7.93 dB for the proposed casing (A4). This means that under controlled conditions the Audiomoth looses approx. 3 dB against the SM4 (for a 1 kHz pure sinusoid, the developers estimated approx. 5 dB). The freezing bag behaves close to no having protection, and the proposed casing

looses 5 dB with respect to the Audiomoth itself. This figure also provides information in separated bands. We detected a high gain of the SM4 below 200 Hz.
We consider this test valuable as music allows testing true dynamic range of
devices and casings, because sometimes real-life performance significantly differs
from datasheets.

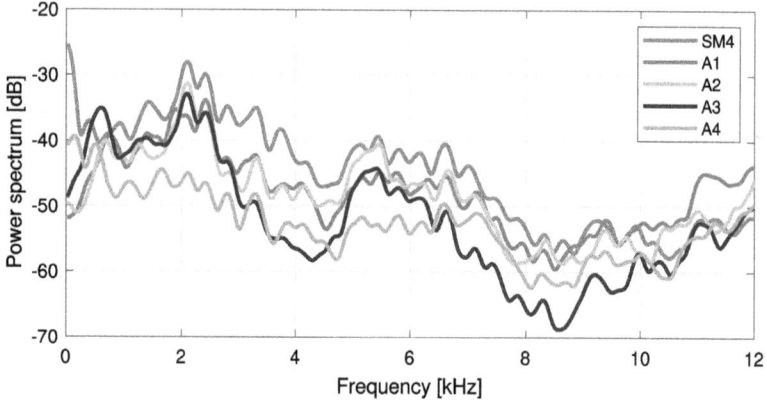

Fig. 4. Power spectrum comparison under controlled conditions.

3.2 Real-Life Experiment

Figure 5 shows the same power spectrum but for real-life conditions (average of
5 recordings in a rainforest –1 min each). The figure shows the expected larger
gain of the SM4 at very low frequencies, but it also shows a linear reduction of
gain for this recorder after 9 kHz. Although expected (from the datasheet), this
behavior was not evident under controlled conditions (the trend was confirmed in
individual recordings). Similar to the previous experiment, all casings behaved
similarly with the exception of the peak at 6.6 kHz, where the proposed casing showed lower gain. Finally, by analyzing individual recordings we found
many noise stamps from the aluminum bag in A3 (presumably due to wind).

Under real-life conditions the average gain differences with respect to the
SM4 were lower for all cases: The Audiomoth lost 0.99 dB (A1), the freezing
bag 2.88 dB (A2), the aluminum paper bag 0.45 dB (A3), and the proposed case
3.4 dB (A4). We also checked for the average correlation among devices. Between
the SM4 and the Audiomoth without protection (A1) it was 86.62±0.71%, mostly
downgraded by the low and high frequency disparities of the SM4 (between 300–
9 kHz the correlation was 95.4 ± 1.85%). The others were computed against
the Audiomoth (A1) for a fair comparison: $Corr = \{A2 : 93.24 \pm 2.88\%, A3 :
91.64 \pm 5.84\%, A4 : 88.03 \pm 2.63\%\}$.

For the third experiment, we tested the five gain levels of the Audiomoth to
determine the optimal one for our proposed casing. Figure 6 shows the average

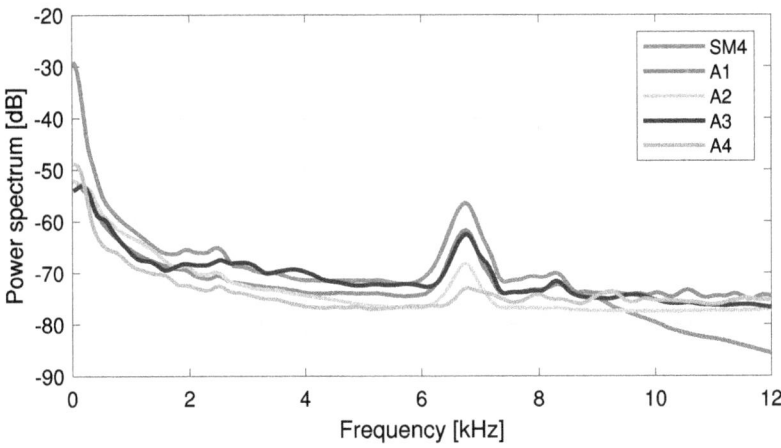

Fig. 5. Power spectrum comparison under real-life conditions.

power spectra of the 50 recordings obtained during two windows within 12 h in the rainforest (some of them with heavy rain). The figure shows how the two lower and the two higher gain levels are close to each other. The loss of gain against the SM4 for each level (from low to high) are: $G = \{14.29 \pm 0.60, 12.74 \pm 0.57, 7.29 \pm 0.73, 2.13 \pm 0.52, -0.54 \pm 1.04\}$ dB. Note how the gain of the high level is even higher than the SM4; however, listening to the individual audios we observed that this result is tricky, because there were many saturation

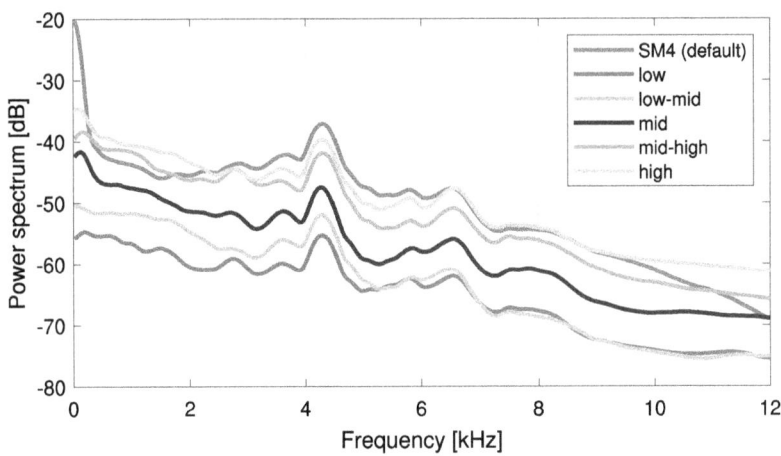

Fig. 6. Gain comparison after a 12 h test.

This experiments showed that our proposed casing, although behaving similar to other options, with default gain presented a slightly lower gain than just using a freezing bag (which behaves as if there was no casing). Therefore, why choosing it? because of the rainforest. Under long-term real-life conditions a robust casing is mandatory. As a toy example, we took both the proposed casing and some freezing bags (filled with cookies) for a field study at a rainforest. After just one week, all freezing bags had insect holes and were wet or even flooded (same problem sometimes observed with the SM4 microphone foam protector), while the proposed casing was not degraded. Moreover, the proposed casing has been used by our research team for more than two years without issues.

3.3   Long-Term Real-Life Test

Figure 7 shows the projection of the recordings in the HxC plane for the two recorders in the long-term experiment. Initially, significant differences between the Audiomoth and SM4 recorders were evident. The Mann-Whitney U test results, summarized in Table 2, confirmed this with extremely low p-values for entropy and complexity (1.46×10^{-199} and 5.51×10^{-201}, respectively), leading to the rejection of the null hypothesis that the distributions are the same. The low correlation values (0.43 for entropy and 0.21 for complexity) further supported these differences. The higher gain of the Audiomoth after 8 kHz and the

Table 2. Statistical Analysis Results and Correlations.

Metric	Mann-Whitney U Test (p-value)	Correlation (Corr)
Before Filtering		
Entropy	1.4598×10^{-199}	0.43
Complexity	5.5122×10^{-201}	0.21
After Filtering		
Entropy	0.0884	0.79
Complexity	7.3909×10^{-5}	0.67

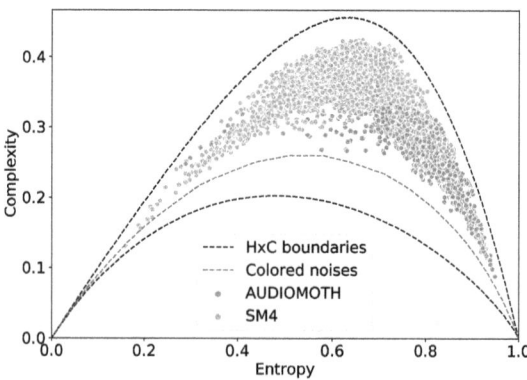

Fig. 7. Distribution of the acoustic samples (EGCI values) in the HxC plane.

abnormally higher low-frequency and lower high-frequency gains in the SM4, as reported in the datasheet of the SM4 microphone https://www.wildlifeacoustics. com/resources/user-guides, were identified as the primary causes of these discrepancies.

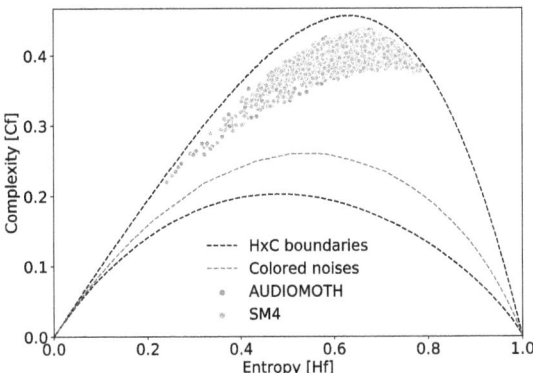

Fig. 8. Distribution of the filtered acoustic samples (EGCI values) in the HxC plane.

To address these discrepancies and achieve a fair comparison, we applied a bandpass filter (order 615) between $500 - 8$ kHz with a Hamming window of length 1024 to all recordings. Figure 8 illustrates the effect of this filtering, showing a significant overlap in the clouds representing the two recorders in the HxC plane. Post-filtering, the statistical analysis revealed an improved alignment in entropy measurements, with the p-value increasing to 0.0884, suggesting that the distributions for entropy are now similar. Although the complexity p-value remained low (7.39×10^{-5}), indicating it did not pass the hypothesis test, it still showed a notable improvement. The correlation values also improved substantially (0.79 for entropy and 0.67 for complexity).

These results underscore the effectiveness of the low-cost Audiomoth casing in aligning with the gold-standard SM4 recorder. By applying the bandpass filter, we mitigated the inherent differences in gain and frequency response between the Audiomoth and SM4 recorders. This preprocessing step effectively aligned the entropy measurements and improved the overall comparability of the data. Thus, with appropriate preprocessing, the low-cost Audiomoth recorder in its proposed casing can be used alongside the professional SM4 recorder, providing reliable and comparable outputs for multisensor research.

4 Conclusion

In this work, we proposed a protective casing for an Audiomoth wildlife recorder designed for long-term monitoring under rainforest conditions, using a professional SM4 recorder as the gold standard. Controlled condition analyses revealed that the proposed casing exhibited a higher gain loss in its default configuration than other protectors, such as a freezing bag, but maintained a comparable overall performance. Real-life tests in a tropical rainforest demonstrated similar results, with the Audiomoth providing more soundscape information than the SM4 recorder. Statistical analyses showed significant differences in acoustic indices like entropy and complexity between the devices due to their frequency responses, with p-values of 1.46×10^{-199} and 5.51×10^{-201}, respectively. A bandpass filter was applied to address these differences, effectively aligning the devices' frequency responses. Post-filtering, the entropy distributions became comparable (p-value = 0.0884), and although the complexity p-value remained low (7.39×10^{-5}), it indicated notable improvement. Correlation values increased to 0.79 for entropy and 0.67 for complexity, demonstrating that with appropriate preprocessing, the low-cost Audiomoth recorder in its proposed casing can be reliably compared to the SM4 recorder. This long-term field test confirmed the durability and reliability of the proposed casing, establishing its potential to provide robust and comparable results in multisensor research alongside the SM4 recorder.

Acknowledgments. This work was supported by Universidad de Antioquia, Instituto Tecnológico Metropolitano de Medellín, Alexander von Humboldt Institute for Research on Biological Resources and The Colombian National Fund for Science, Technology and Innovation, Francisco Jose de Caldas -MINCIENCIAS (Colombia). [Program No. 111585269779].

References

1. Beason, R.D., Riesch, R., Koricheva, J.: AURITA: an affordable, autonomous recording device for acoustic monitoring of audible and ultrasonic frequencies. Bioacoustics **28**(4), 381–396 (2019). https://doi.org/10.1080/09524622.2018.1463293
2. Bedoya, C., Isaza, C., Daza, J.M., López, J.D.: Automatic recognition of anuran species based on syllable identification. Eco. Inform. **24**, 200–209 (2014). https://doi.org/10.1016/j.ecoinf.2014.08.009
3. Browning, E., Gibb, R., Glover-Kapfer, P., Jones, K.E.: Passive acoustic monitoring in ecology and conservation. WWF Conservation Technol. Ser. **1**, 75 (2017). https://doi.org/10.25607/OBP-876
4. Colonna, J.G., Carvalho, J.R.H., Rosso, O.A.: Quantifying ecoacoustic activity in the amazon rainforest through information theory quantifiers. PLoS One **15**(7)(e0229425) (2020). https://doi.org/10.1101/2020.02.09.940916
5. Gaitan, D., Isaza, C., Gomez, W., Daza, J.: Categorization of ecosystems based on soundscape analysis: a perspective from image classification. In: 2016 International Conference on Computational Science and Computational Intelligence (CSCI), pp. 762–766. IEEE (2016). https://doi.org/10.1109/CSCI.2016.0148
6. Gibb, R., Browning, E., Glover-Kapfer, P., Jones, K.E.: Emerging opportunities and challenges for passive acoustics in ecological assessment and monitoring. Methods Ecol. Evol. **10**(2), 169–185 (2019). https://doi.org/10.1111/2041-210X.13101

7. Gómez, W.E., Isaza, C.V., Daza, J.M.: Identifying disturbed habitats: a new method from acoustic indices. Eco. Inform. **45**, 16–25 (2018). https://doi.org/10.1016/j.ecoinf.2018.03.001

8. Guerrero, M.J., Bedoya, C.L., López, J.D., Daza, J.M., Isaza, C.: Acoustic animal identification using unsupervised learning. Methods Ecol. Evol. **14**(6), 1500–1514 (2023). https://doi.org/10.1111/2041-210X.14103

9. Hill, A.P., Prince, P., Piña Covarrubias, E., Doncaster, C.P., Snaddon, J.L., Rogers, A.: AudioMoth: evaluation of a smart open acoustic device for monitoring biodiversity and the environment. Methods Ecol. Evol. **9**(5), 1199–1211 (2018). https://doi.org/10.1111/2041-210X.12955

10. Hill, A.P., Prince, P., Snaddon, J.L., Doncaster, C.P., Rogers, A.: AudioMoth: a low-cost acoustic device for monitoring biodiversity and the environment. HardwareX **6**, e00073 (2019). https://doi.org/10.1016/j.ohx.2019.e00073

11. Kohlberg, A.B., Myers, C.R., Figueroa, L.L.: From buzzes to bytes: a systematic review of automated bioacoustics models used to detect, classify and monitor insects. J. Appl. Ecol. (2024). https://doi.org/10.1111/1365-2664.14630

12. Lapp, S., Stahlman, N., Kitzes, J.: A quantitative evaluation of the performance of the low-cost audiomoth acoustic recording unit. Sensors **23**(11), 5254 (2023). https://doi.org/10.3390/s23115254

13. wa Maina, C., Muchiri, D., Njoroge, P.: A bioacoustic record of a conservancy in the mount kenya ecosystem. Biodiversity Data J. **4**(e9906) (2016). 10.3897/BDJ.4.e9906

14. Metcalf, O., et al.: Good practice guidelines for long-term ecoacoustic monitoring in the uk (2023). https://doi.org/10.57711/1sxv-9k96

15. Piña-Covarrubias, E., Hill, A.P., Prince, P., Snaddon, J.L., Rogers, A., Doncaster, C.P.: Optimization of sensor deployment for acoustic detection and localization in terrestrial environments. Remote Sens. Ecol. Conservation **5**, 180–192 (2019). https://doi.org/10.1002/rse2.97

16. Pérez-Granados, C., Bota, G., Giralt, D., Albarracín, J., Traba, J.: Cost-effectiveness assessment of five audio recording systems for wildlife monitoring: Differences between recording distances and singing direction. Ardeola **66**, 311–325 (2019). https://doi.org/10.13157/arla.66.2.2019.ra4

17. Rempel, R.S., Francis, C.M., Robinson, J.N., Campbell, M.: Comparison of audio recording system performance for detecting and monitoring songbirds. J. Field Ornithol. **84**, 86–97 (2013). https://doi.org/10.1111/jofo.12008

18. Rosso, O.A., Carpi, L.C., Saco, P.M., Ravetti, M.G., Plastino, A., Larrondo, H.A.: Causality and the entropy–complexity plane: robustness and missing ordinal patterns. Phys. A Stat. Mech. Appl. **391**(1-2), 42–55 (2012). https://doi.org/10.1016/j.physa.2011.07.030

19. Sánchez-Giraldo, C., Bedoya, C.L., Morán-Vásquez, R.A., Isaza, C.V., Daza, J.M.: Ecoacoustics in the rain: understanding acoustic indices under the most common geophonic source in tropical rainforests. Remote Sensing Ecol. Conservation **6**(3), 248–261 (2020). https://doi.org/10.1002/rse2.162

20. Sethi, S.S., Ewers, R.M., Jones, N.S., Orme, C.D.L., Picinali, L.: Robust, real-time and autonomous monitoring of ecosystems with an open, low-cost, networked device. Methods Ecol. Evol. **9**(12), 2383–2387 (2018). https://doi.org/10.1111/2041-210X.13089

21. Sethi, S.S., et al.: Characterizing soundscapes across diverse ecosystems using a universal acoustic feature set. Proc. Natl. Acad. Sci. **117**(29), 17049–17055 (2020). https://doi.org/10.1073/pnas.2004702117

22. Sueur, J., Farina, A.: Ecoacoustics: the Ecological Investigation and Interpretation of Environmental Sound. Biosemiotics **8**(3), 493–502 (2015). https://doi.org/10.1007/s12304-015-9248-x

23. Sugai, L.S.M., DesjonquÃres, C., Silva, T.S.F., Llusia, D.: A roadmap for survey designs in terrestrial acoustic monitoring. Remote Sens. Ecol. Conserv. **6**, 220–235 (2020). 10.1002/rse2.131

24. Whytock, R.C., Christie, J.: Solo: an open source, customizable and inexpensive audio recorder for bioacoustic research. Methods Ecol. Evol. **8**(3), 308–312 (2017). https://doi.org/10.1111/2041-210X.12678

25. Wrege, P.H., Rowland, E.D., Keen, S., Shiu, Y.: Acoustic monitoring for conservation in tropical forests: examples from forest elephants. Methods Ecol. Evol. **8**, 1292–1301 (2017). https://doi.org/10.1111/2041-210X.12730

Requirements Engineering in Web Applications for Education

L. F. Buitrago-Castro[1] (iD) and M. B. Salazar-Sánchez[2]([📧]) (iD)

[1] Programa de Ingeniería Biomédica, Universidad Autónoma de Bucaramanga – UNAB,
Bucaramanga, Colombia
`lbuitrago411@unab.edu.co`
[2] Bioinstrumentation and Clinical Engineering Research Group - GIBIC, Systems Engineering
Department, Engineering Faculty, Universidad de Antioquia UdeA, Calle 70 No. 52-21, A.A.
1226, Medellín, Colombia
`bernarda.salazar@udea.edu.co`

Abstract. In recent years, the development of web applications for teaching and learning has become a focus of research, leading professionals from different fields to form interdisciplinary teams to work together on the integration and development of such tools. Requirements engineering has enabled researchers to identify and prioritize the needs and specifications that these technological tools must meet in order to have the greatest possible impact on the training process. From the implementation of semi-structured interviews, the evaluation of the needs of the environment, and the analysis of the state of the art, the methodological phases for the requirements engineering of web applications developed for the learning of topics related to the field of the health sciences are approached and prioritized. The methodological and strategic aspects applied in the elicitation of five groups of requirements are presented: (i) content, (ii) pedagogical, (iii) functional, (iv) non-functional, and (v) technical. All groups consider the synergy with the actors involved in the process of developing the application to support the learning of students belonging to health sciences or related programmes. The interaction and prioritization of the strategies proposed for the collection of requirements have allowed the generation of a guide for the fluid, clear and organized development of a web application for teaching in the health sciences. In which the involvement and high synergy of the actors involved promote the development of technological tools that have a greater impact on the acquisition and reinforcement of knowledge and skills.

Keywords: Requirements lifting · Elicitation · Requirements Engineering

1 Introduction

Currently, the accelerated and ever-changing progress of technological development has led society to experience major changes that have not been alien to teaching and learning strategies, which have been led to the incorporation of Information Technology and Communication (ICT) tools, such as web applications, which provide students with new spaces for reinforcing and improving the skills and abilities of each profession [1]. This trend is increasingly evident in undergraduate and postgraduate training programmes, particularly in the health sciences [2]. In this area, the use of simulators and virtual tools allows the provision of simulated clinical environments to consolidate the concepts according to the learning curve of each student, allowing multiple repetitions of the clinical scenario without putting patient's lives at risk [3].

The development of web applications with this approach is a major challenge for software developers (companies and educational institutions), as it requires the application of requirements engineering techniques, such as identifying, analyzing, documenting, and validating both the set of decisions and parameters, in order to optimize the time and costs associated with development, while meeting the learning objectives set [4]. In this way it is possible to provide a complete description of the system: behavior, constraints, specifications, and attributes [5]. These are subdivided according to the Institute of Electrical and Electronics Engineers (IEEE) classification as follows: functional requirements, system attribute requirements (non-functional), external interface requirements, database requirements, and a special category comprising derived requirements such as design and content requirements [6]. This complex process allows developers to understand the particular aspects of the software, taking into account traditional or agile methodologies [7]. The latter, according to some authors, is a good choice for the development of web applications if you want to provide a route that facilitates the delivery of solutions to the customer through the analysis of requirements [8]. The above implies the definition of the macro proposal of the application (functional requirements) and the constraints that this solution must comply with (non-functional requirements) [6].

It is important to emphasize that normally not all the requirements and restrictions raised can be met in the estimated time and with the available resources, so it is essential to prioritize the requirements to identify the set of critical requirements. In this sense, multiple factors can influence the definition of the priority, such as business aspects, customer satisfaction, technical elements, and specific customer requests (importance, adverse effects, risk, time, and costs) [9], which generally leads to the prioritization of design and presentation aspects.

The above implies some limitations, considering that the development of web applications focused on teaching and learning requires the incorporation of methodologies that allow synergy between students and teachers [10], in order to improve the accessibility and literacy of learners in the use of technologies, especially in developing countries. The integration of such tools into higher education programmes has become a basic indicator of quality standards. For this reason, developers have made great efforts in requirements engineering to identify and generalize the content, pedagogical and functional elements that are fundamental to the acquisition of knowledge in any field, such as user authentication, database management, sequential learning, and specific content [11].

All these efforts are aimed at creating learning environments in which the use of technological aids such as mannequins, partial task trainers, simulated patients, and hybrid simulators facilitates the consolidation of knowledge. However, some factors influence the frequent use of a particular type of technological aid. Firstly, there are the factors that motivate students to actively use a tool, and secondly, there are pedagogical reasons why teachers are motivated or not to use the available tools [12]. With the aim of integrating some of these components and demonstrating the relevance of the gathering of requirements to improve such factors, in this work we show and provide a group of guidelines that seek to facilitate the elicitation of requirements in the development of applications. The focus was on the teaching-learning of subjects related to the Programs of the Health Sciences Area. For this, the conditions of purpose (to facilitate a tool for learning support, considering the modern aids and needs of the university community), learning results (likelihood of academic improvement), use (guarantee of permanence), cost-benefit (feasibility of the tool), and impact (effect of the technological aid) were considered. It also highlights the key considerations for analysis, documentation, validation, prioritization, and management in each of the integrated requirements.

2 Methods

The requirements engineering for the design of five applications was addressed by considering the following stages: (i) review and definition of the group of requirements to be met; (ii) specification of the phases to be considered within the requirements gathering; (iii) definition of the actors to be involved in each of the phases; (iv) precision of the strategies for eliciting the different types of requirements; (v) design of the tools and, finally, the (vi) requirements gathering. This project was approved by the Bioethics Committee of the Faculty of Medicine of the University of Antioquia, Medellín, Colombia (F-017–00, Act No. 011).

A systematic search was carried out in the Scopus, Scielo, ProQuest and CSI databases, using combinations of the following keywords: requirements, content, functional, applications, mobile, web, teaching, learning, pedagogical, technical, engineering, medical, health sciences, elicitation, survey, strategies. Besides, to explore the reasons for non-use were included: factors, influence, implementation, applications, web, mobile, teaching, higher education institutions, ICT, use, students, teachers.

The requirements gathering process was based on six main actions: (i) administration, manage, control, and use the application; (ii) selection, to obtain information from documents, questionnaires, and interviews; (iii) analysis, to refine, specify, relate, and verify the users' requirements; (iv) specification, to document the requirements identified; (v) validation, to ensure that the requirements identified are sufficient to achieve the final objectives [14]; and (vi) prioritization, which indicates the impact of each requirement [15]. The interaction between the actors, including the hierarchy and acceptance criteria in each phase, is shown in Fig. 1.

The elicitation of the different types of requirements were addressed by using the following set of techniques: analysis of existing information, surveys, audio and video recording, interviews, history of use, ESRE document and checklist. Each method has an associated objective, which leads to the initial classification of requirements as "hard" or "soft", where the hard ones tend to be more "precise", while the soft ones are more "desirable" and therefore subjective [16]. In this way, a variety of interacting requirements were achieved, allowing the identification of needs and limitations in the development of applications. Thus, for the semi-structured interviews, an instrument was implemented that included a set of questions grouped into the following dimensions of interest: (i) professional and teaching experience, (ii) difficult topics to teach, (iii) study material, (iv) knowledge and use of simulators or web applications, (v) assessment strategies and, (vi) teacher evaluation. And in the case of micro-curricula, the following inclusion criteria were considered: (i) offered by a higher education institution, (ii) certified programs with high quality, (iii) training programs in health sciences, and (iv) great relationship with the proposed contents.

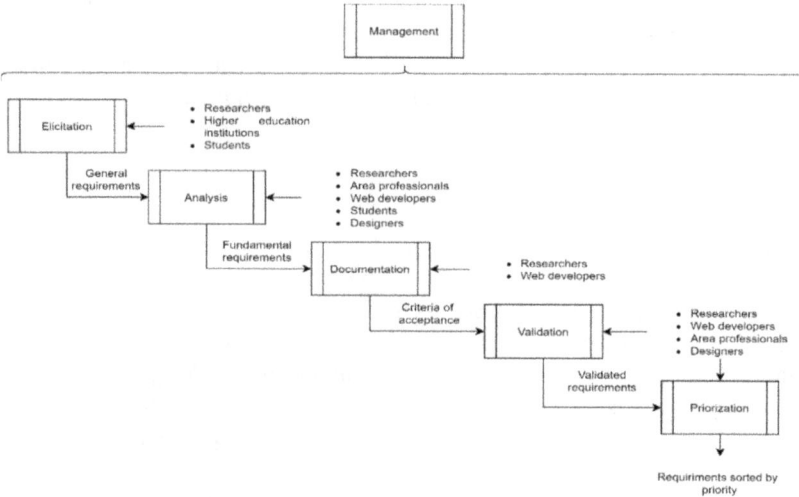

Fig. 1. Methodology and main actors in requirements engineering. The blocks show the stages of the process of requirements gathering, the expected result in each one (output), and the relationship with other actors involved (synergy).

3   Results

In developing web applications to support the learning of students in health sciences or related programs, five sets of requirements have been addressed: (i) content requirements, so that the elements and knowledge integrated into the web application are understood; (ii) pedagogical requirements, to define the structures and strategies through which the content will be addressed; (iii) functional requirements, which provide clarity about the elementary functions that the web application will address; (iv) non-functional requirements, to define the quality and performance parameters that are expected from the tool; and (v) technical requirements, to know the minimum specifications that the development environment and its related elements must meet.

The different types of requirements (content, pedagogical, functional, non-functional and system requirements) have been assigned a specific importance (low, medium and high), considering the possible impact of each on another requirement. A major change in a high-level requirement can cause a cascade of changes to requirements at different levels. In contrast, a low-level requirement may only affect those in the same sub-group. The hierarchical process led to a real definition and sub-grouping of the main actors, which allowed an organized and staged development of the requirements engineering. Figure 2 shows the sub-grouping and synergy between the actors and the different types of requirements. As can be seen, the researchers are in charge of collecting and compiling all the requirements and are in constant contact with all the actors, allowing the communication and global definition of requirements.

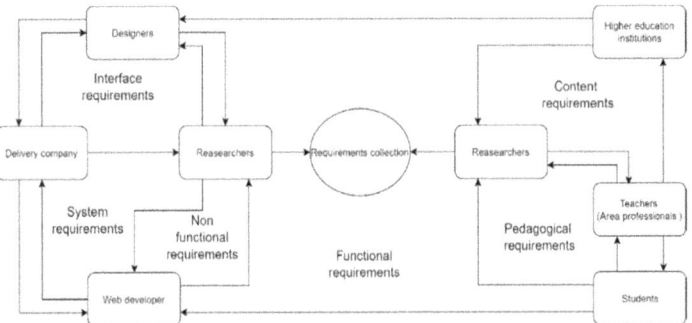

Fig. 2. Relationship between actors and requirements. The actors involved in each stage delimit the different types of requirements. The arrows show the interaction between these actors.

Figure 3 shows the decision flow for removing the essential content requirements. The contents were prioritized for each theme according to the following three aspects: (i) difficulty in teaching, (ii) difficulty in understanding the material by students, and (iii) relevance of the material to clinical practice. As can be seen, each module of the application has a set of themes that make up the "fundamental" content, which can group multiple micro-contents.

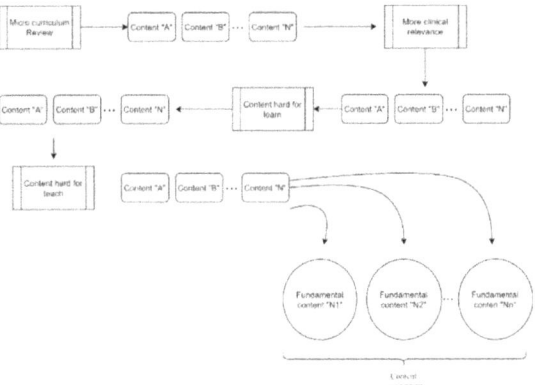

Fig. 3. Stages of content requirement gathering. The blocks indicate the restrictions that filter the contents—finishing the process with distribution in "fundamental contents" according to the correlation between them.

It is also necessary to consider the structures and methods included in pedagogical models, such as: traditional [17], conductivist, constructivist, dialogue-critical, and cognitivist models [18]. In this sense, the selection of the most suitable model for the application is taking into account particular characteristics such as the need that is expected to be met (to support learning from attendance), the target audience (students belonging to health sciences and related programs) and the content to be supplied (particular program, depth of content, type of content). In the case of web applications for the health sciences, the following models have been selected (i) behavioral, which seeks to develop skills through practice and repetition, (ii) constructivist, which focuses on free exploration of knowledge, and (iii) cognitivist, which is based on goal-oriented learning, allowing knowledge to be acquired in an orderly fashion. The convergence of objectives of the three previous models and the use of specific and necessary teaching strategies in Health Science Programs (summary, illustration, analogies, interspersed questions, concept maps and case studies), leads to the establishment of *pedagogical requirements*.

On the other hand, the *functional and non-functional requirements* defined the minimum functionality expected from the system. Where clinical simulation is a specificity of the technological support needed for the learning and acquisition of skills in the professional in training. Therefore, the general and specific functions considered for web applications in this area should take into account, during their development, the analysis of the strengths and weaknesses of similar tools, in order to identify options for improvement or innovation (see Fig. 4).

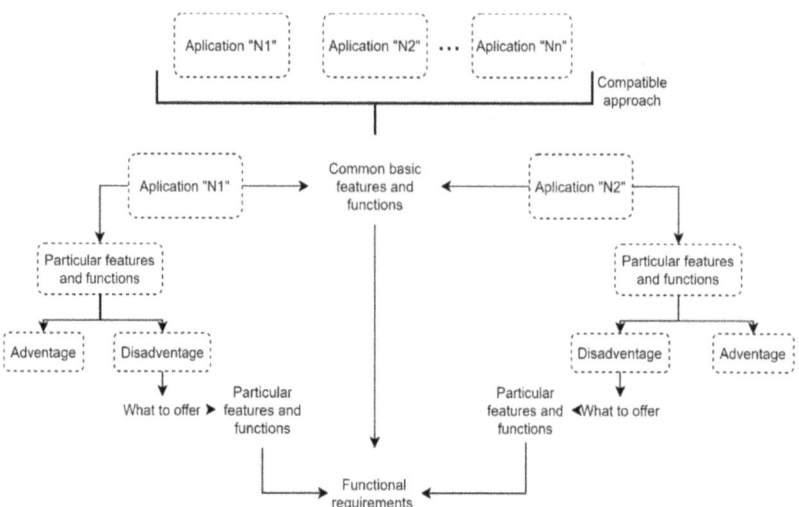

Fig. 4. Lifting of functional requirements. Functional requirements are raised by comparing multiple applications, specifying the fundamental characteristics they all share, and the opportunities for improvement that exist.

The acceptance criteria developed in this type of requirements are oriented towards the optimal functioning of the web application, specifying the essential performance characteristics for the fluid and dynamic interaction between the user and the tool (see

Table 1). The identification of all these requirements leads to the definition of the *fundamental technical requirements*, whose minimum conditions are shown in Table 2. The expected characteristics of the system are related, in which elements from the computational capacity (essential for the design complex models allowing the simulation of more real clinical events) to the graphical capabilities of the web application (facilitating the inclusion of high-resolution structures).

Table 1. Fundamental non-functional requirements. Those that stand out the most are those that affect the performance of the tool, such as efficiency, safety, and usability.

Requirement	Acceptance criteria
Performance	• The application supports multiple concurrent users
Security	• The application achieves with the security protocols for database protection
Efficiency	• The system is capable of processing and simulating in response to the user in less than 2 s
Usability	• The system allows an easy and logical orientation to the different modules and aids
Interface	• The application is responsive • Buttons, bars, and any interaction element are standard throughout the application • The font is legible and comfortable • The resolution of the objects and the screen must be appropriate for different screen sizes

Table 2. Fundamental technical requirements and their acceptance criteria.

Requirement	Acceptance criteria
Multi-platform operation	The application is developed to run on Android, Windows, and iOS to ensure access to all users regardless of device
Online operation	The interaction with the application is online
Calculation capacity	The environment allows the development of models of minimum order 1
Graphic capacity	The environment allows the implementation of high-resolution graphics

4 Discussion

The development and use of simulation tools has become a focus of research in recent years. A recent study presented by Toro et al. highlights the importance of these new technological tools for professionals in training, especially applications focused on the recreation of simulated clinical environments, because they facilitate the acquisition, development, and reinforcement of knowledge and skills [20]. For this reason, the construction of these tools requires a careful process that takes into account as many variables as possible. This process should consider the regulations and the impact that these elements have on the high quality of higher education institutions and the importance of evaluating their possible impact on student learning [21].

For this reason, requirements engineering is used to identify the functional and non-functional elements that facilitate the development of the most complete tool possible. Given the large number of requirements to be considered, it is necessary to agree on those that are fundamental for good development. Context in which functional, non-functional, interface, data, navigation, transactional, economic, environmental, technical, performance, usability, availability and reuse requirements, among others, have been raised [22]. However, those specifically related to the content and pedagogical objective, fundamental elements for the development of applications focused on teaching-learning, have been left behind. This paper suggests the types, order, and hierarchy of requirements considered fundamental for the construction of tools of this type. The order aims to provide a structure that facilitates a fluid process and the hierarchy to demonstrated the cascade effect that they can generate, thus avoiding, as much as possible, the regular meeting of stakeholders that is suggested in agile methodologies given the evolution and changes in the requirements [23].

The above, always considering the actors involved, because as demonstrated by Zary et al. in the development of a virtual environment of clinical cases of patients, it is important to include the opinions of teachers and students not only in each stage of the process, but also in the construction of each requirement [24]. However, considering these two as the only focus of information may limit the perspective, so it is necessary to consider as many actors as possible (see Fig. 2), maintaining a high synergy between them through the researcher. Meanwhile, in terms of content requirements, looking at higher education institutions, as well as students and teachers, gives a broader view of the issues of the common core, facilitating the inclusion of content that may not represent an additional challenge for the parties involved, but favours the construction of a comprehensive tool for consultation, training and self-assessment on the issues of interest.

In recent years, the idea of instructional design has gained ground in educational technologies [25], which *"create experiences that make the acquisition of knowledge and skills more efficient, effective and attractive"* [25]. With this goal in mind, the protocol shown in Fig. 3 was used, which, by defining prioritization criteria, filters the contents to highlight those that may be most relevant and significant. For health science programs, it is suggested that three, in particular, be taken into account: (i) difficulty in learning, so that the technological support provides tools that facilitate the acquisition of knowledge, as stated in the instructional designs; (ii) difficulty of teaching, so that it provides support for teachers; and (iii) relevance to clinical practice. The above does not mean that criteria cannot be added or subtracted, as this will depend on the final objective of each application.

Related to the above, Ortega states the importance of designing a structure that facilitates the creation and implementation of learning environments for e-learning [26], for which it considers the ADDIE instructional design model, an acronym for its phases: Analysis, Design, Development, Implementation, and Evaluation; highlighting the link with pedagogical elements such as meaningful learning and constructivist model. In this context, although this model is relevant for distance learning, it is important to think about what the tool being developed and what the public it is aimed at are looking for, which allows the best model or models to be considered. In this sense, Siemens tries to put together a theory of learning for the digital age, which it calls connectivism, highlighting that most models (constructivist, cognitivist, conductivist) have described learning as a process that take place inside the person, but they do not address the learning that take place outside them, stored and manipulated by technology [27]. Thus, for connectivism, learning occurs when a learner connects to a learning community, understanding the community as a network of individuals who are themselves learning networks [28]. Although the above is true, given the current era, not all technological tools will have environments that allow such interaction, and not because of this will be less valid or useful. The strategy that can serve as a guide for the selection of these elements, which is based on the resolution of a group of questions that allow to clarify which of them can be effectively applied given the objectives of the application, highlighting that for programs in the field of health sciences, at least three models should be analyzed, including the next teaching-learning strategies: (i) the constructivist model, thinking of a free navigation in which the student himself explores what he wants to learn; (ii) the conductivist model, which facilitates the constant repetition of simulations and activities; and (iii) the cognitivist model, which provides a guide and logical order for goal-oriented learning.

Once the content and the structures to display it have been defined, it is necessary to consider the functions that the application will provide, a complex process given the instability generated by the constant change in the characteristics of technological devices [16]. Thus, the definition of requirements by objectives has allowed a more fluid development of this type of requirements [29], being raised from the needs that the system requires to provide future users. This process, although it addresses the possible needs, ignores those that are already supplied by other tools, which is why both the basic characteristics that they all have in common (e.g. the user authentication) and the needs that are satisfied to a lesser extent (e.g. simulation) should be studied by comparison (see Fig. 4).

Then, the suggested methodologies were designed with the objective of considering the opinions, positions, and interests of the potential end-users, integrating them with the characteristics of the pedagogical models that best fit the specified contents and functions that facilitate the teaching-learning process. These enable a logical and organized requirements engineering process to be carried out through hierarchization, always considering the effects and changes that generate the addition or elimination of some requirements. The above does not imply that these cannot be complemented with other strategies proposed for the collection of some type of requirement, such as the strategy suggested by Benfell for the functional requirements, he implements a model called "normative statements", which seeks to solve the problems associated with obtaining tactic knowledge in the requirements lifting phase [30].

Finally, due to the diversity of devices and operating systems present in the market, it is necessary to select typical characteristics of a WEB application during the establishment of the technical requirements (see Table 1), meeting the multi-platform requirement and online operation. However, as mentioned by Babovic et al. selecting the WEB application option leads to the selection of specific technologies to be used in its development [31], in such a way as to guarantee the requirements established for each case, such as calculation capacity and graphic capacity, in addition to high performance in its operation [32]. Therefore, due to its applicability and compatibility with all browsers, Javascript is the ideal language for the development of this type of application. But, due to the difficulty of developing applications that include mathematical modeling (clinical cases, physiological signals, medical devices, etc.) and the need for high performance in response to graphics, it is essential to select a framework such as Backbone.js, AngularJS, AngularJS, React, Ember.js or Vue.js [32].

5 Conclusion

Requirements engineering is a process that allows the orderly and efficient development of technological tools focused on teaching-learning, facilitating the prioritization and selection of functional and non-functional elements that best fit the final objective of the aid. In this context, the inclusion of the most significant number of stakeholders significantly improves the definition of requirements, as long as the researcher in charge manages to maintain a high synergy between them. On the other hand, it is considered of vital importance to raise content and pedagogical requirements, through which it is possible to approach, as much as possible, instructional designs where those topics of greater relevance for the population of interest are included. Likewise, it is relevant to consider the general and particular functionalities of the application, seeking to approach those that can improve the learning experience, helping the student to acquire and strengthen the related topics in the tool. Finally, considering the minimum desired performance characteristics, it favors the construction of a high-level web application that can be used in higher education institutions.

References

1. Cardona, D.M.: Indicadores Básicos para Evaluar el Proceso de Aprendizaje en Estudiantes de Educación a Distancia en Ambiente e-learning basic indicators for assessment the learning process in students of distance education in environment e- learning. Form. Univ. **3**(6), 15–31 (2010)
2. Ventola, C.L.: Mobile devices and apps for health care professionals: uses and benefits. Digit. Storytell. **39**(5), 356–364 (2014)
3. Koh, K.C., Wan, J.K., Selvanathan, S., Vivekananda, C., Lee, G.Y., Ng, C.T.: Medical students' perceptions regarding the impact of mobile medical applications on their clinical practice. J. Mob. Technol. Med. **3**(1), 46–53 (2014)
4. Sharif, N., Zafar, K., Zyad, W.: Optimization of requirement prioritization using Computational Intelligence technique. In: 2014 International Conference on Robotics and Emerging Allied Technologies in Engineering, iCREATE 2014 - Proceedings, no. Ci, pp. 228–234 (2014)

5. Jackson, J.D.E.H.K.: Requirements Engineering. United Kingdom (2017)
6. Society, I.C.: IEEE Recommended Practice for Software Requirements Speciɓcations Software Engineering Standards Committee of the IEEE Computer Society IEEE-SA Standards Board, vol. 1998 (1998)
7. Páez Cárdenas, P., Peralta Arias, D.C., Silva Wanumen, F.L.: Methodology for the elaboration of requirements in applications with web services. Rev. Vínculos **15**, 160–174 (2018)
8. Clerissi, D., Leotta, M., Reggio, G., Ricca, F.: Test driven development of web applications: a lightweight approach. In: Proceedings - 2016 10th International Conference on the Quality of Information and Communications Technology, QUATIC 2016, pp. 25–34 (2017)
9. Berander, P., Andrews, A.: Engineering and Managing Software Requirements (2005)
10. Notari, M.P., Hielscher, M., King, M.: Educational apps ontology. In: Mobile Design Learning: Theories and Application, Churchill, D., Lu, J., Chiu, T.K.F., Fox, B. (eds.) Springer, pp. 83–96 (2016). https://doi.org/10.1007/978-981-10-0027-0
11. Yoshinov, R., Hadjitodorov, S., Kousov, O., Ivanov, P.: Requirements for the e-learning Platform for Bulgarian Education, no. November (2014)
12. Nieto, M.S.: Tecnologías de la Información y de la Comunicación en la Educación. Rev. Mex. Investig. Educ. (2006)
13. Goguen, J.A., Linde, C.: Techniques for Requirements Elicitation* (1992)
14. Escalona, M., Koch, N.: Requirements engineering for web applications: a comparative study. J. Web Eng. **2**(3), 193–212 (2003)
15. Thakurta, R.: Understanding requirement prioritization artifacts: a systematic mapping study. Requir. Eng. **22**(4), 491–526 (2017)
16. Olasoji, R., Preston, D., Mousavi, A.: Requirement engineering for effective mobile learning: Modelling mobile device technologies integration for alignment with strategic policies in learning establishments. In: 2014 Federated Conference on Computer Science and Information Systems, FedCSIS 2014, vol. 2014-Janua, pp. 851–860 (2014)
17. Alejandra, C., Guti, D.: Estrategias de Enseñanza y Aprendizaje. Una Mirada Desde Diferentes Niveles Educativos (2016)
18. Oca, A.O.: Modelos Pedagógicos y Teorías del Aprendizaje (2013)
19. Cruz-barragán, A., Barragán-lópez, A.D.: Aplicaciones Móviles para el Proceso de Enseñanza-Aprendizaje en Enfermería. Salud y Adm. **1**(3), 51–57 (2014)
20. Toro-Troconis, M., Morton, C., Bennie, T., Leppington, C., Hemani, A., Lupton, M.: Design, development and implementation of a mobile learning strategy for undergraduate medical education. J. EAHIL **11**(2), 14–20 (2015)
21. Mesa Jiménez, F. Y., Forero Romero, A.: Las TIC en la normativa para los programas de educación superior en Colombia. Prax. Saber **7**(14), 91 (2016)
22. Alharthi, A.D., Spichkova, M., Hamilton, M.: Sustainability requirements for eLearning systems: a systematic literature review and analysis. Requir. Eng. **24**(4), 1–21 (2018)
23. Asghar, A.R.: Impact and Challenges of Requirements Elicitation & Prioritization in Quality to Agile Process: Scrum as a Case Scenario. In: International Conference on Communication Technologies, pp. 50–55 (2017)
24. Zary, N., Johnson, G., Boberg, J., Fors, U.G.H.: Development, implementation and pilot evaluation of a Web-based virtual patient case simulation environment - Web-SP. BMC Med. Educ. **6**, 1–17 (2006)
25. Merill, M.D.: First Principles Of Instruction. John Wiley (2012)
26. Ortega, C.H.C.: Prototype of learning management system, for the administration of contents and processes, in the teaching of geography with engineering students. In: Innovative and Creative Education and Technology International Conference no. January (2017)
27. Siemens, G.: Connectivism: A Learning Theory for the Digital Age (2005)
28. Necmettin, M.Ş: Pros and cons of connectivism as a learning theory. Int. J. Phys. Soc. Sci. **2**(4), 437–454 (2012)

29. Chawla, S., Srivastava, S., Bedi, P.: Improving the quality of web applications with web specific goal driven requirements engineering. Int. J. Syst. Assur. Eng. Manag. **8**(s1), 65–77 (2017)
30. Benfell, A.: Modeling functional requirements using tacit knowledge: a design science research methodology informed approach. Requir. Eng. **26**(3es), 0123456789 (2020)
31. Babovic, Z.B., Member, S., Protic, J.: Web performance evaluation for Internet of Things Applications. IEEE Access **4**, 6974–6992 (2020)
32. Nikulchev, E., Ilin, D.: Programming technologies for the development of web-based platform for digital psychological tools. Int. J. Adv. Comput. Sci. Appl. **9**(8), 34–45 (2018)

Factors Associated with Dropout in Engineering: A Structural Equation and Logistic Model Approach

Jaime A. Gutiérrez-Monsalve[1][(✉)] , Juan Garzón[2] ,
Maria Francisca Forero-Meza[3] , Cindy Estrada-Jiménez[1] ,
and Angela M. Segura-Cardona[4]

[1] Grupo de Investigación en Innovación Digital y Desarrollo Social INDDES Institución Universitaria Digital de Antioquia (IUDigital – Antioquia), Medellín, Colombia
jaime.gutierrez@iudigital.edu.co

[2] Grupo de Investigación en Ingenierías Multidisciplinar (GIMU), Universidad Católica de Oriente UCO, Rionegro, Colombia
fgarzon@uco.edu.co

[3] Facultad de Ciencias Sociales, Universidad Católica de Oriente; Grupo de Investigación Gibsicos, Rionegro, Colombia
mforero@uco.edu.co

[4] Grupo de Investigación en Educación Superior (GIES), Universidad CES, Medellín, Colombia
asegura@ces.edu.co

Abstract. About 65% of students who start engineering programs do not graduate. This situation causes significant economic losses and social problems for families and society and risks achieving social sustainability worldwide. Sometimes, engineering programs focus on enrolling students rather than providing strategies to secure their academic success, which often leads to student dropout. This study proposes a model to explain and predict engineering dropout through pedagogical, sociodemographic, and institutional factors. Using data from 4127 engineering students (cohorts 2005 – 2019), a structural equation model (SEM) and logistic regression demonstrate that institutional, demographic, and pedagogical variables explain and predict dropout in computer, electronic, environmental, and industrial engineering. According to SEM, institutional, sociodemographic, and pedagogical factors confirm the theoretical model. With Logistic regression as a predictable model, we could identify variables that predict almost 74.8% of student dropouts and 72.4% of student success. Our results provide novel insights to engineering programs and Higher Education institutions to implement curricula and pedagogical strategies leading to decreased engineering dropouts and increased student success.

Keywords: Academic performance · dropout · engineering · Higher Education

J. C. Figueroa-García et al. (Eds.): WEA 2024, CCIS 2223, pp. 225–236, 2025.
https://doi.org/10.1007/978-3-031-74598-0_19

1   Introduction

Higher Education dropout can be understood as partial or definitive academic student termination without obtaining an academic degree (1). There are three types of dropping out depending on the time they abandon the career: 1) early dropout (the student is accepted at a Higher Education institution but does not enroll in a specific program), 2) firstly dropout (the student abandons the career in the first to third academic semester), and 3) late dropout (the student abandon the career having approved more than a half of the credits) (2).When considering institutional factors, dropout can be understood as 1) internal dropout (when the student changes to another program within the same Higher Education institution), 2) institutional dropout (when the students change institution), and 3) dropout of the higher educational system (when the student abandons all formal educational activity) (3). Depending on personal factors, dropout can be understood as 1) dropout caused by internal or personal factors, motivation to study, adaptation to university life, skills, and learning strategies, or 2) dropout caused by external or institutional factors, career profile, teaching methods, professors' attitudes, inflexible schedules, institution's infrastructure, and student environment (4).

Dropout continues to be one of the most severe problems that afflict Higher Education, especially in developing countries. According to Organization for Economic Cooperation and Development (OECD), in 2019, the graduation rate at the theoretical duration of Higher Education programs was 39%. The United Kingdom presented the highest graduation rate (72%), while Chile presented the lowest rate (16%).

Engineering and STEM (Science, Technology, Engineering, and Mathematics) show higher dropout rates than other knowledge areas. Colombia is the second country with the highest Higher Education dropout rate in Latin America at 35% (5). For Cohorts initiated in 2015, the graduation rate was 34.5% in the expected graduation time (31.1% for public and 36.8% for private universities). Regarding areas of knowledge, the highest was in health with 44.3%, followed by education sciences with 37.9%. For areas related to social-human sciences, agronomy-veterinary, graduation fell to 33.7% and 24.2%, respectively.

Regarding geographic distribution, the lowest graduation was observed in rural regions (21.6%). The highest was concentrated in semi-urban (44%) and urban (47.1%) (6). Consequently, Engineering students suffer a series of changes in their first semesters: low academic performance in basic science, little curricular flexibility, lack of professional support, heavy academic load, and less favorable sociodemographic variables generate high dropout rates compared to other areas of knowledge (7).

Different models explain factors associated with Higher Education dropout. Spady's social integration model considers academic performance as one of the leading causes of student dropout (8). In Tinto's model, academic dropout is causally related to academic integration, commitment to learning objectives, and institution characteristics (9). Like Spady and Tinto, Bean (1985) considers academic performance to be one of the direct causal factors influencing the decision to dropout. In this model, academic factors and psychosocial and sociodemographic characteristics affect performance, adaptation, and institutional commitment (10).

Dwek (1986) proposed the social-cognitive theory; the central premise of this theory is that the decision to dropout is directly related to the student's ability to orient himself to the goal and previous academic performance (11). Bandura, in 1990, proposed that dropout depends on the degree of self-efficacy, achievement orientation, and student's previous academic performance (12). Elliot (1999) and (2016) proposed an integrative model where achievement orientation, study strategies, past academic performance, and class size explain students' dropout (13).

Worldwide there is considerable research that intends to use Structural Equation Model (SEM) and Logistic Regression (LR) to explain and predict Academic Performance (AP) and dropout in engineering programs. This research predicts factors related to academic performance and dropout among engineering students to devise better programs that take advantage of students' interests and retain undergraduates in engineering (14). Education quality received in high school, ethnicity, and marriage are essential predictors of dropout (15); models that include sociodemographic, institutional, pedagogical, cognitive and non-cognitive domains are crucial to propose intervention strategies and predict dropout with almost 70% of variance explained (16).

Structural Equation Modelling (SEM) to explain dropout in Higher Education is increasing (17).SEM models complemented with other predictable techniques like logistic regression or decision and classification tree resulted in good strategies in order to prove theoretical dropout models and use it to build early warning system and prevent dropout in Higher Education (18). We propose a novel method to explain and predict dropout in engineering until the effect of the COVID-19 pandemic. We integrate pedagogical, institutional, and sociodemographic variables available in many Higher Education institutions worldwide. Second, we use SEM to confirm the theoretical model to explain dropout in engineering. Third, we propose a logistic regression to predict dropout. Finally, we report risk measures (OR) associated with all variables in a predictive model. These measures help every engineering Higher Education institution to know and manage programs to reduce dropouts in engineering.

2 Method

An Observational, longitudinal, sequential, and Structural Equation Model approach of data obtained from institutional information systems in a private university located in the east of Colombia was extracted until the pandemic COVID-2019. Sociodemographic, pedagogical, and institutional factors were established. Academic records of students who have enrolled since 2005 were selected in order to follow them for at least 15 years. Information from 4127 engineering students was collected from a private university in east of Colombia. This university has eight faculties, namely Agricultural Sciences, Education Sciences, Health Sciences, Economic and Administrative Sciences, Social Sciences, Law, and Engineering.

2.1 Data Collection and Measurement

Variables used to explain the dropout in engineering were genre, age, site of origin, type of high school graduate, and economic income in sociodemographic factors. According to institutional factors, level, program enrolled, subsidy, and scholarship were included. In the pedagogical factor evaluation of teachers in areas related to identity, pedagogy, didactics, teacher age, and teacher salary, they were included, too. As a response outcome, academic performance and early dropout.

2.2 Statistical Analysis of Data

Descriptive analysis was used according to the nature of the variables in all factors. Qualitative ones were reported using frequency and comparative tables. In the case of continuous variables, their distribution was explored from goodness-of-fit, and measures of central tendency and dispersion were used to describe the sample's characteristics.

An independent Chi-squared test was used to identify significant statistical differences between undergraduate dropout and qualitative variables. Analysis of variance ANOVA or non-parametric tests such as Kruskal-Wallis was used to identify statistical differences according to quantitative variables. Post-hoc was performed using Tuckey-HSD to identify homogeneous groups. If data did not distribute parametrically, Dunn's posthoc was used with the Bonferroni correction.

Variables measured at the student level are described as independent. The adjusted ORs were calculated, and the variables with the highest student dropout risk were identified. The model was validated using the Hosmer-Lemeshow criterion, and the ROC curves relating to specificity and sensitivity were proposed. This model allows us to determine which variables predict dropout among undergraduate engineering students.

A canonical discriminant analysis was proposed to validate if a correct classification was achieved between dropout students. The classification rules that would allow discriminating selectivity, absorption per year, new student, and first-timer permanence were assigned. All statistical component was developed in R software using the package candisc.

A confirmatory analysis based on the Structural Equation Model (SEM) validated the sociodemographic, pedagogical, and institutional factors. We consider the mean root square of approximation (RMSEA $< =.8$), comparative fit index (CFI $> =.80$), and tucker lewis index (TLI $> =.80$) according to Alda's criteria.

A logistic regression was performed to identify the association between factors and dropout. Logistic regression allowed for calculating the Odds Ratio (OR) for each variable. The predictive quality was evaluated using the goodness-of-fit criteria and area under the curve (AUC) based on sensitivity and specificity. The model was set with 2/3 of the data and the remaining 1/3 for validation.

3 Results

3.1 Sociodemographic, Pedagogical and Institutional Factors Describes Dropout in Engineering

Regarding gender, 82.24% of women remain in the educational system (even if they do not graduate), compared to 76.61% of men ($p<.001$). According to student trajectories, Level 1 has the lowest number of remaining students, with a percentage of 51.4%. After the students pass the sixth level, the degree of permanence in engineering rises above 90% ($p<.001$). Regarding the programs, electronic engineering is the one that presents the lowest percentage of accumulated permanence (not counting graduation), with 67.22%, compared to the other programs that present accumulated permanence greater than 74% (p<.001). Students from the urban area of Medellin showed higher percentages of accumulated permanence with 94.12%, compared to students from Rionegro (semi-urban), who had a permanence percentage of 78.35% (p<.001).

Students with a subsidy have fewer chances of dropping out (15.9% compared to 21.2% p<.001). It is interesting to note that students with a more significant number of subjects enrolled per semester are less likely to dropout; this is mainly explained because these students probably do not work and may be able to register for more subjects.

Students who cancel and miss fewer subjects are the ones who showed the most remarkable permanence at the end of the study. According to pedagogical and institutional factors, contract full-time professors with sound pedagogy and course management strategies significantly improve permanence rates (79.2% compared to 82.4%, p<.001). Father and mother education with professional and postgraduate studies increment permanence rates (81% compared to 79%, p<.001), good economic incomes in the family (84% to 71%, p<.001), students declare that they have their own house besides rent (84% to 78%, p<.001) and, age (p<.001) affect statistically the permanence rates. These variables permit the establishment of the route in order to confirm the theoretical engineering model of predicting dropout.

3.2   Structural Equation Model to Explain Dropout from Institutional, Demographic and Pedagogical Factor

The path diagram is shown in Fig. 1. This diagram displays all the significant associations with a standardized coefficient between observable and latent variables. Across latent variables, the variable semester did not significantly contribute to the SEM and was dropped from it. According to squared multiple regression, sociodemographic, pedagogical, and institutional variables accounted for 31% of the dropout factor variance.

The SEM coefficients with the significant covariates and standardized Betas are presented in Table 1. SEM was built with 22082 observations with 90 parameters. Standard error estimation was robust, and the NLMINB optimization method was performed in Diagonally Weighted Least Squared (DWLS) to estimate the model. An RMSEA value was equal to .08, suggesting that additional information could be introduced to improve the adequation model. All other fit indices (CFI, TLI, NNFI, NFI, RFI, IFI, and RNI) had values above .99, indicating a good fit.

SEM indicates that engineering academic performance significantly affected engineering dropout (-0.936) (Fig. 1). Negative signs indicate that low values in academic performance (GPA or credits approval rate) correlate with a high risk of undergraduate dropout. The institutional factor impacts academic performance more and correlates positively with academic performance (0.166).

Students with an excellent institutional environment have more probability of staying in school.

Pedagogical and demographic factors show less effect on academic performance. Pedagogical practices favored academic performance (0.053), and Sociodemographic variables did not affect it (-0.014). Academic performance is more affected by institutional and pedagogical factors than sociodemographic ones. We confirm the hypothetical

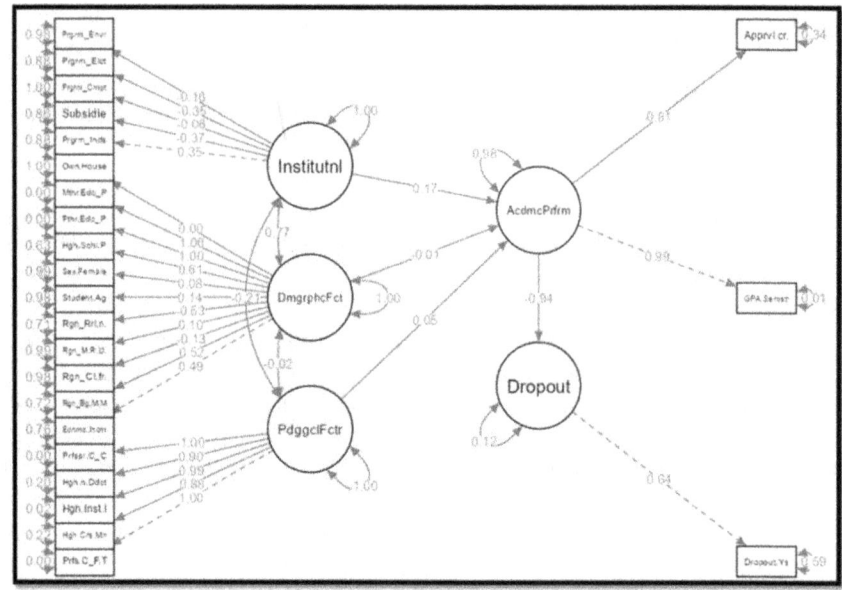

Fig. 1. Path diagram of SEM model which explain Dropout in engineering

Table 1. Structural regression weights, estimates and betas of SEM model which explain dropout in engineering.

Dependent	Predictor	Estimate	SE	
Dropout	Academic Performance	-0.87	0.177	-0.936
Academic Performance	Pedagogical Factor	0.036	0.007	0.053
Academic Performance	Demographic Factor	-0.02	0.004	-0.014
Academic Performance	Institutional	0.327	0.066	0.166

model proposed in Fig. 1 with this model, but it is necessary to incorporate additional information to improve it.

3.3 Logistic Model Approach: Predictable Model

A logistic regression was proposed to predict dropout based on institutional, sociodemographic, and pedagogical variables. In this regression, only those variables in SEM that showed significant effects were included. Table 2 presents model estimates, the OR ratio, and the respective p-value associated with the Wald statistic.

According to results, an undergraduate who received classes from chair professors increases the risk of suffering dropout by 1.28 IC95% [1.18, 1.39] times concerning students receiving classes from full-time professors.

Exciting results were associated with mothers' education: Students who have mothers with professional degrees have a protective effect of 0.73 IC95%[0.93,0.80] to dropout. Increasing economic incomes reduces dropout risk by 0.84 IC95%[0.80,0.89]. If the family of the undergraduate has his own house, the dropout risk has been reduced to 0.68 CI 95%[0.62,0.73]. An undergraduate who lives in an urban region has a protective value of 0.74 IC95%[0.56,0.97], studying computer a protective of 0.63 IC95%[0.56,0.71], and an industrial a protective of 0.66 IC95%[0.58,0.76] compared to the electronic engineering program. To dropout, students with good academic performance have a protective value of 0.24 IC95%[0.23,0.28]. Undergraduates from private high schools have a 1.48 IC95%[1.35,1.62] risk of dropout compared with those from public schools. A high qualification in pedagogy, sex, and subsidy did not affect engineering dropout according to logistic regression.

The sensitivity and specificity percentages were estimated to evaluate the logistic model's predictive capacity. The best model converged with an Aikayke AIC information criterion of 16829, identifying 74.8% of the total students analyzed as dropouts and 72.4% of non-dropouts with a cut-off of 17.6%.

By applying the area under the curve (AUC) criterion, it was found that this value was equal to .81. More variables could be included to increment the AUC must be above 0.90. Figure 2 shows the ROC curve of the analysis performed according to JAMOVI software (19).

4 Discussion

Historically, electronic and computer engineering have had more considerable dropout rates than other engineering programs. Students feel they need to be more motivated during their 2 or 3 initial semesters programs, whereas many programs propose only theoretical studies. Students from electronic and computers engineering could be dropout because many courses in their first semester are associated with theory in mathematics, physics, and calculus, but the practical approach starts at the advanced semester in their academic trajectory (20). Unlike electronics and computer engineering, industrial present relatively lower dropout and higher graduation rates. This result is associated with lower theoretical courses in the first semesters. Many universities have industrial as a program with less semester duration than electronics and computer (21).

Higher Education institutions have eliminated selectivity and admission exams to increase the number of undergraduates enrolling in private engineering programs. Program with high selectivity rates tends to have low graduation rates. This result correlates positively with entrance examinations in engineering programs (22). Several Higher Education institutions propose the entrance examination as an excellent strategy to decrease the dropout risk. Still, this strategy impedes many engineering aspirant studies and affects the economic sustainability of different programs, especially in private Higher Education institutions (23).

Finally, Good grades in math, science, and quantitative reasoning competencies on admission tests were the more predictable variables of dropout in engineering (24).

Table 2. Logistic regression estimates and OR associated to dropout in engineering programs.

Predictor	Estimate	SE	Z	p	Odds ratio	Lower	Upper
Intercept	5.06	0.18	28.61	<.001	157.97	111.68	223.45
Professor.Contract_Chair	0.25	0.04	6.20	<.001	1.28	1.18	1.39
High.pedagogy	0.07	0.07	1.01	0.31	1.08	0.93	1.24
Mother.Education_Professional	-0.35	0.07	-5.22	<.001	0.70	0.62	0.80
Economic.Incomes	-0.17	0.03	-5.80	<.001	0.84	0.80	0.89
Own.House	-0.39	0.04	-9.57	<.001	0.68	0.62	0.73
Region_Big.Met.Medellin	-0.30	0.14	-2.17	0.03	0.74	0.56	0.97
Region_Col.foreign.region	-0.12	0.15	-0.81	0.42	0.89	0.66	1.19
Region_Metrop.Region.U.	-0.05	0.07	-0.67	0.50	0.95	0.83	1.10
Sex.Female	-0.08	0.05	-1.62	0.11	0.92	0.84	1.02
High.School.Private	0.39	0.05	8.25	<.001	1.48	1.35	1.62
Program_Computer	-0.46	0.06	-7.25	<.001	0.63	0.56	0.71
Program_Environmental	0.21	0.07	3.03	0.00	1.24	1.08	1.42
Program_Industrial	-0.41	0.07	-6.12	<.001	0.66	0.58	0.76
Subsidie	-0.05	0.04	-1.14	0.25	0.95	0.88	1.04
GPA.Semester	-1.37	0.06	-24.47	<.001	0.25	0.23	0.28
Approval.coursed.rate	-1.28	0.14	-8.99	<.001	0.28	0.21	0.37

Note. Estimates represent the log odds of "Dropout.Yes = 1" vs. "Dropout.Yes = 0"

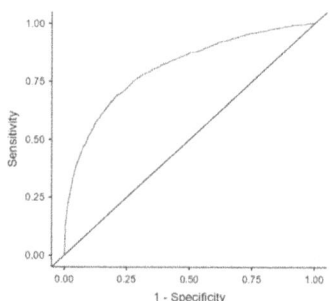

Fig. 2. ROC curve reporting the sensitivity cross specificity of logistic regression model with predict dropout in engineering

The structural Equation Model (SEM) is an innovative technique to describe and explain dropout phenomena in Higher Education. Authors use SEM to confirm that variables associated with academic performance, learning progress, and pedagogical variables explain dropout adequately in students (25). Factors related to social integration, sociodemographics, institutional commitments, and pedagogical strategies enhance predictability and generate resilient environments that favor undergraduate permanence (26). Other studies combine SEM with logistic regression to estimate the risk of undergraduate dropout. In Budapest, researchers propose a combination of SEM and a series of classifier models (decision tree, naive Bayes, linear models, and Deep learning) to predict dropout. The best model to predict dropout has an Area Under Curve (AUC) of 0.81. These results are similar to our findings using only information from institutional data (27). Our results complement the findings of these authors to propose a model to predict dropout without additional investment in new data.

Nowadays, professor contract is a crucial aspect influencing stress, pedagogy, and didactics in Higher Education institutions (28). This research reports that students who learn from chair professors have more risk of dropout than students from full-time professors. According to our knowledge, this is the first research that reports a significant association between professor contracts and dropout in engineering students.

Economics income is another variable that predicts dropout. Students with higher economic incomes reduce their dropout risk due to the best environmental context where they develop their academic activity (29). Providing financial support could diminish in a meaningful manner risk of dropout. Subsidy or scholarships implies that undergraduates are making more significant efforts to stay in their trajectory (30). Mother education is another exciting variable that predicts dropout in engineering students. Students without previous professional degrees, lower socioeconomic backgrounds, and women are more vulnerable to dropouts (31). Finally, the proceeding region of students could affect academic performance and dropout in a university context. The authors concluded that rural students could have low AP and cumulative risk of dropping out compared to those from urban areas (32).

With the validated dropout model, Higher Education institutions will be able to know the variables that explain university dropout and implement effective support programs to prevent student dropout in engineering. As observed in the discussion, this explanatory model complements the variables that explain university dropout in engineering. Similarly, implementing this model will not require that Higher Education institutions invest in additional tests or information to what they already do. The model uses the information available in almost all Higher Education institutions for monitoring engineering students according to law, so executing an early warning system with these variables would not imply additional costs for acquiring new data.

The limitation of the study is associated with the absence of cognitive and non-cognitive variables that demonstrate a good prediction of dropout in engineering undergraduates. Those variables allow for improved Structural Equation Models and prediction. Another limitation is that data come from a private university in Colombia, so the extrapolation of these results could be applied to a Higher Education like this private university.

In future work, we will include cognitive and no cognitive variables in a novel SEM model. According to that, we will develop a model using learning analytics techniques and machine learning to predict the dropout risk of every engineering student.

5 Conclusion

Several prior studies have reported that the graduation rate presented for the first time is one of the most important indicators of the academic management of dropout. It is observed that the Engineering programs have lower graduation percentages statistically compared to the total of other areas of knowledge like health or social sciences. Therefore, these graduation rates must be managed throughout the student's trajectory, and the causes that generate said rates must be identified by pedagogical, sociodemographic, and institutional factors.

The structural equation model confirms that sociodemographic, pedagogical, and institutional factors affect dropout. Therefore, to improve the model adjustment, considering variables at individual factors like cognitive and non-cognitive measures is essential.

Depending on the variables that significantly explain university dropout, professor contract, economic income, having own house, proceeding from the urban region, public high school graduate and academic performance have an incidence on dropout. Therefore, level or semester could be considered because first-semester dropouts occur more frequently.

The logistic model built in this study identified 74.8% of the total students as dropouts and 72.4% as non-dropouts. Engineering faculties could use this indicator to explain undergraduate dropouts.

The authors declare no conflict of interest.

Acknowledgments. Authors knowledge to Universidad Católica de Oriente to support the data, Universidad CES and Institución Universitaria Digital de Antioquia to financial support.

Disclosure of Interests. The authors declare no conflict of interest.

References

1. Heublein, U.: Student drop-out from G erman Higher Education institutions. Eur. J. Educ. **49**(4), 497–513 (2014)
2. Behr, A., Giese, M., Teguim Kamdjou, H.D., Theune, K.: Motives for dropping out from Higher Education—an analysis of bachelor's degree students in Germany. Eur. J. Educ. **56**(2), 325–343 (2021)
3. Choi, H.J., Park, J.H.: Testing a path-analytic model of adult dropout in online degree programs. Comput. Educ. **116**, 130–138 (2018)
4. Sánchez-Hernández, G., Barboza-Palomino, M., Castilla-Cabello, H.: Análisis de la deserción y los factores asociados a la permanencia estudiantil en una universidad peruana. Actualidades Pedagógicas. **1**(69), 169–191 (2017)
5. Guzmán, A., Barragán, S., Cala Vitery, F.: Dropout in rural Higher Education: a systematic review. Front. Educ. **6**, 351 (2021)
6. Giha Tovar, Y., Karime Abadía Alvarado, L., Sánchez Perilla, A., Orlando Valero Quintero, W., Pablo Mondragón Pardo, J., Orlando García Bogotá, O., et al.: Compendio Estadístico Educación Superior Colombiana de la Ministerio de Educación Nacional Contenido. Bogotá; (2016)

7. Veenstra, C.P., Dey, E.L., Herrin, G.D.: A model for freshman engineering retention. Adv Eng Educ. **1**(3), n3 (2009)

8. Behr, A., Giese, M., Teguim Kamdjou, H.D., Theune, K.: Dropping out of university: a literature review. Rev. Educ. **8**(2), 614–652 (2020)

9. Tinto, V.: Classrooms as communities: exploring the educational character of student persistence. J. Higher Educ. **68**(6), 599–623 (1997)

10. Bean, J.P., Metzner, B.S.: A conceptual model of nontraditional undergraduate student attrition. Rev. Educ. Res. **55**(4), 485–540 (1985)

11. Dweck, C.S.: Motivational processes affecting learning. Am. psychol. **41**(10), 1040 (1986)

12. Bandura, A., Freeman, W.H., Lightsey, R.: Self-efficacy: the exercise of control. Springer (1999). https://doi.org/10.1891/0889-8391.13.2.158

13. Elliott, D.C.: The impact of self beliefs on post-secondary transitions: The moderating effects of institutional selectivity. High. Educ. (Dordr). **71**(3), 415–431 (2016)

14. Besterfield-Sacre, M., Atman, C.J., Shuman, L.J.: Characteristics of freshman engineering students: models for determining student attrition in engineering. J. Eng. Educ. **86**(2), 139–149 (1997)

15. Moller-Wong, C., Eide, A.: An engineering student retention study. J. Eng. Educ. **86**(1), 7–15 (1997)

16. Mayra, A., Mauricio, D.: Factors to predict dropout at the universities: a case of study in Ecuador. In: 2018 IEEE Global Engineering Education Conference (EDUCON). IEEE; 2018. pp. 1238–42 (2018)

17. Green, T.: A methodological review of structural equation modelling in Higher Education research. Stud. High. Educ. **41**(12), 2125–2155 (2016)

18. Bäulke, L., Grunschel, C., Dresel, M.: Student dropout at university: a phase-oriented view on quitting studies and changing majors. Eur. J. Psychol. Educ. **37**(3), 853–876 (2022)

19. Şahin, M., Aybek, E.: Jamovi: an easy to use statistical software for the social scientists. Int. J. Assess. Tools Educ. **6**(4), 670–692 (2019)

20. Shmeleva, E., Froumin, I.: Factors of Attrition among Computer Science and Engineering Undergraduates in Russia. Вопросы образования. 2020;(3 (eng)):110–36

21. Lord, S.M., Long, R.A., Layton, R.A., Orr, M.K., Ohland, M.W., Brawner, C.E.: Academic outcomes of international students in chemical, civil, electrical, industrial, and mechanical engineering in the USA. In: 2022 IEEE Frontiers in Education Conference (FIE). IEEE; 2022. pp. 1–7 (2022)

22. Araque, F., Roldán, C., Salguero, A.: Factors influencing university drop out rates. Comput. Educ. **53**(3), 563–574 (2009)

23. Cannistrà, M., Masci, C., Ieva, F., Agasisti, T., Paganoni, A.M.: Early-predicting dropout of university students: an application of innovative multilevel machine learning and statistical techniques. Stud. High. Educ. **47**(9), 1935–1956 (2022)

24. Guarín, C.E.L., Guzmán, E.L., González, F.A.: A model to predict low academic performance at a specific enrollment using data mining. IEEE Rev. Iberoamericana de tecnologias del Aprendizaje. **10**(3), 119–125 (2015)

25. Nikolaidis, P., Ismail, M., Shuib, L., Khan, S., Dhiman, G.: Predicting student attrition in Higher Education through the determinants of learning progress: a structural equation modelling approach. Sustainability. **14**(20), 13584 (2022)

26. Castro-Lopez, A., Cervero, A., Galve-González, C., Puente, J., Bernardo, A.B.: Evaluating critical success factors in the permanence in Higher Education using multi-criteria decision-making. High. Educ. Res. Dev. **41**(3), 628–646 (2022)

27. Nagy, J.T.: Evaluation of online video usage and learning satisfaction: an extension of the technology acceptance model. Int. Rev. Res. Open Distrib. Learn. **19**(1) (2018)

28. Seibt, R., Kreuzfeld, S.: Influence of work-related and personal characteristics on the burnout risk among full-and part-time teachers. Int. J. Environ. Res. Public Health **18**(4), 1535 (2021)

29. Bardach, L., Lüftenegger, M., Oczlon, S., Spiel, C., Schober, B.: Context-related problems and university students' dropout intentions—the buffering effect of personal best goals. Eur. J. Psychol. Educ. **35**(2), 477–493 (2020)
30. Moreira G de O, Passeri, S., Velho, P.E., Ferraresi, F., Appenzeller, S., Amaral, E.: The academic performance of scholarship students during medical school. Rev Bras. Educ. Med. **43**, 163–169 (2019)
31. Kronberger, N., Horwath, I.: The ironic costs of performing well: grades differentially predict male and female dropout from engineering. Basic Appl. Soc. Psych **35**(6), 534–546 (2013). Available https://doi.org/10.1080/01973533.2013.840629
32. Yusuf, F.A., Okanlawon, A.E., Oladayo, T.R.: Investigation into factors affecting students' academic performance in tertiary institutions as expressed by undergraduates. J. Educ. Black Sea Reg. **5**(2), 62–75 (2020)

Geographic Information Management Applied to Land Administration in Colombia Through the Use of Free Software Tools

Jhon Alexander Galindo Ambuila$^{(\boxtimes)}$ and Alvaro Enrique Ortiz Dávila

Universidad Distrital Francisco José de Caldas, Bogota D.C, Colombia
mcic@udistrital.eu.co,jagalindoa@udistrital.edu.co
https://facingenieria.udistrital.edu.co/maestria-ciencias-informacion

Abstract. Globally, the need for territorial entities to have a territorial information system in which the existing real estate and its physical and legal characteristics are registered is identified. This system would facilitate the administration and management of the resources of the same and thus allow the decision-making of different administrative entities according to the various purposes required.

For this reason, free software plays a fundamental role in land administration due to its versatility in being studied, modified, distributed, and improved. It is for this reason that this article exposes a vision of the concept of free software and provides a description of the tools that intervene and facilitate land administration from a flow that starts from the management of databases with the creation of a model that fits the process of cadastral formation in Colombian territory, then describes the customization of forms for field acquisition by mobile device using the model described above. It also details the automation processes for the edition and validation of the information from desktop tools. Finally, it concludes with free tools' role in land administration and how they contribute to the definition of an agile and efficient multipurpose cadastre.

Keywords: QGIS · QFleld · Free Software · PostgreSQL · Land Administration Domain Model (LADM)

1   Introduction

This article offers the reader a general approach to the use of free software in the processes associated with the management of geographic information applied to land administration in Colombia, considering a definition and contextualization of the scope of this type of technology and tools; then, some characteristics of land administration in Colombia will be described, as well as the applications of free software in the process associated with geographic information, analyzing them from a practical point of view.

© The Author(s), under exclusive license to Springer Nature Switzerland AG 2025
J. C. Figueroa-García et al. (Eds.): WEA 2024, CCIS 2223, pp. 237–246, 2025.
https://doi.org/10.1007/978-3-031-74598-0_20

In this sense, it is strategic to support, promote and disseminate the free software movement from extensive, creative and critical use of the opportunities it offers, as is the case of the creation and strengthening of communities that contribute to the work of technological sovereignty, both in public and private institutions, to seek and propose ways to promote access to the population of working tools according to different requirements, in particular, the requirements of the structure and regulations of land administration in Colombia.

2   What Is Free Software?

In this sense, it is important to state that the free software concept has different interpretations due to its English-speaking origin, which has led it to be interpreted as free software in an economic context, but it is really aimed at the power and the right of people to make use of the software. This is why free software can be understood as the freedom of users to run, copy, distribute, study, modify and improve the software [1].

Before defining the guidelines of free software, it is important to clarify the difference between free software and open source. The difference lies mainly in the fact that the free software movement defends the freedom of the users who use computers, in a movement for freedom and justice. On the other hand, the open source idea mainly values practical advantages and does not defend the principles of freedom and justice [2].

It is for this reason that within the free software movement are defined the four freedoms that govern it and that become the basic pillars for its understanding, these pillars are defined in [1] as follows: The freedom to run the program whatever our purpose, the freedom to study how the program works and adapt it to your needs - access to the source code is an indispensable condition for this, the freedom to redistribute copies and thus help your colleague and the freedom to improve the program and then publish it for the good of the whole community - access to the source code is an indispensable condition for this.

Based on these principles, organizations whose objective is the management of geographic information are born, which have appropriated the free software movement. Among these organizations, The Open Source Geospatial Foundation (oSGeo) stands out, leading projects in areas such as Content Management Systems, Metadata Catalogs, Operating Systems, Desktop Applications, Web Mapping, Geospatial Libraries and Spatial Databases, which are fundamental to the management of geographic information applied to land administration.

3   Generation of Community-Based Free Software

The free software movement is as old as the development of computers. However, when computers began to be produced, this concept was not yet defined if actions of reading, modifying, or using parts of the source code were performed to improve or create new programs to achieve the proposed development objectives. This is because the sharing of software allows societies to grow and generates technological sovereignty for both consumers and producers.

Once the guidelines proposed by free software are understood, the community's search for the appropriation of knowledge is understood. This search is constantly strengthened in the search for solutions to different problems that affect people in a particular way and can be applied in a general way, allowing communities around free software to grow daily with different types of resources that contribute to solving different needs.

From the point of view of geographic information, it is evident how this community grows due to the need to satisfy the information production required by the generation of the XXI century and how this is associated with a spatial location. In countries such as Colombia, it is evident that there are growing communities like the group of users of QGIS Colombia, which aims to promote and disseminate the free software QGIS in Colombia [3] through the organization of meetings, workshops and training to share knowledge about QGIS and how it contributes to the management of geographic information.

It's through this approach that we recognize the significance of nations' growth, which is rooted in knowledge and investment in their human resources. This path leads to the establishment of technological sovereignty, a concept that QGIS plays a pivotal role in promoting.

4 Characteristics of Land Administration in Colombia

The term land administration (LA) was established in 1993 by the United Nations Economic Commission for Europe (UNECE) in its Land Administration Guidelines. These guidelines define land administration as: "the processes of recording and disseminating information on ownership, value and use of land and its associated resources. These processes include the determination or "adjudication" of land rights and other land attributes, the measurement and description of these, their detailed documentation, as well as the provision of relevant information to support the land market" [5].

Considering the above, the importance of having a large amount of information to support these processes can be identified. The information will then be both documentary and geographic to adequately support the knowledge of the spatial dynamics of the land resource. [6] already mentioned the need to have geospatial resources that generate value in the entities and optimize their work of land resource management through quality assurance and interoperability of data, services, and other necessary resources.

It is worth noting that under this proposal, initiatives such as the Project for the Modernization of Land Administration in Colombia, which since late 2015, has been supporting technical assistance tasks for the adoption of the ISO 19152:2012 (LADM) standard through the definition of the Colombian profile of this, which is called LADM-COL. This project is financed by the Government of Switzerland, executed by the Economic Cooperation and Development (SECO) of the Embassy of Switzerland in Colombia, and implemented by the Implementation Agency (IA).

It is important to understand the LADM as a conceptual model rather than a data product specification [10]. According to ISO (2012), it is a conceptual model that captures semantics related to land administration based on agreements on "geometry, temporal aspects, metadata, observations and measurements from the field" [4].

The definition of LADM-COL as a conceptual model suggests that it consists of different data models, according to the theme, which aim to facilitate the exchange of territorial data associated with different processes related to land policies, cadastre, and land registries [4].

The Land Administration Domain Model (LADM) came into being in response to the global need for a universally accepted standardized domain model in land administration. This need arose in the early 2000 s, spurred by discussions on technological opportunities and social demands integrated into land policies. The International Federation of Surveyors (FIG) and UN-Habitat, along with the Food and Agriculture Organization of the United Nations (FAO), lent their support to this initiative [10].

5   Importance of Free Software Software in the Development of Geographical Information

The Open Source Geospatial Foundation (OSGeo) is a not-for-profit organization whose mission is to foster global adoption of open geospatial technology by being an inclusive software foundation devoted to an open philosophy and participatory community driven development [7].

The foundation provides financial, organizational and legal support to the broader open source geospatial community. It also serves as an independent legal entity to which community members can contribute code, funding and other resources, secure in the knowledge that their contributions will be maintained for public benefit. OSGeo also serves as an outreach and advocacy organization for the open source geospatial community, and provides a common forum and shared infrastructure for improving cross-project collaboration [7].

One of the projects on which the OSGeo Foundation is working consists of a spatial database spatial database extension for the PostgreSQL DBMS. It provides new types to PostgreSQL geometry, geography, raster, and topogeometry and SQL/MM OGC SFSQL compliant functions for doing GIS work such as cadastral management, back-end for Web mapping services [8].

On the other hand, the foundation mentioned above forged the QGIS initiative, which consists of a tool that, by 2002, imported and visualized Post-GIS data. Subsequently, this tool was provided with the ability to improve layer manipulation and colour layers and display the properties of shapefiles and other vector formats. By 2004, support for raster data was added, and the display of vector data became simple and seamless. This project, launched as one of the first eight OSGeo Foundation projects officially graduated from the incubation phase in 2008. To date, it is a set of Free Software spatial data management applications for GNU/Linux, Unix, Mac OS, Microsoft Windows and Android platforms, dedicated to the field of geographic information systems (GIS) that is capable of supporting the spatial extension of PostgreSQL, PostGIS, and that allows handling raster and vector formats through the GDAL and OGR libraries. It also offers the possibility of being used as a user interface (GUI) of GRASS, using all the analysis power of GRASS and the friendly working environment provided by QGIS, which is developed in C++ and uses the Qt library for its graphical user interface [9].

QGIS is free software and operates under the GNU GPL license, which has an add-on infrastructure, i.e., the user can add many new features by writing his code (add-on development). These add-ins can be written in C++ or Python. Since the QGIS 3.0 generation, QGIS uses Python version 3. X offers developers several links to examples and guides for the "Plugin Builder" as a Python development tool, so it is possible to automate tasks in QGIS. [9].

6   Tools for Data Capture

As previously mentioned, LADM is a set of data models that facilitate the exchange of territorial data. Given the ease of use of this standard, an ecosystem solution that facilitates the management of information in each of the processes of the Multipurpose Cadastre methodology, such as information acquisition, is needed. For this reason, a tool that allows data capture in the field by a reduced model of the LADM-COL profile is identified and integrated with the different tools developed for the Colombian case.

When this need was identified, QField was identified as a tool that facilitates the process of acquiring geographic and alphanumeric information from mobile tools. This tool facilitates the integration of projects developed in QGIS and, in turn, allows them to be deployed anywhere through the application, thus ensuring that fieldwork in the collection of geographic and alphanumeric information is carried out quickly and efficiently.

When the need for efficient acquisition of geographic and alphanumeric information from mobile tools was identified, QField emerged as the ideal solution. This tool not only integrates projects developed in QGIS but also enables their deployment anywhere through the application. This ensures that fieldwork, crucial for the collection of geographic and alphanumeric information, is carried out with utmost efficiency and speed.

Once the tool to be applied is defined, and in line with the zero (0) principle of free software, the application is adjusted and executed. The aim is to configure it into a versatile tool, capable of capturing geographic, alphanumeric, and documentary data in the field for a multipurpose cadastre. It also enables the synchronization and validation of information, based on a structure proposed according to LADM-COL.

It is necessary to use different free software tools that favour the implementation of QField to acquire geographic and alphanumeric information. These applications are UML Editor, QGIS, QGSModelBaker, and QFieldSync. These applications are related to each other, as shown in the following figure (Fig. 1).

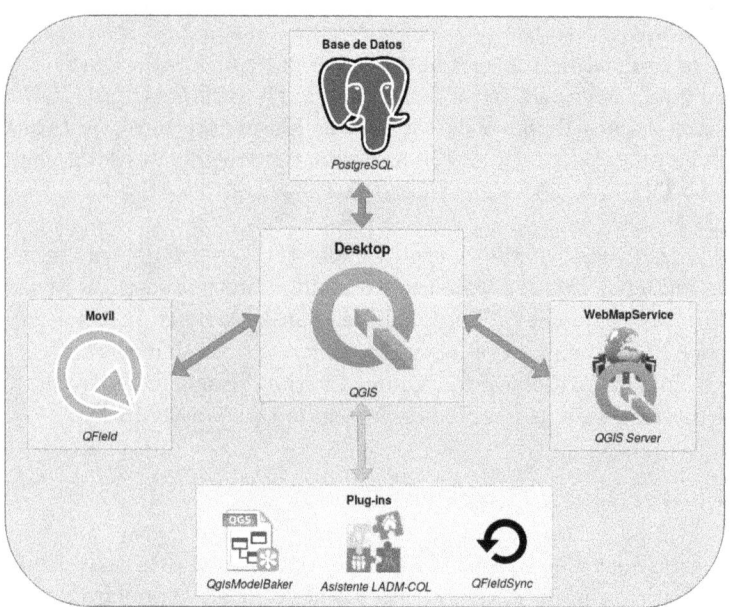

Fig. 1. Schematic of the land administration architecture using Free Software.

The wish to enhance the application of the model-based method motivated the creation of the UML editor [11] and the need for a graphical application that would allow the handling of the INTERLIS data modelling language, which is integrated into the ISO:19152:2012 standard and facilitates obtaining descriptions of computer-processable models, which can be used to initialize databases or transfer LADM data through XML (Fig. 2).

Once the information capture model has been defined, it must be transferred to QGIS so that it can be consumed by QFied in the same way and facilitate the acquisition of information in the field.

For this, we use the QGISModelBaker tool, a QGIS plugin that allows you to quickly create a QGIS project from a physical data model. Moreover, it lets you import, export, and validate INTERLIS models and data into QGIS using graphical control of the ili2db tools. [12]

Because QGISModelBaker facilitates the conversion of INTERLIS files to QGIS layers, these require a configuration inside QGIS that facilitates the use of the forms inside QFied.

Finally, QFieldSync is used, which facilitates the packaging of QGIS projects with the objective of transferring them to QFied and allows the synchronization of projects once the information has been acquired in the field.

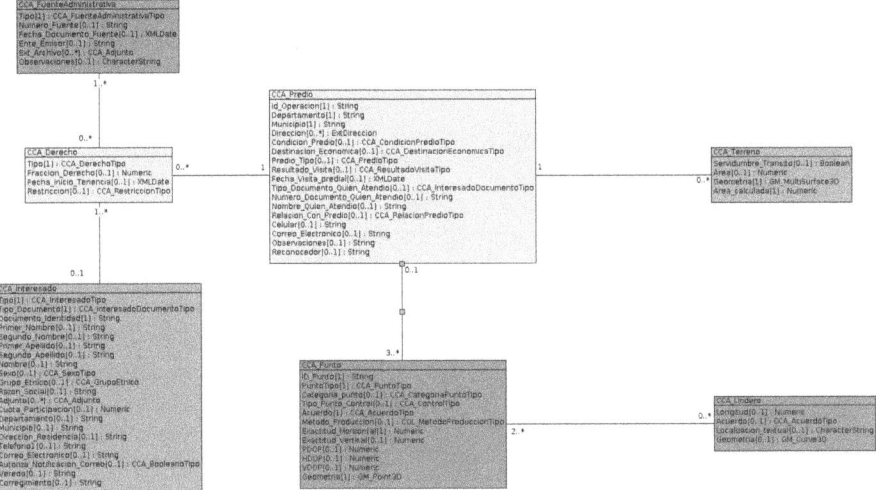

Fig. 2. Relational model for field data capture based on LADM-COL.

7 Plug-in in Data Editing

In acquiring geographic information, it is necessary to perform an editing process, where the topological consistency and accuracy of the information obtained must be defined. This requires an adjustment between the boundaries of the properties, making use of the different iterations in the data capture, which are stored in the PostgreSQL database.

In this development, the information is stored or transformed into point-type geometry. This type of geometry, with its inherent adaptability, facilitates the adjustment and correction of errors in line and polygon representations, empowering developers with a flexible and versatile solution.

Given the importance of the editing process and to reduce errors, mainly due to the intervention of different users in the succession of steps required to edit the data, the plug-in is proposed. This tool would allow users to edit the boundaries between boundaries by adjusting the points that make them up.

Within this development, it is necessary to consider the type of point acquired in the field, differentiating from their level of precision, which assigns them different degrees of importance. The proposed classification consists of: Anchor point, Ground point and Reference point.

Anchor points are the most precise and relevant due to their behaviour in the survey since they are related to a set of properties. A change in them generates variations on a high portion of the captured information, followed by terrain points, which are acquired with a higher level of precision than reference points, and a change in them would affect, to a lesser extent, the boundaries between properties, compared to the impact on the modifications of anchor points. Finally, reference points indicate the location of objects/boundaries on the ground that are not fundamental to the survey (Fig. 3).

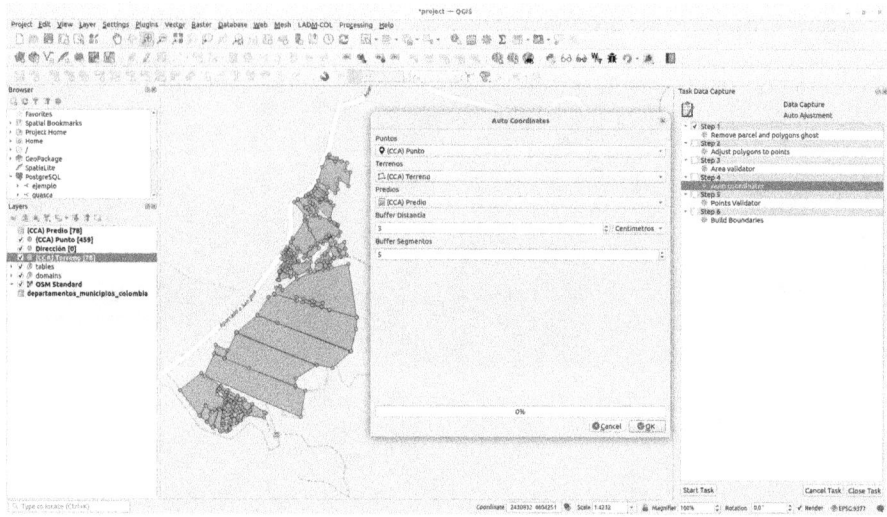

Fig. 3. Plug-in for data editing

8   QGIS Server in Public Inspection

The proposal to develop a tool that allows the approval, rejection, and identification of boundaries, based on the active participation of the land holders in the community, is a testament to our commitment to empowering land holders. This tool not only facilitates communication among the various parties involved in the land administration process but also allows landholders to actively participate in the formulation of their land policies actively, thereby ensuring their voices are heard and their needs are met.

The use of the PostgreSQL database is proposed, which provides a set of facilities for the management of geographic information and its PostGIS extension that has support for the use of both vector and raster data, followed by the need for a geographic server that facilitates the consumption of geographic information from the WMS standards, WFS and WCS defined by the OGC, for this QGIS Server is used, which can work together with QGIS Desktop, maintaining compliance with OGC standards, giving use of configurable printing templates in QGIS Desktop available from the Web Service (GetPrint) and customization of services with Python. When finding compatibility with Python, the Django framework is proposed, which uses Python to develop the Client and will consume the services exposed from the QGIS Server.

Finally, we propose the development of a user-friendly application to support the process of land administration in Colombia. This application will facilitate the geographic and alphanumeric registry of land tenure, empowering land users to easily generate reports on property boundaries, manage roles within the application, and make property-related queries. It will also simplify the interaction of landowners with the approval or rejection of boundary requests, making the land management process more accessible and efficient for all.

9   Conclusions

Our proposal, based on established recommendations and the advantages of free software, presents a unique opportunity to enhance land administration in Colombia. With this software, we can streamline data management, capture both geographic and alphanumeric information in the field, and edit and validate data using desktop tools. The process can then be easily published via the web, improving the overall efficiency and effectiveness of land administration.

Integrating technology into land administration processes not only reduces costs but also enhances the speed of information acquisition. By developing or modifying tools under the free software paradigm, we can further amplify these efficiency gains, offering a promising outlook for the future of land administration in Colombia.

Acknowledgement. I am primarily grateful to my alma mater, the Universidad Distrital Francisco Jos de Caldas (UD), where I learned most of the concepts mentioned in this article. At the university, I had the opportunity to meet the Linux group (GLUD), a pivotal moment that sparked my interest in the philosophy of free software. I am also deeply thankful to my tutor, whose guidance and support have been vital during the research I have done not only for this article but also for my master's degree thesis. Lastly, I thank Swiss Tierras Colombia for the opportunity I had to work with them to develop free software tools for managing cadastral information in Colombia.

References

1. Stallman, R.: Software libre para una sociedad libre. Traficantes de Sueños, Madrid (2004)
2. Why Open Source Misses the Point of Free Software. https://www.gnu.org/philosophy/open-source-misses-the-point.html. Accessed 22 May 2024
3. Grupo de Usuarios QGIS Colombia. http://QGISusers.co/es/. Accessed 12 Aug 2021
4. Agencia de Implementación Suiza, E., Modernización de la Administración de Tierras en Colombia, Bogotá D.C, Colombia (2017)
5. Agencia de Implementación Suiza, I. C, Conceptualización de la Infraestructura de Datos Espaciales para la Administración de Tierras, Infraestructura Colombiana de Datos Espaciales, Bogotá D.C, Colombia (2017)
6. García, F.A., Escobar, A.A., Alvarez, C.A., Guía de elaboración de modelos extendidos del estándar ISO 19152:2012 y del perfil colombiano LADM-COL., Infraestructura Colombiana de Datos Espaciales, Bogotá D.C, Colombia (2018)

7. OSGeo. https://www.osgeo.org/about/. Accessed 23 May 2024
8. OSGeo PostGIS, https://www.osgeo.org/projects/postgis/. Accessed 23 May 2024
9. OSGeo QGIS. https://www.osgeo.org/projects/QGIS/. Accessed 23 May 2024
10. Lemmen, C., Van Oosterom, P., Bennett, R.: The land administration domain model. Land Use Policy **49**, 535–545 (2015)
11. Hirzel, P., UML-Editor Reference ManualThe Art of Modeling, umleditor (2004)
12. OPENGIS.ch QGIS ModelBaker. https://opengisch.github.io/QGISModelBaker/. Accessed 23 May 2024

Statistical Models and Neural Networks in Predicting Income Levels Based on the Maturity Level of the Management System

Alexander Parody Muñoz[1]($\boxtimes$) (iD), Martha Mendoza Hernandez[2] (iD),
Walter Martínez Burgos[3] (iD), Malory Guerra Lara[4], and Margarita Castillo Ramirez[2] (iD)

[1] Libre University, Barranquilla, Colombia
`alexandere.parodym@unilibre.edu.co`
[2] Reformada University, Barranquilla, Colombia
`{m.mendoza,m.castillo}@unireformada.edu.co`
[3] Federal University of Paraná, Curitiba, Brazil
`walter.burgos@ufpr.br`
[4] Sergio Arboleda University, Barranquilla, Colombia
`malory.guerra@usa.edu.co`

Abstract. The need to understand the factors influencing financial indicators, especially those associated with business management, is essential for making sound decisions, maintaining good financial health, strategically planning, and effectively managing risks. **Purpose:** In this research, the impact of management system maturity on the revenue levels of various types of companies in the city of Barranquilla (Colombia) is analyzed. **Methods:** To do this, the maturity levels of 201 companies were measured for two consecutive years prior to the Covid-19 pandemic. During the research process, inferential statistics and Machine Learning tools were applied. This was done with the purpose of identifying which established financial indicators directly affect the maturity of organizations' management systems, highlighting revenue and asset levels as those exhibiting behavior that, when more extensive, leads to better economic benefits. Finally, a Bayesian neural network classifier was used to establish the forecasting capacity of financial indicators and provide key information for the continuous improvement of companies. **Results:** As main findings, it was evidenced that out of the 20 items used to measure the maturity of management systems, 15 showed a statistically significant relationship with the annual income level of the companies. Furthermore, these 15 items achieved an 89.15% of well-classified companies in their income level. Additionally, during the variable selection process with the help of inferential statistics, it was established that the higher the level of implementation of the 15 identified items from the maturity instrument, the greater the economic income of the company.

Keywords: Management systems maturity · financial indicators · Inferential statistics · Neural networks

© The Author(s), under exclusive license to Springer Nature Switzerland AG 2025
J. C. Figueroa-García et al. (Eds.): WEA 2024, CCIS 2223, pp. 247–258, 2025.
https://doi.org/10.1007/978-3-031-74598-0_21

1 Introduction

In the field of research for business development, several studies have been conducted, some of which were carried out to determine the relationship between management systems and company performance, as shown in Nair's article, where they analyzed and observed various aspects of quality management, finding positive links between these practices and various indicators of business performance [1]. Similarly, in Kaynak's article, the results obtained in this study, along with findings previously documented in the literature reviewed in this article, support the positive influence of Total Quality Management (TQM) practices on company performance [2]. Therefore, it is valid to affirm that the success process of creating and developing a company is achieved as a continuous improvement plan is carried out both in the services or products offered by a company and in the processes carried out to materialize them. In this way, the ability to evolve progressively in the life of a company is achieved.

This continuous improvement process has the characteristic of being effective because it examines different variables that directly affect the company, such as overall team efficiency, performance, process time, number of workers, among others. The data is obtained through continuous review of operations and processes, which are carried out to measure company performance, and this continuous improvement allows us to reduce costs and identify factors that enable an optimization process.

This leads us to a very important axis which is measurement; through it, the company's status can be known, and thus, an optimal plan can be implemented to achieve the set improvement goal. It is carried out by obtaining data to quantify the level of efficiency of our process, thus we can easily identify areas for improvement to apply strategies to the processes that require it. This is fundamental because it provides indicators to know if progress is being made towards the set goal or, on the contrary, indicates if the process carried out is not adequate. For this, the processes involved in the business must be identified, then classified, and the respective measurement carried out.

Therefore, if an emerging or already positioned company in the market decides not to implement improvements in the products or services it offers, it is most likely that it will not generate growth, it will be in suspension, or a decrease may occur. In the application of management systems under ISO standards, in the study conducted by Gonzales and Quintero, variables such as sales, assets, liabilities, production, and price were evaluated in certified and non-certified companies, using statistical tools such as ANOVA and mean differences, concluding that companies choosing these systems will have better productivity and competitiveness indices [3].

Thanks to this, Kaziliūnas and others explain in their article the importance of implementing a quality management system for companies, since the performance associated with before and after its use has generated satisfactory performance results. These are associated with different patterns or deficiency factors that organizations did not consider. This system benefits from planning and designing organizational learning mechanisms to increase its capacity and administrative knowledge. These mechanisms help the organization to collect, analyze, store, disseminate, and use relevant information for the organization to create greater efficiency. Due to this, rules such as ISO 9001, which applies the minimum requirements for the implementation of a quality management system in organizations, and ISO 9000, which is based on the documentation of processes such as procedures, are relevant to administrative organization such as the control of a mature quality management system for a company [4].

Continuing with the above and to understand a little more about ISO 9000, Javorcik and Sawada explain that, by obtaining an ISO 9000 certification, many benefits are obtained: a significant increase in sales, a greater flow of company exports, and the ability to generate more employment, but these are not the only effects in favor of obtaining, profits increase, as well as the profitability index, labor productivity, and wages. One of the disadvantages of this certification process is that it is costly; however, the opportunity cost obtained is being able to generate more future profits, since sales volume and company profitability can increase simultaneously [5].

With regard to the above, if we talk about studies based on quantitative processes, it is important to mention Sanchez-Marquez and others, where it was verified that, by using a good quality management system strategy in a market-leading company, it generated an improvement in its productivity performance, proven as a case study approach using real data from two complete years in a leading manufacturing company. This is to improve customer service factor with an analysis of key performance indicators, from balanced scorecards in manufacturing environments [6].

This study consists of, starting from a database that relates the maturity index of management systems with financial indicators, it is intended to know the impact that these indices have on the indicators. From a theoretical point of view, this research allows us to expand knowledge about Quality Management Systems. Likewise, through this analysis, programs and projects can be established in organizations for the strengthening of programs, to achieve maturity in their management systems, with which high levels of quality, profitability, and business productivity are achieved.

From a statistical point of view, multivariate statistical models, logistic regression models, and machine learning tools were applied, which provide us with the facility to know and identify within large volumes of data when an element or factor is directly impacting, either satisfactorily or deficiently, on the result associated with the maturity of the management system. This contribution will provide a model capable of recognizing weaknesses and creating improvements within a company through the proposed indicators and variables, likewise it would assist in making business decisions.

2 Methodology

To carry out this research, a database from the master's thesis in Integrated Management Systems by Guerra Lara and Montes Lopesierra titled "Evaluation of the degree of implementation of quality management systems and their relationship with the economic performance of companies in the hotel sector in the city of Barranquilla and its metropolitan area" [7] was used. This database was constructed through a questionnaire based on categorized questions and responses following the Likert scale. The authors of the thesis used as a reference for the construction of the instrument for measuring the maturity of the management system the theoretical model by Diago & Elguedo [8], in which a structured model of variables was designed according to the following set of interrelated requirements of ISO 9001:2015:

The organizational maturity measurement instrument applied consists of 20 items divided into 5 dimensions, which are: organizational context, stakeholders, planning,

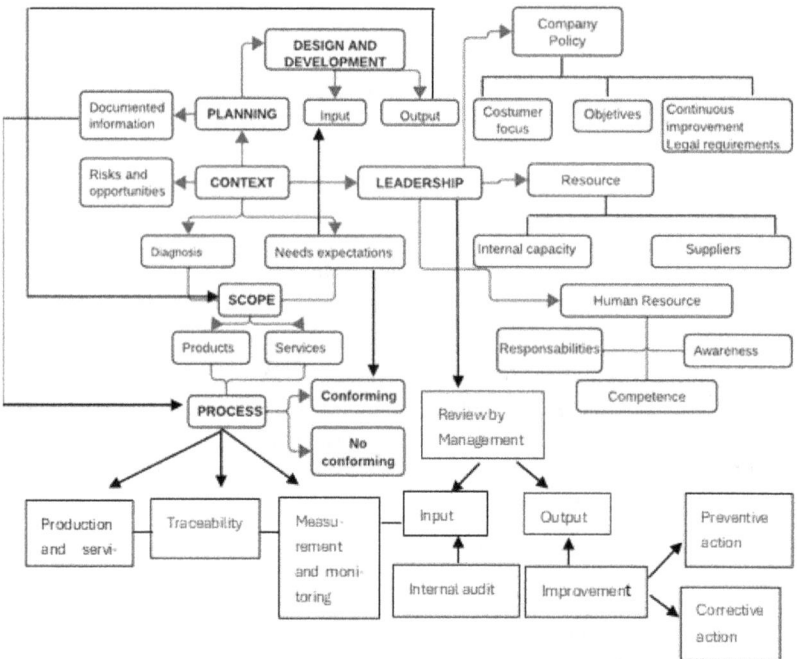

Fig. 1. Interrelationship Model of ISO 9001:2015 Requirements, Diago & Elguedo [8]

leadership, and processes. However, different levels of maturity were assigned a numerical representation to facilitate statistical work, established as follows: Non-existent (1), Initial (2), Intermediate/formalized (3), Advanced and measurable (4), Improved and Automated (5), and Integrated (6). The complete form of the instrument applied to the companies was as follows:

The instrument was applied to 201 companies in the city of Barranquilla, and these companies were also asked whether their annual income level was above 5.001 billion pesos or below this value. This cutoff point was applied as it represented the median of the income level reported by the companies (Table 2).

For the statistical analysis, the initial aim was to determine which items of the tool for measuring the maturity of the management system have a statistical association with the income level presented by the 201 selected companies. For this purpose, the Z-test for comparing means was applied, as the sample size being greater than 30 (sample size of 201) allows the use of this test, where the population variance is estimated from the sample variance [9]. This test allowed the identification of which questions associated with the maturity index of management systems influence the income level of the companies. The hypothesis test compares the average maturity level score between companies with income levels greater than or equal to 5.001 billion pesos and those with income levels less than 5.001 billion pesos. The null hypothesis suggests that there are no differences in the average maturity levels (p-value greater than 0.05), while the alternative hypothesis suggests that there are statistically significant differences (p-value less than

Table 1. Instrument applied to companies. Guerra & Montes [7]

Questions	No-existent	Initial	Intermediate/Formalized	Advanced and Measurable	Improved and Automated	Integrated
Does the organization periodically analyze its environment, considering aspects that may influence it?						
Does the organization define its strategic direction?						
Is there a focal point in management's attention?						
Does the organization identify, analyze, and update information about the needs and expectations of its customers, suppliers, employees, and other stakeholders?						
Is the company planned, along with its strategy and policies?						
Are the company's policies and strategy communicated?						

(*continued*)

Table 1. (*continued*)

Questions	No-existent	Initial	Intermediate/Formalized	Advanced and Measurable	Improved and Automated	Integrated
Does the organization determine and provide the necessary resources for the operation of its processes?						
Is a leadership approach defined?						
Are there spaces for deciding what is important?						
Are daily activities organized?						
Is there tactical planning (for the direction of operational levels) in the company?						
Are product/service processes monitored to control changes?						
Does the organization have defined criteria for the acquisition of goods and services?						
Does the organization identify and control non-conforming processes, products, and services?						

(*continued*)

Table 1. (*continued*)

Questions	No-existent	Initial	Intermediate/Formalized	Advanced and Measurable	Improved and Automated	Integrated
Are non-conforming products and services controlled?						
Does top management review compliance with the strategy, policies, and corporate objectives?						
Does the Organization carry out internal audits at planned intervals to provide information about whether the management model applied complies with the organization's own requirements?						
Does the organization inspect its processes?						
Does the company establish improvement actions when it identifies non-conformities?						
Does the organization identify suitable improvement opportunities to implement in processes?						

Table 2. According to the methodological section, the results of the Z-tests comparing the maturity levels between the two income levels studied are shown:

Questions	P-value	≥ $5.001MM	< $5.001 MM
Periodically analyzes its environment	0,0036	3,83 (1,19)	3,28 (1,00)
Defines its strategic direction	0,0076	3,89 (1,17)	3,37 (1,01)
Center of interest of management	0,1182	N/A	N/A
Has information about needs and expectations	0,1153	N/A	N/A
Plans its strategies and policies	0,1735	N/A	N/A
Communication of strategies and policies	0,5776	N/A	N/A
Determines and provides resources for processes	0,3491	N/A	N/A
Leadership exists	0,4227	N/A	N/A
Decision-making spaces exist	0,3593	N/A	N/A
Organizes daily activities	0,2441	N/A	N/A
Tactical planning exists	0,0205	3,89 (1,17)	3,44 (1,02)
Tracks product processes for control	0,2874	N/A	N/A
Definition of criteria for acquiring products	0,1115	N/A	N/A
Identifies and controls non-conforming aspects (products and processes)	0,0121	3,81 (1,10)	3,29 (1,12)
Non-conforming product control	0,2078	N/A	N/A
Reviews compliance with strategies, policies, and objectives	0,0077	4,08 (1,08)	3,57 (1,00)
Internal audits to determine compliance with organizational requirements	0,0139	3,86 (1,18)	3,34 (1,13)
Performs inspections in its processes	0,1786	N/A	N/A
improvement actions when it identifies non-conformities	0,2538	N/A	N/A
identify suitable improvement opportunities to implement in processes	0,132	N/A	N/A

0.05). Hence, the item from the management system maturity instrument influences the income level of the companies under study.

Subsequently, a Bayesian neural network classifier was trained and validated using only the questions that were statistically significant in the hypothesis test comparison. This was done to measure the predictive capacity of the income level based on the maturity level of the companies under study. All statistical results were generated with the help of Statgraphics version 19 statistical software, and all techniques were applied with a significance level of 5% (95% confidence). This article demonstrates an articulated use of classical inferential statistical techniques with machine learning tools, achieving a synergistic use of the two types of analysis tools.

3 Results

According to the methodological section, the results of the Z-tests comparing the maturity levels between the two income levels studied are shown:

The questions that showed a p-value in the Z-test comparison below 0.05 (see Table 1) were:

Does the organization periodically analyze its environment, considering aspects that may influence it?

Does the organization define its strategic direction?

Is there tactical planning (for the direction of operational levels) in the company?

Does the organization identify and control non-conforming processes, products, and services?

Does top management review compliance with the strategy, policies, and corporate objectives?

Does the Organization carry out internal audits at planned intervals to provide information about whether the management model applied complies with the organization's own requirements?

In all cases where questions were statistically significant related to income level, it was evident that companies with higher maturity levels had higher income levels, as the mean maturity level was higher in the group of companies with annual income above 5.001 billion pesos in all cases.

Based on the above, it is evident to mention that most of the significant questions asked to each company focused on discovering how many were carrying out strategies or practices to achieve incomes higher than the established ones. In view of this, it is observed that most companies are implementing these activities comprehensively, resulting in incomes that reach or exceed 5.001 billion pesos. However, it is worth focusing on practices related to "Planning of strategies and policies," as these show a high proportion of 50% in terms of lack of implementation, even reaching non-existence. This factor does not seem to be so decisive, as it does not significantly affect the ability to achieve the income levels predetermined by the few amounts of companies that exist. It is most advisable to look for companies that have this deficiency to conduct a more comprehensive analysis.

After identifying the questions most related to the income indicator, a neural network was established with them, as seen in Fig. 1. It can be observed how the nodes on the left side refer to the significant questions to consider (such as the number of employees), while the two nodes in the middle and on the right side represent the two possible cases, namely, whether they exceed the income of 5.001 billion pesos or not (Fig. 2).

If we analyze each aspect of the neural network, we find that the blue lines, also known as interconnections, represent the relationships or possible cases of the nodes mentioned earlier. Meanwhile, the nodes found on the right side are the aspects considered whether the income exceeds 5.001 billion pesos or not. Leaving the nodes on the left side referring to the significant questions related to the evaluated indicator.

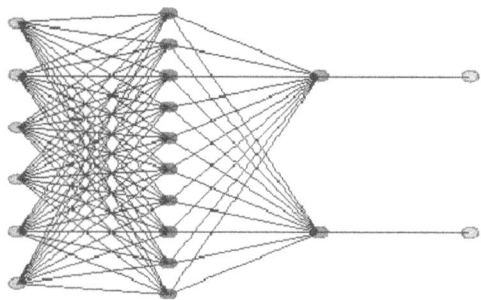

Fig. 2. Neural network for predicting economic income. Source own.

Table 3. Hyperparameters of the generated neural network.

Neural Network Bayesian Classifier	
Classification factor:	Income level
Input factors:	Items: 1, 2, 11, 14, 16, 17
Prior probabilities:	proportional to occurrence in training set
Error costs:	equal for all classes
Selection variable:	random (161)
Number of cases in training set:	160
Number of cases in validation set:	41
Spacing parameter used:	10,4 (optimized by jackknifing during training)

The hyperparameters of the generated neural network are detailed below (Table 3).

Thanks to this, a training set was started, which randomly selects 80% of the data to train and adjust the parameters within the neural network. The remaining 20%, known as the validation set, evaluates the model's performance, making unforeseen adjustments and assessing the performance of the Neural Network (Bayesian Classifier) to predict income levels.

Table 4. Confusion matrix of the neural network

Network Phase	Members	Percentage Correctly Classified
Training	161	81,87%
Validation	41	80,48%

The trained neural network achieved good results by obtaining an 81.87% of well-classified companies according to their income level based on the maturity of their management system. Once the network was trained, the validation phase results showed that 80.48% of the selected companies to validate the network's capability were well classified (Table 4). This demonstrates that the network provides a high level of reliability in identifying companies with annual incomes above 5,001 million pesos. Furthermore, it establishes that the use of inferential statistics and machine learning tools not only allows the construction of highly reliable forecasting models but also enables the understanding of the dynamics of variable relationships and interactions, making it possible to build prediction algorithms with low margins of error.

4 Conclusions

According to the results, this study has provided solid evidence of the impact of management system maturity on the income level of the companies under study. It was evident that the higher the maturity level of the company, the higher the annual income, contrasted with companies with lower maturity in their management system, especially when there is greater development in the following aspects of management systems: periodic environmental analysis, defining strategic direction, planning strategies and policies, determining and providing resources for processes, organizing daily activities, tactical planning, monitoring product processes for control, defining criteria for acquiring products, identifying and controlling non-conforming aspects (products and processes), controlling non-conforming products, reviewing compliance with strategies, policies, and objectives, conducting internal audits to determine conformity with organizational requirements, employing improvements when there are non-conformities, and identifying improvement opportunities.

Neural network analysis demonstrated that items associated with management system maturity could be a reliable input for estimating company income behavior and using that information as input for designing action plans to improve company income levels.

In various studies examined in this article, a key point is observed, which is the positive impact of implementing management systems on business performance. This study specifically focuses on how these systems affect financial indicators. In seeking to compare other research, which may encompass similar results, for example, the work of Javorcik and Sawada (2018) highlights how the adoption of ISO 9000 certification leads to increased profitability, sales, exports, and job creation, which in turn can influence a company's financial indicators. Similarly, in the study by González and Quintero (2014), two hypotheses were confirmed: the first being "certified companies present differences in financial variables compared to non-certified ones," and the second being "certified companies present differences in at least the variables studied for a given level of significance."

In conclusion, it is demonstrated the positive impact of adequate development of the management system on the financial performance of companies, and with the combined use of inferential statistics and machine learning, it is possible not only to predict the company's annual income level but also to use this information for the proper development of continuous improvement plans for the company.

References

1. Nair, A.: Meta-analysis of the relationship between quality management practices and firm performance—implications for quality management theory development. J. Oper. Manage. **24**, 948–975 (2006). https://doi.org/10.1016/j.jom.2005.11.005
2. Kaynak, H.: The relationship between total quality management practices and their effects on firm performance. J. Oper. Manage. **21**, 405–435 (2003). https://doi.org/10.1016/S0272-696 3(03)00004-4
3. Gonzales, D.M., Quintero, R.D.: Estudio para la medición del impacto de la implementación de sistemas de gestión de calidad bajo el estándar NTC ISO 9001:2008 en las empresas de los diferentes sectores económicos de Barrancabermeja y su área de influencia. Revista Citecsa, Volumen **4**, 184–206 (2014)
4. Kaziliūnas, A, Vyšniauskienė, L.: Impact of different quality management system implementation patterns on performance outcomes. Mykolas Romeris University (MRU) **8**, pp. 140–155 (2014)
5. Javorcik, B., Sawada, N.: The ISO 9000 certification: little pain, big gain. European Economic Review, Volumen **105**, 103–114 (2018). https://doi.org/10.1016/j.euroecorev.2018.03.005
6. Sanchez-Marquez, R, Albarracín Guillem, J.M, Vicens-Salort, E, Jabaloyes Vivas, J.: Diagnosis of quality management systems using data analytics – a case study in the manufacturing sector. Comput. Indust. **115**, 103–183 (2020). https://doi.org/10.1016/j.compind.2019.103183
7. Guerra Lara, M.B, Montes Lopesierra, W.: Evaluación del grado de implementación de los sistemas de gestión de calidad y su relación con el desempeño económico de las empresas del sector hotelero en la ciudad de barranquilla y su área metropolitana. (Tesis de maestría). Facultad de ingeniería, Ingeniería industrial, Universidad autónoma del Caribe, Barranquilla. (2017)
8. Diago, V., Elguedo A.: Evaluación del grado de implementación de los Sistemas de Gestión de Calidad y su relación con el desempeño académico de las Universidades e instituciones Universitarias de la ciudad de Barranquilla y área metropolitana. Master Thesis. Dir. Fuentes-Morales, Bulmaro Adrián & Marquez Rodríguez, Patricia Beatriz. Master en Sistemas de Gestión. Universidad Autónoma del Caribe. Colombia (2017)
9. Llinás, H.: Estadística inferencial. Barranquilla: Ediciones Uninorte (2010)

Author Index

J. C. Figueroa-García et al. (Eds.): WEA 2024, CCIS 2223, pp. 259–260, 2025.
https://doi.org/10.1007/978-3-031-74598-0

Printed in the USA
CPSIA information can be obtained
at www.ICGtesting.com
CBHW050252041124
16857CB00004B/125